CICS
PRIMER

CICS PRIMER

Liz Ryan

Ryan Computing Services, Inc.

 ® SCIENCE RESEARCH ASSOCIATES, INC.
Chicago, Henley-on-Thames, Sydney, Toronto

A Subsidiary of IBM

Acquisition Editor	Micheal J.Carrigg
Project Editor	Richard Myers
Copy Editor	Kathleen West
Design & Composition	Interface Studio
Cover	Holly Rifkind/Interface Studio

Acknowledgments are listed on page 317.

Library of Congress Cataloging in Publication Data

Ryan, Liz, 1939-
  CICS primer.

  Includes index.
  1. Electronic digital computers—Programming.
2. CICS (Computer system)   I. Title.
QA76.6.R93   1986   001.64'2   85-11941
ISBN 0-574-21940-4

Printed in the United States of America

10 9 8 7 6 5 4 3 2 1

Contents

Preface

The subject of this book is how to write application programs for use with CICS, a data communication system that many companies use to maintain and access large computerized data bases. CICS stands for Customer Information Control System. However you will probably never hear CICS called by this formal name. It is almost always referred to by the letters C-I-C-S, often spoken like the single word "kicks."

The book is designed to teach the concepts and programming skills that you would use in the first year or so if you were hired as an application programmer in a company that uses CICS. As a starting point, the book assumes that you have already learned to write computer programs in the COBOL language, that you understand basic computer terms like *compiler* and *debugging*, and that you know how data is represented within a computer. However, unless you have already worked in a fairly large computer installation, you probably aren't exactly sure what a data communication system actually does and why it's needed. The first two chapters of the book describe how a typical company uses computers to manage and communicate with its data base, and how CICS and similar systems fit in with other parts of the overall computer system.

When new programmers arrive on the job, they traditionally receive a brief introduction to the new environment and then are given an initial programming assignment. The first assignment isn't complicated and doesn't take long to complete. The idea is to get the programmers to use the computer system as soon as possible. They will learn the system fastest by using it to accomplish a defined task. This book uses the same philosophy. Beginning with Chapter 3, each chapter is followed by programming exercises that give you practice at the CICS commands you've learned so far.

To be successful as a programmer you need to know more than how to write correct COBOL statements. You also need to use good judgment about the way you design programs, test them, and prepare them for use by other people. Of course, good judgment requires experience that must be gained over a long period of time. However, to be useful the experience must be viewed against a background of general concepts. Therefore, as the text introduces CICS commands it also points out related concepts that apply to the data base and data communication environment in general. By keeping these concepts in mind you will be prepared to apply your skills to data systems other than CICS alone. Many of the discussion questions that follow each chapter are intended to help you see how these general concepts apply in real situations.

The author and publisher thank the following reviewers for their helpful comments: Lucy McJunkin, Fox Valley Technical Institute; Sandy Fabyan, Columbus Technical Institute; and Philip David Jones, University of North Alabama.

1 Introduction to Data Base/ Data Communications

Introduction

We begin this book in the same way that programmers often begin a new job. If you report for work for the first time in a large computer installation, you can expect the first day to be devoted to introductions. Your manager will spend some time talking to you about the company and how the programs you will write fit in with the company's business. Then you will get a tour of the computing facility, be introduced to many of the people who work there, and be told the names or numbers of a great many devices that attach to the central computer. Your manager doesn't really expect you to remember the names of all these people or to be able to describe in detail what each piece of computing equipment does. The purpose of the tour is to help you form some general impressions that will become clearer as time goes on.

You can think of the first two chapters in this textbook as the written equivalent of that first day's orientation. The intent is to give you a general impression of the kind of business and computer facility that uses CICS, and to point out the people and parts of the computing system that will be most important to you as you work with CICS.

If you have worked in a large computer installation before, you may already be familiar with some of the introductory information. However, you may still benefit from a review of the *terminology* used to describe computer hardware and systems concepts in the CICS environment. Each computer manufacturer and system developer tends to coin new terms that may be used differently, or not at all, by other developers and manufacturers. This book uses the same terminology that you will encounter in IBM manuals that describe CICS and the system hardware and software used with CICS.

Of course no two computer facilities are alike, so this discussion will have to be more general than a tour of an actual facility. But you know that, in general, the CICS system is devoted to allowing users at terminals to access data stored on a central computer. This is a computing environment referred to as *data base/data communications* or DB/DC. There are some characteristics of the data base/data communications environment that are shared by virtually all facilities of this type. These are the characteristics that we want to point out in this chapter.

Objectives

After completing this chapter, you will:

- Be familiar with the hardware and system terminology used in CICS installations.
- Be able to describe the roles of other computer specialists you will work with as a CICS application programmer.
- Be able to discuss the factors that affect work activity in a company that uses CICS.

The Data Base and Data Files

As people describe the computing facility to you, they will refer again and again to the *data base*. You have probably heard and seen this term in several contexts since you began studying programming. For example, you may have seen advertisements for personal computer programs designed to manage data bases, or you may have seen descriptions of classes about data base design. And you may have heard bank tellers or airline reservations clerks explain that service is delayed because "the data base is down."

But you may have noticed that the term "data base" is not always used in exactly the same way. Sometimes it's used in a very general sense to mean any collection of data. In this general sense a list of the names, locations, and menu specialties of your favorite restaurants would be considered a data base. Unless you are in the business of reviewing restaurants, however, it's unlikely that you would use CICS to maintain your restaurant list.

On the other hand, when used in its most formal sense, data base applies only to a few special types of information collections. In this formal sense many of the data collections for which CICS is used cannot be considered data bases at all. Therefore, throughout this book, you will see the term *data file* much more often than *data base*. However, in the normal working environment, which we are describing here, you are apt to hear *data base* used to refer to any collection of information that has the following characteristics:

1. It's relatively large. Later we'll discuss the size of a typical data base. For now, we'll say simply that it occupies a significant amount of space.
2. It's stored on some type of direct access device in such a way that a computer program can find a particular data item without having to search through a lot of other items. A collection of data like this is called a *direct access file*.
3. It's important to the business of your company. (Many texts and manuals use the term *enterprise* in place of *company* in order to make clear that data bases can exist within private organizations, public institutions, and other "non-business" settings. For the sake of simplicity we'll use the term *company* although we also intend to include other types of settings.)
4. It's used by many people at once. For example, the computer operator may look at a display screen and tell you, "There are 200 users online to the data base right now."
5. It contains information needed throughout the business. For example, your tour might take you through the accounting department, the warehouse, and marketing research. In each of these areas you would see people at computer terminals using the same data base for their own job requirements. Because a data base permits information from different parts of the company to be combined, it is said to be *integrated*.

Many direct access files satisfy all the requirements except the last. That is, they can be large, important, and accessible to many people simultaneously, but not satisfy this definition of data base because they are not integrated. Such a file usually contains rather specialized data like personnel records or descriptions of parts used in manufacture. These are the kinds of data files that you will work with most often in the CICS environment. However, CICS can also be used with "true" data bases, such as data bases created by the IBM Information Management System (IMS). The chapter "Accessing DL/1 Data Bases" describes how CICS is used to manage access to IMS data bases.

Each of the characteristics of a data base makes a requirement upon the computer facility. It may affect the hardware or software required, the kinds and schedule of work performed, or the rules by which the computer is used. If you know that a company uses CICS, you can expect certain things to be true about its computer facility.

Hardware

Let's start with the computer hardware. First, of course, there is the computer itself. It actually consists of several separate "boxes" or units; for example, the central processing unit (CPU) and memory (also called *processor storage*) units. Attached to the computer are peripheral devices which perform various types of input and output functions. They include magnetic tape drives, printers, and direct access storage units such as you would see in any computer room. In a CICS facility, two types of peripheral devices are especially important: the direct access storage devices where the data base resides, and the transmission control devices which permit communication between the computer and online terminals.

Direct Access Storage

We said earlier that the data base is "relatively large" and that it resides on direct access storage devices. This is a good time to try to pin down what is meant by "relatively large."

The data base is recorded on direct access storage *volumes*. Although there are different types of direct access storage volumes, the most commonly used is the *disk* or *disk pack*. The common expression is that the data is *on disks*, so we will refer to "disk" instead of "volume."

You may be familiar with the *floppy–disks, diskettes,* used on many personal computers. One way to get a feeling for the size of data base you will find in a CICS facility is to compare the disks used there to the personal computer's floppy disk. The most common floppy disk is 5¼ inches in diameter. Information is recorded on one or both sides of the floppy disk, depending upon the type of personal computer system in use. A floppy disk with information recorded on both sides holds about 400 thousand characters.

The disks that you would find in most CICS facilities hold more than 160 *million* characters—about 400 times as much information as a floppy disk. A data base that fills only one of these disk volumes would be considered relatively small.

The largest disks in use today have capacities of more than 800 million characters, 2000 times the capacity of a floppy disk. Some CICS installations have data bases that fill twenty or thirty of these large direct access storage volumes.

You may not see any of the disks themselves; often, they are permanently sealed in the direct access drive that reads and writes them. Other types of disks can be moved from one drive to another. Direct access storage devices can differ in other ways besides whether or not their volumes can be removed. Your CICS facility may use several types of devices, and the CICS programs must be able to process data even if it is moved from one device type to another.

The device in which the volume is placed is called a direct access storage device or *disk drive*. The disk drive is attached to a storage controller, which in turn, is attached to a channel, and then to the computer. The storage controller and channel are examples of boxes which will be pointed out to you, but whose names and numbers won't be important to you at first. The point to remember is that there are several connections or links between the computer and the data. We will return to that point later when we discuss system reliability.

Transmission Control Devices

There are also several connections between the computer and the terminals used to access the data base. Figure 1-1 shows a typical arrangement.

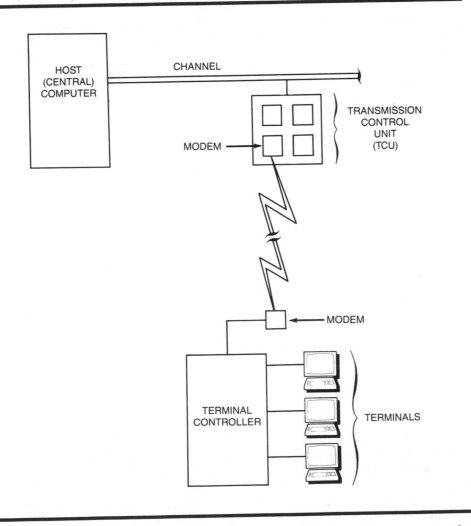

**Figure 1-1
Communications
Path from Central
Computer**

A *transmission control unit* is attached, via a channel, to the computer. The transmission control unit houses *modems* which encode and decode signals from a *phone line*. On the other side of the phone line is another modem which attaches to a *terminal controller*. The terminal controller can connect to one or several *terminals*.

On a typical tour you would see many different kinds of terminal devices.

Most would probably be some type of video display terminal, but you could also see printers, with or without keyboards, various types of computers, and special purpose terminals like optical scanners. Some would access the CICS computer by dialed phone connection, others would be directly cabled.

The point to keep in mind is that the application programs you write will have to communicate with users at many different types of terminals which can be connected in various ways to the central computer.

System Reliability

Remember that your company depends upon its data base in order to conduct its daily business. Consider this in light of the many links you observed between the computer and the data base, and between the computer and the users at their terminal devices. A failure in any of these links makes the data inaccessible to some or all users. With the data base inaccessible, work comes to a halt in many parts of the business. Sometimes the effect is dramatic. Picture a hundred or so impatient truck drivers, with their rigs in line at the warehouse, unable to load or unload because the warehouse management data base is down. Or picture a manufacturing process at a standstill because additional parts cannot be distributed.

To protect against such failures, the computing facility installs extra (or *redundant*) hardware to provide duplicate backup links. Figure 1-2 shows a direct access storage volume mounted on a drive that is connected to the computer through a single controller and channel. Figure 1-3 shows how the same drive would be installed to provide backup connections. Each device in the path has been duplicated. Additional drives are attached to the storage controller. But there is also an additional storage controller so that the drives can be reached through either controller A or B. The channel is duplicated in a similar way, so that each controller can be reached through two channels. Although not shown in the figure, the computer itself can also be duplicated.

You may want to trace out some of the possible paths between the computer and the direct access drive shown in Figure 1-3. Keep in mind that the CICS programs you will write must function correctly no matter which path may be in use.

As you would expect, hardware redundancy is also used for the communication links. Again, the CICS programs must function correctly even if a user must move from one terminal type to another.

Software

As the preceding description suggests, a CICS facility can be quite a complex environment. Its size, the number of users being served simultaneously, the variety and interconnections of the hardware, all contribute to the complexity. You may wonder whether your CICS application programs will also be very complex.

Fortunately, the operating system used to support CICS, and CICS itself, are designed to deal with much of the complexity. For example, CICS keeps track of what type of terminal was used to invoke your program, and translates your input and output statements into the correct form for the terminal. CICS and the operating system work together to simplify your program's access to the data base. Your program will refer to a data base or file by name. CICS keeps

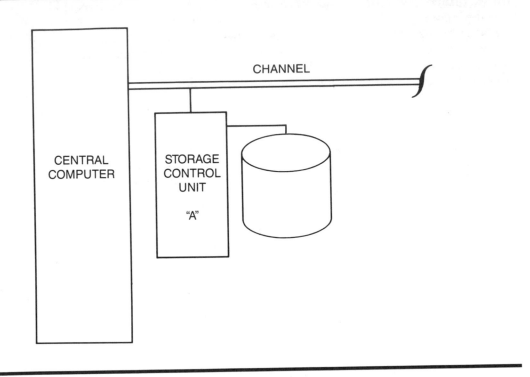

Figure 1-2
Path from Central Computer to Direct Access Storage

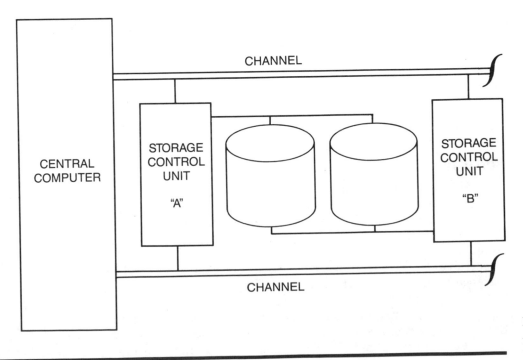

Figure 1-3
Alternate Paths to Direct Access Storage

track of where each file is located, and the operating system keeps track of which paths can be used to reach the required volume.

You can think of the software as residing in several layers within the computer. The innermost layer is the operating system. The operating system is in contact with the computer's hardware—for example, the processor or processors, data-storage devices, and communication lines. The outermost layer contains application programs like the ones you will be writing. They are closest to the user and may be the only part of the system that the user recognizes. CICS resides in an intermediate layer, between the operating system and the application programs. It serves as a "go-between," translating the requirements of the application programs to a form that the operating system can recognize. Let's look at each layer in a little more detail.

Operating System

The operating system is responsible for controlling:

- The various hardware devices attached to the computer.
- The scheduling of work. Remember that at any one time there are many CICS users requesting service from the system. There may be other terminal users at the same time requesting service, and there will probably be some *batch* jobs also awaiting service. The operating system controls how the computer is shared among all these potential users.

The operating system is not designed for use within any particular type of business. For example, when the operating system writes data onto a direct access storage device, it makes no difference whether the data contains numeric values that are part of a calculation in astronomy, digits that represent black or white dots in an X-ray scan, or the collected works of William Shakespeare. Similarly, when a job or terminal request enters the system, the operating system schedules it according to what resources are available, what resources are needed, and how important the local installation has declared the request to be. Because the operating system works only with objects and requests that are defined in terms of computer hardware and resources, the same operating system can be used by a university, a hospital, or an aircraft manufacturer.

Application Programs

In contrast to the operating system, the application programs are concerned almost exclusively with the business your company is in, and as little as possible with details of hardware. Your company may decide at any time to replace its direct access storage devices with new or different models, or to buy a new type of terminal for its employees to use. It would be unacceptable if application programs had to be changed whenever a hardware change like this took place.

This textbook describes how to write application programs for use with CICS. Besides learning new programming statements that are part of the CICS programming environment, you will learn about some general characteristics of application programs written for the DB/DC environment. As an example, each program you write will be small and designed to complete its job very quickly. The people who use the program will usually be looking for some very specific information or requesting a service that must be completed within one or two seconds.

This is quite a different request than one requiring a great deal of computation—

for example, a request for an earnings projection based on a mathematical model of the economy. Let's look at one way in which the two types of request are different.

A user would submit a request for the earnings projection and then go on to do other work. The projection might be completed in an hour or so or perhaps overnight depending upon the relative importance of the request. However, while the projection was being prepared, the user's terminal would be free and could be used for other work. The preparation of the projection is said to be done *offline*.

On the other hand, in the DB/DC environment, a user requests information or service that must be supplied immediately. The user waits for the results to be returned to the terminal. Until the results are received, the terminal is not free to be used for other work. The request is said to be for *online* service.

You will hear the terms online and offline (or batch) used frequently. As discussed in more detail later, the computer will perform both types of work throughout the day.

DB/DC System

CICS resides in the software layer between the operating system and the application programs. It is less general than the operating system because it is designed to support a particular type of processing—DB/DC processing. However, it is more general than the application programs because it is not specifically tailored to your company's business. For example, CICS is used by manufacturers, retailers, banks, insurance companies, and hospitals.

CICS controls the communication between application programs and users, and access by application programs to the data base. To do this it acts as a go-between between the application programs and the operating system. That is, it makes use of the operating system in order to provide services to the application programs.

The middle software layer may include other go-between types of software. CICS is often used together with one or more *data management* systems. The data managed by these systems is contained in true data bases; that is, data bases as defined in the most formal sense of the term. You may encounter data management systems with the following acronyms: IMS, SQL/DS, DB2, and others. Besides providing a link between the operating system and CICS application programs, CICS also provides a link between CICS applications and these data management systems. Therefore, CICS programs can access data managed by IMS and the other systems listed above. But to do so they must use programming statements that are specific to the data management system. That is, you must know when you write the program that the data is in a particular type of data base.

The middle software layer may also contain systems that are not DB/DC systems. You will probably use a terminal to write your CICS programs and to get them compiled. While you do so, your terminal will be controlled by a terminal system other than CICS. One way this is done is to use dial-up connections from the terminal. You dial one number to connect to CICS and another to connect with the other terminal system. Another way is to have the terminals directly connected to the operating system. Each time you sign on at a terminal, the operating system will ask you which terminal system you want to use.

Keep in mind that the operating system must schedule work requests from users of *all of the terminal systems*, not just from CICS terminals.

People

Just as the DB/DC environment's complexity requires that different types of software work together, it requires cooperation among people who have different specialties. As you are introduced to people on your tour, you will be given their name and their job title. Here we'll list some of the job titles you'll hear, and we'll describe how each job fits in with your job as application programmer.

Users

The people you need to have most in mind as you do your work are the people who will use your programs. In this book, we'll call them simply *users*. Many texts and programming manuals refer to the online user as the *terminal operator*. However, we will reserve the term *operator* for the person who operates the central computer. This makes it easier to keep in mind that the computer operators have knowledge and responsibilities that you will need to draw upon as you do your job. It also allows us to point out that the operator, like all of the people discussed in this section, is also a user of CICS programs.

Operators

You have seen that the central computer may be used to support many kinds of work at the same time—some of which may not be in any way related to the data base. The operations staff has to ensure that all categories of work receive the service they need. The operators must understand the requirements of each group of users, and what computer resources each type of work needs. Above all, the operators must be able to recognize when things are going wrong, and to know what to do or whom to call to get things fixed. Part of the job of designing an application program is deciding how the program can recognize problems and make them known to the operators. To do a good job of this, you need to think of the operator as another user of your program.

Data Base Administrator

Because the data base is so critical, a great deal of effort must go toward protecting it. We have discussed the hardware redundancy used to be sure the data base is accessible in spite of hardware failures. However, we haven't said anything about damage to the data itself. What happens if the volume on which the data is stored fails? What if a magnetic field or, more likely, a human error causes the data to be erased? Or what if incorrect data is entered?

Each facility defines its own set of procedures to prevent these problems and to recover when they occur. (For they do occur.) The *Data Base Administrator* is responsible for defining the procedures and making sure they are carried out.

There are also procedures and programming standards that define how data is organized and named. These are important so that information from different parts of the company can be combined in the integrated data base. All of the procedures include guidelines for designing and writing application programs, so you will work with the data base administrator when you are planning a new program.

System Programmers

As an application programmer you will be most concerned with the outermost layer of software. You will learn how to write COBOL programs that use CICS to perform functions like communicating with user terminals and accessing direct access files. That is, you will learn about the CICS *programming interface.*

System programmers are most concerned with the innermost layer of software and how it communicates with CICS and other software in the middle layer. Their knowledge of CICS will be primarily about the CICS *system interface.*

Remember that the operating system and CICS are more general than application programs—they are not designed specifically for your company. However they include many *optional features* that can be selected and combined in different ways. The system programmers are responsible for understanding these options and choosing the ones needed for the kinds of applications your company will use.

You will work with the system programmers to be sure that they understand what your programs need to do, and that you understand which system options have been provided for you to use. You will probably also need help from system programmers from time to time when you find that CICS or the operating system have not responded as you expected to your program's requests.

Activity

If you toured the computing facility during business hours, you would find that most of the work being done by the computer was online work requested from CICS and other terminal systems. Some users will have submitted offline work too. These requests will be placed in a *service queue* on direct access storage awaiting service. The operating system will read a few of them at a time into the computer's memory for processing. During those instants when the computer has caught up with all the online requests, the operating system will direct it to work on the offline requests. However if there are a large number of online users, these offline requests will receive very little service.

At night, however, the activity is quite different. The terminal systems may not be available at all, but if they are there will be very few users. The computer will have more opportunity to do the offline work.

Much of the offline work will have to do with the data base. You will hear a lot about *data base maintenance* jobs which may have to be run at night and be finished before CICS can be started the next morning. For example, copies of the data base must be made periodically, usually when the CICS terminals are not in use. Remember that the data base may be very large, so data base maintenance can take several hours. The focus of night shift activity is on completing data base maintenance before morning so that the online work can begin when the day workers arrive. This explains why you may not be able to test your CICS programs at night without making special arrangements.

There are other kinds of variations in activity that have to do with your particular company. They will often affect the timing of your work. For example, if your company files its income tax in October, you will find that September is not a good time to begin changing certain accounting programs. Therefore, as a programmer, you may have to complete your work by a specific deadline determined by your company's operational schedules.

Summary

The term *data base* is not always defined in exactly the same way. This chapter defines data base as you would be most apt to hear it used on the job. In this sense a data base is a collection of information that has a number of characteristics we have listed. Given an understanding of what we mean by *data base*, we can make some general statements about what a CICS computing facility is like.

CICS belongs to a category of systems called *data base/data communication* or DB/DC systems. In the DB/DC environment, the hardware used to access the data base and to communicate with terminal users is critical. There are several devices that link together to form the path between the computer and the data base and between the computer and the user terminals. To protect against failures along this path, "redundant" hardware is used. The redundancy creates alternate paths that can be used if one path fails.

The hardware redundancy together with the large number of simultaneous users create a complex processing environment. The operating system and the DB/DC system—in our case, CICS—work together to insulate application programs from this complexity.

The operating system resides in an inner layer of software on the computer. It is responsible for controlling the computer hardware and for scheduling the various kinds of work requested by users.

The DB/DC system lies in a middle layer of software and serves as go-between to request operating system services needed by application programs.

Application programs reside in the outer layer of software, closest to the user. Their purpose is to handle specific requests from users, and they are concerned as little as possible with details of the computer hardware. This allows the application programs to work correctly even if data is moved to a new type of storage device, or a user moves to a different type of terminal.

As an application programmer you will work together with people in several different jobs. They include users, computer operators, data base administrators, and system programmers.

The work performed by the computer can be divided into online and offline (batch) processing. During the day, priority is given to online requests by users of CICS and other terminal systems. During the evening, however, priority is given to offline processing, especially *data base maintenance* work which must be completed before morning when the day workers arrive at work.

Your work as an application programmer is affected not only by the computer hardware and software, but also by the requirements of your particular company. In particular, the schedule of your work and deadlines you may have to meet are affected by deadlines important to the company's operations.

2 Introduction to CICS

Introduction

Chapter 1 described CICS as a "go-between" that translates the requirements of application programs into requests for services from the operating system. In this chapter, we'll list the several types of services that CICS provides to application programs and describe, in general, the five component parts of the CICS system itself.

To write a CICS application program you must learn some new programming statements. Chapter 3 will introduce the first of these, but first you need to know how to go about compiling a program and getting it into a form that can be tested. This chapter lists the steps required to do this.

To get ready for Chapter 3s programming exercise, you will also want to try signing on to CICS just to make sure that your *userid* and *password* have been set up correctly. The chapter concludes by describing how to do that.

Objectives

After completing this chapter, you will be able to:

- Describe the function of the five CICS components.
- Describe the sequence of steps required to prepare a CICS application for testing.
- Describe how CICS processes a user's transaction request.
- Sign on to CICS.

CICS Services

The main purpose of CICS is to allow you to write DB/DC application programs without becoming involved with details of the computer hardware and operating system. The intent is not solely to make the programming job easier or more pleasant, but to increase the *system independence* of the applications. The applications developed by your company will be used for many years. During their lifetime, the company will make many changes to the computing environment. Faster and larger disk drives or improved terminal devices may be installed. It's important that these changes can be done without forcing the application programs to be changed.

To meet this objective CICS provides five different types of service. Figure 2-1 shows CICS as made up of five *components*, each responsible for a particular type of service. The figure also shows that each component interfaces with some part of the computing environment. Let's look quickly at each component, beginning with Data Handling Functions and proceeding clock-wise in the figure.

Data Handling Functions

The *data handling* functional component interfaces, through the Data Base

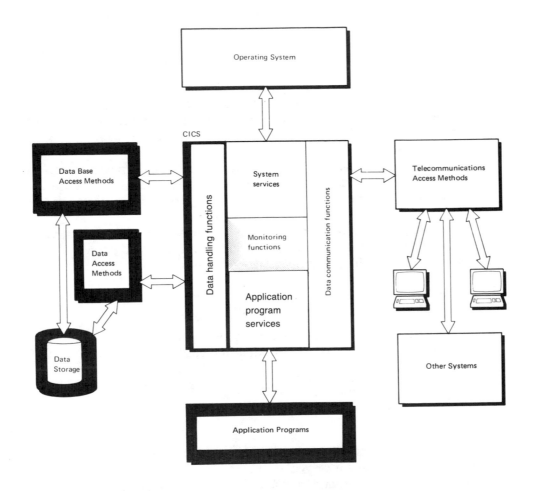

**Figure 2-1
CICS Software
Components**

Access Methods and Data Access Methods, with direct access storage. Notice the distinction between *Data* Access Methods and *Data Base* Access Methods.

The Data Access Methods are part of the operating system, and control input and output requests directed to direct access files. The Data Access Methods are present in every computer that uses CICS.

The Data Base Access Methods are part of Data Base Management systems that your company may use in addition to CICS. Chapter 1 mentioned that data management systems could be used with CICS and listed the acronyms of some of these systems: IMS, SQL/DS, and DB2. If your company uses one or more data management systems they will reside with CICS in the "middle layer" of software described in Chapter 1.

When you write a CICS application program to read from a direct access file, you do not use the usual COBOL input/output statements. That is, you do not code a file description and you do not use a READ statement. Instead you request CICS to read the data for you. CICS translates the request into a form that can be handled by either the Data Access Methods or a Database Access Method. This interface is represented in Figure 2-1 by two-way arrows.

However when your program requests that CICS read or write some data, the data handling component must perform some additional processing. Most important, it must take steps to preserve the *integrity* of the data base. *Data base integrity* means that the data base correctly represents the most recently entered data values, and that the data is recorded in a form that the access methods can continue to process. The chapter "Data Security and Integrity" contains a detailed discussion of data integrity. Here we will briefly point out three situations in which CICS must take action to ensure that data integrity is protected.

The first is while a program is updating data. Because many users may be accessing a given data base at the same time, it will often happen that two or more users need to update the same item at the same time. If one user started to update an item and a second user were permitted to begin updating the same item, the results would be unpredictable. CICS prevents this by ensuring that one user's update is complete before allowing another user to begin updating the same item. The chapter "Random Access of Data Files" will present a detailed example of an attempted *simultaneous update*.

Secondly, data integrity must be protected in case an update request is canceled or interrupted. Suppose that an online user entered a data update request, but that the application program being used terminated abnormally before it completed the update. The user can recognize that the request was not completed and resubmit the request. But if some part of the data had already been changed, the new request will be changing, not the original value, but some intermediate (that is, partly updated) value. CICS prevents this problem by recognizing that the application program has failed and restoring the data to the value that existed before the program attempted to modify it. The chapter "Data Security and Integrity" describes this process in detail.

Finally, the DB/DC system must protect data integrity when the *system*— either CICS itself or the operating system—fails. To do this, CICS keeps a *journal* of each data change. The journal is maintained on a magnetic tape or direct access storage device. When CICS is restarted it will automatically read the journal and use its contents to restore the data bases.

System Services

At the top center of the CICS system as illustrated in Figure 2-1, is the *system services* component. This text will discuss three types of system services:

1. Program Management

When a CICS user requests service or information, the program management component must determine which application program provides the requested service. It then loads the program from a library of CICS application programs into the computer's memory so that the program can be run. The next chapter describes how an application program that you have written gets into the CICS library, and how CICS recognizes when your program is needed for a user request.

2. Storage Control

Within the computer, a section of memory is assigned to the CICS system. Both CICS itself and the CICS application programs loaded by program management reside in this area. CICS manuals typically refer to the computer's memory or processing storage simply as *storage* or sometimes as *internal storage*. *Storage control*, then, refers to controlling that part of memory that has been assigned to CICS. When program control must load a new application program, it calls upon storage control to find space for the program. Other programs call upon program control when they need space to store data or to build control blocks.

3. Task Control

Chapter 1 said that the operating system is responsible for scheduling the work within the computer. Chapter 1 also referred to several types of work that might be performed by the computer. There is online CICS work, of course, and some offline work. There may also be a terminal system besides CICS whose users request online work. The unit of work that can be scheduled by the operating system is called a *task*. The operating system does not schedule each CICS user's work individually. Instead the operating system considers CICS and all its users to be a single task, and assigns computer resources to CICS or to another task that performs non-CICS work.

Note: CICS also uses the term *task* for the work that it schedules. As a CICS application programmer, you will be concerned almost exclusively with *CICS tasks* rather than the tasks that are managed by the operating system.

When the operating system assigns the computer to perform CICS work, the CICS task control component determines which CICS *user* will receive service. So the operating system and CICS share work scheduling responsibility. The operating system schedules work among CICS and non-CICS tasks, and CICS schedules work among CICS users.

Let's look briefly at how the operating system does its scheduling. Keep in mind that the computer's central processing unit (CPU) can execute only one instruction at a time, so at any instant the CPU is working on only one task. In large computers, there are normally several tasks awaiting processing by the CPU. The operating system must determine which task will receive CPU service at a given instant. The goal is to be sure that each task gets some amount of service over a period of time—say a second or so. Then the central processor is *time-shared* by the users. The general term for this process is *multi-tasking*.

At an instant in time a task may be either *active* or *inactive*. A task is inactive if it is waiting for some resource other than the CPU. For example, if a task is waiting to receive data from direct access storage, it is inactive. The central processor cannot perform useful work for this task until the requested data has been received. The task is said to be in an I/O wait.

When a system schedules work, it considers only active tasks. To choose from among the active tasks, the system considers the relative *priority* of each task. Tasks with higher priorities are given preference. The operating system looks at the priority of CICS compared to other tasks scheduled by the operating system. CICS looks at the priority of each user task it schedules.

We will not discuss multi-tasking in detail. However, we will point out two features of the multi-tasking method used by CICS.

a. Priority CICS calculates a priority for each task it must schedule. The priority is based upon priority values that a system programmer can pre-assign to the *individual user*, the *terminal which the task is serving*, and *the application program* the task is using.

b. Need for brevity When CICS task control selects a CICS task to receive service, the task will continue to receive service until it becomes inactive. Remember that there may be many CICS users awaiting service, and each user expects to receive a response from the computer within a few seconds. You have to be careful in writing your application program to be sure that it will not do very long and uninterrupted calculations or procedures. Otherwise your program can monopolize the system and lock out other CICS users.

Data Communication Functions

The *data communication* component of CICS is pictured on the right side of the CICS system in Figure 2-1. It interfaces, through the Telecommunication Access Methods, with the user terminals and with other computers.

CICS supports more than fifty different types of terminals. You may have wondered how you can write a program to send information to a user terminal when you don't know what kind of terminal you will be communicating with. The answer is that you use a facility called *Basic Mapping Support* to describe how you want the information to appear on the user's terminal. The Basic Mapping Support translates this description into the correct form for the terminal that is communicating with your program. Basic Mapping Support is one part of the data communications component.

The data communications component also includes two facilities that allow communication between computers. The first of these facilities, *Intersystem Communication* (ISC), allows a CICS system to communicate with a DB/DC system in another computer. The second DB/DC system can be either another CICS system or IMS, a widely used data base management system.

The second facility for communicating with other computers is designed to support *distributed processing*. This is a term that you are apt to hear in the DB/DC environment, so we will define it briefly.

Distributed Processing

Distributed processing describes the situation in which a central computing facility is linked to smaller "satellite" computers some distance away. Each satellite computer has a data base used in the work that goes on at its location. The central computer maintains a data base that combines the data from all of the satellite computers.

Distributed processing is commonly used where a company has branch offices, each of which is responsible for managing some set of accounts. The branch office uses its own computer to maintain data about the accounts managed by the branch. Periodically, usually at the close of each business day, the branch computer sends the updated branch data to the central computer.

If the branch office receives a request for information about an account it does not manage, the branch computer can route the inquiry to the central computing facility.

Notice that the central data base may not have up-to-the-minute information about the branch office accounts. If an account is changed at the branch office in the morning, the record of the change will not be placed in the central data base until evening. However if someone at the central facility needs to know the exact current status of a particular branch office account, the central computer can request this information from the satellite computer.

Monitoring Functions

In the center of the CICS system illustrated in Figure 2-1 is a component labeled "Monitoring Functions." These functions are used principally by systems programmers and data base administrators, and involve collection of information about how the CICS system is used. For example, the monitoring functions can be used to record how often a particular direct access file is modified. This text will not be concerned with the monitoring functions.

Application Program Services

As an application programmer you will be most concerned with the Application Program Services component shown at the lower center of the CICS system in Figure 2-1. This component includes the facility that allows you to code CICS commands into COBOL, and also PL/1 or Assembler language, programs. The facility is called the *Command Level Translator* and will be discussed below. In addition to the Command Level Translator for writing programs, CICS provides facilities for testing and debugging programs, checking command syntax interactively, and for tracing program execution. These facilities will be discussed in the chapters "CICS Program Concepts" and "Test and Problem Determination Tools."

Preparing a CICS Program

The previous section introduced the Command Level Translator as part of the Application Programming Services component. In order to get started to write CICS programs you need to know how to make the translator work. We'll begin by describing how the translator fits into the program preparation process.

Figure 2-2 shows the usual sequence of steps required to prepare a program for execution under the operating system. You have probably used a sequence like this for your previous programs. The figure shows that a program, which we call PROG, passes through two processes before it can be executed. The first is the *compile* process which translates the source program, made up of program language statements, into an *object module*. The object module contains the computer-level, binary-encoded equivalent of the source program.

The second process is the *link edit* which combines the PROG object module with any previously prepared programs that PROG will call upon during execution. These previously prepared programs are found in a "library" data set stored on direct access storage. The result of the link edit step is a single *load module* (called a *phase module* on some operating systems). The load module is essentially the complete package of programs, in binary form, ready for execution. If PROG is to be executed, the operating system will read

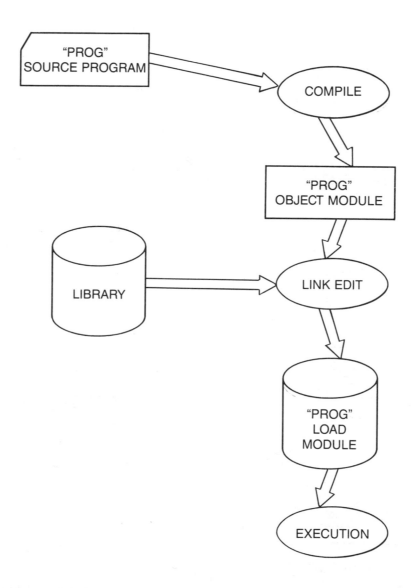

**Figure 2-2
Preparing Standard
Application Program
for Execution**

the load module into computer memory and schedule it for execution.

Figure 2-3 shows the program preparation sequence for CICS programs. Notice that at the beginning of the process there is a new step performed by the Command Level Translator. Remember that the CICS Command Level Translator permits CICS commands to be coded into your COBOL source program.

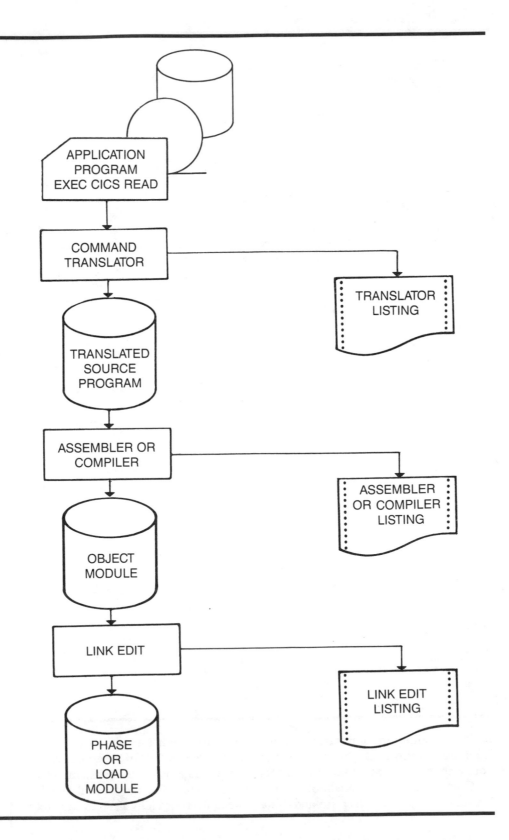

Figure 2-3
Preparing CICS
Application Program
for Execution

But the statements are not recognized by the COBOL compiler. If you tried to compile the program without going through the translator, COBOL would reject each of the CICS statements. The Command Translator's function is to translate the CICS commands into a form that the COBOL compiler will accept. The Command Translator's output is a source program that contains only standard COBOL statements. CICS provides a translator for PL/1 and assembler language programs as well as for COBOL.

You request translation of your program by submitting Job Control Language or an online terminal request defined by the system programmers at your computing facility. The request is similar to the requests you have probably submitted in the past to compile a COBOL program.

Figure 2-3 shows that, like the compiler or assembler and the linkage editor, the command translator produces a listing. As you would expect, the translator's listing contains information about any errors found in the CICS commands that the translator processed. If you request them, the translator can also provide a listing of the translated source program or a cross-reference list of the CICS commands that you used in the program.

You request optional output as well as other optional processing from the translator by placing a control statement at the beginning of your program. For example, your COBOL program might be preceded by a control statement like:

CBL CICS(SOURCE SPACE2)

This statement requests SOURCE, a listing of the translated program, and SPACE2 which causes the listing to be double-spaced.

Coding CICS Commands

Figure 2-4 shows a CICS command as you would code it in a COBOL program, and as it would be translated by the CICS command translator for COBOL.

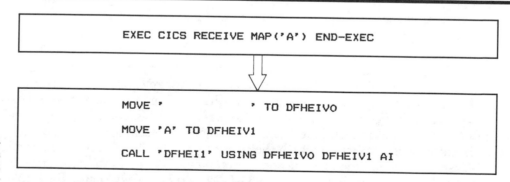

Figure 2-4
CICS Command as
Translated by CICS
Command Translator

```
EXEC CICS RECEIVE MAP('A') END-EXEC
```

```
MOVE '          ' TO DFHEIVO

MOVE 'A' TO DFHEIV1

CALL 'DFHEI1' USING DFHEIVO DFHEIV1 AI
```

The general format of CICS commands is EXEC CICS followed by the name of a CICS *function* and one or more *options* and terminated by END-EXEC. In Figure 2-4 the function is RECEIVE, and the option is MAP. The value A enclosed in parentheses is an *argument* of the option MAP. (RECEIVE is a CICS function that will be introduced in Chapter 3.)

The COBOL command translator translates each command into a sequence of COBOL statements like those shown in Figure 2-4; a sequence of MOVE statements followed by a CALL statement. The MOVE statements assign values to COBOL data variables, like DFHEIVO and DFHEIV1. These variables are named and declared automatically by the translator.

When your program is executed, the CALL statement passes control to the CICS *Execution Interface* program which is part of CICS. The Execution Interface program interprets the values passed to it by the CALL statement. In Figure 2-4, these are the variables DFHEIVO, DFHEIV1, and AI. It then passes control to the program within CICS that performs the requested function. Chapter 3 will look at the Execution Interface more closely.

Executing a CICS Application Program

When we introduced the Program Management service earlier in the chapter, we said that the program management service function (or *program manager*) is responsible for loading a CICS application program into the CICS region where it can be run. The sequence of events is this:

1. A CICS user enters a *transaction request* from his or her terminal.

   In the DB/DC environment, a *transaction* is the unit of work that is performed in response to a single user request. The user has a list of transaction names that can be requested. Each transaction name is associated with a service that the user requires. That is, the user does not know the names of *programs*, but only the names for *services*.

2. The program manager looks up the name of the service requested by the user and finds the name of the program that performs that service.

   To do this, the program manager looks in a table called the *Program Control Table*. You will get to know this table as the PCT. It contains the name of every transaction that can be requested by a CICS user. The entry for a particular transaction gives the name of an application program. The PCT is maintained by a system programmer.

3. If the program is not in the CICS region, the program manager finds the program in the CICS application library and loads it for execution.

   The reason for using the PCT may not be immediately obvious. Chapter 1 pointed out the importance of system independent application programs that do not have to be changed if the computer hardware or operating system change. It's also important that the CICS users don't have to "relearn" how to use transactions if the application programs are changed. For example, suppose that an application program has been written to perform a transaction that the users call AUD1. The users then find that they occasionally need to perform a slightly different type of transaction which they want to call AUD2. You may find that it's easiest to modify the existing application program to perform both trans-actions. The entries for both AUD1 and AUD2 in the PCT will name the same application program. Later on, you may decide to write separate programs for AUD1 and AUD2. When the programs have been tested, the PCT entries for AUD1 and AUD2 can be changed so that each names the correct new program. The user will continue to type AUD1 or AUD2, and has no reason to care whether the transactions are done by a single program or two different ones.

The Programmer's View

From this description you can see that the way to run your program is to:

1. Link edit the program into the CICS application library.
2. Define a name for the work your program does. This is the *transaction name*. It has to be a name that isn't already in the PCT.
3. Ask the system programmer to put the transaction name into a PCT entry and set the entry to contain the name of your program.
4. Sign on to CICS and enter a transaction request using the transaction name you defined.
5. The CICS program manager will then load your program into the CICS region. The next chapter will describe this sequence in more detail.

In practice, you will find that a set of transaction names have been placed in the PCT so that you can test a program without having to get a new transaction name put into the PCT. The system programmer will tell you what transaction name to use to test the program and how to link edit your program so that the program manager can find it. But these names are just for testing the program; they aren't known to the CICS users. When the program has been tested and is ready for general use, the PCT entry for a transaction name known to the users will be changed to point to your program.

The User's View

Typically, the user doesn't think in terms of running programs, but in terms of requesting transactions. From this point of view, three steps are involved:

1. Sign on to CICS.
2. Enter a transaction request.
3. Enter any additional information the transaction may require.

You will have to perform this sequence in order to test your program, so let's see how each step is done.

Signing On to CICS

To sign on to CICS you need a user identification name (*userid*) and a *password* that allows CICS to verify that you are the person authorized to sign on with this particular userid. When you identify yourself by signing on, CICS can determine your priority and the CICS resources you are authorized to use. (You may remember that CICS uses your priority as one factor in scheduling work you request.)

You will begin the sign on process by using a terminal either to type in a request to sign on, or to select CICS from a menu of available systems. For this description, we'll assume that a menu is not available and you must type in the request.

Signing on to CICS is itself a transaction, so you request it by entering a transaction request. The transaction name for signing on is CSSN—you simply type this four letter transaction name and press the ENTER key on your terminal.

From the earlier discussion, you know that the CICS program manager will find the name of the program that performs the sign on function and will load the name into memory for execution. However, most users don't know about this step. They know only that when they type CSSN, a display like the one shown in Figure 2-5 appears on their terminal screen.

You then enter your userid into the "Name" field, and your password into the "Password" field. You will have to change your password periodically, and to do so you just type a new password after the words "New Password = ".

```
PLEASE SUPPLY PERSONAL DETAILS

NAME=

PASSWORD=

NEWPASSWORD=
```

Figure 2-5
Typical CICS Sign
on Panel

Usually, when you type into the password and new password fields, you won't see the characters displayed on the screen. This is so no one can discover your password by reading it from the terminal screen.

When the sign-on process is finished, you receive the message:

SIGN-ON IS COMPLETE

Entering the Transaction Request

In some computing facilities, after sign on is complete CICS displays a menu of transactions that can be performed. Figure 2-6 shows this type of menu. The four-letter codes in the left-most column are *transaction identifiers*. We have been referring to these as transaction names. These are the codes the CICS program manager will look up in the PCT to find out which application program to load.

```
                VACATION PLANNING SYSTEM

KEY CHOSEN TRANSACTION CODE,THEN PRESS "ENTER"

    CODE    FUNCTION

    VAC1    FOR COUNTRIES AND DATES
    VAC2    TO SELECT A VACATION
    VAC3    TO PRINT CONFIRMATION DETAILS
    VAC4    TO ARRANGE AUTOMOBILE RENTAL
```

Figure 2-6
Typical Transaction
Request Menu

If there is no menu, you have to type a transaction request. You have already entered a very simple transaction request in order to sign on. In general, a transaction request consists of a transaction code, which can be from one to four characters long, and then any data required for the particular transaction. For example, suppose that a college CICS system provides a CICS transaction named SCDL to type out the schedule of any course listed in the course catalog.

To request the schedule for a course called CHEM 160, you might type:

SCDL CHEM 160

In this example, SCDL is the transaction name or code. CHEM 160 is data that will be processed by the application program that produces the schedule.

The next chapter will describe how CICS processes a user's transaction request.

Summary

In order to permit system independent DB/DC application programs to be written, CICS provides five types of services. This chapter names these services and the CICS component that performs each one.

The data handling component supports access to data bases and direct access files. It also provides facilities for preserving data integrity.

System services perform task control, program management, and storage control.

The data communications component supports communications with many types of terminals and, in a distributed processing environment, with other computer systems.

The monitoring functional component can be used to collect data about how CICS is used.

Application programming services support preparation of CICS application programs. This includes a command translator available for use with COBOL, PL/1, and Assembler languages to permit CICS commands to be coded into the source program. The translator replaces each CICS command with a sequence of source language instructions that, during execution, will assign values to parameter variables and invoke the CICS Execution Interface Program. This chapter showed how a CICS command looks before and after translation by the COBOL command translator.

Users invoke CICS application programs indirectly, by typing a transaction request that names the service they wish to be performed. The CICS program manager uses a table called the Program Control Table (PCT) to find which application program performs the requested service. This chapter outlined how you prepare a CICS application program and make it available for selection through the PCT. It also described how to sign on to CICS and enter a transaction request.

3 A CICS Transaction

Introduction

In Chapter 2, you saw how a CICS user invokes an application program by entering a transaction request at the terminal. This chapter will describe what goes on inside the CICS region in response to the transaction request. The description will include a discussion of some of the major parts of CICS involved: the Data Communications Component, and the Program Management and Task Management functions of the System Services Component. It will also introduce some of the major CICS control blocks and tables.

Next, to prepare for writing your first CICS program, you will be introduced to two CICS commands, SEND and RECEIVE. In the exercise, you will use these commands to communicate with an online user. (Of course, in this case, *you* will be the "user" as you enter transaction requests to try out your program.)

The chapter concludes with a discussion of some factors to consider when you write programs for the DB/DC environment. The terms *reenterable, quasi-reenterable, conversational,* and *pseudo-conversational* are defined in this section.

Objectives

After completing this chapter, you will be able to:

■ Describe how the CICS Terminal Control Program processes terminal input and output.
■ Describe how the CICS Task Control Program handles a transaction request.
■ Identify the major CICS tables and control blocks used when a task is initiated for a user's transaction request.
■ Write a CICS program that receives input from a user terminal and sends a message to the user terminal.
■ Define the terms *reenterable, quasi-reenterable, conversational,* and *pseudo-conversational.*

Transaction Processing

The CICS Region

We said earlier that the operating system assigns CICS a section of the computer's memory, and that CICS and the CICS application programs execute from that part of memory. We have been using the term CICS *region* for this part of memory. However with some operating systems, it might be called the CICS *partition* or *address space*. We will continue to use the term CICS region.

As Figure 3-1 shows, when the operator starts CICS, the program modules that make up CICS are loaded into the CICS region. These modules contain the CICS components we listed in Chapter 2. As CICS begins to execute, it reads some *tables* into the region. The tables, which are prepared by the system programmer, describe the computing facility and the way in which CICS is to operate.

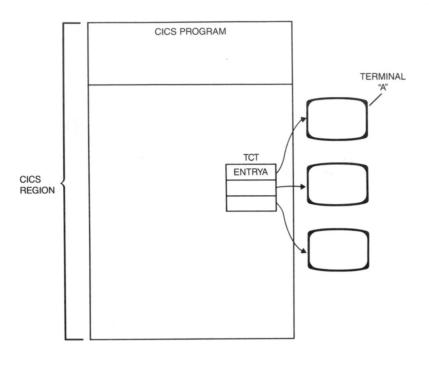

**Figure 3-1
CICS Region with
Terminal Control
Table (TCT)**

In Chapter 2, we introduced the *Program Control Table* (PCT) that lists the application programs available to CICS users. In Figure 1 another table, the *Terminal Control Table* is shown. You will usually hear the Terminal Control Table referred to as the TCT. The TCT has an entry for every terminal that can be used to communicate with CICS. This is the table that allows the CICS data communications function to know the characteristics of the terminal that was used to invoke your program.

Besides reading the tables into memory, CICS builds *control blocks* in its region. These are data areas that CICS will use to keep track of various processes. For example, the discussion to follow will introduce the *Task Control Area* or TCA. CICS builds a TCA to keep track of each CICS task that it initiates.

Many CICS manuals distinguish carefully between tables and control blocks, but you will find that programmers often use the terms interchangeably. The distinction is that tables are built by someone at your computing facility and placed on direct access storage where CICS can read them. Control blocks are built by CICS within the CICS region.

Reading the Transaction Request

We assume that after CICS has been started, a single user whom we will call USERA has used terminal A to sign on to CICS. After USERA signs on, the CICS region would be as shown in Figure 3-1.

We have mentioned the TCT which contains an entry for each terminal available to CICS. In Figure 3-1 we have labeled the TCT entry that describes terminal A as ENTRYA. Besides describing the terminal itself, ENTRYA contains several data fields that CICS can use to keep track of what terminal A is being used for. When USERA signed on to CICS, information about USERA—a user identification code, security and priority information—was placed in some of those fields. CICS will refer to this information as USERA continues the terminal session. For example, when USERA enters a transaction request, CICS will check the authorization information to see whether USERA is permitted to use the required application program.

Now assume that USERA enters a transaction request:

SCDL CHEM 160

Within the CICS data communications component is a program called the *Terminal Control Program* or TCP. (You may be wondering how many of these acronyms, like TCP, you will encounter as you read about CICS. To make things a little easier at first, we will use both the full name and acronym for these new terms. But you will probably find that you soon begin to use the acronyms quite naturally.)

The Terminal Control Program reads the input from the terminal and obtains a control block in which to store the input. The control block is called a *Terminal Input/Output Area* (TIOA), and it is built in space that the CICS Storage Control Program (SCP) provides in response to a request from the Terminal Control Program. The TCP moves the input into the Terminal Input/Output Area (TIOA) and places the address of the TIOA in ENTRYA.

Figure 3-2 shows the tables and control blocks as they exist at this point.

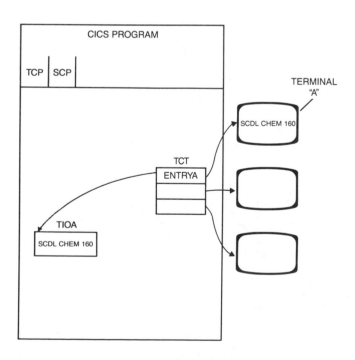

Figure 3-2
CICS Region with
Terminal Input
Output Area

The TCT entry for terminal A points to the TIOA where the terminal input SCDL CHEM 160 has been placed.

Initiating a Task

Within ENTRYA is a field used to keep track of the tasks that are executing for terminal A. Since no transaction has yet been started for USERA, ENTRYA will show that there is no task in process for terminal A. Therefore, the TCP will determine that the input just received from the terminal must be a request to *start* a transaction.

The Terminal Control Program (TCP) requests the *Task Control Program* to initiate a new task. (The acronym for the Task Control Program is *KCP*. This unusual acronym illustrates that making acronyms up is almost as difficult as remembering them—especially if you need an acronym for the *Task* Control Program, but the *Terminal* Control Program was invented first.)

Figure 3-3 summarizes the task initiation process; you may want to refer to Figure 3-3 as you read the following description.

The Task Control Program (KCP) checks the Program Control Table (PCT) to determine whether there is an application program that matches the transaction identification code SCDL. For our example, the program to perform transaction SCDL is called SCHEDULE, so the Program Control Table (PCT) entry for SCDL contains the name SCHEDULE.

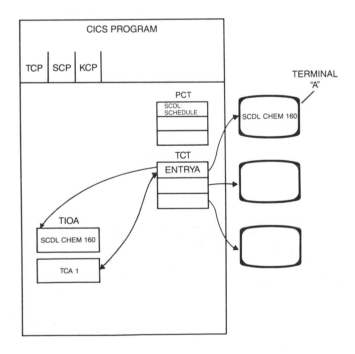

Figure 3-3
CICS Region After
Initiation of Task

The Task Control Program (KCP) then initiates a task to execute SCHEDULE. This involves creating a Task Control Area (TCA) for the new task, and "connecting" the task to terminal A by address pointers that connect the TCA to ENTRYA.

Notice that the TCT entry for terminal A points to the task control area, and the task control area points back to the TCT entry.

ENTRYA's pointer to the TCA shows that there is a task in process for terminal A. Therefore, if the Terminal Control Program (TCP) reads additional input from terminal A, the TCP will recognize that the input is not a new transaction request but data to be used in the current transaction.

When the TCA has been created, the CICS Program Control Program (PCP) is invoked to find the SCHEDULE program. As will be discussed later, SCHEDULE might already have been loaded into the CICS region in response to another user's transaction request. For now, assume that SCHEDULE is not already in the CICS region. The Program Control Program (PCP) will look in a table called the *Processing Program Table* (PPT) to find out where SCHEDULE is located within the CICS library. Using this information, the Program Control Program (PCP) will load SCHEDULE into storage.

Let's summarize the situation at this point—and review some terminology at the same time:

USERA has requested some work (a *transaction*) by entering a *transaction request* made up of a *transaction identification code* (SCDL) and data (CHEM 160) to be processed.

The CICS *Terminal Control Program* has recognized the transaction request and requested the *Task Control Program* to initiate a *task* to perform the transaction.

The Task Control Program has determined that a program called SCHEDULE is required to perform the SCDL transaction, and has requested *Program Control* to invoke SCHEDULE. SCHEDULE has been loaded into the CICS region, and it is associated with a task.

The task is *active* because it is waiting for service from the CPU. CICS will calculate a priority for the task, and schedule the task for processing according to its priority relative to other active CICS tasks. Remember that CICS calculates the task priority based upon priorities that have been assigned to the user (USERA), to the terminal in use (A), and to the application program (SCHEDULE) that the task is running.

Programming a Transaction

So far you've read how to code CICS commands into programs, how to get a program into the CICS library, and how to enter a transaction request to test a program. It's time to write a program and actually try all of this. Your first program will read some input from the user's transaction request and send a reply to the user. To do this you will learn the CICS commands to send and receive simple one-line terminal messages. In later lessons you will learn to send and receive full screens of data.

The RECEIVE Command

Think again about the SCHEDULE program used in the example above. When CICS assigns the CPU to process USERA's task, it will begin to execute program

SCHEDULE. One of the first things SCHEDULE must do is to read the data (CHEM 160) that USERA entered as part of the transaction request.

Remember that when you write a CICS application program, you don't use the input/output statements that are standard to your programming language. Instead, you use CICS commands—terminal commands for input/output for terminals, and file control commands for reading and writing the data base.

The command used to obtain input from the terminal is RECEIVE. We say that RECEIVE "obtains" input, rather than "reading" it, because the Terminal Control Program (TCP) performs the actual terminal read. When the SCHEDULE program begins to execute, the input data is already in a Terminal Input/Output Area (TIOA) within the CICS region. The function of the RECEIVE command then is to make the data in the TIOA available to the application program.

The general form of the RECEIVE command is:

EXEC CICS RECEIVE INTO (data area) LENGTH (data area)
END-EXEC

Here and throughout this text we will use upper case to indicate parts of the command that must be placed in the program exactly as shown. Lower case indicates that a variable name or value from the program must be substituted. As shown above, data area names must be entered as arguments of the INTO and LENGTH options.

The LENGTH data area must be a two-byte binary field. In COBOL it is defined:

PIC S9(4) COMP

Prior to execution of the RECEIVE, the value in LENGTH specifies the maximum length of data that can be accommodated in the INTO data area. The INTO data area may be any area whose length is greater than or equal to the size specified in the LENGTH argument.

When the RECEIVE command is executed, the TCP moves data from the TIOA into the data area specified for the INTO option and places the length of the data in the data area indicated by the LENGTH argument. If the input message is shorter than the INTO data area, the TCP moves the message into the area but leaves untouched the part of the INTO area that is beyond the message length. If the program were then to process the entire message area rather than the part indicated by LENGTH, it would find "garbage" in the rightmost positions.

The following sequence of COBOL statements illustrates how a program might correctly use the RECEIVE command:

```
WORKING-STORAGE SECTION.
77   LEN  PIC S9(4) COMP VALUE +8.
01   INPUT-MSG  PIC X(8).

MOVE 8 TO LEN.                    [begin loop]
MOVE '        ' TO INPUT-MSG.
EXEC CICS RECEIVE INTO (INPUT-MSG) LENGTH (LEN) END-EXEC.
IF INPUT-MSG EQUAL TO 'END' ...[exit loop]
```

Here the programmer has defined an eight-byte area, INPUT-MSG, to receive input from the terminal. Remember that the user's input may be less than eight characters. In fact, to terminate the transaction, the user is expected to type the three characters END. The MOVE statement preceding the RECEIVE command is important. To see why, read through the following case.

Suppose that the RECEIVE command is in a programmed loop that is exited only when the program receives the END message from the user. Assume that, in the previous trip through the loop, the program received BROCCOLI as the input message. Therefore, INPUT-MSG is equal to BROCCOLI. Now imagine that the MOVE statement has been omitted, and the program issues the RECEIVE command again. This time, the user has typed END. The program RECEIVES the new input message into INPUT-MSG and tests to see whether INPUT-MSG is equal to END. But without the preceding MOVE statement, INPUT-MSG will *not* be equal to END, instead it will be equal to ENDCCOLI.

Notice that the program also resets the value of LEN before each execution of the RECEIVE command. This is important because each time CICS executes a RECEIVE command, it places the number of characters received into the LENGTH argument. Therefore, the value of the LENGTH argument may be changed each time the RECEIVE command is executed.

The program illustrated above could have checked the LENGTH argument, LEN, to find how many characters the user typed. When the user typed END, the RECEIVE command would have set LEN to 3. The program could then have tested only the first three characters of INPUT-MSG. However, testing only part of the input area would be less straightforward to program. Since INPUT-MSG is small, it is easier and more efficient to simply reset INPUT-MSG before issuing the RECEIVE command.

Suppose that the user types *more* characters than you allowed for in defining the size of your input area. In this case, the TCP moves only the number of characters specified by the value of the LENGTH argument. The remaining characters are lost. In this situation, CICS sets the LENGTH value to the length of the message as it was typed by the user. For the example program, suppose that the user types ASPARAGUS. Then, after the RECEIVE command is completed, INPUT-MSG will contain ASPARAGU and LEN will have a value of 9.

As you will see in the next chapter, CICS regards this as an error condition. The next chapter discusses how CICS applications can be programmed to handle error conditions.

Figure 3-4 shows a segment of a COBOL program that uses the RECEIVE command. Notice how the data areas used as arguments for the INTO and LENGTH options have been defined in the working-storage section. Notice too, that like all CICS commands in COBOL programs, the RECEIVE command is terminated by END-EXEC. For the rest of this book, we will not show the END-EXEC in the definition of each new command.

The SEND Command

The CICS command used to send messages to the online user is, not surprisingly, called the SEND command. As shown below, the general form of the SEND command is similar to that of the RECEIVE command:

EXEC CICS SEND FROM (data area) LENGTH (data area) [ERASE]

Here and throughout this text, we use brackets ([ ]) to indicate a field, like the ERASE option, that may be omitted. Remember that, although we will not continue to show it, every CICS command must terminate with END-EXEC.

```
IDENTIFICATION DIVISION.
    .
    .
    .
WORKING—STORAGE SECTION.
    77    MSG—LENGTH PIC S9(4) USAGE IS COMP.
    01    INPUT—MSG.
          02    TRANS—ID        PIC X(4).
          02    FILLER          PIC X(1).
          02    MESSAGE         PIC X(5).
    .
    .
    .
PROCEDURE DIVISION.
    MOVE 10 TO MSG—LENGTH.
    .
    .
    .
    EXEC CICS RECEIVE INTO (INPUT—MSG) LENGTH (MSG—LENGTH) END—EXEC.
    .
    .
    .
```

**Figure 3-4
COBOL Program
with CICS RECEIVE
Command**

When the SEND command is executed, the number of characters indicated by
the LENGTH argument are moved from the FROM data area to a TIOA for
transmission to the terminal. Remember that you must define a value for each
character you send to the terminal. The following sequence of COBOL statements illustrates a programming error that can have spectacular effects at the
user's terminal.

```
WORKING-STORAGE SECTION.
77   LEN  PIC S9(4) COMP VALUE  +20.
01   OUTPUT-MSG PIC X(15).

MOVE 'USER MESSAGE 15' TO OUTPUT-MSG.
EXEC CICS SEND FROM (OUTPUT-MSG) LENGTH (LEN) END-EXEC.
```

Here the programmer has defined an output area, OUTPUT-MSG, that is
15 bytes in length. But the SEND command's LENGTH argument specifies
that 20 bytes be sent to the terminal. CICS will transmit the 20 bytes beginning
at OUTPUT-MSG to the terminal.

The effect depends upon what the five bytes that follow OUTPUT-MSG
in memory happen to contain. If they contain character values, the user will
simply see a strange message. For example:

USER MESSAGE 15PLEAS

However, the remaining five bytes might also contain non-character values that have special meaning to the terminal hardware. In this case, the user's display may flash, or the terminal might beep or disconnect altogether.

Notice that neither the RECEIVE nor SEND command includes a parameter to specify "which terminal" the command is to address. The TCP always directs the input/output to or from the terminal that was used to initiate the transaction. (And, as you remember, the TCP can determine which terminal that is by following the address pointers from the task's TCA to the TCT entry for the terminal.)

Figure 3-5 shows a segment of a COBOL program that uses the SEND command. In this case, the ERASE option has been used. When ERASE is coded, it causes the screen to be cleared before the message is displayed. This is useful to eliminate confusing screen "clutter" caused by data left on the screen from previous processing. However the ERASE option must be used with care so as not to erase information that the user hasn't had a chance to read or may need to refer to during the transaction.

```
IDENTIFICATION DIVISION.
        .
        .
        .
WORKING—STORAGE SECTION.
01    OUTPUT—MESSAGE.
        02    MSG—ID      PIC X(4).
        02    FILLER      PIC X(1).
        02    MSG—TXT     PIC X(35).
        .
        .
        .
PROCEDURE DIVISION.
        .
        .
        .
      MOVE 'INV1' TO MSG—ID.
      MOVE 'INVOICE NOW BEING PRINTED' TO MSG—TXT.
      EXEC CICS SEND FROM (OUTPUT—MESSAGE)
            LENGTH(30)
            ERASE END—EXEC.
        .
        .
```

**Figure 3-5
COBOL Program
with CICS SEND
Command**

In Figure 3-5, the FROM area containing the message to be sent is 40 characters long. Notice that the message to be sent is contained in OUTPUT-MESSAGE which begins with a four-character message identifier (MSG-ID). MSG-ID is followed by a single blank and then by the actual text to be sent. The message INVOICE NOW BEING PRINTED contains 25 characters. Therefore, the LENGTH argument is 30, the sum of 4 + 1 + 25; it specifies the actual number of characters to be sent. As shown in this example, the value may be less than the length of the FROM data area. The output message could be any string of characters; it is not necessary to include a message identifier when sending messages to the terminal.

Terminating the Transaction

There is only one additional CICS command required to complete the first programming exercise. That is, RETURN, the command used to terminate a CICS transaction.

It is coded:

EXEC CICS RETURN

In Chapter 4, we will discuss other ways to terminate a CICS program and will introduce an option that can be used with RETURN.

For now, however, we will consider the RETURN command as shown above and as used in a program like the one described in this chapter's programming exercise. The program performs three steps:

1. RECEIVE a message from the user.
2. SEND a message to the user.
3. Terminate using the RETURN command.

In this context, the RETURN command causes control to return to the CICS Task Control Program, the KCP. As we have seen, the KCP initiated a task to execute the program; now the task will be terminated. If you review the steps that the KCP performed during task initiation, you can guess some of the steps that it will perform to terminate the task. The TCA that was created in space obtained from Storage Control will no longer be needed, so the space can be freed. The address of the TCA that was in the terminal's TCT entry will be replaced with a zero. This will allow the TCP to recognize the next input from the terminal as a new transaction request. If no other user has requested the same application program, the program's space in the CICS region can also be freed. Essentially, after task termination, all traces of the task will be removed from the CICS region.

Testing your CICS program

Let's review the steps involved in completing the programming exercise.

First, of course, you must write the program and enter it into the computer. Although the CICS commands are new to you, the process of entering this program is no different than the process you have used for other programs.

Secondly, the program must be translated by a CICS Command Translator. You need to know the job control statements used in your computing facility to invoke the translator. Possibly the Command Translator will find errors in your program. You should scan the output listing for error or warning messages.

Thirdly, the program file produced by the Command Translator must be compiled. As always, you should scan the compiler listing for error messages.

The fourth step is the link edit. In order to write the job-control statements for this step, you need some information about the CICS system you will use to test your program.

Remember that the linkage editor will place your program, ready for execution, in a load module library. We have seen that you execute a CICS program by typing a transaction request that specifies a transaction identification code. A CICS table, the PCT, matches the transaction code to a program name; another table, the PPT, gives the location of the named program. You must direct the linkage editor to place your program's load module into a CICS program library, and to name the load module so that CICS Program Control can find it. Then to test the program, you must use a transaction code that is connected, by the PCT and PPT, to your program.

You may find that your program doesn't work the first time. In later chapters, we will introduce some debugging tools that can be used to find program errors. At this point, however, the programming exercises are quite straightforward, and sophisticated debugging tools should not be needed. If you find that the program doesn't work, check carefully the listings produced by the Command Translator and Compiler. Make sure that there are no error or warning messages that you might have missed, and confirm that you didn't omit any statements or make other errors in entering the program. Think through the CICS transaction processing steps described at the beginning of the chapter, and try to identify at which point the problem occurred.

If CICS didn't load your program at all, check the output from the link edit step to verify that your program was placed in the correct CICS library and named as you intended. Make sure you entered the transaction request correctly.

Did the program begin to execute? Might it have executed in a way that you couldn't see? For example, perhaps it wrote blanks onto the screen instead of the intended message, or wrote the message and then erased the screen so quickly that you couldn't detect it.

Finally, most programmers find that talking through a program with another person helps them to find errors. It's OK to ask for help; in general, it will not be true that all programs except yours work perfectly.

There is one other source of error to be considered. When you typed the transaction request, did you enter data that your program couldn't handle? In Chapter 4, you'll find out how to prevent unexpected user input from causing your program to fail. An important part of designing a program for DB/DC applications is to make the program "input-proof." For this first exercise, though, incorrect input can easily cause your program to fail.

Programming Strategies

You have seen how an application program is loaded into the CICS region, and you have read about some of the tables and control blocks that also reside in the CICS region. Now we need to think about how the CICS region looks in a "real-world" DB/DC computing environment. We know that, in such an environment, there can be well over a thousand online users at a time. Is there a program in the region for each user? How large a CICS region would be required to hold a thousand application programs plus CICS itself and its tables and control blocks? If you consider that the computer must also have space for the operating system and for non-CICS work, you may begin to suspect that this is an unworkable situation. In practice, the size of the CICS region can sometimes be a problem, but fortunately, the requirement is not so great as the questions above would suggest.

There are two characteristics of online processing that make it unnecessary that there be an application program in memory for each user.

First, when there are a large number of users, it's unlikely that each is using a different program. We will take advantage of this fact by designing programs so that they can be shared by more than one user at a time.

Secondly, most of the time an online user isn't interacting with a program at all. Most of a user's time is spent either reading and thinking about how to respond to messages from a program, or physically entering data—typing characters from the keyboard. Clearly, there is no reason for a program to wait in memory, occupying space, while the user stares at the screen. Nor is the program needed while the user enters data; we've already seen that the data is physically read by the TCP, not by an application program.

We will look first at the question of how programs can be shared. Then we will see how applications can be written so that a program needn't be present in the CICS region during user "think time," and during terminal input/output operations.

Sharing Programs

In general, a program stored in a load module library contains instructions and data areas. When the program is in memory and being executed, the CPU reads and performs each instruction in turn—or as directed by branch instructions. If an instruction is executed that causes the controlling task to become inactive—like a request for input/output or for one of the other external resources that will be discussed in later chapters—CICS makes a note of which instruction to start with when the CPU is next assigned to the task.

If the program doesn't contain instructions that change the program's own instructions or data, there's no reason that several tasks cannot use the same program. The program is merely present in memory where the CPU can read it. The program doesn't change when the CPU reads an instruction from it. If several tasks use the same program, CICS just has to keep track of where each task "left off" and will continue when the CPU is assigned again to the task. In some publications, this is described as *maintaining a separate thread of control* for each task, and the sharing of a program by several tasks is called *multi-threading*.

Remember, however, that multi-threading is only possible if the program isn't changed during execution, and this applies to both the instructions and to the data areas of the load module. Programs written in compiler languages like COBOL or PL/1 do not modify their own instructions, but what about the data areas? If a shared program modified data within the program, then task A might process data that another task had stored in the program while task A was inactive.

To understand how this potential problem is avoided, we must distinguish between two kinds of data. *Constant* or *static* data are unchanged during execution; they may be contained in the load module along with the program's instructions. *Variable* or *working-storage* data are changed during execution. If a program is to be shared, this data may not be part of the load module. All programming languages supported by CICS permit the programmer to easily keep the static and working storage separate.

Reenterable Programs

Refer again to the COBOL program shown in Figure 3-5. The Working-Storage section defines a data area that is 40 bytes in length. The MOVE statements move *constant* data, INV1 and INVOICE NOW BEING PRINTED, into working-storage fields. The load module produced from this COBOL program will include the constant data, but it will not include the 40 bytes of space for working storage. Instead, it will simply include an indicator that 40 bytes of working storage are required. When the load module is loaded into memory for execution, as shown in Figure 3-6, the program instructions and constant data are allocated space in memory. This space can be shared, because it will not be altered when the program executes. The working storage is allocated separate space which cannot be shared. Each task that executes the program will have its own copy of working storage. To summarize, each task executes the same instructions and uses the same constant data, but processes its own version of working storage data.

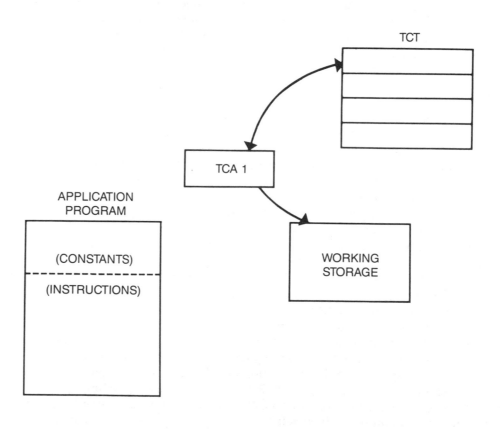

Figure 3-6
Application Program
Load Module and
Working Storage

A program that is not modified during execution is called *reentrant* or *reenterable*. COBOL programs are normally reentrant. PL/1 programs are reentrant if the programmer is careful to use STATIC storage only for data that will not be modified. Writing reentrant assembly language programs requires more attention on the part of the programmer, but is not difficult once the required statements are learned.

Quasi-Reenterable Programs

In reading CICS publications, you may encounter the term *Quasi-reenterable*. This describes a program that modifies itself at some point during execution, but which *restores itself* to the original unmodified form before executing the next CICS command. Such a program can be shared. To understand this, we need to look again at how CICS handles *multi-tasking*.

Once CICS assigns the CPU to process a CICS task, say TASK1, no other CICS task can execute until TASK1 becomes inactive. TASK1 becomes inactive only when it must wait for an external resource of some kind. However, a CICS task may request an external resource only by executing a CICS command. Therefore, between CICS commands, TASK1 cannot lose control to another CICS task. TASK1 can "temporarily" modify the program because no other task will use the program until TASK1 executes the next CICS command.

Quasi-reenterable programs are not recommended. It's easy to inadvertently change the program logic so that a quasi-reenterable program fails to restore itself. Such an error can cause failures that are hard to debug because they will not occur consistently. It is not difficult to write reentrant programs for CICS, and this should be regarded as the correct programming practice.

Conversational Transactions

The program you will write for this chapter's programming exercise performs a simple message-response transaction. That is, the program reads data entered with the transaction request, responds with a message, and terminates. This is different than a *conversational* transaction in which the application program sends a question to the user, the user enters a reply, and then the application program returns an answer.

Consider the following example of a conversational transaction:

A user enters a request for a vacation tour planning transaction. The transaction request includes data specifying a desired destination and vacation dates. Now a program-user "conversation" begins. The program responds with a list of tours available and their price. The user examines the list and selects a desired tour. The user's choice is recorded, and the program sends back a confirmation of reservations. This completes the transaction.

If the vacation tour planning transaction is called VAC1, a single program might process it as shown in Figure 3-7. In this case, the program and other storage areas required remain in the CICS region while the user ponders the tour choices.

However, suppose that the transaction were handled by two separate programs as shown in Figure 3-8. The user enters the initial request using the VAC1 transaction code. The initial program sends the choice of tours and then terminates. When the user enters the final selection, the second program is initiated to record the choice and confirm reservations. The transaction appears the same to the user, but in this case no memory space was tied up by a program awaiting the user's decision. Space is also saved because each of the two programs is much smaller than the single large one.

From the user's point of view, the transaction still *appears* to be conversational, but no truly conversational program is involved. Therefore, the transaction is described as *pseudo-conversational*. As shown in Figure 3-8, the VAC1 transaction is terminated by a form of the RETURN command that names the

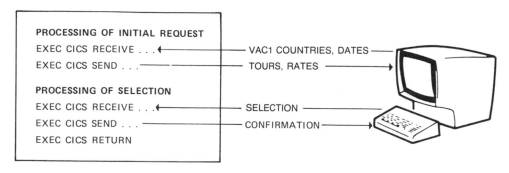

**Figure 3-7
Conversational
Transaction,
User View**

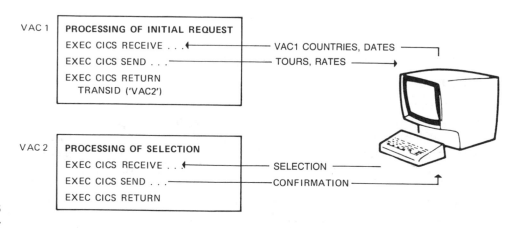

**Figure 3-8
Pseudo-
Conversational
Transaction,
User View**

transaction to be used when input is received again from the terminal. Chapter 4 will discuss this use of the RETURN command.

In the previous example, two separate transactions (VAC1 and VAC2) have been used. However, a pseudo-conversational transaction doesn't always involve more than one transaction.

Figure 3-9 shows a transaction, called PSEU, which processes a single data value received from the user. After processing the data, PSEU terminates but specifies (TRANSID "PSEU") that it is to be initiated again when the user enters the next input. PSEU continues to terminate and be reinitiated until the user enters the characters END which signify that there is no more data to be processed.

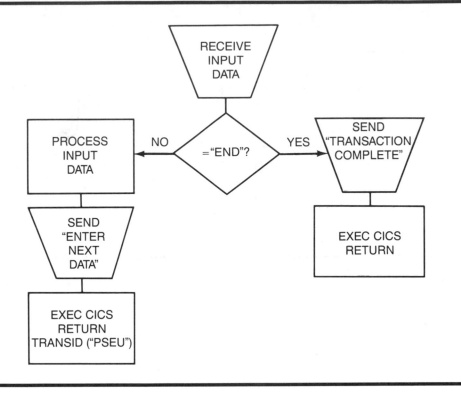

Figure 3-9
Flow of Pseudo-Conversational Transaction

Summary

Before the first CICS user transaction has been started, the CICS region contains the CICS program modules, CICS tables, and control blocks.

The CICS program that performs input/output operations for terminals is the Terminal Control Program (TCP). The TCP uses a CICS table, the Terminal Control Table (TCT) which has an entry for each terminal that CICS controls. The TCP builds a control block, called a Terminal Input/Output Area (TIOA), to hold input received from a terminal. The TIOA is built in space provided by the CICS Storage Control Program. When the TCP reads input from a terminal that has no task in progress, the TCP recognizes that the input is a transaction request.

In response to a transaction request, the TCP requests the Task Control Program (KCP) to initiate a CICS task. A Task Control Area (TCA) control block is built to keep track of the task; its address is placed in the TCT entry for the terminal used to enter the transaction request.

The Program Control Program (PCP) uses two tables, the PCT and PPT, to find the application program required for the transaction request, and to load the program for execution.

CICS application programs use the RECEIVE and SEND commands to obtain input from, and send output to, user terminals. When an application program has completed its processing, it uses the CICS RETURN command to return to the CICS KCP for task termination.

When more than one transaction requires the same CICS application program, the program can be shared by the tasks, because CICS programs must be either reenterable or quasi-reenterable.

In order to make most efficient use of the CICS region, conversational transactions can often be programmed as pseudo-conversational transactions. This means that the transaction may be handled by more than one program. Each program terminates as soon as it has sent the user a request for more input; the next program will be started when the user enters the required input. A program may also name *itself* as the transaction to be started to process the user's next input. In this case, the pseudo-conversational transaction involves only a single program which is reinitiated each time the user enters new input.

The programming exercise for this chapter provides practice in using the RECEIVE, SEND, and RETURN commands.

DISCUSSION QUESTIONS

1. What is the distinction between a *table* and a *control block*?
2. The TCA and the TCT entry for the terminal associated with the task are linked bidirectionally; that is, each contains the address of the other. In this chapter, what uses were identified for:
   a. The TCT entry address in the TCA?
   b. The TCA address in the TCT entry?
3. Distinguish between the PCT and PPT.
4. Distinguish between *conversational* and *pseudo-conversational* transactions.

EXERCISE

Write a program to:

1. Receive the following input from a terminal:

   code LAX01 AB12345 BOOKENDS

   The input consists of four fields separated by a blank character. The lengths of the fields are 4, 5, 7, 30 respectively. The illustrated input shows typical values that might be entered for each field; *code* represents the transaction identification code assigned for testing your program.
2. Respond to the user with the message INPUT RECEIVED.
3. Terminate.

Test your program using various input values. Check to see what happens if you enter an input string of 60 characters.

4 | CICS Program Concepts

Introduction

This chapter is divided into the following four sections:

1. Handling Exceptional or Error Conditions
2. Program Linkage
3. Addressing Areas Outside the Program
4. The Command Language Interpreter

By way of introduction, we'll say a few words about each of these topics.

Exceptional or Error Conditions

In the exercise for Chapter 3, you wrote a program that uses the RECEIVE command to obtain input entered as part of the transaction request. When you tested your program, you may have experimented with entering a transaction request containing more characters than you had specified in the RECEIVE command's LENGTH option. We remarked in Chapter 3 that CICS regards this as an error condition. If you tried a long transaction request you discovered that when CICS recognized the error, it sent a message to the user and terminated execution of your program. In this chapter, you will find out how your program can handle errors like this and prevent CICS from terminating your program when the error occurs.

Program Linkage

At the end of Chapter 3, we introduced the term *pseudo-conversational* and showed how a particular transaction could be separated into two separate transactions. This section shows how to program a pseudo-conversational transaction. This includes how to terminate one program and arrange for a second program to be invoked when the user enters the next terminal input. It also describes how the first program can pass information to the second program.

The Program Linkage section also discusses how a CICS application program can transfer control to a separate program—that is, a program that has not been linked into the same load (or phase) module.

Addressability

When a program transfers control to another, it usually needs to pass some data to the program that is to be invoked. The subject of passing data between programs is related to a more general question of how a program can get at data that is in the CICS region, but is not in the program's working storage. Often, for example, a program needs information that is contained in CICS control blocks or tables. This Addressability section describes how to access several types of such information.

Command Language Interpreter

When you wrote your program, you may have found that you didn't get all the CICS commands and options written correctly the first time. If so, you received an error message from the CICS command translator or from the COBOL compiler. Then you had to change the program and try again, by repeating the command translate—compile—link edit sequence again. Many CICS facilities use a programming aid called the *Command Language Interpreter* that lets you test CICS commands from your CICS terminal *without* going through this sequence. If your CICS facility uses the Command Language Interpreter you will want to use it for the rest of the programming exercises. This chapter describes what the Command Language Interpreter can do, and how you can use it.

Objectives

After completing this chapter, you will be able to:

- Program an exception-handling routine to handle abnormal conditions detected during execution of a CICS command.
- Use the CICS HANDLE, IGNORE, and NOHANDLE commands to specify where control is to be transferred when a CICS command detects an exceptional condition.
- Program a pseudo-conversational transaction.
- Use the CICS LINK and XCTL commands to transfer control to a separate CICS application program.
- Write programs that refer to data that lies outside the program's working-storage and load module.
- Use the Command Language Interpreter to verify the syntax of CICS commands.

Part 1: Handling Exceptional Conditions

The general term for an error or other abnormal situation that occurs during execution of a CICS command is *exceptional condition* or simply *exception*. The term "exception" might cause you to think that these conditions occur so rarely that you needn't be too concerned about them—rather like being struck by a meteor. In the programming sense, however, exceptional conditions occur frequently and are something you need to plan for carefully when you design your programs. When you consider that each application program may be executed hundreds or thousands of times each day, it's not surprising to realize that a program encounters exceptional conditions many times in the course of the day.

When you tested your program for the last chapter's exercise, you may have caused it to fail by entering a longer transaction request than allowed by the LENGTH option of the program's RECEIVE command. If you did, CICS would have terminated execution of your program and sent a terminal message that looked like:

TRANSACTION name PROGRAM progname ABEND AEIV

The field called *name* would be replaced by the name of the transaction you used to test your program. The *progname* field would be replaced by your program's name. ABEND stands for Abnormal End, and AEIV is a code to tell you that the ABEND was caused by "incorrect data length".

As a programmer, you may already be accustomed to seeing messages like this. However, to most users they are confusing to say the least. If your programs are to be useful, you will have to "protect" users from abnormal terminations and from messages the users may not understand.

You can do this by requesting CICS to allow your program to handle certain exception conditions. When CICS recognizes an exception, it checks to see whether it is one of the exceptions your program can handle. If so, it transfers control to the section of your program that you defined to handle the exception.

Since your first program wasn't set up to handle the "incorrect data length" situation, CICS took a *default action*. For most exceptions, the default action is to terminate the program and issue the standard-form error message described above. The message was adequate for you to test the program. It told you that "the program doesn't work if I do this." But now you need to find out how to send a message that the user will understand; for example: "Your transaction request has too many characters. Please try again."

First, each exceptional condition that CICS can detect is identified by an *exception name*. For example, the "incorrect data length" exceptional condition we've been discussing is named *LENGERR*. If you want your program to check for and handle this condition, you code a command to inform CICS that LENGERR is to be handled by your program and *not* by the default CICS exception-handling module. You do this by using the HANDLE command described below.

You may also request that CICS simply ignore certain exception conditions. To do this you code either the IGNORE command, or the NOHANDLE option on a particular CICS command. Both these approaches are described below.

The HANDLE Command

You use the HANDLE Command to specify that your program will handle particular exceptional conditions, and to identify a location in the program that should receive control when the condition is detected.

The command is written:

EXEC CICS HANDLE CONDITION name(argument) ... name(argument)

The option *name* identifies the exceptional condition to be handled. *Argument* is the label of a statement or location in the program. When the named condition is detected, CICS will transfer control to the specified location. A single HANDLE command may specify handling for up to twelve conditions by repeating the name(argument) field multiple times.

Figure 4-1 shows how the HANDLE command might have been used in the programming exercise for Chapter 3. As shown here, the HANDLE command must be executed before the command that detects the error condition. In a COBOL program, the label specified (TOOLONG in Figure 4-1) is a paragraph name. The labeled routine receives control via a "go to depending on"—not via a "perform."

The part of your program that handles an exceptional condition is called an *exception routine*. Your exception routine receives control as described above, performs some processing to handle the exception, and then either branches back into the application program or terminates. In Figure 4-1, the TOOLONG routine sends an error message and then terminates by executing the CICS RETURN command.

Figure 4-2 shows another example of an exception-handling routine. Here the exception-handling routine doesn't terminate processing, but performs some

```
IDENTIFICATION DIVISION.
PROGRAM-ID. CICA01C.
*  *  *  *  *  *  *  *  *  *  *  *  *  *  *  *  *  *  *  *  *
*                                                          *
*                                                          *
*                                                          *
*  THIS PROGRAM RECEIVES INPUT DATA FROM A TERMINAL        *
*  AND SENDS A CONFIRMING MESSAGE BACK TO THE              *
*  TERMINAL.                                               *
*                                                          *
*                                                          *
*                                                          *
*  *  *  *  *  *  *  *  *  *  *  *  *  *  *  *  *  *  *  *  *
ENVIRONMENT DIVISION.
DATA DIVISION.
WORKING-STORAGE SECTION.
77  LEN     PIC S9(4) COMP VALUE +49.
01  INPUT-MSG.
    02 TRANS-ID   PIC X(4).
    02 FILLER     PIC X.
    02 ITEM-NO    PIC X(5).
    02 FILLER     PIC X.
    02 CUST-NO    PIC X(7).
    02 FILLER     PIC X.
    02 DESC       PIC X(30).
01  OUTPUT-MSG    PIC X(27).
PROCEDURE DIVISION.
    EXEC CICS HANDLE CONDITION LENGERR (TOOLONG) END-EXEC.
    EXEC CICS RECEIVE INTO (INPUT-MSG) LENGTH (LEN)
            END-EXEC.
    MOVE 'INPUT RECEIVED' TO OUTPUT-MSG.
    MOVE 14 TO LEN.
    EXEC CICS SEND FROM (OUTPUT-MSG) LENGTH (LEN) ERASE
            END-EXEC.
    EXEC CICS RETURN END-EXEC.
TOOLONG.
    MOVE 'INPUT EXCEEDS 49 CHARACTERS' TO OUTPUT-MSG.
    MOVE 27 TO LEN.
    EXEC CICS SEND FROM (OUTPUT-MSG) LENGTH (LEN) ERASE
            END-EXEC.
    EXEC CICS RETURN END-EXEC.
    STOP RUN.
```

**Figure 4-1
HANDLE Command
and Exception-
Handling Routine**

processing and then transfers control back into the normal program flow.

The HANDLE command (labeled 1) in the figure defines the ENDFILE statement (labeled 2) as the location to receive control when an end-of-file condition is detected. The ENDFILE paragraph formats a message for the user and transfers to DISPLAY-RECORD to send the message. (Don't be concerned with the particular commands used to send and receive messages. They will be discussed beginning with Chapter 7.) The user then enters a response to the message, and processing continues.

Notice that the exception-handling routine uses a GO TO statement to transfer control back into the normal program flow. This illustrates again that the exception-handling routine is, both logically and physically, part of the larger program. It is *not* a separate unit that is "called" by CICS when an exceptional condition is detected, nor is it an "extension" of the CICS command processing routines.

```
PROCEDURE DIVISION.
  (1) EXEC CICS HANDLE CONDITION
                        ENDFILE (ENDFILE) END-EXEC


                        .
                        .
                        .

PAGE-FORWARD.
    MOVE FLDC TO FLDD.
    MOVE FLDB TO FLDC.
    MOVE FLDA TO FLDB.
                        .
                        .
                        .

DISPLAY-RECORD.

    EXEC CICS SEND MAP('XDFHCMC') ERASE END-EXEC.
REPEAT.
    EXEC CICS RECEIVE MAP('XDFHCMC') END-EXEC
    IF DIRI EQUAL 'F' THEN GO TO PAGE-FORWARD.
    IF DIRI EQUAL 'B' THEN GO TO PAGE-BACKWARD.
    GO TO SMSG.
(2) ENDFILE.
    MOVE 'END OF FILE' TO MSG10.
    MOVE DFHBMASB TO MSG2A.
    GO TO DISPLAY-RECORD.
PAGE-BACKWARD.
    IF FLDC EQUAL ZEROS GO TO TOO-FAR.
    MOVE FLDC TO FLDA.
    MOVE FLDC TO FLDB.
    MOVE FLDD TO FLDC.
    MOVE ZEROS TO FLDD.
    IF FLDA NOT EQUAL KEYI THEN ADD 1 TO FLDA.
    EXEC CICS RESETBR DATASET('FILEA') RIDFLD(FLDA) END-EXEC
    GO TO  BUILD.
                        .
                        .
                        .
```

**Figure 4-2
Transferring Control
From an Exception-
Handling Routine**

The IGNORE Command

Rather than specifying a routine to handle a particular exceptional condition, you may use the IGNORE command to specify that no action is to be taken when the condition occurs. In this case, CICS will not check for the condition at all.

IGNORE is written:

EXEC CICS IGNORE CONDITION name ... name

As in the HANDLE Command, *name* identifies a condition, and up to 12 names may be listed.

Let's see how the program of Figure 4-1 might have used the IGNORE command. In place of the HANDLE command, the program would include an IGNORE command of the form:

EXEC CICS IGNORE CONDITION LENGERR END-EXEC.

Then the program would have been modified to test the value of LEN after the RECEIVE command had been executed. Remember that CICS will not move more characters from the TIOA than the LENGTH option allows, and that after moving the characters it sets the LENGTH option argument to the number of characters moved. Therefore, if LEN were greater than 49 after the RECEIVE command, the program should branch to TOOLONG.

When you specify IGNORE for a condition, you must be sure that your program tests for the condition and takes any corrective actions required to prevent incorrect processing. If the program in our example had included the IGNORE command, but had not tested the LEN value, then the program would complete processing using only the first 49 characters of input. The program would not detect, and so could not let the user know, that the final input characters had been lost.

The NOHANDLE Option

In addition to the HANDLE and IGNORE commands, CICS provides a NOHANDLE option that can be coded in any CICS command. If NOHANDLE appears, it specifies that no action is to be taken for any exceptional condition that may arise during execution of that single command.

Returning to the program of Figure 4-1, let's see how it might use the NOHANDLE option. Now neither the HANDLE nor the IGNORE command are coded. Instead, the RECEIVE command is changed to:

EXEC CICS RECEIVE INTO (INPUT-MSG) LENGTH (LEN) NOHANDLE END-EXEC.

Remember that the NOHANDLE option applies only to the execution of this *particular* RECEIVE command.

Because of the NOHANDLE option, CICS would not test for the LENGERR exception. Therefore, the program would have to test for a LEN value greater than 49 and take corrective action just as discussed above when the IGNORE command was used.

Programming Considerations

Once a HANDLE or IGNORE command has been executed for a named condition, the specification remains in effect until the task terminates or until another HANDLE or IGNORE command is executed for the same condition. The HANDLE or IGNORE command in effect—the most recently executed one—for a given condition is said to be the *active command* for that condition. The routine identified in an active HANDLE command is called the *active exception routine* for the condition.

Exception routines are usually more general than the TOOLONG routine of our example. There are two reasons for this:

First, a single routine may be used to handle several different exception conditions. Later in this chapter, we will see how a routine can determine *which condition* caused the routine to be invoked.

Second, a given condition may be detected by more than one command. As you learn more CICS commands, you will encounter commands other than RECEIVE that detect the LENGERR condition. The exception routine may need to take different actions depending upon the CICS command that detected the

① EXEC CICS HANDLE CONDITION LENGERR (WRONGLN)

② EXEC CICS HANDLE CONDITION LENGERR (TOOLONG)

③ EXEC CICS RECEIVE INTO (RECAREA) NOHANDLE

④ EXEC CICS IGNORE CONDITION LENGERR

Figure 4-3
Sequence of
HANDLE Commands

condition. How to determine *which command* detected the condition will also be discussed later in this chapter.

Figure 4-3 shows a sequence of commands that define exception–handling conditions for LENGERR. The figure illustrates that:

At Point 1, WRONGLN becomes the active exception–handling routine for LENGERR.

At Point 2, WRONGLN is superceded by TOOLONG which becomes the active routine.

At Point 3, WRONGLN is still the active routine, but the RECEIVE command will not check for LENGERR—or for any other exception—because the NOHANDLE option has been coded.

At Point 4, IGNORE becomes active for LENGERR. Until a HANDLE command is executed, CICS commands will not check for LENGERR.

Point 4 of Figure 4-3 shows that a HANDLE command for a given condition can be "canceled" by an IGNORE command for the same condition. The effect of IGNORE is *not*, however, the same as had the HANDLE command never been executed. Remember that before a HANDLE command had been executed, CICS would have detected LENGERR and taken default action—abnormal task termination. When IGNORE is in effect, CICS will not detect the condition and, therefore, will take no action. In order to return to the original situation in which CICS takes a default action for LENGERR, a program must execute a HANDLE command of the form:

EXEC CICS HANDLE CONDITION LENGERR END-EXEC

In this form of the HANDLE command, the condition is named, but no label argument is specified. This identifies the CICS default exception routine as active for the LENGERR condition.

The ERROR Condition

In addition to named exception conditions that may be detected by CICS commands, there is a general exception condition called ERROR. If a CICS command detects a condition for which no HANDLE is active, CICS will transfer control to the active exception routine for the ERROR condition (assuming an exception routine for ERROR has been defined). This permits you, for instance, to write one general exception-handling routine that will receive control for all exceptional conditions *except* conditions for which you write specific exception-handling routines. For example, the command:

EXEC CICS HANDLE CONDITION ERROR(MOST) LENGERR(TOOLONG)
END-EXEC.

would cause CICS to transfer control to MOST for any exceptional condition except LENGERR. If LENGERR were detected, control would be transferred to TOOLONG.

Looping on Exception Conditions

Remember that exception routines often contain CICS commands, and that exceptional conditions may arise in executing these commands just as any others. In programming exception routines, you need to be careful that a command within the routine cannot detect one of the conditions which the routine is designated to handle.

For example, suppose you have identified an exception routine called RTN1 as the active exception routine for a number of conditions including LENGERR. Assume that CICS detected an *incorrect terminal input* exception during execution of a RECEIVE command in your program, and that RTN1 was also the active exception routine for that condition. Now RTN1 has been entered for the condition caused by incorrect terminal input. You have coded RTN1 to SEND the user an error message and request that the user enter revised data. RTN1 then executes a RECEIVE command to obtain the new data.

Now let's look at what happens if RTN1's RECEIVE command detects LENGERR. For example, perhaps the value of the LENGTH argument had, through some error, been set to zero. Then the RECEIVE command would detect LENGERR; control would transfer to RTN1 which would execute a RECEIVE command; the RECEIVE command would detect LENGERR.... This is referred to as "looping on the exception condition." Your program would continue in this loop until CICS detected that a time limit had been exceeded. Meanwhile, your looping program would have locked out other active CICS tasks.

A general way to prevent looping on the exception condition is to begin each exception-handling routine with a HANDLE command to temporarily make another exception routine active for the conditions this routine would normally handle. This second exception routine could be the CICS default exception routine, or it could be a simple routine of your own. Often such a routine does nothing more than send an error message like:

Error—notify programmer. Exception xxxxxx in exception routine.

Now your original exception routine can perform its processing. If CICS detects an error during the processing, control will transfer to the temporary exception routine rather than looping back into the first one. When the exception routine completes its processing, it should execute a HANDLE command that restores itself as the active exception routine for the same list of conditions. It can then branch back into the application program.

The next two sections of this chapter, which describe program linkage and addressability, also provide additional information about exception handling.

Part 2: Program Linkage

Chapter 3 introduced the term pseudo-conversational and showed, in Figure 3-8, an example of how a pseudo-conversational transaction is programmed. Now let's look more closely at how one application program (VAC1 in the Chapter 3 example) arranges for a second application program (VAC2) to be executed.

The TRANSID Option

Recall that VAC1 terminated with the statement:

EXEC CICS RETURN TRANSID ('VAC2')

When the command returns control to CICS, the *Program Control Program* (PCP) is called to process the TRANSID parameter. The PCP stores the transaction code in the TCT entry for the user's terminal. The space occupied by VAC1, its associated storage areas, and any associated control blocks is freed. When the user enters the next input (the "selection" in Chapter 3's example), the TCP reads the input and, because of the TRANSID information stored in the TCT entry, interprets the entire input string as data. That is, the TCP doesn't look for a transaction identification code in the input data. Instead, it retrieves the code from the TCT entry. Processing then proceeds just as though the user had typed the transaction code as the first part of the input string.

Modular Programming

We mentioned that the pseudo-conversational process uses CICS region space efficiently because no program or working-storage are needed during user think time. We also remarked that space was saved during processing, because the VAC1 and VAC2 programs were each smaller than the single program that would have been required had the pseudo-conversational technique not been used.

This is one of the advantages of *modular programming*, in which a transaction is programmed as several individual programs rather than as a single large program.

Consider again the example transaction:

SCDL CHEM 160

which requests the class schedule for a course called "Chemistry 160."

Figure 4-4 lists the steps that might be involved as the SCHEDULE program processes the request.

This is an *inquiry-response transaction*, not a conversational one, so we cannot use a pseudo-conversational process to save storage. Nevertheless, there is advantage to be gained from programming the transaction as several small programs instead of a single large one.

Notice that Step 5, Error Messages, is not required unless the request's data (CHEM 160) is incorrect. Consider too that a large part of the work involved in the transaction is performed in Steps 2 and 3—searching and reading the department file. In a university DB/DC environment, there would probably be other transactions besides SCDL that need to search and read department files.

Assume that a program to read department files has already been written and placed in the CICS library under the *program name* DEPTREAD. Assume also that there is a generally available program called ERMESG that, given an error number, formats an error message, transmits it to the user, and terminates the task. Figure 4-5 shows how a program, SCDLPROG, to process the SCDL transaction might be designed to make use of DEPTREAD and ERMESG.

Step 1:	Read and Interpret Request
Step 2:	Find and Read department = CHEM file
Step 3:	Find and Read CHEM course = 160 schedule
Step 4:	Format and Send Response (Terminate Transaction)
Step 5:	Error Messages: (Unknown department or Unknown course) Format and Send Error Message (Terminate Transaction)

Figure 4-4
SCDL Transaction,
Processing Steps

Notice that SCDLPROG performs only Steps 1 and 4 as outlined in Figure 4-4. It invokes DEPTREAD to perform Steps 2 and 3, and invokes ERMESG to perform Step 5. When SCDLPROG invokes DEPTREAD and ERMESG, it needs to pass them data as argument values for processing. For example, SCDLPROG passes DEPTREAD the department name (CHEM) and course number (160) requested by the user. DEPTREAD uses this information to find and read the correct record from the department files. After reading the file, DEPTREAD needs to return the record, or the address of the record, that contains the information requested by SCDLPROG. DEPTREAD also returns a completion code, indicating whether the record was successfully read, to SCDLPROG.

In order to write programs like SCDLPROG, you need to know how to invoke another program and how to pass data back and forth with another program. Remember that we are discussing programs that are located *outside your program's load module* and that do not share working-storage with your program.

We will look first at the CICS commands that you can use to *invoke* another program. The "Addressability" section will discuss the question of accessing data that lies outside your program.

You will probably find that, in a new programming job, many assignments will involve modifying or writing a module that works together with existing modules to perform a transaction. Therefore, you will need to know how a program transfers control to another program. CICS provides two commands for this purpose.

The LINK Command

You use the LINK command to invoke a program in such a way that control can return to your program, the "calling" program. For example, the SCDLPROG program would use LINK to invoke DEPTREAD. The command is written:

EXEC CICS LINK PROGRAM (name)

where *name* is the name by which the program you want to receive control is identified in the PPT. That is, it is a *program name* and not a transaction identification code.

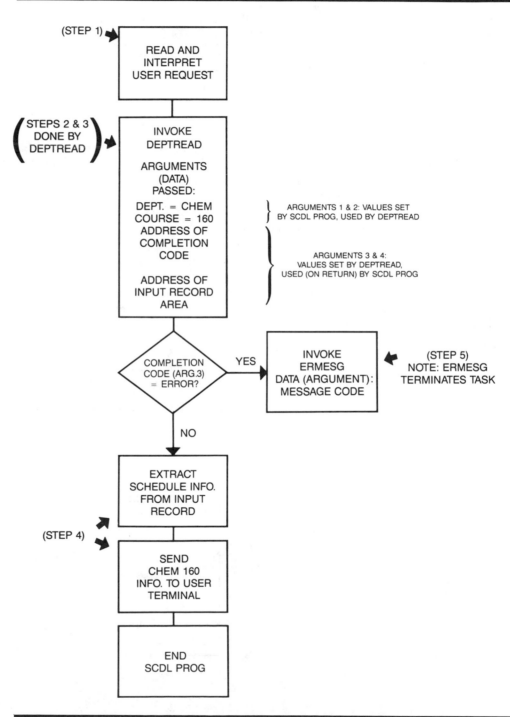

(STEP 1)

READ AND INTERPRET USER REQUEST

$\left(\begin{matrix} \text{STEPS 2 \& 3} \\ \text{DONE BY} \\ \text{DEPTREAD} \end{matrix} \right)$

INVOKE DEPTREAD

ARGUMENTS (DATA) PASSED:

DEPT. = CHEM
COURSE = 160
ADDRESS OF COMPLETION CODE

ADDRESS OF INPUT RECORD AREA

ARGUMENTS 1 & 2: VALUES SET BY SCDL PROG, USED BY DEPTREAD

ARGUMENTS 3 & 4: VALUES SET BY DEPTREAD, USED (ON RETURN) BY SCDL PROG

COMPLETION CODE (ARG.3) = ERROR?

YES

INVOKE ERMESG DATA (ARGUMENT): MESSAGE CODE

(STEP 5) NOTE: ERMESG TERMINATES TASK

NO

EXTRACT SCHEDULE INFO. FROM INPUT RECORD

(STEP 4)

SEND CHEM 160 INFO. TO USER TERMINAL

END SCDL PROG

Figure 4-5
SCDL Transaction,
Modular Programming
Approach

Consider the situation illustrated by Figure 4-6. Assume that program A is executing. At a given point, program A issues a LINK command which names program B. Then we say that B is at a *lower logical level* than A. When the LINK command is executed, program A stops executing but is not terminated. Program B is invoked and executes until a RETURN command within program B is encountered. At that time, Program B will be terminated, and control will return to Program A, the calling program. Execution of Program A resumes with the instruction that follows the LINK command.

The RETURN command used by Program B is coded:

EXEC CICS RETURN

This is the same form of the RETURN command which you used in Chapter 3 to end your program. Now, given the concept of logical level, we can understand the RETURN command in a more general sense. RETURN always returns control to the program at the *next higher logical level*. The program you wrote for Chapter 3 was the highest logical level program associated with the task. In fact, it had to be the task's highest logical level program because there was no other. The only program at a higher level was CICS itself, and so your program terminated by returning to CICS.

TRANSID Restriction: Now that the concept of logical level has been introduced, we can state a restriction on the use of the TRANSID option of the RETURN command. The TRANSID option can be coded only in a RETURN command executed by a program at the task's *highest logical level*. If a program at a lower logical level attempts to execute RETURN with TRANSID, CICS detects the INVREQ exceptional condition.

The XCTL Command

Sometimes, especially when a large program has been divided into two or more smaller parts, it isn't necessary to return to the calling program. The XCTL

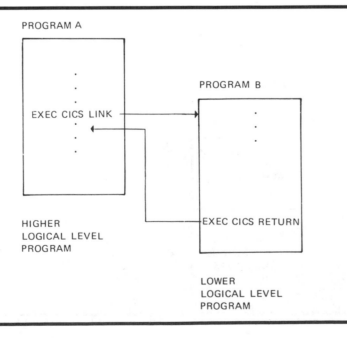

PROGRAM A

EXEC CICS LINK

HIGHER
LOGICAL LEVEL
PROGRAM

PROGRAM B

EXEC CICS RETURN

LOWER
LOGICAL LEVEL
PROGRAM

Figure 4-6
LINK Command and
Logical Level

command is used in this case. For example, the SCDLPROG program would use XCTL to invoke ERMESG, because ERMESG terminates the task rather than returning control to SCDLPROG.

Figure 4-7 illustrates the effect of XCTL. When an application program such as Program Y is invoked by the XCTL command, control passes to the named program, just as it did for the LINK command. However, the calling program will not regain control after XCTL is issued. The calling program is released by the task and can be deleted from storage if it is not required by some other task. When XCTL is used, the "called" program is at the *same logical level* as the "calling" program.

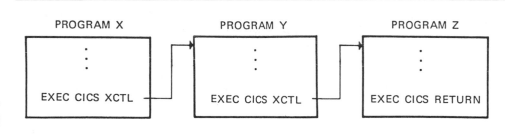

Figure 4-7
XCTL Command
and Logical Level

The XCTL command is written:

EXEC CICS XCTL PROGRAM (name)

where *name* is the same as defined for the LINK command.

When a program that was invoked by XCTL executes a RETURN command, control returns to the program at the next higher logical level, just as we said in our discussion of the LINK command. The program at the next higher level will either be the program that issued the most recent LINK or it will be CICS. Figure 4-8 illustrates the effect of RETURN after a series of XCTL commands. Program Z's RETURN results in control returning to Program A; when Program

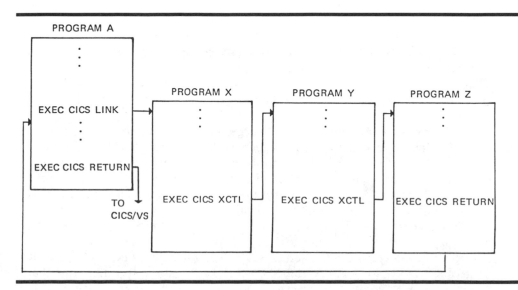

Figure 4-8
RETURN Command
Following XCTL
Series

A executes a RETURN, control returns to CICS because A is at the highest logical level for the task.

Exception Handling with LINK and XCTL

If the program named in a LINK or XCTL command cannot be found, an exceptional condition named PGMIDERR is detected. Figure 4-9 shows how a program might avoid a possible task ABEND by executing a HANDLE command for the PGMIDERR condition before the XCTL is issued.

```
            .
            .
            .
            EXEC CICS HANDLE CONDITION PGMIDERR (NOPROG) . . .
            .
            .
            .
            EXEC CICS XCTL PROGRAM ('PROGRAMB')
            .
            .
            .
END         EXEC CICS RETURN
NOPROG      * * * ERROR DIAGNOSTIC ROUTINE * * *
            GO TO END
```

Figure 4-9
Handling the
PGMIDERR
Exceptional Condition

At this point, we need to think about how exception handling might work within a task like that shown in Figure 4-8. Suppose that Program X has executed a HANDLE command for the LENGERR condition. The exception program identified must be part of Program X, otherwise the label coded as the argument of the CONDITION option would be undefined. Now assume that Program Y has received control and executes a RECEIVE command which detects LENGERR. What is the result?

If CICS attempted to transfer control to the exception routine in Program X, an error could result because Program X may no longer be in storage. Is control transferred to the storage location where the exception routine used to be? That location might now contain some other program not related to this task at all, or it might contain some program's working storage, a control block, or a table.

CICS avoids the problem we have suggested by deactivating a program's exception-handling specifications as soon as the program executes a LINK or XCTL. In Figure 4-8, default exception handling would be in effect when Program X receives control from A; when Program Y receives control from X, and when Program Z receives control from Y. Therefore, each program must provide its own exception-handling routines.

When a program RETURNs to a higher logical level program, the exception-handling routines of the higher logical level program are reactivated. In the example shown in Figure 4-8, when Program Z executes the EXEC CICS RETURN, control returns to Program A, *and* the exception-handling specifications that were active in Program A before the LINK command are reinstated.

Part 3: Addressability

In most cases, when one program passes control to another it needs also to pass data to that program. Control can be passed directly, using LINK or XCTL, or indirectly, as in a pseudo-conversational transaction. In any case, the data is not in the program or working-storage area of the program that receives control. This raises the general question of how your COBOL program can find and process data that is in the CICS region, but that is not defined within the program itself.

So far, we have touched upon three instances when a program might need to do this:

1. Remember that when the user enters data at the terminal, the input is moved into a control block called the TIOA. Later, when your program issues a RECEIVE command, the data is moved from the TIOA into areas you defined in working storage so that the program can examine and possibly modify the data. The move operation and the working-storage space for the data could be eliminated if the program could simply address the data within the TIOA.
2. As we discussed above, a program that invokes another directly or indirectly needs to pass data to the invoked program.
3. In the discussion of exception-handling we said that an exception routine may need to determine what CICS command and what exceptional condition caused the routine to be entered. As you might expect, this information is contained in a CICS control block—in the CICS region, but not in the program or its working storage.

This section discusses each of these situations. But first, let's review the general case. Figure 4-10 shows how an application program looks when it has been loaded into the CICS region for execution. A typical reenterable program requires two separate areas in memory—the area in which the load module (instructions and constant data) resides and the working storage area for variable data.

COBOL programs can address data in either of these two areas directly. In your program you refer to a variable by name, and in the compile-link edit-program load sequence, the reference is translated into an address in memory where the variable is stored.

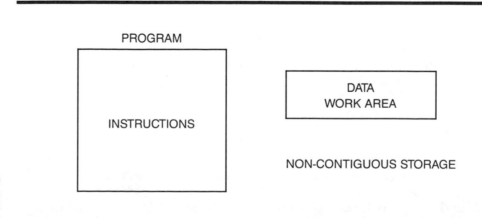

PROGRAM

INSTRUCTIONS

DATA
WORK AREA

NON-CONTIGUOUS STORAGE

**Figure 4-10
Application
Program as Loaded
for Execution**

Address Formation

The process of translating a reference to a named variable into an address in memory is called *address formation*. There are two steps involved in address formation. First, the name of a program variable must be associated with an address *relative to* some defined "reference point" location. For example, we know that a constant like INVOICE BEING PRINTED resides in the program area. During compilation, it is assigned a location relative to the beginning of the program—like "bytes 30 through 50." A variable in working storage is assigned a location relative to the beginning of the working storage. The compiler makes this assignment based upon the variable's description contained in a COBOL DATA DIVISION statement. (If several programs are linked together into a single load module, the linkage editor is also involved in determining relative addresses, but we'll ignore this step for purposes of this brief discussion.)

The second step is the formation of the data's *absolute* location within memory when the program is loaded for execution. During the loading process, the memory locations of "reference points," like the first byte of the program area and the first byte of working storage, are stored in a location that the program can access. Then the relative addresses from the compile step can be adjusted to absolute addresses by adding the absolute address of the appropriate reference point. This adjustment is performed by instructions generated by the compiler and is "invisible" to you, the programmer, unless you study the listing of the object module produced by the compiler.

To return to the earlier example, if the program is loaded into memory location 20000, then the absolute address of the INVOICE BEING PRINTED constant must be 20030. Once the absolute address of a reference point is accessible to a program, the program is said to have *addressability* to the data addressed relative to that reference point.

Normally, a program has addressability to data within the program and within the program's working storage. To obtain addressability to data outside these two areas, the program must:

1. Describe the external data so that the compiler can calculate an address *relative to* an area in which the data will be stored.
2. Obtain addressability for the area in which the data is stored.

Defining External Data

Although you have written COBOL programs in the past, you may not have utilized the statements used to describe external data, because they are used only in rather advanced programming.

In a COBOL program, data outside the program and the working storage are defined in the LINKAGE SECTION. Within the LINKAGE SECTION, the program must define both the data and a four-byte binary field to receive the address of the area (the reference point address). Figure 4-11 shows a segment of a COBOL program's LINKAGE SECTION. Two external data areas, DATA-AREA-1 and DATA-AREA-2, are defined.

The first area defined in the LINKAGE SECTION, BLL-CELLS, is the area in which reference point addresses will be placed during execution. This area is called the *Base Linkage Locator (BLL Cell)* list, and it must be the first 01 level in the LINKAGE SECTION. As shown, the BLL Cell list begins with a variable (called FILLER in the figure) that will receive the address of the BLL

Cell list itself, because the list is also external to the program. The next two cells in the BLL Cell List (AREAPTR1 and AREAPTR2) will contain the addresses of the data areas DATA-AREA-1 and DATA-AREA-2.

The relationship between the entries in the BLL Cell list and the data areas to be referenced is determined by position. The first BLL Cell (FILLER) will be used to address the BLL Cell list (the first 01 level data area); the second entry (AREAPTR1) to address the second 01 level data area (DATA-AREA-1), and so on. The entries in the BLL Cell list must all be defined at the 02 level. If you want to define subfields of the other data areas, like DATA-AREA-1 and DATA-AREA-2, you can define them at any level.

```
LINKAGE SECTION.
01 BLL-CELLS.
   02 filler   PIC S9(8) COMP.
   02 AREAPTR1 PIC S9(8) COMP.
   02 AREAPTR2 PIC S9(8) COMP.

01 DATA-AREA-1.
   02 FIELD ...
   02 FIELD ...
   02 FIELD ...
         .
         .
         .

01 DATA-AREA-2.
   02 FIELD ...
   02 FIELD ...
   02 FIELD ...
         .
         .
         .
```

**Figure 4-11
LINKAGE SECTION
Defined in COBOL
Program**

By setting up the LINKAGE SECTION, you provide the compiler the information it needs to assign relative locations to the external data areas. That is, the compiler knows where each of the 02 level fields defined within DATA-AREA-1 is located relative to the address that, at execution time, will be found in the second position of the BLL Cell list.

Defining the LINKAGE SECTION is a COBOL language technique that has nothing to do with CICS. That is, you may need to reference external data in non-CICS programs, and to do so you would set up the BLL Cell list just as we've described above. However, the next step is to code your program so that the *absolute address* of each reference point will be placed in the appropriate BLL Cells. For example, at execution time, the BLL Cell you called AREAPTR1 must be set to the absolute address of the data area you called DATA-AREA-1. This does not happen automatically. You must code instructions to obtain the address and place it in the correct BLL Cell. We will see how to do this in two CICS programming situations we listed above.

Accessing the TIOA

Think back to the program you wrote for the last chapter's exercise. It issued a RECEIVE command to obtain terminal input. CICS processed the RECEIVE command by moving terminal data from the TIOA into your program's working storage—the area defined by the command's INTO option. Let's look at how you can change the program to process terminal input data as it is stored in the TIOA—without moving it into your program's working storage.

The TIOA is an external data area, so the first change to your program would be to set up a BLL Cell list defining the TIOA. Assume that the name you used as argument of the INTO option was INPUT-MSG and that your WORKING-STORAGE section defined INPUT-MSG as follows:

```
01 INPUT-MSG.
    02 TRANS-ID    PIC X (4).
    02 FILLER      PIC X.
    02 ITEM-NO     PIC X(5).
    02 FILLER      PIC X.
    02 CUST-NO     PIC X(7).
    02 FILLER      PIC X.
    02 DESC        PIC X(30).
```

This describes a copy of the TIOA. That is, the data stored within the TIOA is arranged just as described here. You can use this same description within the LINKAGE SECTION to describe the TIOA, so you need only to move the description to the LINKAGE SECTION and include a BLL Cell list. Here is an example of such a LINKAGE SECTION definition:

```
LINKAGE SECTION.
01 BLL-CELLS.
    02 BLLPTR      PIC S9(8) COMP.
    02 RECPTR      PIC S9(8) COMP.
01 TIOA-MAP.
    02 TRANS-ID    PIC X(4).
    02 FILLER      PIC X.
    02 ITEM-NO     PIC X(5).
    02 FILLER      PIC X.
    02 CUST-NO     PIC X(7).
    02 FILLER      PIC X.
    02 DESC        PIC X(30).
```

Now you're ready to code the instructions to get the address of the TIOA into the BLL Cell you defined for that purpose. (In the example, this is the cell called RECPTR.) To do this you will use another form of the RECEIVE command. This RECEIVE command is written:

EXEC CICS RECEIVE SET (*variable*) ...

where *variable* is the name of the BLL Cell associated with your definition of the terminal input area—RECPTR, in the example shown above.

Note: The command would be extended to include other options like LENGTH or NOHANDLE.

This form of the RECEIVE command moves no data; it simply places the address of the TIOA into the variable named in the SET argument. Your program's references to the named variables in the terminal input area can now be processed correctly. Your program can access the input data simply by referring to CUST-NO and ITEM-NO, just as you did when these locations were part of working storage.

Passing Data to Called Programs

Remember that when the SCDLPROG program, shown in Figure 4-5, invokes DEPTPROG and ERMESG, it must pass data to each of these called programs. This section describes how a COBOL CICS program passes data to a program it invokes, and how a COBOL CICS program can access data that has been passed to it by a calling program.

Let's look first at how a *called* program accesses data passed from the *calling* program. First, you need to know where the data to be passed is physically located. CICS requires that data to be passed via a LINK or XCTL is located in the *calling program's working storage*. Therefore, it is external to the called program, and the called program must define the external data in its COBOL LINKAGE SECTION. For passed data, the LINKAGE SECTION doesn't need a BLL Cell list, but the data area must be called *DFHCOMMAREA*.

Figure 4-12 shows an example. Here program PROG2 is the *called* program. Notice its definition of DFHCOMMAREA.

Now we can look at the command used by the *calling* program to pass the data to the *called* program. The command is of the form:

EXEC CICS XCTL PROGRAM(STEP4) COMMAREA(data area)
LENGTH(data value)

Data area is the name of the data area that contains the data to be accessed by the called program.

LENGTH is required, and its argument gives the length of the area to be passed.

In Figure 4-12, PROG1 is the *calling* program. It invokes PROG2 with the LINK command. Notice that the LINK command is written in the same form as shown above for the XCTL command. The data to be passed, TRANSINF, is part of PROG1's working storage; LENGTH is specified, as required, as four bytes; and PROG2 has defined the passed data area as DFHCOMMAREA.

Although the LINK and XCTL commands are written in the same form, the mechanism that CICS uses to pass the data is not the same. Remember that when XCTL is used, the calling program, its working storage, and other associated storage areas are deleted from memory. When an XCTL specifies COMMAREA, CICS makes a copy of the data to be passed, and then deletes the original data along with other storage associated with the calling program. In the Figure 4-12 example, had XCTL been used, the four bytes of COMMU-NICATIONS-REGION in WORKING-STORAGE would have been copied into a new area of memory; then, PROG1 and all its working storage would have been deleted. PROG2 would receive the address of the new 4-byte area.

In the case of a LINK, this copy process isn't necessary; since the calling program will remain in memory—along with all its data—until it regains control via an EXEC CICS RETURN command. In this case, the called program receives the address of data within the called program's working station.

Pseudo-Conversational Transactions

In a pseudo-conversational transaction, the terminating program may need to pass data to the transaction that will be invoked by the user's next terminal

```
*
* *** PROGRAM IS INCOMPLETE AND WILL NOT EXECUTE ***
*
* * * * * * * * * * * * * * * *
*  LINKING (CALLING) PROGRAM  *
* * * * * * * * * * * * * * * *
*
 IDENTIFICATION DIVISION.
 PROGRAM-ID. 'PROG1'
          .
          .
 WORKING-STORAGE SECTION.
 01  TRANSINF.
     02  FLD1  PIC X(4).
          .
          .
 PROCEDURE DIVISION.
     MOVE 'INVC' TO FLD1.
     EXEC CICS HANDLE CONDITION PGMIDERR(NOPROG) END-EXEC.
     EXEC CICS LINK PROGRAM('PROG2') COMMAREA(TRANSINF)
               LENGTH(4) END-EXEC.
          .
          .
          .
 NOPROG.
*  SEND A MESSAGE TO THE TERMINAL  *
     EXEC CICS RETURN END-EXEC.
```

```
*
* * * * * * * * * * * * * * * *
*  LINKED (CALLED) PROGRAM  *
* * * * * * * * * * * * * * * *
*
 IDENTIFICATION DIVISION.
 PROGRAM-ID. 'PROG2'.
          .
          .
 LINKAGE SECTION.
 01  DFHCOMMAREA.
     02  FUNCTION  PIC X(4).
          .
          .
 PROCEDURE DIVISION.
     IF EIBCALEN GREATER THAN ZERO
               THEN IF FUNCTION EQUALS 'INVC'
          .
          .
          .
```

Figure 4-12
Using LINK
Command with
COMMAREA

input. The COMMAREA is also used for this purpose. The same rules apply for defining COMMAREA in this case as for the LINK and XCTL cases. Remember, the program that is terminating sets up the pseudo-conversational transfer of control by using the RETURN command with the TRANSID option. To pass data to the program that will be invoked through the TRANSID option, you must code another option, COMMAREA, in the RETURN command.

The RETURN command would look like:

EXEC CICS RETURN TRANSID (name) COMMAREA (data area)
              LENGTH (data value)

The program invoked to process the transaction named by TRANSID receives control as though it had been invoked by an XCTL command.

The Execution Interface Block (EIB)

So far we've looked at two kinds of external data references that occur in CICS programs. In the first—direct access to the TIOA—you set up a BLL Cell list and used a form of the RECEIVE command to get the TIOA's address into the proper BLL Cell. In the second case—accessing passed data—you didn't need the BLL Cell list, but you used a special name in your LINKAGE SECTION and then used a new option on the LINK or XCTL command to achieve addressability. The third case of external data reference is the easiest—you need neither a LINKAGE SECTION nor a special CICS command.

In this case, your program will examine fields in a CICS control block called the *Execution Interface Block* (EIB). This is a control block in which CICS places several types of data that application programs often need to examine. For example, the EIB contains the date and time at which the task was initiated. When we discussed exception–handling, we said that your exception routine may need to find out which command detected an exception and exactly which exceptional condition was detected. CICS places this information in the EIB as well.

CICS establishes an EIB for each task during task initiation. Figure 4-13 shows that the TCA contains the address of the EIB as well as the address of the current program's working storage.

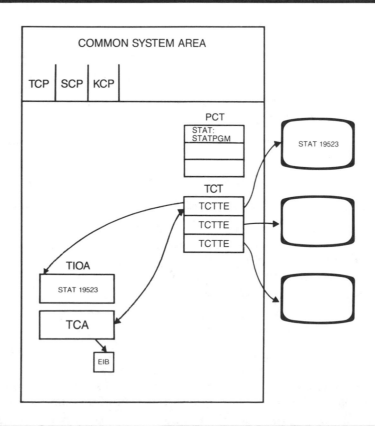

**Figure 4-13
CICS Task with
Execution Interface
Block**

65

Because many application programs need to access data in the EIB, the CICS command translator for each language automatically includes the statements required to obtain addressability to the EIB. The command translator knows the relative location of each field in the EIB and defines this to the compiler. When CICS initiates a task to execute your program, it builds an EIB for the task and makes its address available to your program. All you need to do is use the correct name for each EIB field you want to examine. Figure 4-14 lists the EIB data fields by name.

EIBTIME	Time the task was started
EIBDATE	Date the task was started
EIBTASKN	Task number assigned to the task by CICS/VS
EIBTRNID	Transaction ID
EIBTRMID	Terminal identification
EIBAID	The type of input operation performed on the terminal, such as ENTER, PF3, PF1
EIBCPOSN	Position of the cursor on the screen at time of input
EIBCALEN	Length of the communication area (COMMAREA) passed to an application program which is called in by another application program. COMMAREA allows data to be passed from one program to another when a transaction causes execution of several programs in succession. COMMAREA can also be used to pass data from one task to another.
EIBDS	Contains the name of the last data set referred to in the program
EIBFN	A code representing the function requested by the last CICS/VS command from the application program
EIBRCODE	The CICS/VS response code for the last command received and processed
EIBREQID	Request identifier assigned by CICS/VS to a time management request

Figure 4-14
EIB Fields

Let's look at a few of the fields you will use most often:

EIBTRNID contains the name of the transaction which the task is processing. It is in the form: PIC X(4). You would use this field in a program that handles more than one transaction. For example, here is a COBOL statement that checks to see which transaction has been requested:

```
IF EIBTRNID = 'ADDS' THEN
    MOVE 'FILE ADD' TO TITLE0.
```

The program does not contain any definition for the variable EIBTRNID; that was taken care of by the CICS command translator.

EIBTIME contains the time at which the task was started. It is in the form: PIC S9(7) COMP-3, and expresses time in hours, minutes, and seconds.

EIBDATE contains the date the task is started. It is in the form: PIC S9(7) COMP-3, and expresses the data as year (2 digits) and date (3 digits).

Figure 4-15 shows a COBOL program that moves the date and time from the EIB into working-storage locations. Notice that the WORKING-STORAGE section defines the target variables LDAY and LTIME. However, no definition for EIBDATE or EIBTIME need be coded.

EIBFN, for EIB *function name*, contains a code identifying the function requested by the last CICS command executed. The code is in the form PIC X(2).

```
DATA DIVISION.
WORKING-STORAGE SECTION.
77   Q-LENGTH PIC 9(4) COMP VALUE 22.
01   LOGORD.
     02   LOGTIME.
          03   LDAY PIC S9(7) COMP-3.
          03   LTIME PIC S9(7) COMP-3.
     02   LITEM PIC X(22).
     02   COMMENT PIC X(11) VALUE 'ORDER ENTRY'.
     02   FILLER PIC X(51) VALUE SPACES.
01   XDFHCMLO COPY XDFHCML.
01   FILEA COPY FILEA.
01   L860 COPY L860.
01   DFHBMSCA COPY DFHBMSCA.
PROCEDURE DIVISION.
               .
               .
               .

          MOVE EIBDATE TO LDAY
          MOVE EIBTIME TO LTIME
          MOVE ITEM TO LITEM
```

Figure 4-15
Accessing Data
in the EIB

Figure 4-16 shows the codes in hexadecimal form and the corresponding command.

EIBRCODE contains the response code returned after completion of the most recent CICS command. If an exception condition has been detected, EIBRCODE can be decoded to determine what the exception condition was. EIBRCODE doesn't give the name of the condition, but a value that must be decoded. The code is in the form: PIC X(6).

Figure 4-17 shows that to decode EIBRCODE you must also look at the value of EIBFN. For example, let's see what EIBFN and EIBRCODE would look like after the LENGERR condition has been detected in a RECEIVE command. Look first at Figure 4-16 to find the EIBFN code for RECEIVE. It is 04 02; that is, byte 0 has the hexadecimal value 04, and byte 1 has the hexadecimal value 02. Now refer to Figure 4-17. Follow down the EIBFN Byte 0 column, looking at entries where byte 0 is 04. Exceptions that occur in a RECEIVE command will appear among these entries. The entry for LENGERR shows that EIBRCODE's byte 0 will have a value of E1. The other bytes of EIBRCODE are used to provide additional information for some exception conditions. You will not be required to decode EIBRCODE for any of the programs in this text.

Part 4: The Command Level Interpreter

In the introduction to this chapter, we said that your CICS facility may use

Code	Command	Code	Command
02 02	ADDRESS	0C 02	GETMAIN
02 04	HANDLE CONDITION	0C 04	FREEMAIN
02 06	HANDLE AID	0E 02	LINK
02 08	ASSIGN	0E 04	XCTL
02 0A	IGNORE CONDITION	0E 06	LOAD
04 02	RECEIVE	0E 08	RETURN
04 04	SEND	0E 0A	RELEASE
04 06	CONVERSE	0E 0C	ABEND
04 08	ISSUE EODS	0E 0E	HANDLE ABEND
04 0A	ISSUE COPY	10 02	ASKTIME
04 0C	WAIT TERMINAL	10 04	DELAY
04 0E	ISSUE LOAD	10 06	POST
04 10	WAIT SIGNAL	10 08	START
04 12	ISSUE RESET	10 0A	RETRIEVE
04 14	ISSUE DISCONNECT	10 0C	CANCEL
04 16	ISSUE ENDOUTPUT	12 02	WAIT EVENT
04 18	ISSUE ERASEUP	12 04	ENQ
04 1A	ISSUE ENDFILE	12 06	DEQ
04 1C	ISSUE PRINT	12 08	SUSPEND
04 1E	ISSUE SIGNAL	14 02	JOURNAL
04 20	ALLOCATE	14 04	WAIT JOURNAL
04 22	FREE	16 02	SYNCPOINT
04 24	POINT	18 02	RECEIVE MAP
04 26	BUILD ATTACH	18 04	SEND MAP
04 28	EXTRACT ATTACH	18 06	SEND TEXT
04 2A	EXTRACT TCT	18 08	SEND PAGE
06 02	READ	18 0A	PURGE MESSAGE
06 04	WRITE	18 0C	ROUTE
06 06	REWRITE	1A 02	TRACE ON/OFF
06 08	DELETE	1A 04	ENTER
06 0A	UNLOCK	1C 02	DUMP
06 0C	STARTBR	1E 02	ISSUE ADD
06 0E	READNEXT	1E 04	ISSUE ERASE
06 10	READPREV	1E 06	ISSUE REPLACE
06 12	ENDBR	1E 08	ISSUE ABORT
06 14	RESETBR	1E 0A	ISSUE QUERY
08 02	WRITEQ TD	1E 0C	ISSUE END
08 04	READQ TD	1E 0E	ISSUE RECEIVE
08 06	DELETEQ TD	1E 10	ISSUE NOTE
0A 02	WRITEQ TS	1E 12	ISSUE WAIT
0A 04	READQ TS	1E 14	ISSUE SEND
0A 06	DELETEQ TS	20 02	BIF DEEDIT

Figure 4-16
Function Name Codes
Used in the EIB

an optional programming aid called the Command Level Interpreter. If it does, this is a good time to learn about the Interpreter so that you can make use of it for the programming exercises in the rest of this course.

You use the Command Level Interpreter from your CICS terminal by entering a CICS transaction request. The transaction name for the Command Level Interpreter is either CECS or CECI, depending upon the version of the Interpreter that is available to you.

The CECS Transaction

The CECS transaction allows you to enter a CICS command for syntax checking. To check the syntax of a READ DATASET command (which will be introduced in the next chapter), you would enter:

CECS READ DATASET(FILEA)

EIBRCODE Codes

Figure 4-17
Result Codes
(EIBRCODE) in
the EIB

EIBFN Byte 0	Byte	EIBRCODE Bit(s)	Meaning	EIBFN Byte 0	Byte	EIBRCODE Bit(s)	Meaning
02	0	E0	INVREQ	0A	0	D0	SYSIDERR
04	0	04	EOF	0A	0	D1	ISCINVREQ
04	0	10	EODS	0A	0	E1	LENGERR
04	0	C1	EOF	0C	0	E2	NOSTG
04	0	C2	ENDINPT	0E	0	01	PGMIDERR
04	0	E1	LENGERR	0E	0	E0	INVREQ
04	0	E3	WRBRK	10	0	01	ENDDATA
04	0	E4	RDATT	10	0	04	IOERR
04	0	E5	SIGNAL	10	0	11	TRANSIDERR
04	0	E6	TERMIDERR	10	0	12	TERMIDERR
04	0	E7	NOPASSBKRD	10	0	14	INVTSREQ
04	0	E8	NOPASSBKWR	10	0	20	EXPIRED
04	0	EA	IGREQCD	10	0	81	NOTFND
04	0	EB	CBIDERR	10	0	D0	SYSIDERR
04	0	D0	SYSIDERR³	10	0	D1	ISCINVREQ
04	0	D2	SESSIONERR³	10	0	E1	LENGERR
04	0	D3	SYSBUSY	10	0	E9	ENVDEFERR
04	0	D4	SESSBUSY	10	0	FF	INVREQ
04	0	D5	NOTALLOC	12	0	32	ENQBUSY
04	1	20	EOC	14	0	01	JIDERR
04	1	40	INBFMH	14	0	02	INVREQ
04	3	F6	NOSTART	14	0	05	NOTOPEN
04	3	F7	NONVAL	14	0	06	LENGERR
06	0	01	DSIDERR	14	0	07	IOERR
06	0	02	ILLOGIC¹	14	0	09	NOJBUFSP
06	0	04	SEGIDERR	18	0	01	INVREQ
06	0	08	INVREQ	18	0	02	RETPAGE
06	0	0C	NOTOPEN	18	0	04	MAPFAIL
06	0	0F	ENDFILE	13	0	08	INVMPSZ²
06	0	80	IOERR¹	18	0	20	INVERRTERM
06	0	81	NOTFND	18	0	40	RTESOME
06	0	82	DUPREC	18	0	80	RTEFAIL
06	0	83	NOSPACE	18	0	E3	WRBRK
06	0	84	DUPKEY	18	0	E4	RDATT
06	0	D0	SYSIDERR³	18	1	10	INVLDC
06	0	D1	ISCINVREQ	18	1	40	IGREQCD
06	0	E1	LENGERR	18	1	80	TSIOERR
08	0	01	QZERO	18	2	01	OVERFLOW
08	0	02	QIDERR	18	2	04	EODS
08	0	04	IOERR	18	2	08	EOC
08	0	08	NOTOPEN	18	2	10	IGREQID
08	0	10	NOSPACE	1E	0	04	DSSTAT
08	0	C0	QBUSY	1E	0	08	FUNCERR
08	0	D0	SYSIDERR³	1E	0	0C	SELNERR
08	0	D1	ISCINVREQ	1E	0	10	UNEXPIN
08	0	E1	LENGERR	1E	0	E1	LENGERR
0A	0	01	ITEMERR	1E	1	11	EODS
0A	0	02	QIDERR	1E	1	15	NODATARECD
0A	0	04	IOERR	1E	1	2B	IGREQCD
0A	0	08	NOSPACE	1E	2	20	EOC
0A	0	20	INVREQ				

Figure 4-18 shows the response you would receive at your terminal. (The numbers referred to in the following discussion are the circled numbers outside the pictured display screen.)

Line 1 repeats the CICS command whose syntax is to be checked.

The STATUS line (labeled as Line 2) indicates that the command's syntax is being checked.

The entire command is expanded in the lines beginning with Line 3; the expanded command includes the EXEC CICS prefix and lists the options available for the command. Notice that, as shown for the DATASET parameter, the argument of any parameter you have specified is displayed. The names of parameters that are not required, like LENGTH and KEYLENGTH, are displayed in a field delimited by the "less than" and "greater than" signs.

Line 4 is an error message; it indicates that a required parameter, RIDFLD was omitted.

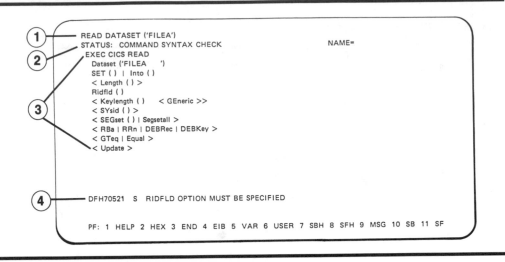

① READ DATASET ('FILEA')
STATUS: COMMAND SYNTAX CHECK   NAME=
② EXEC CICS READ
    Dataset ('FILEA   ')
    SET ( ) | Into ( )
    < Length ( ) >
    Ridfld ( )
    < Keylength ( )   < GEneric >>
    < SYsid ( ) >
③ < SEGset ( ) | Segsetall >
    < RBa | RRn | DEBRec | DEBKey >
    < GTeq | Equal >
    < Update >

④ DFH70521 S RIDFLD OPTION MUST BE SPECIFIED

PF: 1 HELP 2 HEX 3 END 4 EIB 5 VAR 6 USER 7 SBH 8 SFH 9 MSG 10 SB 11 SF

**Figure 4-18
Command Level
Interpreter (CLI)
"Syntax Check"
Display**

The CECI Transaction

The CECI transaction performs syntax checking just as the CECS transaction does. However, the CECI transaction then goes on to *execute* the command online. You may define *receiver variables* to be modified by the command, just as the command would modify a variable in your program's working storage. You may then use the same variable as an input argument to another command. In this way, you can test a sequence of CICS commands to be sure not only that the syntax is correct, but that they perform as you expect. Testing such a series of commands is referred to as a Command Level interpreter *session*.

As you use CECI you will receive a series of three displays as the transaction progresses. The STATUS line identifies each of the three displays. The first display is identical to that shown for the CECS transaction; its status line is "COMMAND SYNTAX CHECK". When the syntax has been checked and verified to be correct, a second display is produced. The STATUS line of the second display is "ABOUT TO EXECUTE COMMAND". The third display, with STATUS "COMMAND EXECUTION COMPLETE" is produced after the command has been executed.

Figures 4-19 and 4-20 illustrate the second and third displays:

Notice that in Figure 4-19, the required RIDFLD parameter has been specified. Otherwise, CECI would have detected a syntax error, and would not prepare to execute the command.

We haven't discussed the READ command shown here. However, it is an input command used to read data from a direct access file. The INTO field, like the INTO field of the RECEIVE command, receives the input data. Fields that are modified when the Command Level Interpreter executes a command, are referred to as *receivers*.

In Figure 4-20, you see the data displayed in the INTO field. The quote mark followed by periods at the end of the field indicates that the length of the data exceeds the display size. You can request that all the data be displayed by positioning the screen cursor in the INTO area and pressing the ENTER key. Figure 4-21 shows how the expanded INTO area would be displayed.

```
      READ DATASET ('FILEA') RIDFLD (000001)
      STATUS:  ABOUT TO EXECUTE COMMAND                        NAME=
       EXEC CICS READ
        Dataset ('FILEA      ')
        SET ( ) | Into ( )
          Length ( )
        Ridfld ('000001')
        < Keylength ( )   < GEneric > >
        < SYsid ( ) >
        < SEGset ( ) | Segsetall >
        < RBa | RRn | DEBRec | DEBKey >
        < GTeq | Equal >
        < Update >




      PF: 1 HELP 2 HEX 3 END 4 EIB 5 VAR 6 USER 7 SBH  8 SFH  9 MSG  10 SB 11 SF
```

Figure 4-19
CLI "About to
Execute Command"
Display

```
      READ DATASET ('FILEA') RIDFLD (000001)
      STATUS:  COMMAND EXECUTION COMPLETE                      NAME=
       EXEC CICS READ
        Dataset ('FILEA')
        SET ( ) | Into ('U000001LIEBERS S      . . . . . . . . . . . . . . . . . . . . . . . . . . . . . . . . . . . . )
        < Length (+00080) >
        Ridfld ('000001')
        < Keylength ( )     < GEneric >>
        < SYsid ( ) >
        < SEGset ( ) | Segsetall >
        < RBa | RRn | DEBRec | DEBKey >
        < GTeq | Equal >
        < Update >



      RESPONSE: NORMAL                    EIBRCODE=X'000000000000'

      PF: 1 HELP 2 HEX 3 END 4 EIB 5 VAR 6 USER 7 SBH  8 SFH  9 MSG  10 SB 11 SF
```

Figure 4-20
CLI "Command
Execution Complete"
Display

```
      READ DATASET (FILEA) RIDFLD (000001)
      EXPANSION OF:            OPTION=INTO         LENGTH= +00080 NAME=
      00000    U000001LIEBERS S      . . . . . . . . . . . . . . . . . . . . . . . . . . . . . . . . . . $
      00064    0000.1 . . . . . . . .










      PF: 1 HELP 2 HEX 3 END 4 EIB 5 VAR 6 USER            9 MSG
```

Figure 4-21
CLI Expanded
Display of INTO Area

Program Function Keys

The bottom line of each display lists optional Command Level Interpreter functions that you can request by pressing the indicated Program Function (PF) key. If your terminal doesn't have function keys, you can simulate pressing the key by placing the cursor under the desired option and pressing ENTER.

We will briefly describe the option selected by each of the function keys.

PF1 selects the HELP function that gives the meaning of each function key and describes generally how to use the Command Level Interpreter.

PF2 causes fields that are displayed as characters to be redisplayed in hexadecimal (HEX) format. Pressing PF2 a second time restores the fields to the original character format.

PF3 ends the session.

PF4 displays the EIB.

PF5 selects the *variable* function which allows you to define simulated variables. The Command Level Interpreter will assign values to each variable and allow you to display the values as the session proceeds. This function will be described in more detail below.

PF6 is used when the command being checked sends data to the terminal. To receive the data, you press PF6 after you have read the ABOUT TO EXECUTE display. You will then receive the terminal message produced by the command.

PF7, PF8, PF10, and PF11 allow the display to be scrolled. PF7 and PF8 scroll a half page; PF10 and PF11 scroll a full page. PF7 and PF10 scroll backward, PF8 and PF11 scroll forward.

The ability to interactively execute CICS commands, including commands that read and write data bases, is a powerful tool. It permits you, for example, to update the data base directly from your terminal. Because of this, many installations limit the CECI transaction to use by system programmers and data base administrators. In other cases, CECI is generally available, but you must have special authorization to execute certain commands.

Defining Variables

If you intend to test a series of commands, it's useful to define variables to store information that will be used later in the session. You can define variables to take the place of variables you would define in your program. You can also define variables that have meaning only to the Command Language Interpreter. For example, suppose you expect to repeat a particular command frequently during a session. Then you can store the entire command in a variable, and later execute the command by entering the variable name in the command field rather than retyping the entire command.

You define a variable by entering a variable name in the NAME parameter (upper right field of display) and pressing ENTER. The first character in the variable name must be an ampersand (&).

You can also define a receiver field as a variable. This allows you to transfer data between two associated commands. Figure 4-22 shows how the INTO area of a READ command is defined as a variable named &SAVEIO.

You can press PF5 to display all the variables you've defined in the session. The display gives the name, length, and current value of each variable. Figure 4-23 shows an example display.

From this VARIABLES display, you can define a new variable simply by

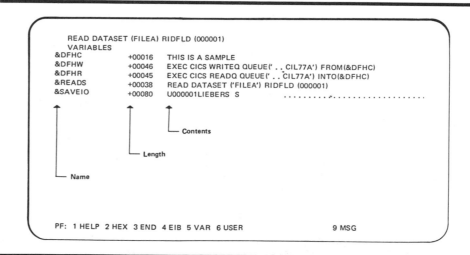

**Figure 4-22
Defining Variables
in CLI Display**

```
READ DATASET ('FILEA') RIDFLD (000001) UPDATE
STATUS:  ABOUT TO EXECUTE COMMAND                          NAME=
  EXEC CICS READ
    Dataset ('FILEA      ')
    SET( ) | Into (&SAVEI0)
      Length ( )
    Ridfld ('000001')
    < Keylength ( )  < GEneric >>
    < SYsid ( ) >
    < SEGset ( ) | Segsetall >
    < RBa | RRn | DEBRec | DEBKey >
    < GTeq | Equal >
    < Update >




PF:  1 HELP  2 HEX  3 END    EIB  5 VAR  6 USER  7 SBH  8 SFH  9 MSG  10 SB  11 SF
```

**Figure 4-23
CLI Defined
Variables List**

```
    READ DATASET (FILEA) RIDFLD (000001)
    VARIABLES
&DFHC            +00016      THIS IS A SAMPLE
&DFHW            +00046      EXEC CICS WRITEQ QUEUE(' . . CIL77A') FROM(&DFHC)
&DFHR            +00045      EXEC CICS READQ QUEUE(' . . CIL77A') INTO(&DFHC)
&READS           +00038      READ DATASET ('FILEA') RIDFLD (000001)
&SAVEI0          +00080      U000001LIEBERS  S      . . . . . . . . . .´. . . . . . . . . . . . . . . . . .

                                        └─ Contents

                            └─ Length

         └─ Name

PF:  1 HELP  2 HEX  3 END  4 EIB  5 VAR  6 USER               9 MSG
```

adding its name to the list and specifying the length and value. You can also modify the value of a variable by typing over the value in the display. Finally, you can delete a variable you no longer need by placing the cursor under the ampersand of the variable name and pressing the ERASE EOF key.

Summary

Each time CICS executes a command, it also checks for exceptional conditions. Unless your program has specified a different action, CICS will handle any exceptional condition by taking a default action. In most cases, this means terminating the task and sending a standard error message to the terminal.

You can override the default exception–handling by using the HANDLE or IGNORE command or by coding the NOHANDLE parameter on a command. You use the HANDLE command to identify a routine within your program that is to receive control if CICS detects a particular exceptional condition. You use the IGNORE command to request that CICS not check for a particular condition. You may code the NOHANDLE parameter on a CICS command to prevent exception–checking for *all conditions* for the duration of *this command only*.

The TRANSID option of the RETURN command is designed for use in pseudo-conversational transactions. The RETURN causes control to return to CICS, at the same time the TRANSID option specifies the name of a transaction to receive control when the user enters the next terminal input.

Memory space can be conserved and common programs can be shared if transactions are programmed as a sequence of small programs (modules) instead of as a single large program. You use the CICS LINK and XCTL commands to transfer control from one program to another.

LINK transfers control to a program at a *lower logical level* than that of the calling program. The calling program remains in memory and will regain control when a program at the lower level executes a RETURN command.

XCTL transfers control to a program at *the same logical level* as the calling program. The calling program will not regain control and can be released from memory.

Issuing a LINK or XCTL deactivates the active exception routines in the calling program. When a program that transferred control through a LINK regains control, its exception–handling specifications are reactivated.

In many programming situations you need to refer to data outside your program and its working storage. To do so, you must:

1. Define the data so the compiler can establish a relative address.
2. Code instructions that, at execution time, will obtain the absolute address of the area that contains the data.

We discussed the COBOL Base Linkage Locator (BLL) Cell list and how to define it in your program's LINKAGE SECTION. The LINKAGE SECTION is used to define external data.

You can process input data stored within the TIOA by defining the data area in a BLL Cell list, and using the RECEIVE command's SET option to obtain the address of the TIOA.

To reference data passed to your program by another program through LINK, XCTL, or RETURN with TRANSID, you define an external data area called DFHCOMMAREA. The calling program places the data into this area by coding the COMMAREA option on the LINK or XCTL command.

CICS stores commonly needed information in a control block called the Execution Interface Block (EIB). An EIB is constructed for each new task as it is initiated. To refer to fields in the EIB you need to know the field name and the form of the data contained in it. You do not need to define the EIB within your program.

If your CICS facility has the Command Level Interpreter, you can use it to test the syntax of your CICS commands before you code them in a program. Some installations also permit you to test the commands by executing them online through the Command Level Interpreter.

The programming exercise for this chapter will give you practice in writing exception routines and in passing control between two programs.

DISCUSSION QUESTIONS

1. How is invoking a program with LINK or XCTL different than using the standard COBOL PERFORM or CALL statement?
2. Assume that a program uses the RECEIVE command to obtain input from the user's terminal. Where is the terminal input processed if the program uses the following commands:
   a. RECEIVE INTO (data area) LENGTH (data area)
   b. RECEIVE SET (data area) LENGTH (data area)
3. Assume that a COBOL program defines an area called DFHCOMMAREA to contain data passed to it by another program. Where is the data if the program receives control via:
   a. LINK command
   b. XCTL command
   c. RETURN with TRANSID option
4. Assume that a sequence of LINK's and XCTL's occurs as shown in Figure 4-8. If programs A and Y each contain a HANDLE command for LENGERR, what will be the result if LENGERR is detected:
   a. in program X?
   b. in program Y?
   c. in program Z?
   d. in program A before the LINK command?
   e. in program A after return from Z?

EXERCISE

Write two programs that perform a pseudo-conversational transaction as follows:

■ Program 1

1. Receives the following message from the terminal:

   A01C LA73532 ABCD1234

   where the message consists of three fields of lengths 4, 5, and 8 characters. The first field is a four character transaction name (shown here as A01C). This message will be passed to program 2 as described below.
2. If the terminal input exceeds the length of the input area, send the message TOO MUCH INPUT—REENTER and terminate the task.
3. If the terminal input is normal, send the message ENTER QUANTITY, then terminate the task and specify a second transaction (for example, B01C) to process the input message which will be passed via COMMAREA.

■ Program 2

1. Check to see that the data was received from the first program. If not, send the message, SEVERE ERROR—NOTIFY SUPERVISOR and terminate the task.
2. Check the input entered in response to the ENTER QUANTITY message. If the number exceeds four digits, send the message ONLY FOUR DIGITS

ARE ALLOWED FOR THE QUANTITY. START FROM BEGINNING. Then terminate the task.

3. If the quantity was entered correctly, send the message "111111 nnnn SHIPPED TO CUST cccccccc."

    "111111" is the 6 character field read by Program 1 as field 2 (LA73532 in example above).

    "nnnn" is the QUANTITY entered in response to Program 1s request.

    "cccccccc" is the 8 character field read by Program 1 as field 3 (ABCD1234 in the example above).

    Notice that this message combines data passed from Program 1 with the quantity entered at the terminal.

4. Terminate the task.

5 Random Access of Data Files

Introduction

At this point, you have written programs that communicate with the user by sending and receiving simple terminal messages. You have some experience with the "communication" part of the DB/DC environment. Now it's time to begin working on the "data" part of DB/DC.

In this and the next chapter, we discuss how random access files are processed in the DB/DC environment. (The terms *direct access* and *random access* are often used interchangeably. However, as you will find in this chapter, *direct-access file* refers to a particular type of random file. We will use *random* as the more general term.)

In this chapter, we will concentrate on *random access* of the files. As an example application, we will use a typical *order entry* application in which selected records must be read from and written into a direct access file. You will practice CICS commands to read, update, add, and delete data records.

When a program modifies a file, provision must be made to be sure that no other program simultaneously modifies the same data. This is necessary to preserve *data integrity* of the file. We will discuss the CICS *exclusive control* feature that is used to protect data integrity.

Objectives

After completing this chapter, you will be able to:

- Describe how CICS maintains data integrity during file update processes.
- Distinguish between *keyed access* (indexed) files and files that are accessed by *relative record number*.
- Use the CICS commands to read, write, update, and delete records from random access files.
- Explain how the READ UPDATE, REWRITE, DELETE, and UNLOCK commands affect CICS *exclusive control* for a file.

Data File Control in the DB/DC Environment

If you have written COBOL programs that read and write data files, you may have processed either *sequential* files or *random access* files. Let's look briefly at some of the differences between sequential and random access files.

Accessing Sequential Files

Many files used outside the DB/DC environment are sequential files. You must read their records in the same order in which they were written. To find a particular record, you begin at the file's first record, and read and check each record in sequence until you reach the desired record.

If you want to modify a sequential file, the operating system must, insure somehow that no other program reads or writes the same file while your modification is in progress. That is, your program must have *exclusive control* of the file.

Usually, you request the exclusive control by using the job-control language. In this case, the operating system grants the exclusive control when your program begins execution. The exclusive control is retained until the program completes execution. You may also have written programs that request and release exclusive control "dynamically," that is, during execution. This allows exclusive control to be held for only part of the program's execution time.

However, whether exclusive control is held for all or part of the program's execution time, the exclusive control for a sequential file applies to the *entire file*.

You can modify a sequential file only by adding records to, or deleting records from, the end of the file. If a data value is to be changed—say in a record RECA in the middle of the file—you have to create a new file by copying all the records that precede record RECA, writing the revised RECA, and finally, copying all the records that follow RECA.

Accessing Random Access Files

You may also have written programs that process random access files. In a COBOL File Description you define such files as *random*. Usually a random file is also *keyed*—that is, each record in the field contains a field identified as the key.

When you read a record from a file like this, you specify the key of the record you want to read. Files like this are most commonly used for performance reasons when a program must access data quickly and in random order. You can perform random access input/output without using a DB/DC system like CICS so long as there's no requirement that the file be shared by several simultaneous users.

In this chapter, we will discuss random access of data files in the DB/DC environment. In this environment, the files are shared by a large number of simultaneous users—each of whom must receive a response to his or her data transaction in a matter of seconds. We will be discussing only random access files. The CICS modules that perform file control, the CICS *File Control Program* (FCP) component, support only random access files. (CICS does permit the use of sequential files, primarily as a means of interchanging information between programs. We will discuss this in a later chapter.)

Order Entry Applications

Order Entry is a typical class of DB/DC application that involves frequent update of the data base. In order entry applications, the company is in the business of selling some type of commodity. The commodity may be items of merchandise like automobiles or furniture, or it may be less tangible like reservations on airline flights. In any case, the data base is used to keep track of the quantity of each item that is available, as well as its price and other descriptive information. When a customer places an order for an item, the order is entered at an online terminal. A transaction is requested to locate the data record that describes the item the customer wants, and to display the "quantity on hand."

Let's assume that an enterprise sells outdoor sports equipment. A customer requests 15 lightweight expedition quality tents, Model XYZ. The person who receives the order enters a transaction request to display information about

TENT XYZ. If the display indicates that there are more than 15 of the tents on hand, the customer order is entered. The order-entry program reduces the "quantity on hand" value by 15, and writes the updated TENT XYZ record into the data base.

Consider the requirements of such an order-entry application:

In order to fill orders promptly, it is important to obtain the information about a particular item of merchandise quickly. The data base definition in Chapter 1 stated that data bases are usually "large." Therefore, to search through the data base record by record for the TENT XYZ information would be impractical. The data base cannot be sequential; it must be organized so that the TENT XYZ record can be retrieved directly or, at least, by reading no more than three or four records. The next section will discuss two common types of non-sequential data organization that can satisfy this requirement.

Data Integrity During Update

Keep in mind that orders for merchandise can be placed from any of several terminals. If TENT XYZ is a big seller, it's not unlikely that two or more customers may be placing an order at the same time, say at 9 a.m. on a Monday morning. We have said that only one transaction can be permitted to update a given data item at a time. Figure 5-1 shows what would happen if the order-entry system permitted both orders for TENT XYZ to proceed in parallel.

As you study Figure 5-1, assume that when the enterprise opens for business on Monday morning there are 200 of TENT XYZ on hand. Customers A and B phone in orders for 50 and 60 tents respectively. The calls are processed by two different people, each of whom enters a transaction to process an order. Task A is initiated to execute the order-entry program for Customer A and Task B for Customer B.

The three right-hand columns in Figure 5-1 show the "quantity on hand" value as seen by Task A and Task B and as represented in the file. We know

ASSUME: QUANTITY ON HAND   200
         TASK A ORDER QUANTITY   50
         TASK B ORDER QUANTITY   60

	ACTIVITY	TASK A	TASK B	FILE
TIME 1	TASK A READS	200		200
TIME 2	TASK B READS		200	200
TIME 3	TASK A UPDATES	150		200
	TASK A REWRITES			150
TIME 4	TASK B UPDATES		140	
	TASK B REWRITES			140

Figure 5-1
Incorrect Data
Caused by Parallel
Update

that after the two orders are processed, the quantity on hand should be 200-50-60 = 90. However, as shown in Figure 5-1, when the two tasks are permitted to proceed in parallel, the quantity shown in the file will be 140. This error would be prevented if Task B were not allowed to read the TENT XYZ record until Task A completed its update. That is, Task A needs to *exclude* Task B from accessing the TENT XYZ record.

We have seen that outside the DB/DC environment, a task which will update a file is usually given exclusive control of the entire file until its update of the file is complete. In the DB/DC environment, however, it is impractical to grant a task exclusive control of the *entire file*. There may be hundreds of other customers waiting who want to order sleeping bags or flashlights. There is no reason to hold these orders for a task that affects only tents. Therefore, in the DB/DC environment, exclusive control is granted for only a part of the data base that will be affected by an update.

Data Independence

At this point, it may seem that programming in the DB/DC environment must be very complex. Does an application program have to include statements that request exclusive control before each update? Suppose the program requests exclusive control, but another task has already been given exclusive control for the same records. Must the program go into some sort of timed loop to ask for the exclusive control periodically until the first task completes?

The answer to all these questions is that the DB/DC system, not the application program, takes care of these matters. Every DB/DC system has an objective of making the application program *independent* of the structure of the data base. As we shall see in our discussion of CICS file control, complete independence may not always be achieved. However, in general, an application program written for use with a DB/DC system will be less complex and very much less dependent on data structure than a similar application written outside the DB/DC system environment.

Consider a COBOL program, written outside the DB/DC environment, that manipulates a data file. This program includes three kinds of statements relative to the file. First, there is the File Description that specifies how the file is organized. Secondly, there are file control statements—OPEN and CLOSE. And, finally, there are the input/output statements, READS and WRITES, GETS and PUTS, which cause data to be transferred to and from the files.

Outside of the program there are job-control statements that allow the operating system to locate the file to be used, and specify whether or not the program requires exclusive use of the file.

By contrast, a program written for use with CICS generally contains only statements (equivalent to READS, GETS, WRITES, etc.) that move logical records.

In order to make the program as independent as possible of the way the file is structured, the files are defined within CICS rather than in the program. The File Descriptions are eliminated. Since a file is described in only one place—a CICS table—rather than in each individual program; it is more convenient to restructure the file. For example, in the CICS environment, a file written using the Indexed Sequential Access Method (ISAM) could be converted for use with the Virtual Storage Access Method (VSAM) without requiring that application programs be rewritten. This textbook will not discuss the features of particular access methods. The point to be understood is that you can write CICS application programs without being familiar with the details of each file's structure.

In CICS programs, the OPEN and CLOSE programming statements are also eliminated. CICS controls all the files. A file is available for access (open) or not (closed) depending upon whether the system programmer has defined the file to the system. All the files defined to the system are normally opened when the DB/DC system is started and remain open while the system is in operation. (An exception is the situation where, for some reason, the system operator must control the availability of a file. Perhaps the file wasn't available when the operator started the DB/DC system. Or a file may be scheduled to be unavailable (during particular periods of the day, for instance) to permit maintenance or batch updates that would interfere with online usage. In these instances, the operator can control the file's open or closed status by using special online operator commands.)

Finally, CICS application programs don't include explicit statements to request exclusive control. CICS is designed to recognize the need for exclusive control from the form or sequence of the program's file input/output statements. That is, the control is requested *implicitly* rather than *explicitly* by specific commands.

Random File Organizations

A record in a non-sequential file is accessed in one of two general ways:

1. The record may contain a KEY. To access such a record, you specify the value of the key in your input/output command. For example, records in the file used by the outdoor sports equipment company might contain a catalog number as key. If TENT XYZ's catalog number were 000-TENT-XYZ, the person who received an order for TENT XYZ would enter 000-TENT-XYZ as part of the transaction data. Your application program would use the catalog number as a READ statement parameter in order to retrieve information about TENT XYZ. The key must be *unique*; that is, no other item may have a catalog number of 000-TENT-XYZ. Files like this are called *keyed access* files. You may also hear them referred to as *indexed files*.
2. The record may be referenced *by location*. In this case, your program accesses the record by specifying its relative position in the file, or its address on the storage device. Files like this are called *direct access* files.

   For example, if TENT XYZ were described by the 317th record in the file, your application program would specify the integer value 317 as a "relative record number" parameter of the READ command. How would the program determine that TENT XYZ is described by record 317? This would depend upon how the particular order-entry system was designed. There might be a table of catalog numbers constructed so that if an item's catalog number is the 317th in the table, the record describing the item is also the 317th record in the file. Or catalog numbers might be coded so that by performing a series of arithmetic operations on the catalog number, the program could obtain the record number.

CICS File Control

The CICS File Control Program allows application programs to read and write non-sequential files using several different access methods. CICS application programs are not completely independent of data structure. Some CICS commands are restricted to use with particular access methods, so you must know whether the file is, for example, a keyed access file or a direct access file.

We will use the Virtual Storage Access Method (VSAM) as the basis for discussion, because VSAM supports the largest subset of CICS function. You should be aware, however, that file control programming for other access methods may differ in some details from the examples in this text.

Reading a Record

To read a record from a file, you use the CICS READ command, shown below.

EXEC CICS READ INTO(data area) LENGTH(data value)
DATASET(data value) RIDFLD(data area)

Notice that, like the RECEIVE command, READ uses the INTO and LENGTH parameters. Both parameters are used exactly as described for RECEIVE. As discussed for the RECEIVE command, SET may be used in place of INTO if you want to process data in the input buffer rather than moving it into working-storage.

LENGTH is not required if all the records in the file are the same length, and if the INTO data area is also the same length. However, the recommended programming practice is to program for the general case whenever practical. Therefore, as illustrated in Figure 5-2, you will normally use the LENGTH option, and define an exception-handling routine for the LENGERR condition. (You may want to review the discussion of LENGERR in the description of the RECEIVE command.)

The DATASET argument is a symbolic name or a character string constant that identifies the file to be read.

All the files that can be accessed by CICS application programs are listed in a table called the *File Control Table* (FCT). Within the FCT each file is identified by a name of up to eight characters. This is the name you specify with the DATASET option.

The FCT contains other descriptive information about the file. For instance: the access method used, the length of logical records, the length of the key, and the location of the key within the record are all contained in the FCT.

RIDFLD stands for *Record Identification Field*. The RIDFLD parameter specifies which record to read. If the file is a keyed access file, called a Key Sequenced Data Set (KSDS) in VSAM, the RIDFLD argument gives the record's key. If the file is a direct access file where a record is identified by its relative location in the file; the RIDFLD argument contains a four-byte binary relative record number. In this case, the option RRN (which has no argument) must also be specified to make clear how the RIDFLD argument is to be interpreted. A file that is accessed in this way is called a Relative Record Data Set (RRDS) in VSAM. You may have seen the terms *relative file* and *nominal* keys used to define files like this in COBOL programs.

When you are processing a keyed access file, you often need to read all the records whose keys fall in a particular range. For example, let's assume that a customer has called the outdoor equipment dealer to order TENT XYZ. However, there are no XYZ model tents available, and the expected availability date is after the customer's planned trip. The customer may then

```
      IDENTIFICATION DIVISION.
      PROGRAM-ID. FCPCOB1.
     *
     * PROGRAM READS A RECORD WITH THE KEY LAX01 IN A DATA SET
     * NAMED MASTER.
     *
     *
     *** PROGRAM IS INCOMPLETE AND WILL NOT EXECUTE ***
     *
      ENVIRONMENT DIVISION.
      DATA DIVISION.
      WORKING-STORAGE SECTION.
      77  LEN PIC S9(4) COMP VALUE 25.
      77  RECORD-KEY PIC X(5) VALUE 'LAX01'.
      01  FILE-AREA.
          02 REC-KEY  PIC X(5).
          02 REC-DESC PIC X(20).
               .
               .
               .
      PROCEDURE DIVISION.
          * ERROR CHECKING *
          EXEC CICS HANDLE CONDITION LENGERR(RTOOLONG)
                    NOTFND(NOREC) ERROR(OTHERR)
                    END-EXEC.
          EXEC CICS READ INTO(FILE-AREA) DATASET('MASTER')
                    RIDFLD (RECORD-KEY) LENGTH(LEN) END-EXEC.
          *** PROCESS RECORD ***
               .
               .
               .
      RTOOLONG.
          * ERROR PROCESSING - THE RECORD READ IS LONGER THAN *
          * NUMBER OF BYTES SPECIFIED IN LENGTH FIELD (LEN) *
               .
               .
               .
      NOREC.
          * ERROR PROCESSING - RECORD WITH SPECIFIED KEY IS NOT *
          * IN THE DATA SET *
               .
               .
               .
      OTHERR.
          * ERROR PROCESSING - OTHER ERROR HAS OCCURRED *
               .
               .
               .
```

Figure 5-2
LENGTH Option
Coded in READ
Command

want to know, "What model tents do you have in stock now?" To find out, your application program would need to display information about all the items whose keys begin 000-TENT.

To handle this requirement, additional READ command options are provided for use with VSAM files.

You use the GENERIC option to inform CICS that the key specified by RIDFLD is only a *partial* key. Then the KEYLENGTH argument specifies the number of characters in the partial key. The KEYLENGTH option is required because when the READ command has been completed, the RIDFLD argument will contain the *full* key of the record that was read. Therefore, the RIDFLD argument cannot be a constant, *and* it must be long enough to hold the complete key.

To answer the customer's TENT question then, a READ statement like the following would be used:

EXEC CICS READ INTO(data area) LENGTH(data area)
DATASET('OUTGEAR') RIDFLD(part key) GENERIC KEYLENGTH(8)

Part-key is a data area of length 12 which contains the value 000-TENT. Assuming that the record found was for TENT ABC, part-key would contain the value 000-TENT-ABC after the READ command had been completed.

Exceptional Conditions

In Chapter 3, we described the LENGERR exception condition which can arise during execution of the RECEIVE command. It can also arise during the READ command if the actual length of a data record exceeds the number of characters specified by LENGTH.

In addition to LENGERR, a number of other exception conditions may arise with the READ command. They are:

1. NOTFND. This occurs when a record with the specified key cannot be found in the file. This would usually indicate that the user had entered an incorrect key as data. Perhaps the user made a simple typing error and entered 000-TENF-XYZ instead of 000-TENT-XYZ as the catalog number. Notice that the program segment shown in Figure 5-2 defines an exception–handling routine for NOTFND.
2. DSIDERR. The file name specified by the DATASET argument does not appear in the FCT.
3. ILLOGIC. VSAM has detected an exceptional condition not covered by other CONDITION categories.
4. IOERR. An unrecoverable input/output error has occurred during the operation.
5. NOTOPEN. The requested file is not open. In this case the online user should be notified that the file is temporarily unavailable and that the transaction should be retried later. (Although you haven't yet learned how to send messages to the computer operator, your program should notify the operator when a requested file is unavailable, so that corrective action can be taken if required.)

Updating a Record

The earlier discussion of exclusive control showed that when a program reads a logical record with the intent of updating the record, the program must obtain exclusive control of the record. Figure 5-1 illustrates how the file could become inaccurate if a second task were to read a record that is being updated.

CICS application programs obtain exclusive control when they execute a CICS READ with the UPDATE option. This is referred to as performing a *READ for UPDATE.*

When the READ for UPDATE has been performed and the data within the logical record has been changed, the program executes a REWRITE command to write the modified record back to the file. Figure 5-3 shows an example of a READ for UPDATE—REWRITE sequence.

When the REWRITE command has been completed, CICS automatically

```
          IDENTIFICATION DIVISION.
          PROGRAM-ID. FCPCOB2.
        *
        * PROGRAM READS AND UPDATES A RECORD WITH THE KEY LAX01 *
        * IN A DATA SET NAMED MASTER. *
        *
        *
        *** PROGRAM IS INCOMPLETE AND WILL NOT EXECUTE ***
        *
          ENVIRONMENT DIVISION.
          DATA DIVISION.
          WORKING-STORAGE SECTION.
          77  LEN PIC S9(4) COMP VALUE 25.
          77  RECORD-KEY PIC X(5) VALUE 'LAX01'.
          01  FILE-AREA.
              02 REC-KEY  PIC X(5).
              02 REC-DESC PIC X(20).
                     .
                     .
                     .
          PROCEDURE DIVISION.
        * ERROR CHECKING *
              EXEC CICS HANDLE CONDITION LENGERR(RTOOLONG)
                        NOTFND(NOREC) ERROR(OTHERR)
                        END-EXEC.
              EXEC CICS READ INTO(FILE-AREA) DATASET('MASTER')
                        RIDFLD(RECORD-KEY) LENGTH(LEN) UPDATE
                        END-EXEC.
          *** PROCESS RECORD ***
                     .
                     .
                     .
              EXEC CICS REWRITE FROM(FILE-AREA) DATASET('MASTER')
                        LENGTH(LEN) END-EXEC.
                     .
                     .
                     .
        RTOOLONG.
           * ERROR PROCESSING - THE RECORD READ IS LONGER THAN *
           * NUMBER OF BYTES SPECIFIED IN LENGTH FIELD (LEN) *
                     .
                     .
                     .
        NOREC.
           * ERROR PROCESSING - RECORD WITH SPECIFIED KEY IS NOT *
           * IN THE DATA SET *
                     .
                     .
                     .
        OTHERR.
           * ERROR PROCESSING - OTHER ERROR HAS OCCURRED *
                     .
                     .
                     .
```

Figure 5-3
Exclusive Control
During File Update

revokes exclusive control. The modified record is then available for access by other tasks.

As shown in Figure 5-3, the REWRITE command has the form:

EXEC CICS REWRITE FROM(data area)
          LENGTH(data value) DATASET(data value)

The FROM and LENGTH options are the same as for the SEND command. The DATASET argument is as described for the READ command.

Exclusive Control Considerations

Remember that when a task executes a READ for UPDATE command, the task is implicitly requesting exclusive control for the selected record. If another task, say TASKA, has exclusive control of the record named in the READ for update command; the requesting task will be placed in a wait for exclusive control. The task, therefore, becomes inactive. CICS will allow the highest priority active task to begin execution. When TASKA relinquishes exclusive control, for example by executing a REWRITE, the waiting task becomes active and will be scheduled for execution depending upon its priority.

In the examples discussed so far, CICS has managed the exclusive control automatically. You didn't have to program requests for control, waits for control, etc. Nevertheless, you need to be aware of when a program has exclusive control and when it does not.

Suppose that TASKA receives exclusive control for a record and then enters a WAIT state before executing a REWRITE. Then other tasks that may be waiting to access the same record must wait until TASKA becomes active, is placed in execution, and completes the REWRITE command. This is why you should write your application programs so they hold exclusive control for as brief a period as possible. REWRITE should follow READ for UPDATE as quickly as possible. Other CICS commands should be delayed until after the REWRITE if program logic permits, because a task may become inactive whenever it executes a CICS command.

The INVREQ Condition: So far, in our discussion of exclusive control we haven't pointed out a practical detail of which you should be aware. When your program receives exclusive control, the control is not necessarily restricted to a single logical record. Depending upon how the file is structured and upon the data or data base access method in use, the *span of exclusive control* may extend over several logical records. This means that your request to update one logical record may have to wait until another task completes its update of another record in the same span of control. It also means that you have to be careful when writing a program that must update more than one logical record. Let's see why.

Consider the following sequence of commands:

> READ UPDATE (for record A)
> READ UPDATE (for record B)

Assume that record A and record B are both within the same span of exclusive control. The first READ obtains exclusive control. The exclusive control will be retained until released, for example, by a REWRITE command.

The second READ requests the same exclusive control, but cannot obtain it. The exclusive control is unavailable because of the first READ command. The task will be placed in the wait state—waiting for itself to release exclusive control. This is, in effect, a permanent wait since the task cannot become active until it releases exclusive control, but it cannot release exclusive control without becoming active.

CICS prevents this permanent wait situation by preventing a *transaction* (remember that a transaction may involve more than one task) from having more than one update operation in progress at a time for a given file. If a second update is attempted for the same data set, the INVREQ exceptional condition is raised. Therefore, in the example above, the second READ would raise the INVREQ condition rather than placing the task into the permanent wait state.

INVREQ may also be raised in a number of other situations. They include:

A REWRITE command not preceded by a READ for UPDATE,
An operation requested that is not permitted for the file type,
A KEYLENGTH argument specifies a key length inappropriate for the file.

The UNLOCK Command: You may find some situations in which, after reading a record for update, your program determines that the UPDATE is no longer required. However, because the record has already been read for UPDATE, the task will be holding exclusive control of the record. You must release the exclusive control so that other tasks may access the record, but you don't want to issue a REWRITE command.

In this situation, you must *explicitly* release the exclusive control by issuing the following CICS command:

EXEC CICS UNLOCK DATASET(data-area)

The DATASET argument specifies the name of the file from which the record was read—the file for which you are holding exclusive control.

If you didn't issue the UNLOCK command, exclusive control would remain in effect—and the record would be unavailable to other tasks—until your task terminated.

Multi-Task Considerations: You've seen how CICS prevents a transaction from entering a permanent wait by attempting to update two records in the same span of control. But there still remains the possibility of two *different* transactions becoming interlocked. In the DB/DC environment, it's not at all unlikely that two tasks might be attempting to update the same record at the same time.

But let's look at a two transaction situation. Consider two tasks, TASK1 and TASK2, that are both updating Files A and B.

Suppose that TASK1 contains the command sequence:

READ UPDATE DATASET('A')
READ UPDATE DATASET('B')

TASK2 contains the command sequence:

READ UPDATE DATASET('B')
READ UPDATE DATASET('A')

Remember that in the multi-tasking environment, a task doesn't normally execute from beginning to end all at once. Whenever a task executes a CICS command, it may lose control of the CPU by entering a wait state. During the period of the wait, other tasks may execute. Therefore, TASK1 and TASK2 may become interleaved in execution so that the commands are actually executed in the order shown in Figure 5-4.

Consider the situation at Point 1 in Figure 5-4. TASK1 has exclusive control of record 338 in File A. TASK2 has exclusive control of record 753 in File B.

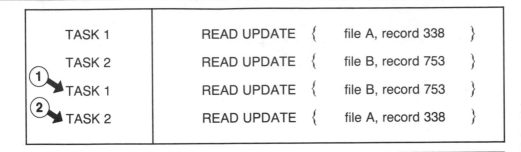

TASK 1	READ UPDATE	{	file A, record 338 }
TASK 2	READ UPDATE	{	file B, record 753 }
TASK 1	READ UPDATE	{	file B, record 753 }
TASK 2	READ UPDATE	{	file A, record 338 }

**Figure 5-4
Perpetual Wait
Caused by Task
Interlock**

TASK 1 is now requesting exclusive control of record 753 in File B—the record TASK2 is holding.

Since the exclusive control is not available, TASK1 will be placed in the wait state. What is required for TASK1 to become active? TASK2 must release control of record 753 of File B. But to release control, TASK2 must regain the CPU. Now look at the command TASK2 intends to execute when it resumes execution (Point 2 of Figure 5-4). As soon as TASK2 resumes, it will execute a READ for UPDATE of record 338—the record that TASK1 is holding. TASK2 will also enter the wait state—waiting for TASK1 to release a record. But TASK1 is waiting for TASK2. Neither task can proceed, because each is waiting for the other.

Each program appears to be correct when viewed alone, but clearly in the real-world DB/DC multi-task environment, the programs don't work correctly.

This type of interlock can be avoided if all programs are written according to a *standard convention*. Just as a country must adopt a convention of driving either on the left or the right, programmers must adopt a convention about the order in which they access multiple files. If both TASK1 and TASK2 had accessed first File A and then File B, the interlock would have been prevented. Each installation defines its own local programming conventions, but a common convention is to access files according to the alphabetical order of their names when a program must access more than one file at a time.

Adding and Deleting Records

The commands we have discussed so far: READ, READ for UPDATE, and REWRITE, are the most commonly used file processing commands in most DB/DC applications.

However, it is sometimes necessary to add new records to a file or to delete records from a file. In the order-entry example, the outdoor equipment company might decide to add bicycles to its line of merchandise. Then records would have to be added to describe the various models of bicycles. On the other hand, the company might decide that it would no longer sell fishing rods and reels. The records for these items would be deleted.

Depending upon how files are organized, it may not be possible to add or delete records in the online CICS environment. These operations may have to be done by a batch program that is run while online terminals cannot access the file. In this section, we will discuss the CICS commands that are used to add and delete records online. In the work situation, you would have to consult with the data base administrator or system programmer to find out whether you can use these commands for a particular file.

The DELETE Command

Often when a record is to be deleted, it must first be read to verify that the record is no longer needed. In this case, you read the record for UPDATE and then delete it. The command to delete a record is written:

EXEC CICS DELETE DATASET(data-area)

The DATASET argument, as usual, gives the name of the file from which the record was read.

The DELETE releases the exclusive control that was obtained by the READ for UPDATE.

Note: A record cannot be deleted in this way if it was read for UPDATE by a READ command that used the GENERIC option.

It isn't necessary to read a record before deleting it; you can delete a record by specifying its key or location. For example:

EXEC CICS DELETE DATASET('OUTGEAR') RIDFLD(catalog-no)

The record-identifying options, RRN, KEYLENGTH, GENERIC, are used for the DELETE command just as described for the READ command.

If KEYLENGTH and GENERIC are used, the command will delete *all the records whose keys match* the partial key given by RIDFLD. To do this, you must also code the NUMREC option. As an argument, NUMREC requires a two-byte binary field which will be set to the number of records deleted—that is, the number of records whose keys matched the specified partial key. Exclusive control will be in effect for the duration of the DELETE operation.

Figure 5-5 shows a COBOL program that deletes a group of records.

The physical effect of DELETE on the file depends upon how the file is structured. For some access methods and file structures, a deleted record is actually removed from the file; the space it occupied is freed and can be used if a new record is added to the file. In other situations, however, the record remains in place and is merely *marked* as "deleted." In this case, the space is not freed and the record can still be read if a program specifies its key or record number. Application programs written for use with these types of file must check each record they read to be sure that it does not contain the "deleted" indicator. You should confer with the data base administrator to find out which type of deletion is performed for a particular file.

The WRITE Command

The WRITE command is used to add new records to a file. The command is of the form:

EXEC CICS WRITE FROM(data-area) LENGTH(data-value)
DATASET(data-value) RIDFLD(data-area)

All the options are as defined for previous commands.

Remember that if the file is a direct access file—as opposed to keyed—you must code the RRN option to clarify the meaning of the RIDFLD argument.

Exclusive control is in effect while the WRITE command is being executed.

You can also add a *group of records* whose keys or record numbers are in ascending sequence. Figure 5-6 shows how to do that.

```
IDENTIFICATION DIVISION.
PROGRAM-ID. FCPCOB5.
*
* PROGRAM DELETES RECORDS WITH THE GENERIC KEYS LA IN A DATA SET *
* NAMED MASTER.*
*
*
*** PROGRAM IS INCOMPLETE AND WILL NOT EXECUTE ***
*
ENVIRONMENT DIVISION.
DATA DIVISION.
WORKING-STORAGE SECTION.
77  RECORD-KEY PIC X(5) VALUE 'LAX01'.
77  REC-DEL    PIC S9(4) COMP.
         .
         .
         .
PROCEDURE DIVISION.
    * ERROR CHECKING *
     EXEC CICS HANDLE CONDITION
               NOTFND(NOREC) ERROR(OTHERR)
               END-EXEC.
     EXEC CICS DELETE DATASET('MASTER') KEYLENGTH(2)
               RIDFLD(RECORD-KEY) GENERIC NUMREC(REC-DEL)
               END-EXEC.
     * NUMBER OF RECORDS DELETED WILL BE IN THE FIELD REC-DEL *
         .
         .
         .
NOREC.
     * ERROR PROCESSING - RECORD WITH SPECIFIED KEY IS NOT *
     * IN THE DATA SET *
         .
         .
         .
OTHERR.
     * ERROR PROCESSING - OTHER ERROR HAS OCCURRED *
         .
         .
         .
```

Figure 5-5
Deleting a Group
of Records

Notice that a new option, MASSINSERT, must be specified in this case. MASSINSERT causes exclusive control to be maintained rather than canceled as each WRITE statement in the group is completed. When all the records in the group have been added, you must use the UNLOCK command to release exclusive control.

If you attempt to add a record whose key matches the key of a record already in the file, the DUPREC exceptional condition is raised.

If there isn't enough space in the file to accommodate a new record, a WRITE command will raise the NOSPACE exceptional condition.

Programming Example

At this point, you may find it helpful to look through a CICS program that uses a number of the commands we have discussed so far.

The flowchart in Figure 5-7 shows a program designed to handle two transactions: a file inquiry transaction (INQY) and an *add new record* transaction (ADDS). The ADDS transaction is programmed as a pseudo-conversational transaction. To add a record, the same program will be entered twice.

```
      IDENTIFICATION DIVISION.                                      00010000
      PROGRAM-ID. FCPCOB7.                                          00020004
      *                                                             00030006
      * PROGRAM ADDS 5 SEQUENTIAL RECORDS BEGINNING WITH THE KEY * 00040002
      * LAX01 TO A DATA SET NAMED MASTER *                          00050002
      *                                                             00060006
      *                                                             00070008
      *** PROGRAM IS INCOMPLETE AND WILL NOT EXECUTE ***            00080008
      *                                                             00090008
      ENVIRONMENT DIVISION.                                         00100000
      DATA DIVISION.                                                00110000
      WORKING-STORAGE SECTION.                                      00120000
      77   LEN PIC S9(4) COMP VALUE 25.                             00130000
      01   RECORD-KEY PIC X(5) VALUE 'LAX01'.                       00140002
      01   FILLER REDEFINES RECORD-KEY.                             00150009
           02 RECORD-KEY-A PIC X(3).                                00160002
           02 RECORD-KEY-N PIC 9(2).                                00170002
      01   FILE-AREA.                                               00180000
           02 REC-KEY  PIC X(5).                                    00190000
           02 REC-DESC PIC X(20).                                   00200006
           .                                                        00210000
           .                                                        00220000
           .                                                        00230000
      PROCEDURE DIVISION.                                           00240000
         * ERROR CHECKING *                                         00250001
           EXEC CICS HANDLE CONDITION                               00260002
                   DUPREC(RECTHERE) ERROR(OTHERR)                   00270006
                   END-EXEC.                                        00280002
           .                                                        00290000
           .                                                        00300000
           .                                                        00310000
           MOVE 'LAX01' TO RECORD-KEY.                              00320002
      MASS-INS.                                                     00330002
           MOVE RECORD-KEY TO REC-KEY.                              00340002
           MOVE 'NEW RECORD INSERTED' TO REC-DESC.                  00350002
           EXEC CICS WRITE FROM(FILE-AREA) LENGTH(LEN)              00360006
                   DATASET('MASTER') RIDFLD(RECORD-KEY)             00370006
                   MASSINSERT                                       00380002
                   END-EXEC.                                        00390002
           ADD 1 TO RECORD-KEY-N.                                   00400002
           IF RECORD-KEY-N LESS THAN 6 THEN                         00410002
                GO TO MASS-INS  ELSE                                00420002
           EXEC CICS UNLOCK DATASET('MASTER') END-EXEC.             00430007
           .                                                        00440002
           .                                                        00450002
           .                                                        00460002
      RECTHERE.                                                     00470003
         * ERROR PROCESSING - RECORD IS ALREADY *                   00480003
           IN THE DATA SET *                                        00490000
           .                                                        00500000
           .                                                        00510000
           .                                                        00520000
      OTHERR.                                                       00530005
         * ERROR PROCESSING - OTHER ERROR HAS OCCURRED *            00540000
           .                                                        00550000
           .                                                        00560000
           .                                                        00570000
```

Figure 5-6
Inserting a Group of Records

91

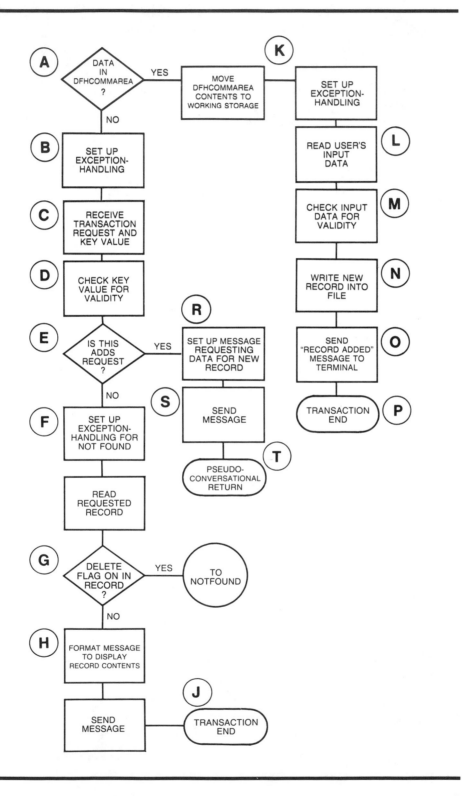

Figure 5-7
Pseudo-
Conversational
File Update, Flow

```
                    DATA DIVISION.
                    WORKING-STORAGE SECTION.
                    77 IN-LNG PICTURE S9(4) COMP VALUE +11.
                    01 IN-MSG.
                         02 TRAN-ID PIC X(4).
                         02 FILLER PIC X.
                         02 KEYNUM PIC 9(6).
                    01 FILEA.
                         02 FILEREC.
                              03 STAT PICTURE X.
                          .
                          .
                          .

                    LINKAGE SECTION.
                    01 DFHCOMMAREA.
                         02 TRAN-ID PIC X(4).
                         02 FILLER PIC X.
                         02 KEYNUM PIC 9(6).

                    PROCEDURE DIVISION.

              (A)   IF EIBCALEN NOT = 0 THEN
                                                   (K)
                          MOVE DFHCOMMAREA TO IN-MSG    GO TO READ-INPUT.

              (B)   EXEC CICS HANDLE CONDITION ERROR(ERRORS) END-EXEC.
              (C)   EXEC CICS RECEIVE LENGTH (IN-LNG) INTO(IN-MSG) END-EXEC.
                    IF IN-LNG NOT = 11 THEN GO TO BADLENG.
              (D)       [CHECK KEY FOR VALID VALUE]
              (E)   IF EIBTRNID = 'ADDS' THEN
                          [ SET UP MESSAGE REQUESTING DATA (R)
                            FOR NEW RECORD]
                          [ SEND MESSAGE]                    (S)
                          EXEC CICS RETURN
                      (T)     TRANSID (EIBTRNID) COMMAREA (INMSG) LENGTH (IN-LNG)
                                  END-EXEC.

              (F)   EXEC CICS HANDLE CONDITION NOTFND (NOTFOUND) END-EXEC.
                    EXEC CICS READ DATASET ('FILEA') INTO (FILEA)
                              RIDFLD (KEYNUM IN IN-MSG)  END-EXEC.
              (G)   IF STAT IN FILEA = HIGH-VALUE THEN GO TO NOTFOUND.
              (H)   [SET UP MESSAGE DISPLAYING RECORD CONTENTS]
                    [SEND MESSAGE TO TERMINAL]
              (J)   EXEC CICS RETURN END-EXEC.

                    READ-INPUT.
                    EXEC CICS HANDLE CONDITION NOTFND (NOTFOUND) ERROR(ERRORS)
                              DUPREC (DUPREC) END-EXEC.
            (L,M)   [RECEIVE USER INPUT FOR NEW RECORD DATA]
                    [CHECK USER INPUT FOR LEGAL VALUES, AND MOVE TO OUT-DATA AREA]
              (N)   EXEC CICS WRITE DATASET('FILEA') FROM (OUT-DATA)
                              RIDFLD (KEYNUM IN IN-MSG)   END-EXEC.
                    [SEND "RECORD ADDED" MESSAGE]
            (O,P)   EXEC CICS RETURN END-EXEC.
                          .
                          .
                          .
```

**Figure 5-8
Pseudo-
Conversational
File Update,
Program Example**

Figure 5-8 illustrates the COBOL program that corresponds to Figure 5-7s flowchart. The blocks within the flowchart are labeled alphabetically, and the same alphabetic labels are shown in the margin of the COBOL program. You may want to refer to the flowchart as you read the following program description; then, study Figure 5-8 to see the programming statements used to perform each step.

The routine begins (Block A) by checking to see whether there is data in DFHCOMMAREA. If not, this is the first entry to the program. Blocks B through D are then executed. At Block E, the program checks to see which transaction (INQY or ADDS) was requested. It does this by checking the EIBTRNID value.

For the INQY transaction (Blocks F through J), the program reads the requested record and, if the read was successful, formats the record data and sends it to the user terminal. Notice the test in block G to check whether the record had been marked "deleted." As discussed for the DELETE command, in some data files deleted records remain in place and are simply marked "deleted." In these cases, you will need to perform a test like that shown here. Once the requested information has been sent to the user, the INQY transaction is terminated (Block J).

Upon the first entry of the ADDS transaction, the program follows through Blocks B through E as for the INQY transaction. Notice that at Block C it reads the transaction request containing the key value for the new record. In Block R the program formats a message requesting the other data fields for the new record. As soon as the message has been sent (Block S), the transaction can terminate. As set up by the pseudo–conversational RETURN TRANSID command (Block T), the ADDS transaction will be invoked again when the user has completed typing the new record's data and pressed the terminal's ENTER key. Notice that the COMMAREA option of the RETURN TRANSID command is used to pass the data in IN-MSG (including the new record's key) to the "next" transaction. In this case, the "next" transaction will be a new invocation of the same ADDS transaction.

When the program is entered the second time, it retrieves the key value from DFHCOMMAREA (Block K) and sets up the required exception-handling routines. It then reads the user's input data from the terminal (Block L), checks it for validity (Block M), and adds the new record to the file (Block N). The program then need only send a concluding message to the terminal and terminate.

Summary

CICS supports the sharing of data bases by several simultaneous users. To do so, it must control data availability, protect data integrity during update, and provide support for developing data-independent application programs.

Order Entry is a typical DB/DC application. It requires that a particular record can be quickly selected from the data base and updated if necessary. Applications of this type usually require non-sequential files. Keyed Access and Direct Access files are two examples of non-sequential files.

We have discussed the CICS READ, REWRITE, UNLOCK, WRITE, and DELETE commands. A special form of the READ command is the READ for UPDATE which obtains exclusive control of the record that is read. Depending upon how the file is organized, the *span* of exclusive control may extend to several records besides the single record you intend to update. The exclusive control is canceled when the REWRITE command is used to replace the record with a modified version, or when DELETE is used to remove the record from the file. Exclusive control can also be canceled explicitly with the UNLOCK command.

You need to be aware of when a task will hold exclusive control, and write your program so it will hold exclusive control for as short a period as possible. If a task holds exclusive control and fails to release it promptly, it can cause other tasks in the system to wait longer than necessary to access the affected records. If a program must access more than one file at a time, care must be taken to reference the files in a standard order so that two or more tasks do not become interlocked.

The WRITE and DELETE commands are provided to add records to a file or to remove records from a file. These commands are not supported for all types of files. The GENERIC, KEYLENGTH, and NUMREC options of the DELETE command can be used together to delete groups of records whose keys begin with the same character string. For some types of files, DELETE causes a record to be marked as "deleted," but to remain physically accessible in the file.

The WRITE command with the MASSINSERT option can be used to add a group of records to a file if the keys for the records are in ascending order. MASSINSERT maintains exclusive control, so the UNLOCK command should follow a series of WRITE MASSINSERT commands.

We have discussed several exceptional conditions that may arise during file operations. They include LENGERR, INVREQ, ILLOGIC, NOTOPEN, DUPREC, NOSPACE, IOERR, and DSIDERR.

DISCUSSION QUESTIONS

1. From your reading in Chapter 5, what characteristics of a data file must the CICS programmer know in order to use the commands discussed?

2. Which of the characteristics you listed in your answer to question 1 can be found in the FCT?

3. Suppose that two tasks become interlocked as illustrated in Figure 5-4. What effects would be observed by the users whose transactions are being processed by the two tasks? Would there be effects noticeable to other online users?

EXERCISE

This chapter's exercise is presented in three parts. You should first write a program that does Part 1 of the exercise. When the program has been completed and debugged, modify it successively to add the functions required by Parts 2 and 3.

The program will read and update a file which we will refer to as FILEA. The records in FILEA are of variable length, but the maximum record length is 80 bytes. All the fields in the record are in character format; there are no numeric fields.

The record layout is shown in Figure 5-9. The key is contained in the NUMB field of each record. The *field names* shown will be used in this description of

NUMBER OF BYTES	FIELD NAME
1	STAT
6	NUMB
20	NAME
20	ADDRX
8	PHONE
8	DATE
8	AMOUNT
9	COMMENT

Figure 5-9
Format of File for
Programming Exercise

the exercise; you may want to use the same names within your program to simplify comparison with the description.

☐ Part 1: Read, Display, and Update a Record

The program begins by reading a user request from the terminal. The request will be in the format:

xxxx func key

where:

xxxx is the transaction code

func is a four-character field that indicates which function is to be performed. For Part 1, func may be equal to DISP or UPDT.

key is a six-character string which gives the key of a record to be selected.

If the requested function is DISP, the program should read the record specified by "key" and display the number, name, and phone number on the terminal. After displaying the data, the task should terminate.

If the requested function is UPDT, the program should read and display the specified record as described above for DISP. The user will *change* the displayed phone number by typing over it and pressing the ENTER key. The program should update the record with the new phone number, and write the modified record into the file.

If func is not equal to either DISP or UPDT, send an error message to the user and terminate the task. Define exception-handling routines for the LENGERR, NOTFND, and NOTOPEN conditions; allow CICS to take default action for any other exceptional conditions that may occur. Your exception-handling routines should send a descriptive message to the terminal and terminate the task.

☐ Part 2: Delete a Record or Group of Records

Modify the program to accept the additional func values: DELR and GDEL.

If the user enters DELR, delete the specified record and terminate the task with the message RECORD DELETED.

If the user enters GDEL, delete all the records whose keys have the same first four characters as the "key" entered by the user. Send a message that reports how many records were deleted. Then terminate the task.

☐ *Part 3: Add a Record or Group of Records*

Modify the program to accept the additional func values: ADDR and MINS.

If the user enters ADDR, add a single record with a key value of "key". The record to be written should have the name field set to NEW RECORD. Place the key value in the NUMBER field, and set all other fields to blanks. When the record has been written, send the user the message RECORD ADDED TO DATASET and terminate the task.

If the user enters MINS, perform a mass insert of ten records to the file. The first record added should have the key value specified in the user's "key" field. Set the record's NAME field to MASS INSERT RECORD, place the key for each record in the NUMBER field, and set all other fields to blanks. When the records have been added, send the message END OF MASS INSERT and terminate the task.

For Part 3, define an exception-handling routine for the DUPREC condition. If DUPREC is raised, write the message RECORD ALREADY IN DATASET and terminate the task.

6 Sequential Access of Random Files

Introduction

In Chapter 5 we discussed how files can be accessed in a random manner, either by using keys or by specifying the location of a record within the random access file. Although random access is critical to DB/DC applications, it is also important at times to *sequentially access* a random access file. That is, you need to view the file logically *as though* it were a sequential file.

For example, suppose your company maintains a file of customer accounts. The record for each customer contains name, address, phone number, credit information, and a list of outstanding orders. Each customer has an account number, and the account number is used as the key for each record.

Often a customer will call to inquire about an order, but will not know his or her account number. If the customer's name is Johnson, you need to read through all the records for customers named Johnson until you find one with the same address or phone number as the customer on the phone. That is you want to *read sequentially* ("browse") through all the Johnsons until you find the right one.

This chapter is composed of two principal sections. In the first section, we will see how you can read a random file sequentially.

The section begins by discussing a typical application which requires this sequential access or "browse" capability. The CICS commands that are used to browse a file are then discussed.

In the second section, we will take a brief look at how files and data bases are constructed. We begin by describing the *physical* structure of example keyed access and direct access files. Next, we contrast the file's *physical structure* with the *logical view* of the file. We show that the form of an application program depends upon the logical view of the database, but that the performance of the program is affected by the physical structure of files.

Objectives

After completing this lesson, you will be able to:

- Write a program that sequentially accesses ("browses") a random file.
- Write a program that updates a file during a browse operation.
- Discuss how to limit the system resources required while a file is being browsed.
- Distinguish between a *keyed* file and a *direct access* (Relative Record Number or RRN) file.
- Describe the physical structure of a VSAM Key Sequenced Data Set (KSDS).
- Describe the structure of a VSAM alternate index.
- Discuss how multiple occurrences of data can be handled when files are integrated.
- Describe how the CICS Indirect Access Chain facility is used.

Applications

Chapter 5 discussed order-entry systems as an example of applications that require non-sequential access to the data base. In this chapter, we will discuss a DB/DC application with quite different requirements. The library card catalog is typical of a class of applications that involve "browsing"; that is, searching sequentially through records in a particular subsection of a file. Other applications of this kind include "automated yellow pages" and merchandisers' catalogs.

Assume that you wanted to see what books about computer programming were available in the local library. You would go to the "card catalog" organized by subject and look through the card file for the first "Computer Programming" entry. Of course, the "card catalog" may not be kept on cards at all; it might be on microfiche or it might be in a file on a computer. So finding the first "Computer Programming" entry might require you to look through the card drawer or microfiche for a card marked CO, or it might require that you use a computer terminal to enter a command to FIND "COMPUTER PROGRAMMING". In any case, your objective is to *establish the beginning position* in the file.

Next you would scan through the file entries that follow the beginning position. If the file is on cards, you will thumb through the individual cards, making notes of the entries that interest you. If the file is on the computer, you will use some sort of DISPLAY or SCROLL command to list the entries in sequence. In either case, you are *sequentially retrieving records* from the file, starting from the beginning position you established previously.

If you reached an entry headed COMPUTER PROHIBITION you would realize that you had examined all the COMPUTER PROGRAMMING entries, so you would *terminate the browse*. Of course, you would also terminate the browse if you reached the end of the file. This would be more likely to happen if your interest were in a topic near the end of the alphabet—"Zymology," for example—instead of in "computer programming."

In summary, the typical flow of a browse operation consists of the three activities shown in Figure 6-1. Namely:

1. Establishing position
2. Retrieving records in sequence
3. Terminating the browse

Browsing a CICS File

A program to browse a CICS file follows exactly the flow shown in Figure 6-1:

1. The CICS command STARTBR is used to *establish position*.
2. Records are *sequentially retrieved* in either "front to back" or "back to front" sequence. The CICS commands used are, respectively, READNEXT and READPREV.
3. The browse is *terminated* by the CICS ENDBR command.

Establishing Position

The STARTBR command with its possible options and parameters looks like:

```
EXEC CICS STARTBR DATASET (name)
    RIDFLD (data-area)
    [KEYLENGTH (data-value)]
    [GENERIC]    [RRN]
    [EQUAL]  ǀ  [GTEQ]
```

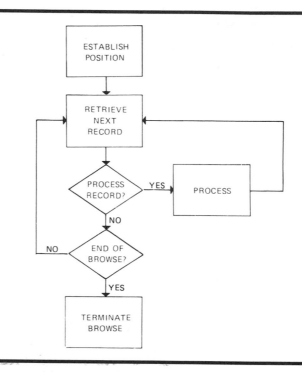

Figure 6-1
Flow of a Browse
(Sequential Access)
Operation

Notice that most of the options are the same as those of the READ command discussed in the previous chapter. However, there is neither an INTO nor a SET option for the STARTBR command. This is because the STARTBR command *does not retrieve* any data; its functions are solely to *initiate the browse* and to *establish the starting position* for the browse.

The DATASET and RIDFLD parameters are required. The RIDFLD, KEYLENGTH, GENERIC, and RRN parameters describe the record with which sequential retrieval is to begin.

Two parameters which have not been discussed previously are EQUAL and GTEQ. For a key sequenced VSAM file they can be used to indicate the type of search to be performed. GTEQ is the default. It specifies that if no record with an exactly matching key can be found, the browse will begin at the record whose key would follow the specified key in the file. By contrast, if EQUAL were specified and no record with matching key were found, the NOTFND condition would be raised.

The other options of STARTBR are as described in the previous chapter for the READ command.

An application program may need to begin a browse at the first record of a key sequenced file, no matter what the record's key is. You can program this in two ways. Either specify a RIDFLD parameter which contains all hexadecimal zeros, or use the GENERIC option with a KEYLENGTH value of 0. In the latter case, the RIDFLD parameter may contain any value; CICS will ignore it. But don't use the EQUAL option with either approach; it would cause the NOTFND condition to be raised.

You may also begin a browse at the *end* of the file and then retrieve records in "back to front" order. To do so, you would use the STARTBR command with a RIDFLD parameter containing hexadecimal FF in every byte. In this case, you should not use the GENERIC, KEYLENGTH, or EQUAL options.

Retrieving Records

Once the browse has been initiated by STARTBR, retrieval of data from the file can begin. This section describes how to retrieve records in either forwards or backwards order.

Forward Retrieval

You use the READNEXT command, written as follows, to retrieve records sequentially in *ascending* sequence.

```
EXEC CICS READNEXT
    INTO(data-area)  I  SET (pointer-ref)
    DATASET(name)
    RIDFLD(data-area)
    [LENGTH(data-area)]
    [KEYLENGTH(data-value)]
    [RRN]
```

Notice that, as for the READ command discussed in Chapter 5, you may use either the INTO or the SET option. INTO specifies that you want the record returned to a work area defined within your program. SET indicates that you want to process the record in the CICS file control buffer; CICS places the address of the buffer into the location specified by the SET parameter argument. You describe the buffer in your program's LINKAGE SECTION as described in Chapter 4, "Accessing the TIOA."

The DATASET and RIDFLD parameters are required. The RIDFLD parameter must be the same as you specified on the STARTBR command that initiated the browse. Otherwise the INVREQ condition will be raised.

LENGTH is required only if you are using the INTO option. In this case you must also set the LENGTH parameter to a value that is not greater than the length of the INTO area. If you are using SET, LENGTH is not required; but you will normally use it so as to obtain the length of the logical record in the buffer. Notice that, because CICS places the record length into the LENGTH parameter, the parameter must not be a constant.

As each record is retrieved, CICS updates the RIDFLD parameter with the *complete* record key. Therefore, the RIDFLD parameter must not be a constant, and it must be large enough to hold a complete key.

Backwards Retrieval

You can browse VSAM files either backwards or forwards. You use the READPREV command for backwards retrieval. It is written:

```
EXEC CICS READPREV
    INTO(data-area)  I  SET (pointer-ref)
    DATASET(name)
    RIDFLD(data-area)
    [LENGTH(data-area)]
    [KEYLENGTH(data-value)
    [RRN]
```

As shown, the options are the same as for the READNEXT command. However, there are some differences between the forward and backward browse.

First, a generic key cannot be used for backward browse operations. If you do issue a READPREV command after a STARTBR with the GENERIC option, CICS will raise the INVREQ condition.

Secondly, the record identified by RIDFLD *must exist* in the file; otherwise, the NOTFND condition is raised. Assuming that you have not changed the value placed in the RIDFLD argument by the STARTBR command, NOTFND can be raised on the first READPREV only if the STARTBR command used the GTEQ option (either explicitly or by default) and the browse position was established at a record whose key is *greater than* the key specified by RIDFLD.

If you specified the equal option with STARTBR, the RIDFLD argument should still contain the same key value. If STARTBR specified GTEQ and a RIDFLD argument of all hexadecimal FF bytes, STARTBR placed the key from the file's last record into the RIDFLD argument. In both these cases, you can be sure the RIDFLD argument contains a legitimate key value unless you have changed the value before issuing the first READPREV.

Remember that backward browse is supported only for VSAM files.

Changing the Direction of a Browse

Suppose that you have initiated a browse and have issued a number of READNEXT commands to browse forward. Now you want to go back and look again at a record you've already retrieved. You can issue a READPREV following a READNEXT command. However, your first READPREV will retrieve the *same record* that was retrieved by the last READNEXT. That is, to change direction and back up a record, you must issue two READPREV commands.

Terminating the Browse

When we talked about the card catalog example we pointed out that the browse would end when you came either to the last record in the file or to an entry for a subject other than "Computer Programming." The first situation, in which the end of the file has been reached, is called the *physical end of file*. In the second situation, the application program must determine, by some appropriate test, that there is no need to retrieve more records. In this situation, the *logical end of file* is said to have occurred.

CICS signals physical end of file by raising the ENDFILE condition. If a forward browse is in progress, ENDFILE will be raised when a READNEXT command is executed *after* the READNEXT command that retrieved the file's last record. In the case of a backward file, ENDFILE is raised by the READPREV command executed after the file's *first* record has been retrieved.

When either physical or logical end of file has occurred, you must terminate the browse operation. The CICS command for this is:

EXEC CICS ENDBR DATASET(data value)

As we'll discuss later in this chapter, a browse operation requires that some system *resources* be allocated to the task that controls the browse. The task will hold these resources until the browse is terminated. It is important for overall system performance that system resources be held for as brief a period as possible. Therefore, your program should issue the ENDBR command as promptly as possible after detecting end of file.

Figure 6-2 illustrates how you could write a COBOL program to browse a keyed access file.

Notice that the STARTBR command specifies a 3 character partial key of LAX, and that the EQUAL option is also specified. Therefore, if the file contains no record whose key begins with LAX, the STARTBR command will cause the NOTFND condition to be raised.

The records that are retrieved in the READ-SEQ paragraph are moved into FILE-AREA. Notice that the LENGTH parameter, LEN, is set to the length of FILE-AREA *before each execution* of the READNEXT command.

The ENDFILE handling routine, END-BROWS, is entered for physical end of file (when the ENDFILE condition is raised) or for logical end of file (when the GO TO END-BROWS statement is executed).

Reestablishing Position

Suppose that you have been browsing some particular area of the file and need to move to an entirely different area. For example, the customer on the phone suddenly reveals that Johnson is his *first name*—his last name is Price. You could terminate the Johnson browse and issue a STARTBR for Price. However, you could also simply *reestablish position* by issuing a RESETBR command.

RESETBR has the following form:

```
EXEC CICS RESETBR
    DATASET(data-value)
    RIDFLD(data-area)
    KEYLENGTH(data-value)
    [GENERIC]
    [GTEQ Ι EQUAL]
    [RRN]
```

DATASET specifies the same name as that of the original STARTBR command.

RIDFLD specifies the location at which the browse should resume. The RIDFLD argument must be the *same data area* that you specified in the original STARTBR command. Before issuing the RESETBR command, you must place the new record identifier (key or Relative Record Number) into the RIDFLD argument.

You may also use the RESETBR command to change the characteristics of the browse. If the STARTBR specified a partial key, using the GENERIC and KEYLENGTH options, you may specify a full key in the RESETBR. Conversely, if the STARTBR specified a full key, you may use the GENERIC and KEYLENGTH options with the RESETBR command. If the file is a VSAM file, you may use the RESETBR to change the type of search; that is, to switch between GTEQ and EQUAL.

Skip-Sequential Processing

With VSAM files, a technique called skip-sequential processing may be used to move forward in a file, skipping over some number of records. To do so, set the RIDFLD parameter of the READNEXT command to the identification of the next record to be retrieved. The READNEXT command will retrieve the record identified by RIDFLD.

```
       IDENTIFICATION DIVISION.                                       00010000
       PROGRAM-ID. FCPCOB12.                                          00020003
      *                                                               00030005
      * INITIATE BROWSE FOR VSAM KEYED FILE USING GENERIC KEY, EQUAL. 00040007
      * THE BROWSE BEGINS AT GENERIC KEY 'LAX..'                      00050007
      * RETRIEVE RECORDS SEQUENTIALLY IN ASCENDING SEQUENCE.          00060007
      * CHECK FOR PHYSICAL END OF FILE AND LOGICAL END OF FILE        00070007
      * (CHANGE IN THE GENERIC KEY).                                  00080007
      *                                                               00090005
      *                                                               00100006
      *** PROGRAM IS INCOMPLETE AND WILL NOT EXECUTE ***              00110006
      *                                                               00120006
       ENVIRONMENT DIVISION.                                          00130000
       DATA DIVISION.                                                 00140000
       WORKING-STORAGE SECTION.                                       00150000
       77   LEN             PIC S9(4) COMP.                           00160002
       77   COMPARE-KEY     PIC X(3) VALUE 'LAX'.                     00170002
       01   RECORD-KEY.                                               00180000
            02   KEY-PFX    PIC X(3) VALUE 'LAX'.                     00190000
            02   KEY-NUM    PIC X(2).                                 00200000
       01   FILE-AREA.                                                00210002
            02   REC-KEY  PIC X(5).                                   00220002
            02   REC-DESC PIC X(20).                                  00230002
                          .                                           00240000
                          .                                           00250000
                          .                                           00260000
       PROCEDURE DIVISION.                                            00270000
      *   ERROR CHECKING *                                            00280000
            EXEC CICS HANDLE CONDITION                                00290000
                      NOTFND(NOREC) ERROR(OTHERR)                     00300000
                      LENGERR(RTOOLONG)                               00310002
                      ENDFILE(END-BROWS)                              00320002
                      END-EXEC.                                       00330004
      *                                                               00340004
            EXEC CICS STARTBR                                         00350000
                      DATASET('MASTER') RIDFLD(RECORD-KEY)            00360000
                      GENERIC  KEYLENGTH(3)  EQUAL                    00370004
                      END-EXEC.                                       00380004
       READ-SEQ.                                                      00390002
            MOVE 25 TO LEN.                                           00400002
            EXEC CICS READNEXT                                        00410002
                      DATASET('MASTER') RIDFLD(RECORD-KEY)            00420002
                      INTO(FILE-AREA) LENGTH(LEN)                     00430002
                      END-EXEC.                                       00440004
            IF KEY-PFX IS GREATER THAN COMPARE-KEY                    00450002
               GO TO END-BROWS                                        00460002
            ELSE                                                      00470002
               NEXT SENTENCE.                                         00480002
            *** PROCESS RECORD ***                                    00490001
                       .                                              00500000
                       .                                              00510000
                       .                                              00520000
            *** LOOP BACK TO RETRIEVE NEXT RECORD ***                 00530002
       END-BROWS.                                                     00540002
            *** TERMINATE THE BROWSE ***                              00550002
                       .                                              00560002
                       .                                              00570002
                       .                                              00580002
       NOREC.                                                         00590000
          *   ERROR PROCESSING - NO RECORDS EXIST ON THE FILE TO MATCH * 00600000
          *   THE SPECIFIED GENERIC KEY ('LAX')                   *   00610000
                       .                                              00620000
                       .                                              00630000
                       .                                              00640000
       OTHERR.                                                        00650000
          *   ERROR PROCESSING - OTHER ERROR HAS OCCURRED *           00660000
                       .                                              00670000
                       .                                              00680000
                       .                                              00690000
       RTOOLONG.                                                      00700002
          *   ERROR PROCESSING - THE RECORD RETRIEVED IS LONGER THAN * 00710002
          *   THE LENGTH SPECIFIED (LEN)                         *    00720002
                       .                                              00730001
                       .                                              00740001
                       .                                              00750001
```

**Figure 6-2
Browse Operation,
Program Example**

Remember that:

■ Skip-sequential processing can be used only to move forward in a file; that is, READNEXT must be the retrieval command.

■ The type of record identification used (full or generic key, RRN or key) must be the same as specified in the preceding STARTBR or RESETBR. If a generic key is used, KEYLENGTH must be coded.

■ If the previous STARTBR or RESETBR specified an EQUAL search and the file does not contain the record specified by RIDFLD, the NOTFND condition will be raised. If you want to continue the browse, you could program the NOTFND exception–handling routine to issue a RESETBR with the same RIDFLD parameter, but using the GTEQ option. This would position the browse to resume at the record whose key is next greater than the key which caused the NOTFND condition to be raised.

Multiple Browse Operations

You may perform several concurrent browse operations, using the same file or multiple files. Each browse must be initiated by a separate STARTBR command. An additional option, REQID, must be used if more than one browse operation is performed for the same file. REQID is coded in every command of each browse operation that refers to the same file. The following is an example of a STARTBR command that initiates one of a set of multiple browse operations against a file called MASTER.

EXEC CICS STARTBR DATASET('MASTER')
RIDFLD(data-area) REQID(3)

The REQID value specifies a two–byte binary value to be used as an identifying number; each command for the same browse operation must include a REQID option that specifies the same identifying number. If a STARTBR is executed and specifies a REQID value in use for a browse currently in progress, the INVREQ condition will be raised.

If the multiple operations are not against the same file, the REQID option is not necessary.

Application of Multiple Browse

You will probably not often be called upon to program a multiple browse. However, the multiple browse is useful when information from the file must be reported in a sequence different from the sequence in which records appear in the file.

Suppose your company is a manufacturing firm, and maintains a file of suppliers for each part used in manufacture. Assume that this supplier file is organized as shown in Figure 6-3, sequenced by part number *within* supplier (i.e., vendor).

Assume that the key for this file is the combination of vendor and part number. Neither part number nor vendor name alone could serve as key because keys must be unique; and there may be many records for the same vendor as well as for the same part number. But the combination of vendor and part number is a unique key, because a particular vendor-part number pair can appear only once in the file. Later in this chapter, we will discuss a different method of defining the key.

VENDOR	PART NUMBER	PRICE	DELIVERY TIME
A	C-0A-001	.53	2
B	C-0A-001	.57	4
B	F-0A-013	.013	2
B	H-1B-027	1.27	3
B	H-3C-015	15.08	4
C	C-0A-001	.62	2
C	H-1B-027	1.43	1
D	H-3C-015	12.43	2
H	F-0A-013	.018	1
H	H-1B-027	1.11	2

Figure 6-3
Supplier File,
Example Contents

If you need a list of all the parts provided by each vendor, you could use a straightforward browse operation. The list will show part numbers within vendor name—the same order as records appear in the file. Your STARTBR command would use the GENERIC and KEYLENGTH parameters to specify a partial key of VENDOR. A series of READNEXT commands retrieves file records sequentially; ENDBR is executed when a new vendor name appears in the RIDFLD parameter.

But suppose you need a list of the part numbers, showing the vendors who supply each part. You need to turn the file "inside out" so that supplier appears within part number. This is less straightforward, but you can do it by using the multiple browse technique as summarized in Figure 6-4.

The program contains two loops, labeled A and B in the figure.

Loop A initiates a browse for each supplier, using supplier name as the key, and retrieves the first record for each supplier by using the READNEXT command. The loop is complete when the first record for each supplier has been read.

Loop B compares the part numbers read for each supplier. The smallest part number and the name of each vendor who supplies it are reported. As each vendor name is reported, a READNEXT command is executed for the corresponding browse operation. This obtains the next part number supplied by the same vendor. The program loops through the part number comparison until all the browse operations have reached an end of file. At that point all the vendors have been listed for each part number.

Updating During a Browse

You cannot use the REWRITE command to replace a record you obtained by a READNEXT or READPREV command. This is because a browse doesn't obtain exclusive control. If you attempt to issue a REWRITE command without exclusive control, CICS will raise the INVREQ condition.

However, if you find that you must update a record that you obtained during a browse, you can do so by rereading the record, using a READ for UPDATE command, and then executing the REWRITE command. The process is shown in Figure 6-5.

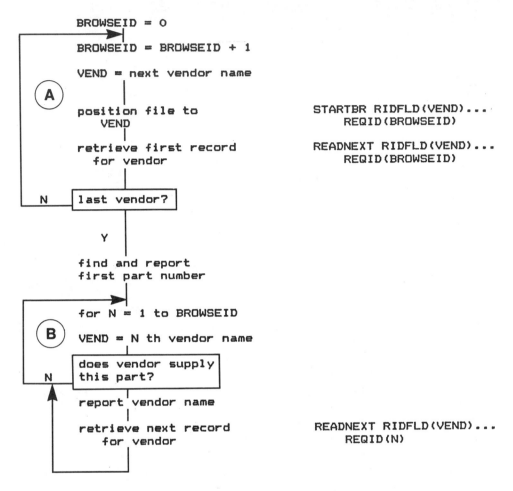

```
         BROWSEID = 0

         BROWSEID = BROWSEID + 1

         VEND = next vendor name

  (A)
         position file to              STARTBR RIDFLD(VEND)...
              VEND                         REQID(BROWSEID)

         retrieve first record         READNEXT RIDFLD(VEND)...
              for vendor                   REQID(BROWSEID)


  N    | last vendor? |


                Y

         find and report
         first part number


         for N = 1 to BROWSEID

  (B)
         VEND = N th vendor name

         | does vendor supply |
  N      | this part?         |

         report vendor name

         retrieve next record          READNEXT RIDFLD(VEND)...
              for vendor                   REQID(N)
```

Figure 6-4
Multiple Browse,
Program Example

The command at Point 1 has read a record during the browse operation.
When it is determined that the record is to be updated, the command at Point
2 is executed to read the record for update. Note that the RIDFLD parameter
is the same as specified in the READNEXT command.

The READ for UPDATE obtains exclusive control so that the command at
3 can be executed to rewrite the record. The REWRITE command releases the
exclusive control.

Resource Usage

In Chapter 5, we discussed how a task could affect overall system performance
by holding exclusive control longer than necessary. This is because many tasks
may require exclusive control of a group of logical records, but the system
grants the exclusive control to only one task at a time. We define *resource* as
an entity, like exclusive control of a record, that is controlled by the system,
and for which tasks must *contend* in order to complete their processing.

```
       IDENTIFICATION DIVISION.                                          00010000
       PROGRAM-ID. FCPCOB16.                                             00020000
*                                                                        00030001
*   BROWSE A FILE AND UPDATE RECORDS AS APPROPRIATE.               *     00040000
*   THE BROWSE BEGINS WITH RECORD 'LAX01'.                               00050000
*                                                                        00060001
*                                                                        00070002
*** PROGRAM IS INCOMPLETE AND WILL NOT EXECUTE ***                       00080002
*                                                                        00090002
       ENVIRONMENT DIVISION.                                             00100000
       DATA DIVISION.                                                    00110000
       WORKING-STORAGE SECTION.                                          00120000
       77  LEN            PIC S9(4) COMP.                                00130000
       77  RECORD-KEY     PIC X(5) VALUE 'LAX01'.                        00140000
       01  FILE-AREA.                                                    00150000
           02  REC-KEY    PIC X(5).                                      00160000
           02  REC-DESC.                                                 00170000
                 .                                                       00180000
                 .                                                       00190000
                 .                                                       00200000
       PROCEDURE DIVISION.                                               00210000
*   ERROR CHECKING *                                                     00220000
           EXEC CICS HANDLE CONDITION                                    00230000
                   LENGERR(RTOOLONG) ENDFILE(END-BROWS)                  00240003
                   ERROR(OTHERR) END-EXEC.                               00250003
           EXEC CICS STARTBR                                             00260000
                   DATASET('MASTER')  RIDFLD(RECORD-KEY)                 00270000
                   END-EXEC.                                             00280000
           MOVE 25 TO LEN.                                               00290000
   (1) EXEC CICS READNEXT                                                00300000
                   DATASET('MASTER')  RIDFLD(RECORD-KEY)                 00310000
                   INTO(FILE-AREA)  LENGTH(LEN)                          00320000
                   END-EXEC.                                             00330000
       *** PROCESS RECORD ***                                           00340000
                 .                                                       00350000
                 .                                                       00360000
                 .                                                       00370000
       *** IF THE RECORD SHOULD BE UPDATED: ***                         00380000
   (2) EXEC CICS READ                                                    00390000
                   DATASET('MASTER')  RIDFLD(RECORD-KEY)                 00400000
                   INTO(FILE-AREA)  LENGTH(LEN)                          00410000
                   UPDATE                                                00420000
                   END-EXEC.                                             00430000
                 .                                                       00440000
                 .                                                       00450000
                 .                                                       00460000
   (3) EXEC CICS REWRITE                                                 00470000
                   DATASET('MASTER')                                     00480000
                   FROM(FILE-AREA)  LENGTH(LEN)                          00490000
                   END-EXEC.                                             00500000
                 .                                                       00510000
                 .                                                       00520000
                 .                                                       00530000
       END-BROWS.                                                        00540000
*   TERMINATE THE BROWSE *                                               00550000
                 .                                                       00560000
                 .                                                       00570000
                 .                                                       00580000
       RTOOLONG.                                                         00590000
*   ERROR PROCESSING - THE RECORD IS LONGER THAN THE *                   00600000
*   SPECIFIED LENGTH (LEN)                           *                   00610000
                 .                                                       00620000
                 .                                                       00630000
                 .                                                       00640000
       OTHERR.                                                          00650000
*   ERROR PROCESSING - OTHER ERROR HAS OCCURRED      *                   00660000
                 .                                                       00670000
                 .                                                       00680000
                 .                                                       00690000
```

**Figure 6-5
Updating a File
During a Browse
Operation**

Examples of System Resources

Space within the CICS region is also a resource. Unlike exclusive control of a record, *region space* is not a single entity that is given entirely to one task at a time. However, tasks must contend for space in the CICS region because only a finite amount is available. At any time, the total requirement for space may exceed the amount of the resource that is available.

We have said that CICS uses buffers to hold data read from, or to be written to, files and terminals. In the case of terminal input/output, the buffer was called a TIOA. For file input/output, the buffers are called simply *file control buffers*. All the buffers are acquired and freed by the CICS Storage Control module. Recall that Storage Control also must provide space for programs to be loaded, for working–storage, and for other CICS control blocks and tables. All these requirements place demands upon the "CICS region space" resource.

An important resource is the CPU itself. CICS Task Control manages this resource, scheduling the CPU among all the active CICS tasks.

Another resource, the *VSAM string* is involved when VSAM files are used. VSAM limits the number of concurrent requests that can be in process for a given file at any one time. The limit for each file is called the *VSAM string number*, and its value is defined for each file by the system programmer. The value is defined in the FCT. If a task requests access to a VSAM file, and the file's string number has not yet been reached, the task is granted access to the file. It is said to "hold a VSAM string."

Whenever a task requires a resource that is not available, the task is placed in the wait state until the resource becomes available. Resources are valuable because their availability determines how quickly a user's transaction can be completed.

For a large number of users to be supported successfully, DB/DC application programs must be designed to use resources efficiently. This means that you must:

1. Know what resources the program requires.
2. Know when the program is holding a resource.
3. Insure that, when a program holds a resource, it *uses and frees* the resource as quickly as possible.

Let's look at these three requirements in connection with a typical browse operation.

Resources Used by Browse

Because browsing is a read-only process, it does not require exclusive control for the file. However, if a VSAM file is being used, a VSAM string is required for each concurrent browse against the file.

The program that controls a browse must remain in the CICS region throughout the entire browse. Browsing usually requires many input/output operations before the browse is complete. Therefore, the storage required for the program is held for a relatively long period of time. Compare, for instance, the amount of input/output activity required for browsing a file to that required for the order-entry transactions discussed in Chapter 5. The order-entry program went directly to a single record of the file, updated the record, and terminated. The browse operation begins at an approximate location in the file, and proceeds to read an undetermined number of records before terminating. From this, you can see that the browse transaction may require considerably more time to complete, so it places a larger demand on the storage resource than does the order-entry transaction. (The difference may not always be so great as suggested by this simple comparison. The order-entry transaction may have to wait to receive exclusive control, thus extending the elapsed time requirement. Since the browsing transaction is read-only, it does not require exclusive control.)

File control buffers are also required for the duration of the browse—a buffer for each file being browsed. If the program uses INTO rather than SET, additional space is required, because the program's working-space must include space for the maximum length logical record.

Limiting the Scope of a Browse

We have already discussed the importance of freeing resources promptly, but we have pointed out that a number of resources will be held for as long as the browse operation continues. Therefore, you need to limit the time required by the browse.

The time requirement is largely determined by the number of input/output operations that must be performed. As we shall see later in this chapter, the design of a data file can affect the number of input/output operations required for a given transaction against the file. However, the application programmer can significantly decrease the input/output requirement by defining transactions so as to *limit the scope* of a browse.

Refer again to the file illustrated in Figure 6-3. Assume that the part numbers are encoded such that the first character indicates a part category, like CONNECTOR or HOSE. If the user were able to request information for only some categories of parts, the browse could be limited to a subset of the file. That is, a *limited file search* could be performed rather than a full file search.

The scope could be limited further if the user could request a more *specific* search. For example, the user might be interested only in receiving a list of vendors who could supply a requested part within less than two weeks. In this case, the browse itself would not be reduced, but the transaction's elapsed time requirement would be reduced because fewer records would need to be formatted and sent to the user.

File Structure

We have discussed CICS commands that read and rewrite records according to a key or record number. We have also discussed commands that add records to, or delete them from, a file. But we haven't discussed how the physical file is structured to permit this type of access. How does the system go about locating a record, given its key? How is a record with a given key physically inserted into the correct position of a file?

You will not be responsible for defining the structure of a file, and your application programs will be quite independent of the file's structure. But you will hear many terms, like *alternate index* and *base cluster* that have to do with physical file structure. This section is intended to give you an overview of concepts and terminology you will be most likely to encounter. We will discuss two general file types: the keyed access file and the direct access file.

Keyed Access Structure

The following discussion is based upon the VSAM Key Sequenced Data

Set (KSDS), although the general concepts apply to other types of keyed access files as well.

In a KSDS, records are stored in *logical order* by their keys. The key is part of each record and appears in the same position in every record. Figure 6-6 illustrates a record whose key is a six-character field beginning in the record's fifth byte.

A KSDS has an index which is used to find a record's *physical* location in the file. The index is a separate file which is ordered physically according to the key of the KSDS. Because the index is a separate file, it is possible to manipulate the data file without the index file. However, for purpose of CICS access, a data file has meaning only when coupled to an index file. (The VSAM term for this couple is *cluster*.)

VSAM divides the data file into groups of physical records; such a group is called a *control interval*. For each control interval, the index file contains the location of its first physical record and the value of the highest key contained in the interval. Therefore, a reference to a data set key causes two operations.

First, VSAM accesses the index file to obtain the entry for the key. This entry gives the location, within the data file, of the control interval that contains the record with the specified key. Next the control interval is transferred from the file into memory, and the logical record with the specified key is made available to the program.

VSAM always transfers an entire control interval, possibly containing many physical records, between memory and external storage. Therefore, the control interval size determines the minimum size of the file control buffer to be provided in the CICS region. The control interval size is also the span of exclusive control for a VSAM data set. Usually either the system programmer or database administrator defines a file's control interval size.

Why is the index file necessary? As logical records are added to and removed from the data file, the physical ordering of the file cannot easily be maintained. Figure 6-7 illustrates how adding new records in their correct *physical* location

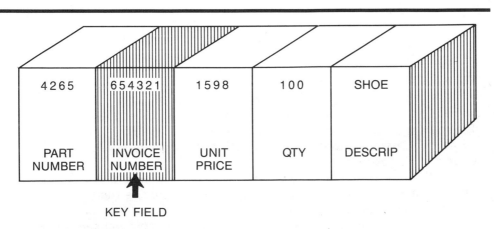

KEY FIELD

KEY MUST BE:

UNIQUE
IN SAME POSITION OF EACH RECORD

**Figure 6-6
Key Field in KSDS
(Key Sequenced
Data Set)**

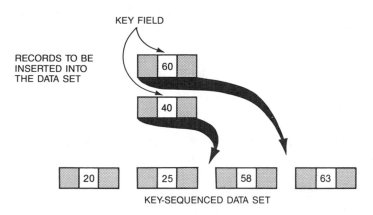

KEY FIELD

RECORDS TO BE
INSERTED INTO
THE DATA SET

60

40

20   25   58   63

KEY-SEQUENCED DATA SET

RECORDS ARE STORED IN KEY SEQUENCE

NEW RECORDS ARE INSERTED IN THEIR COLLATING SEQUENCE

Figure 6-7
Inserting Records
into KSDS

in the file would cause the entire file to be rewritten in order to "spread records apart" to make space for the new record. This is clearly impractical. To prevent this, only the records within a control interval are kept in physical order; the ordering among control intervals is indicated by the index file. In this way, an insertion requires that no more than two control intervals need ever be rewritten.

Direct Access Files

VSAM supports two types of direct access files. In this text, we will discuss only the VSAM Relative Record Number (RRN) file type. Files accessed by record number do not require an index. The system can calculate the location of the required record from its record number. To allow this, all records in a VSAM RRN file must be the same length.

When a direct access file is originally created, "empty" records are scattered throughout to provide slots for inserting new records. When a record is deleted, it is simply marked "empty", a new record may later be inserted in the empty slot.

A VSAM RRN file is divided into control intervals as described above for the VSAM KSDS.

Advantages of each Organization

As the foregoing discussion suggests:

■ A given record can be located more quickly in a direct access file than in a keyed access file because the extra overhead of accessing the index file is eliminated.
■ Applications that require a great deal of new record insertion and record deletion are better suited to keyed access files than direct access files. This is because the management of free space is more flexible in the keyed access file.
■ If variable length records are required, VSAM direct access files cannot be used.

Alternate Indexes

In Chapter 5, we said that a key must be unique. However, in this chapter we have seen two examples of situations in which a file has apparently been accessed by a key that is not unique. The first example was the card catalog. In a library card catalog neither the title, author, nor subject are unique keys. Nevertheless, these are the three record fields by which the catalog is normally accessed. The second example was the manufacturing parts list illustrated in Figure 6-3. The "natural" way to access this file is to use either supplier name or part number as the key. But in order to define a unique key, we used the *combination* of supplier name and part number. The program examples then used the GENERIC option to, in effect, access the file by supplier name.

For VSAM files, there is another "way around" the unique key requirement; it is a feature called *alternate index*. Recall that a VSAM KSDS is actually a cluster of two files; the data file and an index file. For each data file there must be one index file that is physically ordered according to a unique key that defines a logical ordering of the data file according to the same key. We call this index file the *prime index*. For the example of Figure 6-3, the prime index would map the unique supplier-part number key to a location within the data file. For the library card catalog, the prime index might be based upon the book's "shelf code," or perhaps the title-author combination. We refer to the cluster of data file and prime index as the *base data set*.

The existence of an index file is "transparent" to the CICS application program. The programs use the DATASET option to refer to a file name which is defined in the FCT. CICS commands do not indicate in any way that the DATASET is actually a cluster. That information appears only in the FCT.

The VSAM access method permits *alternate index* files to be constructed in addition to the prime index for a file. An alternate index is organized by a different key than is the prime index. And the key for an alternate index need not be unique. Therefore, for the file illustrated by Figure 6-3, two alternate index files might be built; one organized by supplier name, the other by part number. The data file would then be part of three clusters—the base data set, and a cluster for each alternate index file. Each cluster is represented in the FCT by a different name; an application program may use any of the three names as a DATASET parameter.

Assume that for the file represented by Figure 6-3, the cluster with alternate index by supplier name is called VENDFILE. A task executes the following STARTBR command:

EXEC CICS STARTBR DATASET('VENDFILE') RIDFLD(VENDOR)

Here VENDOR is equal to B.

The file will be positioned at the first appearance of Vendor B. When the first READNEXT command is executed, the record will be retrieved, but an exceptional condition, DUPKEY, will be raised. DUPKEY is raised by the READ, READNEXT, or READPREV command when a duplicate key is detected in the file. In the Figure 6-3 example, if a series of READNEXT commands were executed following the STARTBR, the DUPKEY condition would be raised *three* times—for every supplier B record *except* the last one.

Whenever an alternate index is being used, the program must provide an exception routine for the DUPKEY condition. Otherwise, when DUPKEY is raised, CICS will terminate the task. Besides the DUPKEY requirement, there is one other programming consideration related to alternate indexes. If a file is to be updated, it should always be updated by reference to the *base data set*.

Alternate Index Structure

In order to understand how the VSAM alternate index feature works, you need to know that an alternate index does not index the data file; it indexes the prime index.

Figure 6-8 shows an alternate index for a student name file. Within the data file, each student has a unique student number. This number is the *prime index* key value. The prime index, therefore, maps student number to data file location. The *alternate index* is organized by student name. For each student name, there is a pointer to the matching student numbers in the prime index.

Notice that because "name" is not unique, the alternate index contains multiple entries for names like Johnson and Lopez that appear more than once in the data file.

Consider what happens when a READ command is executed using an alternate index. VSAM finds the key entry in the alternate index file. This entry contains a pointer to the prime index file. VSAM then accesses the indicated entry in the prime index file and obtains the location of the target logical record within the data file. This location is then used to access the data file.

The READ command appears the same whether an alternate index or the prime index is used. However, the use of the alternate index causes three files to be accessed instead of two. Because of the extra file access, a transaction that uses an alternate index will require more time to complete than one which uses the prime index. This serves to illustrate that the run-time efficiency of

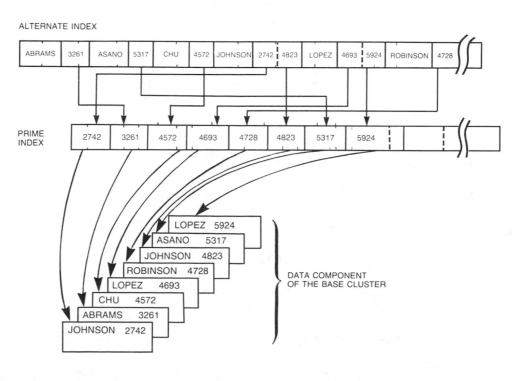

**Figure 6-8
VSAM Alternate
Index**

115

a program cannot always be judged by the number of statements in the program. The fact that a programming statement is *concise* does not necessarily imply that it can be performed efficiently.

Integrating Data Files

The term *data base* has been used very little in this and the preceding chapter. Most often we have referred to searching the *file*, updating the file, etc. The reason for this is that in most of our examples the files did not satisfy all the requirements of the data base definition given in Chapter 1. In particular, the examples have usually not been integrated files. For example, a library card catalog isn't used in all parts of the library business. However, CICS facilities do support collections of information that, considered together, are integrated. In this section, we will look at how such file collections are structured.

When a data base is integrated to contain information used throughout a business, decisions must be made about how to handle *multiple occurrences* of information.

Let's see what we mean by multiple occurrences. The file shown in Figure 6-3 is typical of a file that would be used by a purchasing department. For that purpose, the records would probably also contain information like the name and phone number of the supplier's sales representative.

The accounting department would have a file containing information about suppliers too. That file would contain the supplier's name, address, and current account information.

The site security department might also have a file about suppliers, listing for each supplier the names of service personnel authorized to be in high security areas.

Some information, in particular the supplier's name, appears in all three of these files. That is, the supplier's name is "multiply occurring." If Vendor A goes out of business or changes address, all three files would have to be changed. The accounting department might find out about the change and update their file, but the purchasing and security departments wouldn't know of the change until they discovered it as they went about their own duties.

For practical reasons, it's desirable to limit multiple occurrences of data. If the vendor name appeared in only one place, it would have to be updated only once. And as soon as it was updated, the changed information would be available throughout the business. This is part of what we mean when we talk about *integrated databases*.

Let's see how multiple occurrences can be eliminated when files are integrated. Generally speaking, there are two approaches.

One is to have many files, each containing quite specific information, that can be used in combination by particular applications. For example, the manufacturing company might choose to have a single file that described vendors and another file that described parts. The vendor file would include each vendor's full name, mailing address, and phone number. The parts list would contain the information shown in Figure 6-3, but in place of a 40 character "supplier name" field there would be a four character supplier code. An application that needed to find the name and address of part XYZ could read the part file with a key of "XYZ" and obtain the supplier code. Then, in a separate operation, the vendor file would be read, using the supplier code as key. Later in this chapter, a CICS facility called *indirect access chains*, which simplifies programs of this kind, will be discussed.

The second approach is to have a single file, but structure it so that no data is multiply occurring. Figure 6-9 shows how parts list data might be structured in this type of file.

Notice that the file contains two types of records. One record type contains the main *root* information about a vendor. The second record type is a *data record* that describes a part. But there is a relationship between the two record types. The part descriptor records are connected to the root record describing the vendor who supplies the part. The "connection" between the root record and the data records might be defined simply by position; that is, the data records could follow the associated root record in the file. Or the connection might be defined by a chain of pointers. The root record for a vendor would contain, for example, the relative record number of the first data record for that vendor. Each data record would contain a similar pointer to the next data record for the same vendor. The pointers could go in both directions. That is, each data record could contain a pointer, not only to the *next data record* but also to the *previous data record* for the vendor. The bidirectional chain allows a data record to be conveniently deleted—or connected to a different root record—by modifying the *next record* pointer in the previous record and the *previous record* pointer in the following record.

VENDOR			
NAME	ADDRESS	PHONE	DELIVERY TIME
A			

PART			
NUMBER	PRICE	DELIVERY TIME	
C-0A-001	.53	2	

VENDOR			
NAME	ADDRESS	PHONE	REPRESENTATIVE
B			

PART			
NUMBER	PRICE	DELIVERY TIME	
C-0A-001	.57	4	

PART			
NUMBER	PRICE	DELIVERY TIME	
F-0A-013	.013	8	

**Figure 6-9
Single File Approach
to Eliminate
Duplicate Records**

CICS Indirect Access Chains

A CICS facility called Indirect Access Chains can be used to define a data base made up of physically separate files.

Figure 6-10 shows a data base constructed using the separate file technique. Look at the two files in the left half of the figure. The first is organized by part name sequence; the part name is its access key. Each record of the part name file contains a part number field. The second file is organized by part number. The part number contained in the first file can be used as a key to find a record in the second file. Taken together, the two files describe parts.

Notice that each parts record contains a supplier number that can be used to access a third, supplier, file. The supplier file contains direct pointers to accounts payable records that tell what bills have been received from the supplier.

Suppose that you are writing an application program that must find information about the supplier of part name: BOLT, 2 INCH. As shown by Figure 6-10, three separate file accesses are required. The first reads the *partname* file to obtain a key to be used in a second READ which accesses the *parts* file. The supplier number from the parts record must then be used to obtain the supplier number key that, in turn, is used to access the *supplier* file.

It looks as though each inquiry would require a sequence of three READ commands, each specifying a different DATASET parameter. Not only is such a program tedious to code, but it has the disadvantage of being dependent upon the physical structure of the data base. If application programs were written that way, the company couldn't combine the part number file with the partname file unless it were willing to rewrite many application programs. In other words, the programs wouldn't meet the DB/DC objective of data independence.

To provide data independence, CICS permits an *Indirect Access Chain* to be defined in the FCT. Let's see how the Indirect Access Chain would simplify your program.

An FCT entry would be defined for the Indirect Access Chain just as though it were a file. The entry defines part name as the key to be used to access the Indirect Access Chain, just as though the chain were a keyed file. Additional fields in the FCT entry define the sequence of accesses required to reach the supplier file given the part name.

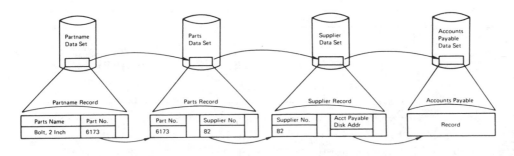

**Figure 6-10
Separate File Approach
to Eliminate Duplicate
Records**

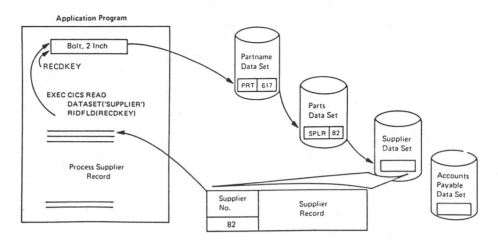

Figure 6-11
Application Program
Referencing Indirect
Access Chain

Figure 6-11 shows how the application program would look.

The example illustrated by Figure 6-11 assumes that SUPPLIER is the name by which the Indirect Access Chain is defined in the FCT. The program is written just as if there were really a single file called "SUPPLIER" that was organized by part name.

The program issues a single READ command which uses the FCT entry name SUPPLIER as the DATASET parameter and specifies the part name BOLT, 2 INCH as key. This single command causes a chain of three file accesses, shown to the right in the figure, to be performed.

This is what we mean by *data independence*. The same program could be used to read an actual file that contained supplier records with part name keys. The processing that takes place in response to the program's READ command is determined by the FCT entry, not by statements within the program itself.

Summary

In Chapter 5, we discussed applications that require transactions to quickly read or update a *selected* record. Because of these requirements, files that are part of a data base are physically structured for non-sequential access. However, many DB/DC applications also require transactions that read a file *sequentially*.

CICS provides the *browse* facility for this purpose. A browse operation consists of three steps: establishing the beginning position, sequentially retrieving records, and terminating the browse.

A browse operation can retrieve records in the sequence in which they appear in the physical file, or in sequence according to their keys. A task may have multiple browse operations active against the same file concurrently. Browsing is a read-only operation, but a task may use the READ for UPDATE command, discussed in Chapter 5, to update a file that is being browsed by the same task.

A browse operation can require a long elapsed time. Therefore, it is important to be aware of the *resources* the browse requires. The browse operation must be kept as brief as possible so that the resources will not be tied up unnecessarily. You should issue the ENDBR command as soon as either physical or logical end of file have occurred, and you should design browse transactions that encourage the user to confine the browse to a small subsection of the file.

Random access files are physically structured so that a record can be accessed according to its key or physical location. Two structures were discussed:

Keyed access files allow a record to be accessed according to the value of a *key* contained within each record. Such files actually consist of a *cluster* of two files: the data file, and an index file. The index file is physically organized according to the unique key. To access a selected key, the DB/DC system first reads the index file to determine where the logical record containing that key is located in the data file. Therefore, each logical record retrieval requires two file accesses, one to the index file and a second to the data file. The two accesses are performed in response to your single READ command.

For VSAM KSDS files, alternate indexes may be defined in addition to the *prime index file* described above. An *alternate index* file permits the data file to be accessed by a different key than the prime index key. The alternate index file contains pointers to the prime index file; so using an alternate index causes a single command to perform three file accesses. The key used by an alternate index file is not necessarily unique; the DUPKEY condition is raised when a CICS command accesses a record that is not the only (or final) record with the specified key. Except for providing an exception routine for the DUPKEY condition, a CICS application program that uses an alternate index is the same as a program that uses the prime index. The program refers to the file by a DATASET name whose FCT entry defines the alternate index structure and the base data set to which it is related.

Direct access files are accessed by specifying the desired record's actual *location* within the file. No index is required, so this structure is the most efficient for retrieving a selected record. However, direct access files are less easy to use for some applications than are keyed access files. This is particularly true of applications that must frequently insert new records into the file.

When data files are integrated, it is usually found that some data items are used in several different contexts; that is, they are "multiply occurring." To maintain the same data in several different areas of the file would increase file size and complicate the task of keeping information current. Two approaches to handling multiply occurring data were discussed. First, the data can be structured into several physically separate files that can be linked together by pointers or keys. Alternatively, the data might be structured into a single physical file containing several different record types that can be linked together.

CICS supports the first, physically separate file, approach with the Indirect Access Chain facility. Application programs refer to an Indirect Access Chain as though it were a single file. The FCT describes the sequence of file accesses that must be performed to obtain the required data by accessing a series of separate, linked files. When your READ command is issued, the sequence of required accesses is performed automatically.

DISCUSSION QUESTIONS

1. The following questions refer to the program shown in Figure 6-2.
   a. Could the program be modified to perform backwards retrieval simply by replacing the READNEXT command with a READPREV command?
   b. The statement MOVE 25 TO LEN is executed each time through the loop. Could the program be improved by placing the statement before the loop so that it would be executed only once?
   c. What is the logical end of file condition for the browse operation?
   d. What is the value of the RIDFLD parameter, RECORD-KEY

      ■ When STARTBR is executed?
      ■ When END-BROWS is reached?
      ■ Between the two points described above?

   e. Can you suggest a change to any CICS commands that would reduce the program's CICS region space requirement?
   f. What is the file's maximum record size?
   g. What is the file's key? (Give the key's location in the record and its size.)

2. Suppose the function of the program in Figure 6-2 were to be performed using an Alternate Index:
   a. What alternate key would be defined?
   b. How would the program have to be changed?
   c. How would the revised program compare to the original in terms of resource usage?

EXERCISE

For this exercise, you are to write an application program to browse the same file used in Chapter 5s Exercise. The user will enter a transaction request like the one shown in Figure 6-12. The browse should begin with the key specified by the transaction request and should continue until *physical* end of file occurs.

The program should check the AMOUNT field of each record retrieved.

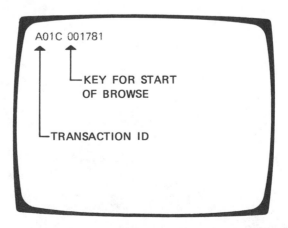

Figure 6-12
Transaction Request
for Programming
Exercise

When the browse has been terminated, the program is to report the number of records that have an AMOUNT value greater than 50. (Note that the AMOUNT field, like all the fields, is a character string, not an arithmetic value. Therefore, you will have to use the character constant 00005000 for the comparison with the AMOUNT field.)

If the browse finds no records with an amount greater than 50, display the message THERE ARE NO ENTRIES WHOSE BALANCE IS GREATER THAN $50.

If the key entered is invalid, terminate the task after displaying INVALID INPUT KEY.

If the transaction request is too long, terminate the task after displaying INVALID TRANSACTION FORMAT PLEASE REENTER.

If FILEA is not open, terminate the task after displaying FILE NOT AVAILABLE, TRY AGAIN LATER.

7 Advanced Terminal Control: The CICS Basic Mapping Support

Introduction

So far your CICS programs have used simple one-line messages to communicate with the terminal user. In most DB/DC applications, however, you will need to make use of the entire display screen to send information to, and receive data from, the user. By presenting information a screen at a time, you can convey a large amount of information in a form that the user can read and understand quickly.

This chapter opens with a discussion of some of the factors to consider when you decide how your program will present information to the user. These factors include both the *content* and *format* of the information. Content means how the information is *expressed*—basically, the words you choose and the way you combine them. Format has to do with the way information is laid out on the screen, and how various terminal device features like blinking, color, and levels of brightness are used.

Terminals don't all support the same features, so the format of information is determined partly by the kind of terminal device used to run your program. But, when you write a program, you have no way of knowing what terminal device will be used. Often your user will have a choice of several terminals, and will simply choose the one that is most convenient at the time. Besides, after you have written the program, someone may decide to buy an entirely new kind of terminal device that wasn't available when you wrote the program. For these reasons, you need to write application programs that are *device independent*—that is, that do not contain any instructions or data that apply to only one kind of device.

This chapter describes how you can write CICS application programs that (1) communicate effectively with the user, and (2) are also device-independent. You will use a CICS facility called *Basic Mapping Support* or *BMS*. BMS allows CICS application programs to specify the format of a terminal message in device independent terms. A user who runs the application program from two different terminal devices will receive messages that contain the same information, but may look different because CICS formats each message for the terminal device in use. The application program is the same in both cases. In order to achieve this, you must create BMS *maps* and place them in a library where CICS can find them when your program is run. There are two types of BMS maps. A *physical map* describes how a message should look on a particular kind of device. A *symbolic map* describes where each information field will be placed in the message. The maps are not part of your program, but CICS will use them together with your program in order to transmit messages correctly to the terminal device. This chapter describes how to construct both types of maps, and how CICS uses the maps when your program is run.

Objectives

After completing this chapter, you will be able to:

- Discuss factors to consider when designing the way in which data will be displayed on the terminal screen.
- Describe how to construct physical and symbolic BMS maps and how they are used by CICS.
- Describe how CICS selects the correct physical map set for a particular type of terminal device.
- Write the macro statements required to define physical and symbolic BMS maps.

User-Application Interaction

So far you have used two CICS commands for communicating with terminal devices. The SEND command transmits a string of characters to the terminal. The RECEIVE command allows your program to process a string of characters that has been read from a terminal—either by moving the characters into your program's working-storage or by allowing your program to access the characters in the input buffer. You can use the SEND and RECEIVE commands in this way for transmitting simple one-line messages, but you need more sophisticated commands when messages use the full terminal screen. We will use the term *panel* to refer to a full screen of information as it appears on a terminal screen.

Using the full-screen features of terminal devices involves more than writing input/output commands. Writing programs that are easy to learn and use requires careful design of the interaction between program and user. We will look first at some things to consider as you design a program.

Design Considerations

For the previous chapter you wrote a program that browsed a file, collecting information from selected records. After reading all records in the file, the program returned a single line of summary information to the user. Usually, however, the user needs to see more than summary information.

For example, assume for the same exercise that the user needed to telephone each person whose record shows a balance greater than fifty dollars. This would mean that your program must display information from each data record that shows the required balance. When you design the program, you need to consider questions like the following:

> Which fields from each record should be displayed?
> How many records should be displayed at a time?

These questions deal principally with message *content*. To answer them, you must know the *meaning* of each field of data, and you must understand how the information is to be *used*. Suppose the data base contained twenty accounts with a balance greater than fifty dollars. A user who intends to telephone each person immediately wouldn't want to see a panel displaying all twenty of the records at once. It would be confusing to be talking with the third person on the list while looking at a panel of twenty accounts. In this case, the user would want to see only the information from one record at a time. On the other hand, if the user wanted to compare this list of accounts with another list, it would be most useful to look at the information a screen at a time.

To define the content of a panel then, you must understand what the user intends to do with the displayed information.

But message *content* is only the first design consideration. Your ultimate goal in designing the program is not merely to *transmit data* to the terminal, but to *communicate information* to the user. Just as in any other form of communication, you must know your audience in order to communicate effectively. Are the users specialists in a particular field? How much training and experience have they had? How are they accustomed to expressing information?

For example, if you design a program to be used by research chemists, the users will not want to see (or type) "hexachloroethane" instead of "C2 Cl6." On the other hand, if your users are not chemists, they won't want to learn chemical formulas in order to use a data base that contains information about chemicals.

People in many other professions also have their own ways of expressing information. You need to take these into consideration when you design programs that interact with the user.

In addition to content and expression, your program design must consider message *format*. How will the information *look* and, on interactive devices, how will it *behave*? That is, will it blink? Can the user type over it?

The format must allow the user to pick out important data quickly and accurately. For example, it's important to know at a glance whether 5139 is an account balance, part of a phone number, or the street number.

Format may include such features as:

- Where the cursor is positioned
- How fields are placed relative to each other in the panel
- The relative *size* of the characters or symbols used
- *Highlighting*, achieved by intensified display, underlining, blinking, or use of color
- Whether a field is protected or modifiable
  This not only determines whether the user can enter data into the field, but may control how the cursor moves from one field to another.
- Whether the user can select the field with a lightpen device

Terminal Control

You have probably seen many terminal devices that don't support all the format features listed above. For example, many devices do not display colors and many don't allow use of a lightpen. As this would suggest, format must depend upon the terminal device being used.

Terminals also differ in more obvious ways—for instance, in the amount of information they can display. A common screen size is 30 lines of 80 characters, a total of 2400 characters. Various device types display either more or fewer characters—for example, 24 lines of 40 characters.

In order to control the format of a display, a program must transmit *control codes* to the terminal device in addition to the information that will be displayed. Control codes specify, for example, where message text is to appear on the screen, and whether the text should be displayed in color.

Figure 7-1 illustrates a panel that might be used for data entry. The cursor is shown as darker in the illustration; on the actual terminal screen it might be blinking so that its position can be seen readily. The display includes a number of identifiers–"Name," "Salary," "Job Title," "Phone." Following each identifier is a blank space which represents a *modifiable field*—that is, an area the user can type information into.

As we've said, in order to produce a panel like this a program must transmit both the text to be displayed and control codes that define how the text is displayed. The text and control codes are contained within a *data stream* transmitted to the terminal device. Let's look at the data stream required to produce this panel on an IBM 3277 terminal device.

The data stream is shown in Figure 7-2. The characters that are to appear on the screen are shown in dark print. All other fields shown in the figure are control codes.

The first four codes and the ETX code at the end of the stream control the transmission itself. When you used the SEND command in earlier programming exercises, the CICS Terminal Control Program took care of producing these codes and transmitting them to the terminal device.

The remaining codes specify *format*. Let's look at the codes required to format the first line of the panel shown in Figure 7-1.

The SBA code stands for Set Buffer Address. The SBA and the 50 which comes after it specify that the following field is to be placed in position 50 of the buffer. On a 3270 device that displays forty character lines, buffer position 50 corresponds to the tenth position of the second line of the display.

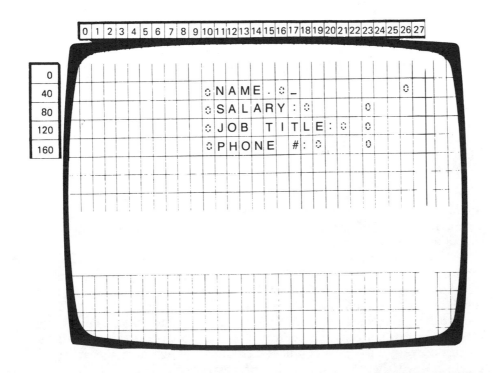

Figure 7-1
Typical Data
Entry Panel

The SF code signals the beginning of a field; ATTR is an *attribute byte* that specifies characteristics of the field, like brightness and whether or not the user can type over the field. Next come the characters (NAME:) to be displayed in the field.

The field following NAME: appears empty on the display screen, but an attribute byte is required to produce it. The attribute byte specifies, among other things, that the field can be modified from the terminal keyboard. The IC code denotes *Insert Cursor*, and causes the cursor to be positioned at the beginning of this field.

If you wanted to produce the panel shown in Figure 7-1, you could write your program to create a *character string* containing the hexadecimal values of the control codes intermixed, as shown in Figure 7-2, with the characters to be displayed. You could then use the SEND command to transmit the character string—containing both codes and text—to the terminal. But if you did that your program would not be device independent, because each type of terminal can require different control codes. In order to use your program, everyone would have to use just one type of terminal device. Your program would be said to build a *native data stream*—that is a data stream designed for a particular device. Notice that a native data stream is both *device dependent* and *format dependent*. The native data stream—and therefore, the program that constructs it—would have to be changed if you wanted to change either the format of the message panel or the terminal device on which it was to appear.

Device and Format Independence

In the chapters on accessing the data base, we discussed why it's important for application programs to be device independent. That is, why programs should not have to be changed if the data base is moved to a different type of data storage device. Device independence is equally important for programs that use terminal devices. Most DB/DC installations have many different types of terminal. Even if that weren't so, it would be unwise to design an application program "tailored to" any single terminal type. Users want to be able to purchase new terminals that might be, for example, less expensive, more energy efficient, or easier to read than the ones they have now. And it's important that they can do this without rewriting hundreds of applications programs.

If the terminal changes, the panel format may have to change as well. For example, we have already seen that terminals don't all display the same number of characters.

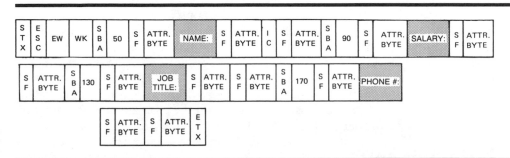

**Figure 7-2
Data Stream for
Terminal Output**

Even if the terminal device doesn't change, you may find that you need to change the format of a message panel. When users begin to gain experience with an application program, they often request changes in the panel's format. It may turn out that "We need to see field A directly above field B," or that "This field needs to be highlighted so we can pick it out quickly." For these reasons, you want to be able to change the format of a panel without reprogramming; that is, your programs should be both *format independent* and *device independent*.

In order to be device and format independent, your program can't contain a native data stream. But the terminal device must receive a native data stream in order to format information correctly. The solution is for CICS—not the application program—to construct the native data stream. But somehow you have to describe to CICS how you want each panel to appear. You cannot put the description in your program because the program would then be format dependent. So the panel descriptions must come from somewhere outside the application program. As we will discuss later in detail, you describe panels by creating BMS maps that are separate from your application program. The rest of this chapter will describe BMS maps and how they are built. Chapter 8 will discuss how your programs use the BMS maps.

Basic Mapping Support

Basic Mapping Support (BMS) is the name of the CICS component used to permit device independent terminal communication. To do this, BMS must provide two distinct services for application programs. First, BMS must construct the native data stream required to produce the desired panel on the user's terminal device. This means that BMS must produce control codes appropriate to the terminal device in use and place the codes correctly in the stream.

Second, BMS must provide a way for the application program to refer to data fields in the native stream. To understand this second requirement, consider the panel shown in Figure 7-3.

The panel contains some constant title information: "Inventory Status," "Item Number:," "On Hand:". In addition, it displays an item number LAX810, and a number-on-hand value 325. These two information fields contain variable information. It's up to the application program to find the correct item number and number-on-hand, and to place these values into the proper position of the panel.

The native data stream for the panel is shown at the bottom of the figure. (The CC fields which separate the displayed information fields each represent one or more control code bytes of the type detailed in Figure 7-2.) Let's suppose that the application program has obtained the value for the item number from a user's transaction request, and the "on-hand" value from the data base entry for item LAX810. The program has read these values into working-storage variables, say ITEMNO and ONHANDNO. In order to produce the required display panel, the program must move the values of ITEMNO and ONHANDNO into the proper position in the native data stream. The program cannot do this directly, because the stream does not exist within the program; and the program doesn't know the format of the stream. Otherwise, the program would no longer be device independent. Since BMS builds the stream, there must be a mechanism for *BMS* to:

INVENTORY STATUS

ITEM NUMBER: LAX810
ON HAND   :   325

DATA STREAM

| C C | INVENTORY STATUS | C C | ITEM NUMBER: | C C | LAX810 | C C |

| ON HAND   : | C C | 325 | C C |

Figure 7-3
Output Panel and
Data Stream

(C C = CONTROL CHARACTERS)

1. Know that it needs to place values from the program into the native data stream
2. Receive the correct values from the application program
3. Place the values in the proper position in the native data stream

The mechanism which allows BMS to accomplish this is the BMS map.

Each panel that contains variable data requires a *pair* of BMS maps: a *physical map* and a *symbolic map*. The physical map describes the format of a panel as it will appear on a particular terminal type. The symbolic map defines the relationship between symbolic variable names in the application program and fields in the panel.

Assume that the panel shown in Figure 7-3 is required for an application that can be run from any of four different terminal types. Then four physical maps must be required for the panel; one for each of the four possible terminal types. Physical maps reside in a load module library, just as do CICS application programs. They are used at *execution time*; they are loaded into the CICS region when a CICS task executes one of the BMS operations described in the next chapter.

The same application would require just one *symbolic map* for the panel. A symbolic map is required for each panel that contains variable data. Symbolic maps reside in source libraries. They are used at *compile time*; they are incorporated into the application program by means of a COPY statement.

You define both physical and symbolic maps by using a set of BMS macro instructions which are written in the syntax used by the IBM 370 Assembler. The macro instructions will be discussed in a later section of this chapter; first, we will examine in more detail how the physical and symbolic maps are used.

Physical Maps

Figure 7-4 shows the procedure for producing a physical BMS map.

The first step is to assemble the BMS macro instructions. You then link-edit the assembler output (object file) into a CICS load library. You can link-edit the object files for more than one physical map together into the same library member as long as the maps were *defined for the same device.* The maps whose object files are link-edited together are collectively called a *map set.* Generally, you would group into the same map set all the maps for panels used in a single application or group of related applications.

A map set must have a name, just as a program in a load module library has a name; it must also have an entry in the *Processing Program Table* (PPT). The name is made up of two parts. The first part of the name is a *generic name* that you may choose and that can be up to seven characters long. The second part of the name is a single-character suffix. The suffix indicates the type of device for which the map set is to be used.

When a CICS program executes a BMS command, it must identify the map set that contains the required map. It does this by specifying the *generic name.* BMS then adds a one-character suffix to the generic name; the suffix identifies

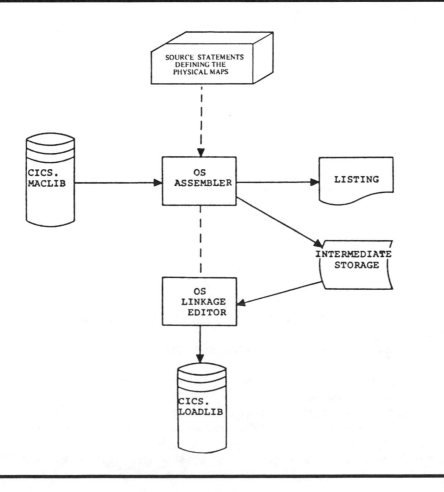

**Figure 7-4
Producing a BMS
Physical Map**

the type of terminal from which the application program was invoked. (As you may remember, the terminal type can be obtained from the TCT.) As an example, suppose you have written an application program that produces four message panels; we will call them panels A, B, C, and D. Assume also that the program can be invoked from *three* different terminal types.

In this situation, there must be three physical map sets—one for each type of device. For convenience, you will probably combine the map for each of the four panels into a single map set. Each map set will contain maps for Panels A, B, C, and D.

Each map set will have the same generic name, but a different suffix. For each map set, you must use the suffix that identifies the type of terminal the map set is for. When you prepare the Job Control Language to link-edit each map set, you must specify the complete name—generic name followed by suffix. Suppose you have chosen the generic name MAP1 for a map set. Then the map sets for various devices would have names like MAP1M, MAP1P, and MAP1K.

Your application program will use a map by issuing a CICS command that names both the map and map set. For example:

CICS   SEND MAP ('A') MAPSET ('MAP1')

When the SEND command is executed by a CICS task, BMS will receive control and consult the task's TCT entry to determine which device type is in use. If it finds, for example, that a Model 3767 is being used, it will append a P to the generic name and request map set MAP1P. If MAP1P were not already in storage, it would be loaded in much the same way a CICS program is loaded.

Figure 7-5 shows that MAP1*P* is loaded into the CICS region to support communication with a 3767 terminal. The figure also shows that if the same application program were executed by a second task that had been invoked from an 80-column model 3270; CICS would use map set MAP1*M* when it executed the SEND command.

If CICS finds no entry in the PPT for the map set name including suffix, for example MAP1M, it looks for a map set whose name is the same as the generic name without suffix, for example MAP1. This feature allows a single map set, appropriate to several different device types, to be generated and used in the absence of a map tailored for a specific device.

Symbolic Maps

Symbolic maps are independent of device type. Therefore, in the example we have been discussing, only one symbolic map set is required. The symbolic map set will contain the symbolic maps for Displays A, B, C, and D.

Figure 7-6 shows the process for producing a BMS symbolic map.

Just as for the physical maps, the first step is to assemble the BMS macro instructions. As the next section of this chapter will discuss, the same macro instructions can be used for specifying the symbolic map as for the physical map; only one parameter must be changed.

The physical map sets were built from the assembler's object file output. The symbolic maps come from another assembler output, the SYSPUNCH file. As shown here, the file is directed to a library that contains cataloged source statements. There is no required naming convention for symbolic map sets. The application program will contain a COPY statement that, together with the Job Control Language for compiling the application program, identifies the map set to be used.

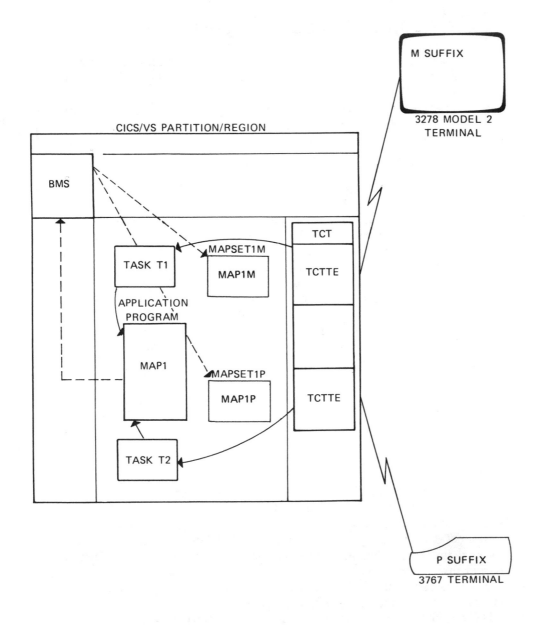

Figure 7-5
Loading BMS Map
for Required
Terminal Type

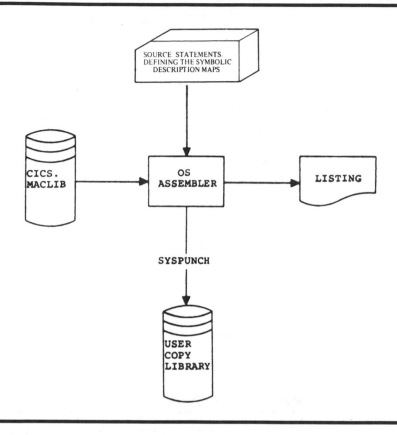

**Figure 7-6
Producing a BMS
Symbolic Map**

Figure 7-7 illustrates part of a COBOL source program which uses a symbolic map.

Note the COPY statement indicated by the circled 1 in the Figure. Its effect is to copy the symbolic map set identified by XDFHCMK into the source program. The symbolic map contains only COBOL statements. Keep in mind the distinction between the *symbolic maps* that contain COBOL statements produced by the assembly step, and the *BMS macro instructions* that serve as input to the assembly. In the section "Format of Symbolic Map," later in this chapter, you will see an example of a set of BMS macro instructions and the symbolic map they produce.

The COBOL statements from XDFHCMK define symbolic working-storage variables CUSTNO1, PARTNO1, and QUANT1 which are referred to by the statements indicated by the circled 2. Later in this chapter, we will see exactly how the symbolic variables are defined. Here, the points to observe are that:

- The COPY statement is used to insert the symbolic map into the program
- The symbolic map is made up of COBOL statements which get "compiled into" the application program

Creating BMS maps

BMS maps are created by using BMS macro instructions (often called simply "macros"). The macro instructions are written in the syntax required

133

SOURCE LISTING

```
******************************************************************
*   ORDER ENTRY SAMPLE PROGRAM                                   *
******************************************************************
 IDENTIFICATION DIVISION.
 PROGRAM-ID. XDFHOREN.
 ENVIRONMENT DIVISION.
 DATA DIVISION.
 WORKING-STORAGE SECTION.
 77   ERROR-FLAG PIC 9.
 01   XDFHCMKI COPY XDFHCMK.
 01   FILEA COPY FILEA.
 01   L860 COPY L860.
 01   DFHBMSCA COPY DFHBMSCA.
*
 PROCEDURE DIVISION.
*
*                                               HANDLE CONDITIONS
     EXEC CICS HANDLE AID CLEAR(ENDA) END-EXEC.
     EXEC CICS HANDLE CONDITION MAPFAIL(MAPFAIL)
                              NOTFND(NOTFOUND)
                              ERROR(ERRORS) END-EXEC.
*
*                                               CLEAR MAP
     MOVE LOW-VALUES TO XDFHCMKO.
*
     EXEC CICS SEND MAP('XDFHCMK') ERASE END-EXEC.
******************************************************************
*                                               PROCESS INPUT   *
******************************************************************
 RECEIVM.
     EXEC CICS RECEIVE MAP('XDFHCMK') END-EXEC.
*
     MOVE 0 TO ERROR-FLAG.
     MOVE DFHBMFSE TO CUSTNOA, PARTNOA, QUANTA.
******************************************************************
*                                               CHECK DATA      *
******************************************************************
*
     IF CUSTNOI NOT NUMERIC THEN
        MOVE DFHBMBRY TO CUSTNOA MOVE 1 TO ERROR-FLAG.
*
     IF PARTNOI NOT NUMERIC THEN
        MOVE DFHBMBRY TO PARTNOA MOVE 1 TO ERROR-FLAG.
*
     IF QUANTI NOT NUMERIC THEN
        MOVE DFHBMBRY TO QUANTA MOVE 1 TO ERROR-FLAG.
*
*                                               DATA ERROR-REENTER
     IF ERROR-FLAG = 1 THEN
        MOVE DFHBMASB TO MSG2A
        EXEC CICS SEND MAP('XDFHCMK') END-EXEC
        GO TO RECEIVM.
******************************************************************
*                                               READ CUST RECORD*
******************************************************************
*
     EXEC CICS READ DATASET('FILEA') INTO(FILEA) RIDFLD(CUSTNOI)
                                               END-EXEC.
     MOVE CUSTNOI TO CUSTNO.
     MOVE PARTNOI TO PARTNO.
     MOVE QUANTI TO QUANTITY.
     MOVE EIBTRMID TO TERMID.
******************************************************************
*                                               WRITE VALID ORDER*
******************************************************************
```

**Figure 7-7
Using a Symbolic
Map, Program
Example**

by assembler language. Figure 7-8 summarizes this syntax and shows an example BMS macro instruction. (The meaning of the macro shown will be discussed later; for now, the important thing is to compare its syntax with the model shown above the instruction.)

Notice in the example that the symbol MAPSET begins in column 1. It is separated by blanks from the operation code DFHMSD. The operation code, in turn, is separated by a blank from the first parameter, TYPE.

Each parameter field, except the last, is followed by a comma to indicate that additional parameters follow. The example shows how an instruction can be continued onto additional statement lines. The STORAGE parameter field is followed by a comma signifying that another parameter follows. The next columns are left blank until column 72 which contains a non-blank character, in this case, an X. The non-blank column 72 indicates that the instruction is continued in the next statement line. As required by the illustrated rules of syntax, the first field of the continuation line begins in column 16.

Comments may be inserted after the last parameter field. They must be separated from the final parameter field by one or more blank columns. A common error in writing macro instructions is to separate two parameter fields by a blank instead of by a comma. The assembler then interprets the fields that follow the blank not as parameters, but as comments.

Three macro instruction operation codes are used to define BMS maps and map sets. They are:

1. DFHMSD to define the *map set*
2. DFHMDI to define each *map*
3. DFHMDF to define each *field* within a map

Figure 7-9 illustrates four maps defined in one map set.

In the figure, the DFHMSD macro defines the beginning of the *map set*. The

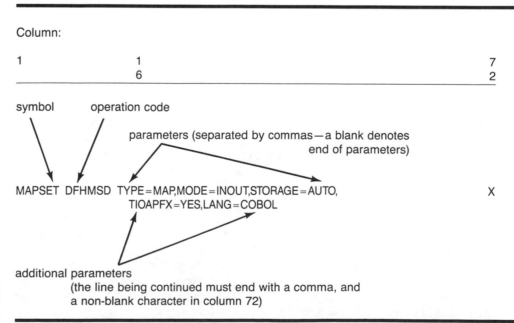

Column:

```
1                    1                                                          7
                     6                                                          2
```

symbol   operation code

parameters (separated by commas—a blank denotes
                                    end of parameters)

MAPSET DFHMSD TYPE=MAP,MODE=INOUT,STORAGE=AUTO,   X
                TIOAPFX=YES,LANG=COBOL

additional parameters
        (the line being continued must end with a comma, and
        a non-blank character in column 72)

**Figure 7-8
Format of BMS
Macro Statement**

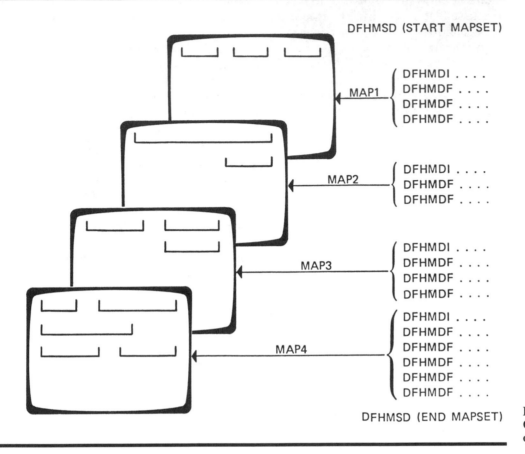

DFHMSD (START MAPSET)

MAP1 { DFHMDI . . . .
DFHMDF . . . .
DFHMDF . . . .
DFHMDF . . . .

MAP2 { DFHMDI . . . .
DFHMDF . . . .
DFHMDF . . . .

MAP3 { DFHMDI . . . .
DFHMDF . . . .
DFHMDF . . . .
DFHMDF . . . .

MAP4 { DFHMDI . . . .
DFHMDF . . . .
DFHMDF . . . .
DFHMDF . . . .
DFHMDF . . . .
DFHMDF . . . .

DFHMSD (END MAPSET)

**Figure 7-9
Organization
of Map Set**

DFHMDI macro defines the beginning of a *map*. The first map, called MAP1 in the illustration, has three fields; one DFHMDF macro is coded for each field.

The second DFHMDI macro defines the start of the second map, MAP2, of the map set. Two DFHMDF macros define the two fields in MAP2. The third map is defined by the DFHMDI macro followed by three DFHMDF macros. The fourth map evidently contains five fields, because its DFHMDI macro is followed by five DFHMDF macros. Finally, another DFHMSD macro is coded to indicate the end of the map set.

The same three macros are used to generate both physical and symbolic maps. The TYPE parameter of the DFHMSD macro indicates whether symbolic or physical maps are to be produced. Some parameter fields are used only during creation of a physical map, others only during creation of a symbolic map. However, parameters are ignored if they are not needed for the type of map being created. Therefore, it is usually most convenient to prepare a single sequence of macro instructions that contain parameters for both symbolic and physical maps. The sequence is assembled once to produce physical maps; then the TYPE parameter is changed and the instructions are assembled again to produce symbolic maps. (The order here is not important. That is, symbolic maps could be created first and then the physical maps.)

Map Set Definition: the DFHMSD Macro

The DFHMSD macro instruction is used to name and describe the characteristics of a map set. At this time, we will discuss only the most commonly used parameters, which are shown in Figure 7-10.

The TYPE parameter indicates whether a physical map set (TYPE = MAP) or a symbolic map set (TYPE = DSECT) is to be created. The DFHMSD macro that marks the end of a map set definition sequence must have a TYPE = FINAL parameter.

The MODE parameter indicates whether the map set to be defined will be used to read data *from* the user terminal (MODE = IN), to send data *to* the user terminal (MODE = OUT), or both (MODE = INOUT).

The LANG parameter is required for generating symbolic map sets; it specifies what source language is to be used in the symbolic map. As shown in the figure, LANG may specify COBOL, PL/1, or ASM.

TERM names the terminal type for which the map set is to be generated. For example, TERM = 3270-2 defines the IBM 3278 Model 2 terminal device. You can find a list of terminal types and their names by consulting the IBM *CICS Application Programmer's Reference Manual*. The TERM parameter is ignored during generation of symbolic maps.

The TIOAPFX = YES parameter is required to allow the BMS maps to be referenced by CICS commands. If it is not included, your program will fail at execution time because the terminal input/output data will overwrite control data contained in the TIOA. This parameter is produced automatically if STORAGE = AUTO, discussed below, is coded.

For COBOL programs, the STORAGE = AUTO parameter field must be coded if the application program will refer concurrently to more than one map within the same map set. If it is omitted, the symbolic maps in the map set will share the same storage, so that the information for each map will overlay the previous map.

Map Definition: the DFHMDI Macro

The DFHMDI macro instruction names and describes the characteristics of a

```
MAPSET NAME          DFHMSD   TYPE = {DSECT
(1 to 7 Characters)                   MAP
                                      FINAL

                             ,MODE = {IN
                                      OUT
                                      INOUT

                             ,LANG = {ASM
                                      COBOL
                                      PLI

                             ,TERM = type

                             ,TIOAPFX = {NO
                                         YES

                             ,STORAGE = AUTO
```

**Figure 7-10
Format of DFHMSD
Macro Statement**

137

specific map. In a given map set, there must be one DFHMDI macro for each map. Figure 7-11 shows the DFHMDI macro and its most commonly used parameters.

The SIZE parameter specifies, in terms of lines and columns, the size of the area the map will occupy on the screen. The line and column values must be between 1 and 240.

LINE, COLUMN, and JUSTIFY define the position of the map on the screen. LINE specifies the line on the screen that will correspond to the top line of the map. JUSTIFY indicates whether the map is to be aligned with the right or left side of the screen. COLUMN gives the column on the screen that corresponds to the first column of the map; columns are counted from the side of the screen indicated by JUSTIFY.

Figure 7-12 shows the effect of these parameters. A BMS map is shown positioned in a display panel as defined by the SIZE, JUSTIFY, COLUMN, and LINE parameters. JUSTIFY=RIGHT has been specified, so the map is right-

name	operation	parameters
Map Name	DFHMDI	SIZE = (line, column)
		,LINE = 1 to 240
		,COLUMN = 1 to 240
		,JUSTIFY = LEFT | RIGHT
		,TIOAPFX = NO | YES

**Figure 7-11
Format of DFHMDI
Macro Statement**

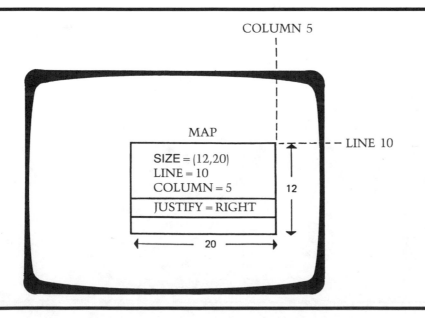

**Figure 7-12
Justification of BMS
Map on Display
Screen**

justified in the Figure. Because the map is right-justified, COLUMN = 5 specifies that the *rightmost* column of the map should appear in the fifth column from the *right* side of the screen. If JUSTIFY were omitted, the map would be left-adjusted.

Field Definition: the DFHMDF Macro

The DFHMDF macro instruction defines a field within a map. Figure 7-13 illustrates a panel which contains nine fields, each defined by a DFHMDF macro.

The first field, in the upper right corner of the panel, contains variable data. The application program will insert an appropriate value during execution.

The second field, DESCRIPTION, is a constant. The field should be defined as *protected* so that the user will not accidentally type data over it.

The third field, to the right of DESCRIPTION, is a field into which the user may type data. Therefore, this field is *unprotected*, and the cursor is to be positioned in the field's first character position.

The next (fourth) field consists only of a *field stopper* that is used to define the field as *autoskip*. When the cursor is moved to the field stopper position, the display will automatically cause the cursor to skip to the next unprotected field on the screen. The next unprotected field, in the illustrated case, is the sixth field which follows the STOCK NUMBER constant field. It is followed by another field stopper, the display's seventh field.

Figure 7-14 illustrates the DFHMDF macro instruction and its major parameters.

The field name is an optional field, but it must be used if the application program will place data into the field or refer to data contained in the field. You don't need to include a field name for constant fields, like STOCK NUMBER in Figure 7-13.

POS defines the position of the field *within the map*. For example: POS (3,1) means that the field will begin in line 3, column 1 of the map. Remember

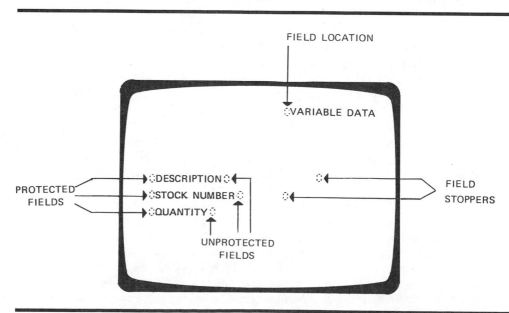

**Figure 7-13
Display Panel
with 9 Fields**

name	operation	parameters
Field Name	DFHMDF	POS = (LINE, COLUMN)
		,ATTRB = (codes) ,
		,INITIAL = 'constants'
		,LENGTH = 1 to 256
		,JUSTIFY = LEFT ¦ RIGHT ,BLANK ¦ ZERO)

Field Name, 1 to 7 characters, is optional

ATTRB codes:

ASKIP	NUM
PROT	UNPROT
BRT	NORM
FSET	IC
DRK	

Figure 7-14
Format of DFHMDF
Macro Statement

that each field begins with an attribute byte, so POS describes where the attribute byte will appear in the map. Suppose that you want to define a field that contains eight bytes of data. Then, the field will actually take up nine bytes, because one byte is required to set the attributes. POS defines the position of the attribute byte in the map. The field's next data byte will appear in the next byte position—line 3, column 2 in this example.

You can display a map anywhere on the screen. For example, if you want the map to appear in the lower right corner of the screen, you could define the *DFHMDI* LINE and COLUMN parameters to 25 and 60 respectively. This does not change the position of fields *in the map*. The field you defined with POS (3,1) will still begin in line 3, column 1 *of the map*. However, if the map is displayed at line 25, column 60 of the screen, the field will begin in line 28, column 60 *of the screen*. Remember that POS defines position in the map. The position in the map will match the position on the screen only if you display the map in line 1, column 1 of the screen.

Some versions of CICS require you to code the DFHMDF macros in the same order as their fields appear in the map—in a top to bottom, left to right sense. This is not required in later CICS versions, but most people find it easier to understand a map that has been coded in this way.

ATTRB defines the characteristics (attributes) of each field. Some attribute values are not supported on all types of terminals. If an attribute does not apply to the terminal in use when the application program is executed, BMS will ignore the attribute. The possible values are listed on the following page:

ASKIP	The field will be skipped by the cursor.
PROT	The field cannot be modified from the user terminal.
UNPROT	The field is unprotected to allow the user to enter data from the terminal.
NUM	The terminal will accept only numeric characters—numerals, decimal point, or minus sign—in this field. This is equivalent to pressing the Numeric Lock key on the keyboard.
BRT	This field is to be highlighted on the screen.
NORM	This field is to be displayed at normal brightness.
DRK	This field is not to be displayed or printed. This attribute is used on input maps to prevent display of sensitive data, such as passwords, entered by the user.
IC	The cursor is to be positioned in the first position of this field when the map is displayed. IC may be specified only for the first unprotected field *in the map*. If it is omitted, the cursor will be displayed at line 1, column 1 *of the screen*.
FSET	On input, this field is to be transmitted to the application program whether or not the user has modified the field. Normally, when an application program reads a map from the terminal, only those fields that have been modified are transmitted. This attribute will be discussed further in the next chapter.

INITIAL specifies that the field will initially contain the value indicated in quotation marks. This parameter is most often used to define constant data, such as headings. However, the application program may modify the field if a field name has been defined for this DFHMDF macro.

LENGTH defines the length of the field *not counting the attribute byte*.

At this point, you have seen the three BMS macro instructions with their most common parameters. To see how CICS interprets the macros to produce BMS maps, refer to Figures 7-15 and 16 as you read the following discussion.

Figure 7-15 shows a formatted display; Figure 7-16 illustrates the BMS macros used to define the display.

In Figure 7-16, the beginning DFHMSD macro specifies that a physical map set whose generic name is MAPSETA is to be generated for use with an IBM 3270 Model 2 terminal device. A symbolic map set can be generated by changing the TYPE parameter value from MAP to DSECT. The symbolic map set will contain COBOL language statements as specified by the LANG parameter of the DFHMSD macro. The maps generated will be used for both input and output. Note the TIOAPFX = YES parameter that is required.

There is only one DFHMDI macro; therefore, a single map will be created. The DFHMDI parameters specify that the map will be named MAPA; it will be 6 lines by 40 columns in size; and its upper left corner will appear in line 6, column 10 of the display. The macro defines the position of the upper left corner because no JUSTIFY parameter has been coded, and JUSTIFY = LEFT is the default option. Had JUSTIFY = RIGHT been coded, the LINE and COLUMN parameters would define the position of the map's upper right corner.

The nine DFHMDF macros each describe a field within MAPA. The application program will refer to data in only the CUSTNO, CUSTNAM, and AMOUNT fields, so names are coded for only these three DFHMDF statements.

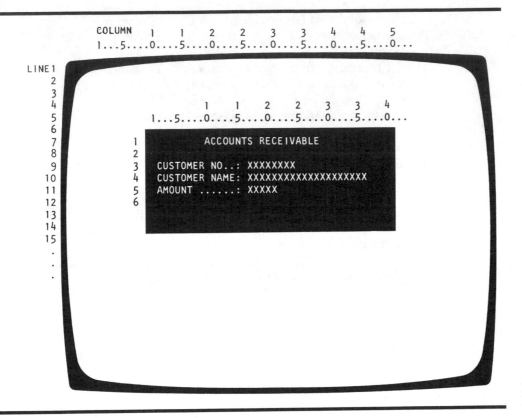

Figure 7-15
Example BMS Display

Let's look at the DFHMDF macro for the CUSTNO field. The POS parameter specifies that the field will begin in line 3, column 16 of the map. The LENGTH parameter specifies that the field contains eight bytes of data. The ATTRB parameter specifies that the field will be *unprotected*, and that when the map is sent to the terminal, the cursor will be moved to this field. Figure 7-17 shows how the CUSTNO field will appear within the map.

Notice that the field occupies *nine* positions in the map—space for the attribute byte and the eight data bytes. The attribute byte always occupies the first byte of a field, so the first data byte will appear in line 3, column 17. When the map is displayed on the screen, the cursor will appear in the first data byte.

Figure 7-15 shows the entire MAPA as it would appear if displayed at line 7, column 8 of the terminal screen. The X's represent the unprotected fields. Notice in Figure 7-16 that these fields have all been defined with the UNPROT attribute.

Comparing Figure 7-16 to the BMS definition of Figure 7-15, you can also see that the heading ACCOUNTS RECEIVABLE will be highlighted on the display, and that the cursor will appear in the first position of the CUSTNO field.

Note that the BMS definition concludes with a DFHMSD macro which specifies TYPE = FINAL. A common error is to omit the concluding macro. If this macro is omitted, no BMS map will be produced, but you will receive an assembler listing with a very large number of error messages.

```
COL 1    COL 9   COL 16                                     COL 72

MAPSETA DFHMSD TYPE=MAP,                                     X
               MODE=INOUT,                                   X
               LANG=COBOL,                                   X
               TERM=3270-2,                                  X
               CTRL=FRSET,                                   X
               TIOAPFX=YES
MAPA     DFHMDI SIZE=(6,40),                                 X
               LINE=6,                                       X
               COLUMN=10
         DFHMDF POS=(1,9),                                   X
               ATTRB=(PROT,BRT),                             X
               INITIAL='ACCOUNTS RECEIVABLE',                X
               LENGTH=19
         DFHMDF POS=(3,1),                                   X
               INITIAL='CUSTOMER NO..:',                     X
               ATTRB=PROT,                                   X
               LENGTH=14
CUSTNO   DFHMDF POS=(3,16),                                  X
               ATTRB=(UNPROT,IC),                            X
               LENGTH=8
         DFHMDF POS=(3,25),                                  X
               ATTRB=ASKIP,                                  X
               LENGTH=1
         DFHMDF POS=(4,1),                                   X
               INITIAL='CUSTOMER NAME:',                     X
               ATTRB=PROT,                                   X
               LENGTH=14
CUSTNAM  DFHMDF POS=(4,16),                                  X
               ATTRB=UNPROT,                                 X
               LENGTH=20
         DFHMDF POS=(4,37),                                  X
               ATTRB=ASKIP,                                  X
               LENGTH=1
         DFHMDF POS=(5,1),                                   X
               INITIAL='AMOUNT.......:',                     X
               ATTRB=PROT,                                   X
               LENGTH=14
AMOUNT   DFHMDF POS=(5,16),                                  X
               ATTRB=(NUM,UNPROT),                           X
               LENGTH=5
         DFHMSD TYPE=FINAL
```

Figure 7-16
Example BMS Map
Set Definition

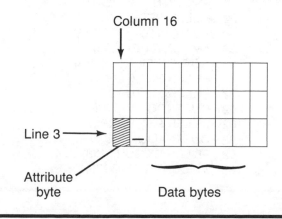

Figure 7-17
Field Within
BMS Map

Format of Symbolic Maps

The BMS macros of Figure 7-16 can be reassembled with the DFHMSD macro changed to specify TYPE = DSECT. This will produce the symbolic map shown in Figure 7-18.

Notice that the map defines two level 01 symbols: MAPAI and MAPAO. The names are generated from the map name, MAPA, and a suffix I for input maps or O for output maps. Because MAPA is to be used for both input and output (MODE = INOUT), it must define both MAPAI and MAPAO. Examine first the format of the input field definition which follows MAPAI. It begins with a twelve-byte filler. This is the TIOA prefix which is produced by the TIOAPFX = YES parameter; it allows the map to be referenced by CICS commands. Next are four symbolic names associated with the CUSTNO field. Note that each name consists of the field name CUSTNO with a one-character suffix. The first variable, CUSTNO*L*, will be set to a two-byte value giving the *length* of the CUSTNO field. The next variable CUSTNO*F* names a single-byte *flag* field that is set during input operations. The same byte can also be referenced by the name CUSTNO*A*; this is because for output operations the byte will contain the *attribute* definition for the CUSTNO field. Lastly, the CUSTNOI variable is defined; this is the eight-byte area that contains the *customer number* value as entered by the user. Notice that the eight-byte length of CUSTNOI matches the LENGTH = 8 specification of the DFHMDF macro. The symbolic map defines each of the three fields, CUSTNO, CUSTNAM, and AMOUNT

```
01      MAPAI.
        02   FILLER PIC X(12).
        02   CUSTNOL      COMP PIC S9(4).
        02   CUSTNOF      PICTURE X.
        02   FILLER REDEFINES CUSTNOF.
          03   CUSTNOA   PICTURE X.
        02   CUSTNOI   PIC X(8).
        02   CUSTNAML     COMP PIC S9(4).
        02   CUSTNAMF     PICTURE X.
        02   FILLER REDEFINES CUSTNAMF.
          03   CUSTNAMA   PICTURE X.
        02   CUSTNAMI   PIC X(20).
        02   AMOUNTL      COMP PIC S9(4).
        02   AMOUNTF      PICTURE X.
        02   FILLER REDEFINES AMOUNTF.
          03   AMOUNTA   PICTURE X.
        02   AMOUNTI   PIC X(5).
01      MAPAO REDEFINES MAPAI.
        02   FILLER PIC X(12).
        02   FILLER PICTURE X(3).
        02   CUSTNOO   PIC X(8).
        02   FILLER PICTURE X(3).
        02   CUSTNAMO   PIC X(20).
        02   FILLER PICTURE X(3).
        02   AMOUNTO   PIC X(5).
```

Figure 7-18
COBOL Statements Generated for Symbolic BMS Map

in this same format: the data field itself preceded by a two-byte length field and a one-byte flag/attribute field.

Now look at the 01 level MAPAO definition. This defines the symbolic names used to refer to the fields for *output*. This definition, and the definitions of CUSTNOA, CUSTNAMA, and AMOUNTA that appeared above, would not appear had the map been generated for input only. Conversely, had the map been generated for output only, the symbols MAPAI, CUSTNOI, CUSTNAMI, and AMOUNTI, and the flag byte names CUSTNOF, CUSTNAMF, and AMOUNTF would not have been defined. In the INOUT case, both output names and input names are defined. If you examine the layout of the MAPAO and MAPAI definitions, you will find that the effect of the MAPAO definition is only to provide an alternate name for the data fields CUSTNOI, CUSTNAMI, and AMOUNTI which were first defined in the input section.

Notice that the symbolic map defines only those fields that were *named* by a DFHMDF macro; the application program can refer to only these fields. Some maps contain no variable data at all; for instance, the display may contain a standard message to the user. Since the application program does not need to refer to any fields within such a map—neither to place data into the display nor to read data from the terminal—no symbolic map need be generated.

Now that you are familiar with the basic format of a symbolic map, we introduce one additional DFHMDF parameter that can be used to produce slightly different symbolic maps.

The GRPNAME parameter allows a field to be divided into subfields that can be addressed by the program. The use of the subfields is strictly for programming convenience. The physical characteristics of the field apply to all the subfields; that is, the length and attribute apply to the entire field.

```
MONTH    DFHMDF   POS = 1, LENGTH = 2,GRPNAME = DATE,ATTRB = NUM
DAY      DFHMDF   POS = 3, LENGTH = 2,GRPNAME = DATE
YEAR     DFHMDF   POS = 5, LENGTH = 2,GRPNAME = DATE
```

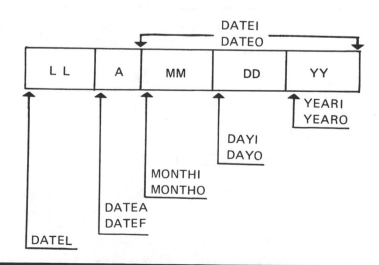

**Figure 7-19
Use of GRPNAME
Parameter of
DFHMDF**

Figure 7-19 shows how the GRPNAME parameter is written and illustrates the symbolic map that would be generated.

Extended Attributes

Earlier in this chapter, we observed that terminal devices differ in the capabilities that they offer. BMS provides a number of parameters which permit maps to use particular device features. We will not discuss all of these, but we will discuss a group of features, called extended attributes, which apply to devices in the IBM 3270 family of terminals. In order to make use of these features, the DFHMSD macro must include an EXTATT = YES parameter.

Figure 7-20 lists the BMS parameters that specify extended attributes. These parameters may be coded in any of the three BMS macro instructions. If conflicting attributes are defined by two or more macros, they are resolved according to the order of precedence DFHMDF, DFHMDI, DFHMSD. That is, a value specified for a particular *field* overrides a value defined for the map or the map set. Similarly, a value specified for a *map* overrides a value defined for the map set.

The meaning of each parameter is defined below:

COLOR When coded in a DFHMSD or DFHMDI macro, specifies the default color for the map set or map respectively. When coded in a DFHMDF macro, specifies the color in which a field is to be displayed.

HILIGHT Defines how fields with the BRT attribute will be displayed on the screen. OFF causes the highlighting request to be ignored. REVERSE causes the field to be displayed in reverse color. BLINK and UNDERLINE are self-explanatory.

VALIDN Controls the use of input fields. MUSTENTER specifies that the user must enter data into a field; MUSTFILL specifies that the user must enter data into *every position* of a field. When VALIDN is specified, the user must meet the input requirements in order to move the cursor out of the input field.

```
,COLOR = DEFAULT ¦ BLUE ¦ RED ¦ PINK

        ¦ GREEN  ¦ TURQUOISE ¦ YELLOW

        ¦ NEUTRAL
```

```
,HILIGHT = OFF ¦ BLINK ¦ REVERSE

          ¦ UNDERLINE
```

```
,VALIDN = (MUSTFILL,MUSTENTER)
```

Figure 7-20
Extended Screen
Attributes

Summary

DB/DC application programs must be designed carefully to communicate information meaningfully to the terminal user. The content, mode of expression, and format of user messages must be considered in light of the particular application and user community.

The choice of message format is determined ultimately by the capability of the terminal device being used. Terminal types differ not only in their capabilities, but also in the control codes required to produce a given format. In order to allow application programs to be device and format independent, control code sequences are generated by CICS from format specifications defined outside the application program.

The CICS Basic Mapping Support (BMS) uses physical and symbolic maps to produce terminal-specific formatted displays. The maps are generated from BMS macro instruction sequences that must be assembled.

Physical maps define the message format. They are link-edited into a CICS load module library and are defined by an entry in the PPT. Physical maps are named with a terminal-identifying suffix; at execution time, when a BMS map command is executed, the physical map for the terminal device in use is loaded into the CICS region.

Symbolic maps are placed into source language libraries from which they are copied into the application program at compile time. Their purpose is to define symbolic names by which the program can refer to data contained in terminal input/output messages.

The chapter introduced the three BMS macro instructions, DFHMSD to define a *map set*, DFHMDI to define a *map*, and DFHMDF to define a *field* within a formatted display.

DISCUSSION QUESTIONS

1. Consider the native data stream shown in Figure 7-2.
   a. How would the stream have to be modified if the same format were to be displayed on a terminal device that supported an 80 character, instead of 40 character, screen width?
   b. If the display generated by the native stream in Figure 7-2 were defined by BMS maps, how would the BMS macros be modified to adapt to the 80 character wide screen?
   c. For the situation described in Part b, how would the application program have to be changed?

2. Assume that the user has entered the following data into the display shown in Figure 7-15:

   > 2839100 entered in CUSTOMER NO. field
   > 15.75   entered in AMOUNT field

   After reading from the device using map MAPA shown in Figure 7-18, what would be the value of each of the variables listed below?

   CUSTNOL   _____
   CUSTNOI   _____
   CUSTNAML   _____

CUSTNAMI	_____
AMOUNTL	_____
AMOUNTI	_____
CUSTNOO	_____
CUSTNAMO	_____
AMOUNTO	_____

3. In Figure 7-8, what would be the effect of omitting the comma after "STORAGE = AUTO"?

4. Assume the display shown in Figure 7-1 was produced using BMS.
   a. Where might the cursor be located just after the display is transmitted to the terminal?
   b. For each of the possible locations you listed for part a, how would the placement be achieved?

5. How many fields would you expect to see defined in a symbolic map used to generate the display shown in Figure 7-13?

6. For the display defined by the map shown in Figure 7-16, what would be the effect of the following changes?
   a. Add HILIGHT = BLINK to the DFHMDI macro
   b. Add HILIGHT = UNDERLINE to the DFHMDI macro and HILIGHT = BLINK to the DFHMSD macro
   c. Add HILIGHT = UNDERLINE to the DFHMDI macro, HILIGHT = REVERSE to the DFHMSD macro, and HILIGHT = BLINK to the second DFHMDF macro
   d. Same as part a plus add EXTATT = YES to the DFHMSD macro
   e. Same as part b plus add EXTATT = YES to the DFHMSD macro
   f. Same as part c plus add EXTATT = YES to the DFHMSD macro

EXERCISE

In this exercise, you are to prepare the BMS macro instructions to generate a physical and symbolic map for the panel shown in Figure 7-21. The map will be named ARMAPC1; it will be used for both input and output to an IBM 3270 Model 2. (You may find it helpful to refer to Figure 7-16 as an example.) Include parameters for both physical and symbolic maps, but specify that a physical map is to be generated.

Position all the fields as shown in the panel at the top of Figure 7-21; the lengths of the variable fields are shown in the table at the bottom of the figure. The X's in the display indicate data to be entered by the user, except that the TOTAL value will be computed and displayed by the application program. Assume that the title TOTAL is also to be supplied by the application program.

The leading line should be highlighted. The cursor should be positioned at the first data entry field, and should move automatically from the end of that field to the next unprotected field. Leave the cursor at the end of the last data entry field.

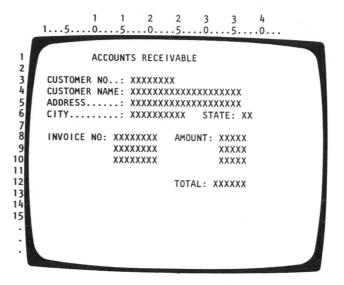

```
                    1   1   2   2   3   3   4
          1...5....0....5....0....5....0....5....0...
    1          ACCOUNTS RECEIVABLE
    2
    3     CUSTOMER NO..: XXXXXXXX
    4     CUSTOMER NAME: XXXXXXXXXXXXXXXXXXXX
    5     ADDRESS......: XXXXXXXXXXXXXXXXXXXX
    6     CITY.........: XXXXXXXXXX    STATE: XX
    7
    8     INVOICE NO: XXXXXXXX    AMOUNT: XXXXX
    9                 XXXXXXXX            XXXXX
   10                 XXXXXXXX            XXXXX
   11
   12                            TOTAL: XXXXXX
   13
   14
   15
    .
    .
    .
```

FIELD	NUMBER OF BYTES
CUSTOMER NO	8
CUSTOMER NAME	20 MAX.
ADDRESS	20 MAX.
CITY	10 MAX.
STATE	2
INVOICE NO	8
AMOUNT	5
TOTAL	6

Figure 7-21 Panel and File Format for Programming Exercise

8 BMS Input/Output Commands

Introduction

This chapter continues the discussion of CICS Basic Mapping Support (BMS). In the previous chapter, you saw the native data streams that are *transmitted to* a terminal device in order to produce a formatted panel. In this chapter, you will see what a native data stream looks like when it is *read from* the terminal device into the computer. Your program doesn't process these native data streams directly. Instead, the program issues a CICS command RECEIVE MAP command which causes BMS to map variable data from the native data stream into locations in working storage. BMS performs this mapping by using the symbolic BMS map.

In a similar way, your program uses a SEND MAP command to cause BMS to construct a native data stream for transmission *to the terminal device*. This chapter will introduce both the RECEIVE MAP and SEND MAP commands.

The BMS maps and commands are used to build formatted display panels that include several fields with different attributes. These panels are particularly useful for presenting information that comes from several fields of a data base record. Occasionally, however, you will need to display a full screen of information that is simply a long text message. For example, you may need to display *Help Text*—text that describes how to use a particular feature of an application. The text is too long to fit on a single line of the terminal screen, but it does not need to be divided into fields with different attributes. CICS supports this type of terminal message with the SEND TEXT command.

The second part of this chapter discusses the SEND TEXT command. It also introduces the technique of building a panel display with a series of SEND commands that do not cause transmission to the terminal. Each SEND command specifies the ACCUM parameter that directs BMS to build the native data stream for this SEND command, but to hold the stream in memory. Each SEND ACCUM command adds to the native data stream. When the native data stream for an entire panel has been built, you issue a SEND PAGE command to transmit the accumulated native data stream. In this chapter, you will see how SEND PAGE is used for unformatted text displays. In the next chapter, we will see how a similar technique can be used for panels built from BMS maps.

Objectives

After completing this chapter, you will be able to:

- Describe the native data stream *received from* an IBM 3270 terminal device.
- Discuss two ways to determine what key the user has pressed (ENTER, PF Key, or PA Key) to complete an input operation.
- Define the function of Modified Data Tags, and discuss how they are set and cleared.

- Write a CICS program to send and receive data using BMS maps.
- Write a CICS program to build a display containing an unformatted text message.

Part 1: Sending and Receiving BMS Maps

Input Data Streams

In Chapter 7, we looked at native data streams used to produce displays on the terminal device. But we haven't yet looked at a native data stream that is the result of *reading from* the terminal device. Your programs will not have to interpret these input data streams—just as they do not have to build the output data streams. But in order to know how to process input received from the terminal, you need to understand generally what is contained in a native input data stream. Our discussion applies to any terminal device that is compatible with the IBM 3270 terminal type.

Suppose that your program has used a SEND MAP command to display a panel that contains several *unprotected* fields. The user studies the panel, types information into one or more of the unprotected fields, and presses ENTER. CICS Terminal Control will then issue a read to the terminal. In response, Terminal Control receives a native input stream which contains data and control codes for only those *fields that were modified by the user*.

For example, consider the display shown in Figure 8-1.

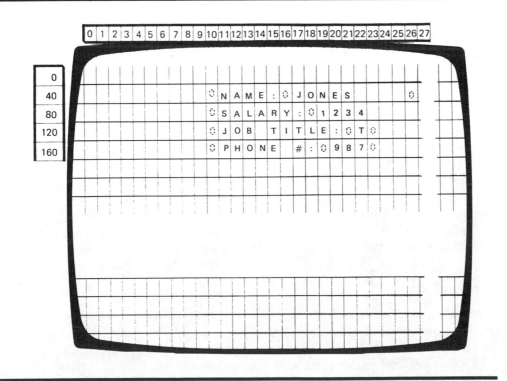

Figure 8-1
Example Terminal
Display

The display contains four unprotected fields, following the NAME, SALARY, JOB TITLE, and PHONE # titles respectively. Assume that the user has entered the values shown: JONES, 1234, T, and 987 into the unprotected fields. If the display were now read from the terminal device, the native stream shown in Figure 8-2 would be transmitted from the device to the computer. (Remember that the native stream transmitted from the terminal is not the form in which your application program will process the data. BMS will extract information from this stream and move it into working-storage locations specified in the symbolic map so that your program can process the input data.)

Notice, in Figure 8-2, that the fields that contained the *titles* (NAME, SALARY, JOB TITLE, and PHONE #) were not transmitted. These are protected fields that cannot be modified. Suppose that the user did not fill in all of the unprotected fields. For example, suppose the PHONE # field were left blank. Then the native data stream would not contain the unprotected field following PHONE #. Only fields that have been modified will appear in the native data stream.

Notice the control codes contained in the stream; most of them are familiar to you from the previous chapter's discussion of output streams. However, you have not seen the *Attention Identifier* (AID) byte before. The AID (Attention Identifier) byte occurs only in input streams. It specifies which terminal function the user employed to initiate the data transmission. For example, the user might have pressed the ENTER key, one of the Program Function (PF) keys, or a Program Attention (PA) key.

Modified Data Tags

Since the terminal device returns only modified fields, it must have some way to keep track of fields in the display and tell which fields have been modified. The mechanism used for this is called a Modified Data Tag (MDT). The terminal hardware maintains a MDT for each unprotected field being displayed. The MDT is associated with the beginning buffer address of the unprotected field. The hardware sets an MDT "on" when its associated field is modified.

MDT's can also be set and reset by commands from the computer. You may remember from the previous chapter that the FSET attribute parameter of the BMS DFHMDF macro can be used to force a field to be transmitted in response to a read command even if the user didn't modify the field. Now that you know about MDT's you can recognize that the FSET attribute works by causing BMS to send a command that sets the field's MDT on.

Once set, an MDT stays "on" until a command from the computer turns it off. You are responsible for making sure that MDT's are turned off (cleared) before you display each new panel. If an MDT is left on and another display is sent to the terminal, the leftover MDT will cause its associated buffer locations

**Figure 8-2
Data Stream Input
From Terminal**

S T X	C C	A I D	CURSOR POSITION	S B A	57	JONES	S B A	99	1234	S B A	142	T	S B A	180	987	E T X

to be transmitted as part of the next read—even though the buffer locations may not contain data meaningful for the current panel. Your program might go on to map these meaningless bytes into working-storage variables, resulting in an exception condition or incorrect results.

Later in this chapter, we will discuss several ways to clear MDT's.

Receiving BMS Maps

Now that you've seen what an input native data stream looks like, let's see what happens after the stream has been read. Assume that the Terminal Control Program has read the native stream into a TIOA. When an application program issues a *RECEIVE MAP* input mapping command, BMS removes the control characters, formats the data as specified by the input map, and places the formatted data into a buffer. The data may either be processed in the buffer or moved into your application program's working-storage, depending upon the parameters you code in the RECEIVE MAP command. In either case, your program accesses the input data by using the names defined in the symbolic map.

The previous chapter discussed the layout of data in a symbolic map. Remember that an input map defines three names for each field. You may want to refer back to that chapter's Figure 7-18 to review the layout of the input map.

Let's assume that, in the BMS symbolic map definition, you assigned the name CUSTNAM to the first field of the panel shown in Figure 8-1. Then the three names generated in the application program will be CUSTNAML, CUSTNAMF, and CUSTNAMI. When BMS has mapped the native stream from the terminal device, the working-storage locations defined by these names will have the following values:

CUSTNAML   The number of characters the user entered into the field. In the Figure 8-1 example, the value will be *5*.

CUSTNAMF   A flag byte. We will discuss this byte later in this section.

CUSTNAMI   The value entered by the user. In this case, *JONES*.

The first variable, CUSTNAML, is a two-byte field that gives the number of characters entered by the user. Therefore, the value must always be less than or equal to the length of the unprotected field itself. If the user enters no data in a field, the value will be zero.

A user may leave a field blank either by moving the cursor through the field or by pressing the End of Field (EOF) key. If the EOF key is used, the value in the length variable is unpredictable, but the *flag byte* (CUSTNAMF in this example) will be set to a hexadecimal 80.

Therefore, in order to tell whether the user has left a field blank, you check first the flag byte (CUSTNAMF) and then the LENGTH parameter (CUSTNAML).

The RECEIVE MAP Command

You use the RECEIVE MAP command to get data from a BMS map that has been read from the terminal. The RECEIVE MAP command is written.

EXEC CICS RECEIVE MAP (name) MAPSET (name)
           INTO (data-area)   I   SET (pointer-reference)
           TERMINAL [ASIS]   I   FROM (data-area)   LENGTH (data-value)

The names you specify in the MAP and MAPSET parameters are, respectively, the map name specified on the BMS DFHMDI macro and the generic map set name specified on the DFHMSD macro.

You can specify these names as literal constants, like:

EXEC CICS RECEIVE MAP('MAPA') MAPSET('MAPSET1') ...

You can also use variable names to specify the names. For example,

EXEC CICS RECEIVE MAP(MAPNAME) MAPSET(SETNAME) ...

The SET and INTO parameters are used much the same as in other RE-CEIVE commands you've used. However, with the RECEIVE MAP command, you have three choices: you may use either *SET* or *INTO*, or *neither*. Let's look at the three possibilities:

1. If your MAP parameter specified a literal constant like 'MAPA', you may omit both SET and INTO. In this case, BMS will map your input into the working storage-area defined by your symbolic map.

   If your MAP parameter specified a variable name, you must code either INTO or SET as described below.
2. The INTO parameter defines a data area for BMS to map the input data into. The data area must be laid out in the same format as a BMS input map, and must have space for all the named fields defined in the symbolic map.
3. The SET option specifies that BMS should obtain space to map the input data into. The space will be somewhere in the CICS region, but outside your program's working-storage. The SET parameter gives the name of a BLL Cell that defines the layout of the input area.

   There is one difference between the effect of a SET parameter in RECEIVE MAP commands and its effect in the commands you've used so far. Before, SET allowed your program to process input data from within the TIOA. This meant that CICS didn't have to move the data into another area. But in this case the TIOA contains *native stream data*—not the mapped data your program needs to process. Therefore, BMS must obtain new space from the CICS region, map the native data stream from the TIOA into the new space, and then return to your program. There is, therefore, some data movement performed even if you specify SET. However, since BMS maps into a storage location outside your program, using SET still saves space in program working-storage.

You will almost always use the TERMINAL parameter that is the default for the RECEIVE MAP command. TERMINAL specifies that the data to be received is located in the current *terminal buffer*. The alternative is to specify FROM which requests that BMS map native stream data that has been stored in a program location.

Normally when BMS maps terminal input, it converts any lowercase characters to uppercase. If your program needs to distinguish between lowercase and uppercase input, you should code the ASIS option of the TERMINAL parameter so that the conversion will not be done.

Interrogating the AID Byte

Recall that the native input stream contains an AID byte that tells how the user terminated the last input sequence—that is, whether the user pressed RE-TURN, used a PF Key, etc. However, notice that the symbolic BMS map does not provide any space for receiving this information. In order to check the contents of the AID byte, your program can examine a field in the Execution Interface Block called the EIBAID field. Whenever CICS processes any terminal input command, it moves the AID byte from the native input stream into the EIBAID field.

To make it easier to check EIBAID, CICS provides a source library member called DFHAID that defines a list of symbolic names you can use to stand for the hexadecimal code values. You use a COPY statement to include DFHAID in your program at compile time. Your program can then refer to the symbolic names defined by DFHAID. For example, to see whether the user pressed the ENTER key, you could use this COBOL statement:

IF EIBAID EQUAL DFH*ENTER* ...

DFHENTER is defined by DFHAID as the hexadecimal AID code for the ENTER key. If you didn't use DFHAID, you would have to look up the hexadecimal code and use it in the IF statement instead of the symbolic name DFHENTER.

Figure 8-3 shows the symbolic names defined in DFHAID.

You can also check the AID byte indirectly by providing an exception-handling routine for a particular attention type. This will be discussed in the "Exception Conditions" section of this chapter.

SYMBOLIC NAME	3270 FUNCTIONS
DFHCLEAR	CLEAR KEY
DFHENTER	ENTER KEY
DFHOPID	OPERATOR IDENTIFICATION CARD READER OR MAGNETIC SLOT READER (MSR)
DFHMSRE	EXTENDED (STANDARD) MSR
DFHTRIG	TRIGGER FIELD
DFHPA1	PA1 KEY
DFHPA2	PA2 KEY
DFHPA3	PA3 KEY
DFHPEN	LIGHT PEN ATTENTION
DFHPF1	PF1 KEY
DFHPF2	PF2 KEY
•	•
•	•
•	•
DFHPF24	PF24 KEY

Figure 8-3
Symbolic Names for Attention Sources

BMS Output Mapping

You've just seen how a RECEIVE MAP command causes BMS to move data variables *from* a native data stream *into* a symbolic map. Next we'll look at how your program causes data values to be moved *from* a symbolic map *into* a native data stream, ready for transmission to the terminal. The first step is to place the variable data to be displayed into the working-storage variables defined by the symbolic map. Then you issue a *SEND MAP* command to cause BMS to map the data from the symbolic map together with data in the physical map. The result is a native data stream that is placed into a TIOA for transmission to the terminal. Figure 8-4 illustrates the sequence.

Remember that the symbolic output map defines three variables for each data field. As shown at the top of the figure, the first two variables, define the *length* and *attributes* of the field. The third variable contains the data itself. Your program needs to supply a value only for the data variable itself—not for

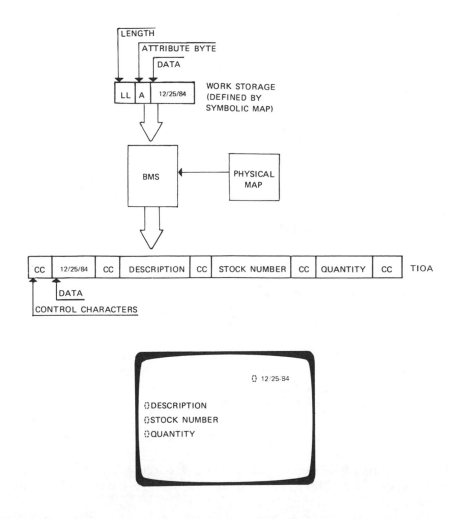

Figure 8-4
Building Output
Data Stream from
BMS Map

the length and attribute variables. For example, if the symbolic map named the first field on the panel as DATE, your program would place the value 12/25/84 into the variable DATEO. The variables DATEL and DATEA were set correctly when the BMS maps were generated.

The SEND MAP Command

The format of the CICS SEND MAP command is:

```
EXEC CICS SEND MAP (name) MAPSET (name)
                FROM (data-area) LENGTH (data-value)
                DATAONLY  ¦  MAPONLY
                ALARM
                CURSOR (data-value)
                ERASE  ¦  ERASEAUP
                FREEKB
                FRSET
```

The MAP and MAPSET parameters are as defined for the RECEIVE MAP command above.

FROM specifies the name of the work area that contains the data to be mapped. You must specify FROM if the MAP value is a variable name. If the program specifies the MAP value as a literal constant, you can omit FROM. In this case, BMS will use data from the work area defined by the symbolic map.

LENGTH need be specified only if the length of the data to be mapped is less than the total length of the area specified by the FROM option.

DATAONLY and MAPONLY indicate what information is to be included in the output mapping operation. There are three possibilities:

1. If neither DATAONLY nor MAPONLY are coded, BMS *merges* data from the symbolic map with constant data defined in the physical map. The resulting data stream, therefore, consists of *both fixed and variable* information.

2. MAPONLY indicates that *only constant* data defined in the physical map is to be displayed. That is, the panel would contain any characters you defined with the INITIAL parameter of DFHMDF macros as well as the attribute codes defined by the map. You would use MAPONLY to display a "blank panel" for data entry. The user would see a panel consisting of only title fields and blank unprotected fields. When you code MAPONLY you do not code FROM, because the physical map is the only source of data required.

3. DATAONLY is the converse of MAPONLY. It specifies that *only variable data*, located in the symbolic map or FROM area, is to be transmitted. Suppose a panel is currently displayed that shows data from record N of a data file. Now you want to display data from record N+1. Instead of retransmitting the entire panel, including title information that is constant, you would use the DATAONLY parameter. BMS would then map and transmit only the data fields found in record N+1.

The remaining parameters specify control functions related to the physical characteristics of IBM 3270 type terminals. Some of these functions can also be specified in the physical BMS map.

ERASE causes the screen to be erased before the requested map is displayed.

ERASEAUP specifies that only the unprotected fields be erased. ERASEAUP causes all MDT's to be reset and leaves only constant fields on the screen.

FRSET resets all MDT's set by previous data entry operations, but does not alter the data visible on the screen.

FREEKB causes the keyboard to be unlocked as soon as the panel has been displayed on the terminal. The keyboard locks automatically as soon as the user sends input to CICS—for example, when the user presses the ENTER key. The keyboard remains locked until a program unlocks it or the user presses the RESET key. If you want the keyboard to be unlocked *every time any map in an entire mapset is displayed*, you can specify CTRL = FREEKB in the BMS *DFHMSD* macro.

CURSOR specifies the buffer position at which the cursor should be displayed. The argument value must be a halfword binary value in the range zero to the size of the screen being used. This parameter overrides any cursor position specified in the BMS maps. Notice, however, that the position of the cursor will depend upon the size of the screen. For example, if a screen's width is 40 bytes, byte 45 will be the fifth column of the second line. If the screen's width is 80, byte 45 will be close to the middle of the first line. The technique is also error-prone. If you change the map, you must remember to change the CURSOR argument. You can also easily miscalculate and specify a buffer location in a protected area of the screen. Because of these disadvantages, you should use either of the following two alternative methods to position the cursor:

1. Code the IC attribute in the DFHMDF macro for the field in which you want the cursor to be positioned.
2. Move the value minus one (– 1) into the length value for the field in which the cursor is to be placed. Then code CURSOR *without an argument value* in your SEND MAP command. BMS will place the cursor in the first field for which it finds a length value of minus one. (This overrides the effect of any IC attributes specified in the BMS map.)

ALARM indicates that the IBM 3270 audible alarm should be sounded when the map is displayed.

The ERASEAUP function can be requested, as described above, by a parameter of the SEND command. It may also be requested in an independent command:

EXEC CICS ISSUE ERASEAUP END-EXEC.

Like the ERASEAUP parameter, the effect of the command is to clear all unprotected fields and reset any MDT's. In addition, the command positions the cursor in the first unprotected field and unlocks the keyboard.

Exception Conditions

There are two common exception conditions that may occur during BMS SEND or RECEIVE operations.

MAPFAIL occurs during input mapping if the native data stream contains no Set Buffer Address (SBA) character. This usually indicates that the user has accidentally pressed ENTER (or a PA key or PF key) before entering any data. Ordinarily, every native data stream will contain an SBA unless the user entered no data at all in a formatted screen, or the display received had not been formatted by BMS. This second case would occur if the user had just begun a session by entering a transaction request, but your program issued a RECEIVE MAP instead of a RECEIVE command.

The invalid map size condition, INVMPSZ, occurs if the map size specified exceeds the width of the display screen.

It is possible that both exception conditions may occur during the same operation; in this case the MAPFAIL condition will be raised before INVMPSZ.

The HANDLE AID Command

Besides defining exception-handling routines for MAPFAIL and INVMPSZ, you may also define a routine to receive control for various types of attention conditions. Then, whenever the user presses one of these keys, CICS will transfer control to the routine you specified for that key. This is an alternative to examining the EIBAID location after a RECEIVE command.

The HANDLE AID command is written:

> EXEC CICS HANDLE AID   keyname (label) ... keyname (label)

Keyname names a possible source of the terminal attention signal. For example:

PA1, PA2, etc. name Program Attention keys.
PF1, PF2, etc. name Program Function keys.
CLEAR or ENTER, which specify the keys of the same name.
ANYKEY for attention from any PA Key, any PF Key, or the CLEAR key if you have *not specified* the key in a HANDLE AID command.

For example:

> EXEC CICS HANDLE AID PA1 (RETRY) PF3 (QUIT)
> (where RETRY and QUIT are labels defined in your program)

Assume that the user causes an attention signal and your program issues a RECEIVE MAP command to receive the input. After completing the RECEIVE MAP command, CICS will transfer control to the handling routine defined for the attention-signalling key pressed by the user. If the user pressed a key you had not specified in a HANDLE AID command, control will return to the program statement following the RECEIVE MAP command. If an exception condition occurs during the RECEIVE MAP operation for which a HANDLE AID applies, the AID–handling routine will receive control before the exception–handling routine.

Programming Example

Before you begin work on the Exercise for this chapter, you may find it helpful to look at a CICS program that uses many of the features we've discussed.

Figure 8-5 shows a segment of a COBOL program to browse through the same NAME, AMOUNT, NUMBER file you have used in programming exercises. The user's transaction request specifies the key of the first record to be retrieved. The program retrieves four records, beginning with the requested record, and places the data into a BMS map for display. Figure 8-6 shows the BMS map and the panel it produces. Notice the messages at the bottom of the panel. They describe how the user can specify whether to browse forward or backward from the current position. The first field on the panel is unprotected. The user can type the *next request* specification in this field or use a PF Key. The user can also press PF3 to terminate the program.

```
                    IDENTIFICATION DIVISION
                    PROGRAM-ID. BROWSE.
                    ENVIRONMENT DIVISION.
                    DATA DIVISION.
                    WORKING-STORAGE SECTION.
                        77   I  PIC 999 USAGE IS COMP.
                        77   KEY PIC 9(6) VALUE IS ZERO.
                        01   FILEA.
                            02  FILEREC.
                                03 STAT PICTURE X.
                                03 NUMB PICTURE X(6).
                                03 NAME PICTURE X(20).
                                03 ADDRX PICTURE X(20).
                                03 PHONE PICTURE X(8).
                                03 DATEX PICTURE X(8).
                                03 AMOUNT PICTURE X(8).
                                03 COMMENT PICTURE X(9).
                        01   MAPC  COPY  MAPC.
                    PROCEDURE DIVISION.
```
(1)
```
                    EXEC CICS HANDLE CONDITION ERROR (ERRORS)
                            MAPFAIL (BAD-INPUT)
                            NOTFND (NOTFOUND)
                            ENDFILE (ENDFILE) END-EXEC.
                    EXEC CICS HANDLE AID  PF3 (END-IT)
                            PF1 (PAGE-FORWARD)
                            PF2 (PAGE-BACKWARD)  END-EXEC.
                               .
                               .
                               .
```
(2)
```
                    EXEC CICS STARTBR DATASET ('FILEA') RIDFLD (KEY) END-EXEC.
                    PAGE-FORWARD.
                      MOVE 1 TO I.
                    NEXT-LINE.
                      EXEC CICS READNEXT INTO (FILEA) DATASET ('FILEA')
```
(3)
```
                                    RIDFLD (KEY) END-EXEC.
                      IF STAT EQUAL HIGH-VALUE THEN GO TO NEXT-LINE.
                      IF I=1 MOVE NUMB TO NUMBER10
                            THEN MOVE NAME TO NAME10
```
(4)
```
                            THEN MOVE AMOUNT TO AMOUNT10.
                      IF I=2 ...
                               .
                               .
                               .
                      ADD 1 TO I.
                      IF I NOT EQUAL 5 GO TO NEXT-LINE.
```
(5)
```
                    DISPLAY-RECORD.
                      EXEC CICS SEND MAP ('MAPC') ERASE END-EXEC.
```
(6)
```
                    REPEAT.
                      EXEC CICS RECEIVE MAP ('MAPC') END-EXEC.
```
(7)
```
                      IF DIRI EQUAL 'F' THEN GO TO PAGE-FORWARD.
                      IF DIRI EQUAL 'B' THEN GO TO PAGE-BACKWARD.
                      GO TO BAD-INPUT.
                               .
                               .
                               .
```

**Figure 8-5
Program Example,
Using BMS Map to
Report Browse Results**

MAPC Definition

```
MAPSET      DFHMSD  TYPE=&SYSPARM, MODE=INOUT, CTRL=(FREEKB,FRSET),          X
                    LANG=COBOL,TIOAPFX=YES,EXTATT=YES
MAPC        DFHMDI  SIZE=(13,40)
DIR         DFHMDF  POS=(1,1),LENGTH=1,ATTRB=(BRT,UNPROT,IC)
            DFHMDF  POS=(1,3),LENGTH=1,ATTRB=(ASKIP)     FIELD STOPPER
            DFHMDF  POS=(1,15),LENGTH=11,INITIAL='FILE BROWSE',              X
                    COLOR=BLUE,HILIGHT=UNDERLINE
            DFHMDF  POS=(3,1),LENGTH=6,INITIAL='NUMBER',COLOR=BLUE
            DFHMDF  POS=(3,17),LENGTH=4,INITIAL='NAME',COLOR=BLUE
            DFHMDF  POS=(3,32),LENGTH=6,INITIAL='AMOUNT',COLOR=BLUE
NUMBER1     DFHMDF  POS=(4,1),LENGTH=6
AMOUNT1     DFHMDF  POS=(4,30),LENGTH=8
NAME1       DFHMDF  POS=(4,9),LENGTH=20
NUMBER2     DFHMDF  POS=(4,1),LENGTH=6
AMOUNT2     DFHMDF  POS=(4,30),LENGTH=8
NAME2       DFHMDF  POS=(4,9),LENGTH=20
NUMBER3     DFHMDF  POS=(4,1),LENGTH=6
AMOUNT3     DFHMDF  POS=(4,30),LENGTH=8
NAME3       DFHMDF  POS=(4,9),LENGTH=20
NUMBER4     DFHMDF  POS=(4,1),LENGTH=6
AMOUNT4     DFHMDF  POS=(4,30),LENGTH=8
NAME4       DFHMDF  POS=(4,9),LENGTH=20
MSG1        DFHMDF  POS=(11,1),LENGTH=39,COLOR=BLUE,                         X
                    INITIAL='PRESS PF1 OR TYPE F TO PAGE FORWARD    '
MSG2        DFHMDF  POS=(12,1),LENGTH=39,COLOR=BLUE,                         X
                    INITIAL='PRESS PF2 OR TYPE B TO PAGE BACKWARD   '
MSG3        DFHMDF  POS=(13,1),LENGTH=39,COLOR=RED,                          X
                    INITIAL='PRESS PF3 TO TERMINATE                 '
```

```
                    FILE BROWSE

     _

     NUMBER          NAME              AMOUNT
     #####   nnnnnnnnnnnnnnnnnnnn  $$$$$$$$$
     #####   nnnnnnnnnnnnnnnnnnnn  $$$$$$$$$
     #####   nnnnnnnnnnnnnnnnnnnn  $$$$$$$$$
     #####   nnnnnnnnnnnnnnnnnnnn  $$$$$$$$$



     PRESS PF1 OR TYPE F TO PAGE FORWARD
     PRESS PF2 OR TYPE B TO PAGE BACKWARD
     PRESS PF3 TO TERMINATE
```

Figure 8-6
BMS Map Defined
for Program Example

Let's go through the program in some detail:

1. The program begins by defining exception-handling routines for the BMS exception MAPFAIL, the file-handling conditions NOTFND and ENDFILE, and the general condition ERROR. It then issues a HANDLE AID command specifying that control should transfer to END-IT if the user presses PF3, PAGE-FORWARD for PF1, and PAGE-BACKWARD for PF2. (To conserve space, only the PAGE-FORWARD label is included in the illustration.)

2. Assume that the key for the first record to be retrieved is in the working-storage variable KEY. The program initiates the browse with the STARTBR command, then continues through the PAGE-FORWARD code to the NEXT-LINE loop.

3. The READNEXT command reads a record into FILEA, using the key value in KEY. If the retrieved record has been marked *deleted* (STAT EQUAL HIGH-VALUE), it is ignored.

4. The NUMBER, NAME, and AMOUNT values from the record are then moved into the BMS map MAPC. The figure shows the program statements required to move values into the first output line (NUMBER1, NAME1, and AMOUNT1) in the map. Notice that the *output* symbolic map names, like NUMBER1O are used.

5. After placing data from four records into the BMS map, the program issues the SEND MAP command to display the map.

6. The RECEIVE MAP command awaits the user's input. After scanning the panel, the user may press PF3, PF1, or PF2. If so, the HANDLE AID command executed earlier causes control to transfer to END-IT, PAGE-FORWARD, or PAGE-BACKWARD respectively.

   Control passes *after* the RECEIVE MAP command is completed. Notice that, since the user has not typed into the panel, no SBA character is transmitted and the RECEIVE MAP command will raise the MAPFAIL condition. However, the HANDLE AID takes precedence over the HANDLE CONDITION. CICS transfers control to the routine specified to handle the PF Key, not the routine specified to handle the MAPFAIL condition.

7. Instead of pressing a PF Key, the user might type a character into the DIR field on the screen and then press ENTER. In this case, control returns to the statement following the RECEIVE command. The program then tests the value of DIR (note that the *input* symbolic map name DIRI is used), and transfers to PAGE-FORWARD, PAGE-BACKWARD, or BAD-INPUT, depending upon the contents of DIRI.

   Suppose the user accidentally presses *PF4*. If the user had typed nothing into the panel before pressing the PF Key, the MAPFAIL exceptional condition would be raised and control would transfer to BAD-INPUT.

   Assume, on the other hand, that the user had typed into the panel before pressing PF4. Since the program has not specified a routine to handle PF4, control would return to the statement following the RECEIVE command. If the user had typed an F or B into the panel before pressing the PF Key, the Forward or Backward request would be honored. Otherwise, the program would transfer control to BAD-INPUT.

Part 2: Text Building

So far, we have discussed how to send and receive short one-line messages and formatted full-screen panels. In many situations, however, you will need to display a "page" or several lines of text. No formatting is required except that the text must be displayed within margins determined by the width of the display device. You may also want to display a header line at the top of the panel and a trailer line at the bottom, and you may want to display a page number in either the header or trailer line. This type of requirement is referred to as *text building*. Notice that text building is very similar to a *text printing* requirement. That is, the display panel will look like a page of printed text. In fact, the techniques we will discuss here may be used to send text to a printer terminal as well as to a display device.

Text-Building Example

Figure 8-7 shows an example of a page of *Help Text* that is to be displayed at the user's terminal.

This page includes a *header line* that includes a page number, and a *trailer line* as well as the text itself. For the present, let's focus only on the text.

Assume that the text of the message is stored as a single-character string within a program's working-storage. There are no subfields within the text, the entire string is to be displayed without special attributes. The user will not modify the text, so the program has no need to move received data into working-storage. Only one service is required from BMS—to segment the text according to the width of the terminal device in use. This is referred to as the BMS *Text Building* support.

Figure 8-7 shows how the text would look on a 40 column screen. Figure 8-8 shows the same text as BMS would display it on a 20 column screen.

BMS segments the text stream into lines that will fit on the display screen, breaking the stream at word boundaries. The application program may insert *New Line* characters into the stream to cause line breaks for paragraphing or other required text patterns. For example, the character string defined within the program would include a New Line character before the sentence beginning, "You may also... ."

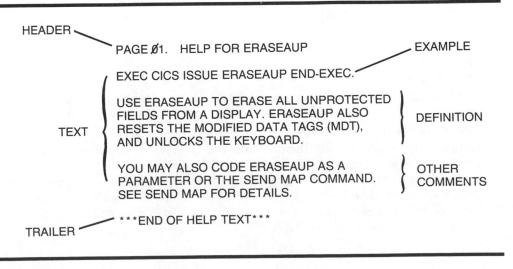

Figure 8-7
Example of Text-
Building Display

```
PAGE 01.   HELP FOR ERASEAUP

EXEC CICS ISSUE ERASEAUP
END-EXEC.

USE ERASEAUP TO ERASE ALL
UNPROTECTED FIELDS FROM A
DISPLAY. ERASEAUP ALSO
RESETS THE MODIFIED DATA
TAGS (MDT), AND UNLOCKS THE
KEYBOARD.

YOU MAY ALSO CODE ERASEAUP
AS A PARAMETER OF THE SEND
MAP COMMAND. SEE THE SEND MAP
FOR DETAILS.

***END OF HELP TEXT***
```

**Figure 8-8
Text-Building
Display Formatted
for Narrow Screen**

CICS provides text building support through BMS. You can use a single SEND command to transmit the entire page, or you can use a series of SEND commands to build a complete page in memory. For example, suppose the text is stored in three sections within your program. The first section is the *Example* line that shows how ERASEAUP is specified in the ISSUE command. Next comes a *Definition* section that tells what ERASEAUP does. Last is an *Other Comments* section—in this case, the comment about ERASEAUP as a SEND MAP parameter. Your program could issue three SEND TEXT commands, one for each section of the text, but specify that the text is simply to be *accumulated* in a buffer rather than being sent to the terminal. After the complete message had been built, you would issue a SEND PAGE command to display the complete message at once.

You can build long messages that are longer than a single page. That is, they must be displayed as a series of panels. In this chapter, we will discuss only single-page text displays; the following chapter will describe facilities for multiple-page text displays.

You don't use BMS *maps* in order to do text building, because the display panel is not separated into fields with different attributes.

Application Programming for Text Building

If the text you want to display is constant, you can simply define it within your program as a series of character string constants. Or your program might read the text from a data file into working-storage character strings. When you send text to be formatted, BMS begins with the first nonblank character in the text stream. Therefore, if you want blanks to appear at the beginning of a line, you must code a nondisplayable nonblank character followed by blanks and then by the text for display.

To send the text, you code a SEND TEXT command like:

```
EXEC CICS SEND TEXT FROM (data-area)
          LENGTH (data-value) [ERASE]
```

The parameters are all as defined for previous versions of the SEND command. Notice that the LENGTH parameter is required. It specifies the length of the text stream, not the line length for the display. If the length of the text exceeds the capacity of the screen, BMS will display the data in multiple pages. However, the resulting display may not be satisfactory from the standpoint of user convenience. Generally speaking, you should either insure that the text can be displayed in a single page or use the page-building facilities described in the next chapter.

Building Multiple-Block Text Displays

The SEND TEXT command in the form just described causes the text to be transmitted immediately to the terminal. However, sometimes you may need to *accumulate* an entire page a little at a time. For example, suppose you are reading text from a direct access file. The text to be displayed may be in several different records that you want to combine on a single display panel. Instead of reading all the records and then formatting them all at once, you might want to read a record and format it before reading the next record. But instead of transmitting each piece as it's formatted, and letting the user see the panel "grow" gradually, you can hold the formatted text in memory and then transmit it all at once when you've built the entire page. This is more efficient because it requires only one terminal output operation per page. When you format a panel this way, the display is called a *multiple-block* display. Each section of the display that is formatted at one time is called a *block*.

You can use these optional parameters to build a multiple-block display:

```
ACCUM
HEADER (data-area)
TRAILER (data-area)
JUSTIFY (data-value)   I   JUSFIRST   I   JUSLAST
CURSOR (data-value)
```

The *ACCUM* parameter indicates that this SEND TEXT command is part of a cumulative text building operation. When ACCUM has been specified, the text in the FROM area will be formatted but not transmitted until you issue another BMS command, SEND PAGE. We will describe the SEND PAGE command in the next section.

HEADER indicates that the specified data area contains information that is to be formatted at the top of the page being constructed. The line PAGE 01. HELP FOR ERASEAUP in Figure 8-7 is an example of a header block.

TRAILER is similar to HEADER except that trailer information is formatted at the bottom of the page. If BMS is forced to segment the text into multiple pages, the TRAILER specified here will appear at the end of each succeeding page. The concluding line ***END OF HELP TEXT*** in Figure 8-7 is an example of a trailer block.

Your program must construct header and trailer blocks in the format described in the section "Preparing Header and Trailer Data."

JUSTIFY, JUSFIRST, and JUSLAST allow you to align a block of text vertically on the page. The three options are mutually exclusive; their meanings are:

JUSTIFY specifies the display line number at which the first line of the page is to be displayed. The data must be expressed as a halfword binary value. JUSFIRST specifies that the data is to be placed at the top of the display. JUSLAST specifies that the data is to be positioned at the bottom of the page.

CURSOR specifies the character position in which the cursor is to be displayed when the page is displayed. It is a halfword binary value greater than zero.

Not shown is the NOEDIT parameter which specifies that BMS should not insert device-dependent control characters like carriage return, line feed, etc. If NOEDIT is specified, the application program must insert the characters as required. Notice that, in this case, the application program becomes both device and format-dependent. Therefore, you will not normally use the NOEDIT option.

The SEND PAGE Command

After you have issued SEND TEXT ACCUM commands to build the entire multi-block message, you use a SEND PAGE command to transmit the message to the user's terminal. SEND PAGE is written:

EXEC CICS SEND PAGE [TRAILER(data-area)]

The optional TRAILER parameter causes the information in *data area* to be formatted at the bottom of the last page. You can specify TRAILER here rather than as a parameter of the SEND TEXT ACCUM command to insure that the trailer appears only on the *last page* of the text message. Your program must construct the trailer block in the format described under "Preparing Header and Trailer Data."

Program Example

Figure 8-9 shows the sequence of SEND commands required to produce the panel shown in Figure 8-7, including the header and trailer lines. Assume that the header text has been built in the working-storage area HEAD, the trailer in END-HELP, the example command in EXAMPLE, the definition in DEF, and the other comments in COMMENTS.

The trailer block is specified in the SEND PAGE command rather than in a SEND TEXT ACCUM command. The result is the same so long as the entire page, with header and trailer, can fit on a single page of the output device.

Figure 8-9
Example Text-Building Command Sequence

```
EXEC CICS SEND TEXT FROM (EXAMPLE)
          LENGTH (30) ACCUM
          HEADER (HEAD)
          ERASE   END-EXEC.

EXEC CICS SEND TEXT FROM (DEFINE)
          LENGTH (120) ACCUM
          END-EXEC.

EXEC CICS SEND TEXT FROM (COMMENTS)
          LENGTH (80) ACCUM
          END-EXEC.

EXEC CICS SEND PAGE TRAILER (TRAIL)
          END-EXEC.
```

Preparing Header and Trailer Data

Your program must construct header and trailer blocks in the format illustrated by Figure 8-10.

The meaning of each field is:

LL a two-byte field that contains the length of the *data*, not including the prefix.
P defines a character that will be used to specify the position of the page number in the block. If automatic page numbering is not required, as in the case of a single-page display, this one-byte field should contain a blank character.
C is a one-byte control field used by BMS.
DATA is the text of the header or trailer information. It may contain new-line characters. If you want a page number to appear in the header or trailer line, DATA will contain a field for the page number. In the figure, this field is shown as PPPPP, because you define the field by using the P character described above. The field you define for the page number may be up to five bytes in length.

Suppose you want the page number to appear after the characters *Page No.* in a header block, and you have specified the character $ in the P field described above. Then you would define the DATA part of the header block as Page No. $$$$$. BMS will replace the $ field with the current page number. Leading zeros are not suppressed. Note that the page number field may occur anywhere after the four-byte prefix field of the header or trailer. Each new SEND PAGE command causes the page number to be reset to 1.

Figure 8-11 shows how the header block for the panel shown in Figure 8-7 would be constructed. Notice that the length field value does not include the length of the prefix area. The character used to mark the page number field is #.

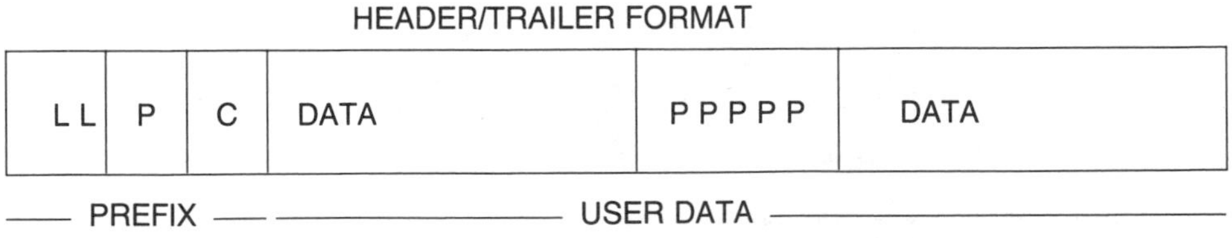

HEADER/TRAILER FORMAT

L L	P	C	DATA		P P P P P	DATA

—— PREFIX —— ——————— USER DATA ———————

**Figure 8-10
Format of Header and Trailer Areas for Text-Building**

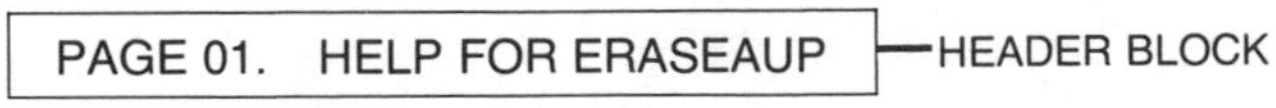

PAGE 01. HELP FOR ERASEAUP ├─HEADER BLOCK

PROGRAM DEFINITION

```
01 HEAD.
   02    FILLER      PIC S9(4)   COMP VALUE (27).
   02    FILLER      PIC XX   VALUE '#'.
   02    HDRDATA     PIC X(27)   VALUE 'PAGE ##.   HELP FOR ERASEAUP'.
```

**Figure 8-11
Example Header Area Coded for Text-Building Display**

Summary

The native data stream transmitted *from* an IBM 3270 terminal contains control codes and data for only those fields whose Modified Data Tags (MDT) have been set. The terminal hardware sets an MDT when a user modifies a field at the terminal, or when the BMS map forces the MDT "on." When you send a new display to the terminal, you must ensure that all MDT's are cleared—that is, reset to "off."

MDT's are cleared when:

1. You erase the screen by coding the ERASE parameter in a SEND command or by executing an ISSUE ERASE command.
2. You erase the *unprotected* areas of the screen by coding the ERASEAUP parameter in a SEND command or by executing an ISSUE ERASEAUP command.
3. You SEND a map for which you have coded the CTRL = FRSET option in the DFHMSD macro.
4. You code the FRSET option on a SEND command.

When an application program issues the RECEIVE MAP command, BMS removes control codes from the native stream in the TIOA and formats the data as specified by the input map. The application program can then access the data using names defined in the BMS symbolic map.

During an input operation an Attention Identifier (AID) byte is transmitted as part of the native stream. BMS places the AID byte into the EIBAID field of the EIB where it can be interrogated by the application program. An application program may also use the HANDLE AID command to define handling routines for the various possible attention sources.

The SEND MAP command is used to transmit a display defined by BMS maps to the terminal. An application program may specify that only the constant parts of a map, only the variable parts of a map, or the entire map be transmitted. Various device control functions may also be requested in the SEND MAP command.

BMS also supports display of *text information* that has not been defined by physical and symbolic maps. When an application program issues a SEND TEXT command, BMS formats the text stream by segmenting it into lines of length appropriate to the width of the terminal device. A SEND TEXT ACCUM command can be used to cause BMS to format the text block, but to hold it in a buffer rather than transmitting it immediately. You can issue several SEND TEXT ACCUM commands in order to accumulate an entire text block for display. When the entire block has been formatted, you issue a SEND PAGE command to transmit the block to the terminal. BMS text building support can also display header and trailer information that you have constructed according to a required format.

DISCUSSION QUESTIONS

1. How can you tell that the native stream shown in Figure 8-2 is an input stream?
2. Figure 4 illustrates an output stream generated by BMS:
   a. What can you say about the use of the DATAONLY and MAPONLY parameters in the SEND command that transmitted this stream?

b. How many fields are represented in the stream?

c. Apart from the STX and ETX transmission codes, do you think the stream is complete? Why?

d. Assume that after reading the screen, the user presses the ENTER key. What would be the result?

3. A working-storage location OPINSTR is defined as follows:

> PICTURE X(22) VALUE 'ENTER PAGING COMMANDS.'

Code a command to display this message.

EXERCISE

In this exercise, you will use the maps generated in the last chapter's exercise. Refer back to Figure 7-21 of the previous chapter if you need to review the screen layout.

Your program should begin by displaying the map ARMAPC1 on the terminal.

The user will enter data in the unprotected fields and press the ENTER key. Your program will receive the map and compute the AMOUNT total.

Next the program will send the TOTAL title and value to the terminal and terminate the task.

If the user presses PF1, your program should clear the screen of any data entered and allow the user to start over.

The user may also use the CLEAR key to cancel the task. If the task is cancelled, display the message *TRANSACTION CANCELLED* and terminate the task.

9 Advanced Mapping Applications

Introduction

The previous chapter discussed two types of message panels:

1. a formatted panel defined by a BMS *map*,
2. a text panel, consisting of one or more text *blocks* and optional header and trailer *blocks.*

In this chapter, you will learn to produce two additional types of formatted message:

1. A single panel consisting of *several* BMS maps and optional header and trailer *maps.* We will refer to a panel made up of several BMS maps as a *page-formatted panel.*
2. A message, consisting either of BMS maps or text blocks, which is made up of a *series of panels.* This is referred to as a *multi-page* message. The user views the message a panel at a time by entering terminal commands to request "next page, please," "back up a page," or "display page *n.*"

In the second part of the chapter, you will learn how to send any of these four types of messages to a terminal other than the terminal that was used to initiate the transaction. Using this facility, called *message routing,* a user can invoke a CICS transaction to produce a formatted message and then send the message to other users or to another terminal—for example, to a high-quality printer.

Objectives

After completing this chapter, you will be able to:

- Discuss the rules for displaying several BMS maps on a single panel.
- Distinguish between multi-page formatted messages and multi-block unformatted messages.
- Write a program to produce a single-page formatted panel.
- Write a program to produce a multi-page, formatted, message.
- Describe how a user controls display of a multi-page, formatted, message.
- Write a program to route a message to another terminal (*not* the terminal used to invoke your program).

Part 1: Advanced Mapping to the Direct Terminal

In Part 1 of this chapter, we will discuss:

1. Building panels that consist of several BMS maps.
2. Building a *formatted* message that exceeds a single panel in length.

Using Multiple BMS Maps in a Single Panel

The exercise for the chapter "Sequential Access of Random Files" required a program to browse sequentially through an accounts receivable file, find all the records showing a balance greater than 50, and then report how many such records were found.

In many situations the user needs to see, not the summary count of "records found," but *detail information* from each record found. In the accounts receivable example, the user might ask for a program to "browse the file and whenever you find a record with a balance greater than 50, display the account number, name, and phone number." The account number, name, and phone number would be the detail information required from each record.

Your program will produce an output message that consists of an optional header, then a *detail message* for each of the records you found, and an optional trailer record at the bottom of the panel. Each detail message will be in the same format—in fact, it will be defined by a single BMS map—but each time it appears it shows information from a different record in the accounts file.

The detail message in this example would probably fit on a single line of the display screen. However, you can format the detail in any way you wish by describing the layout in a BMS map. A BMS map used for this purpose is referred to as a *detail map.*

Figure 9-1 shows a panel produced for a transaction of this kind. Here the display is a single page and is made up of three maps: a header map that contains title information, a detail map that reports account number, account name, and account balance, and a trailer map that gives the total of all the balances displayed. Notice that the single detail map is displayed five times. The display shown results from seven output requests by the application program: one for the header map, five repetitions of the detail map, and one for the trailer map.

As we will discuss, header and trailer maps are special types of BMS maps. They are not the same as the header and trailer *blocks* discussed in the text-building section of the preceding chapter. Remember that text building did not use BMS maps.

Figure 9-1 is a simplified example because the five repetitions of the detail map fit on the display screen at the same time. When we refer to Figure 9-1s display as *single-page* display, we are defining *page* for a terminal device as "the area of the terminal on which data can be displayed or printed at one time".

We will also discuss the common situation in which a transaction may produce more information than can fit on a single page. Figure 9-2 shows a multiple-page message similar to the single-page message shown in Figure 9-1.

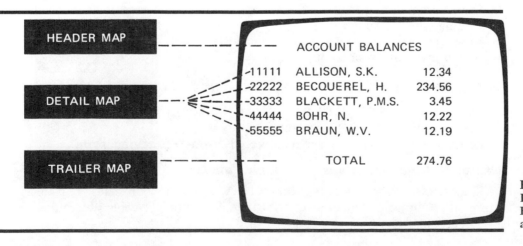

Figure 9-1
Panel showing
Header, Trailer,
and Detail Maps

```
    ACCOUNT BALANCES      PAGE 1              ACCOUNT BALANCES      PAGE 2

    11111  ALLISON, S.K.      12.34           74567   GAMOW, G.          30.15
    22222  BECQUEREL, H.     234.56           75678   GEIGER, H.         55.75
    33333  BLACKETT, P.M.      3.45           87891   HAHN, O.           14.10
    44444  BOHR, N.           12.22
    55555  BRAUN, W.V.        12.19                   PAGE TOTAL        100.00
    61234  COCKCROFT, J.      25.00                   FINAL TOTAL       474.76
    62345  EINSTEIN, A.       15.00
    63456  FERMI, E.          60.00

           PAGE TOTAL    374.76
```

Figure 9-2
Example of Multiple-Page Message

Each page of the message in Figure 9-2 is made up of a header map, a detail map, and a trailer map. In this case, the header map contains a variable page number. The final page of the message, shown to the right, actually has two trailer maps. The first is the same as the trailer map on the first page; it gives the total for the detail shown on the *page*. The second trailer map gives the total for *all pages* of the output message; it will appear only on the last page of the message.

Multi-Page Messages: User's View

In order to use a transaction that produces a multi-page message like the one shown in Figure 9-2, a user goes through four steps.

1. Enter a transaction request.
2. Receive a panel like the one in Figure 9-2. It contains the type of detail information the user requested; however, the message makes it obvious in some way that this is the first page of a multi-page message. That is, the user must be able to recognize that there is more information waiting to be displayed. The example of Figure 9-2 does not make this very clear; here the user has to know that "the transaction isn't over until the FINAL TOTAL appears."
3. Read the displayed page of the message and, when ready, *signal that the next page may be displayed*. We will see that there is a standard BMS procedure by which the user controls the paging operation.
4. Continue paging through the output message until the entire message has been received. The final page of the message should contain some indication that there is no more information to follow; in Figure 9-2, this is indicated by the FINAL TOTAL map.

Multi-Page Messages: Programming View

From the programmer's point of view, there are four steps that the application program must perform.

1. It must define how the message is to "look" on the terminal device. In the context of BMS, this is done in terms of BMS maps, including two new types of map: the header and trailer maps.
2. The program must build the output message. It does so by using BMS output

commands with an ACCUM option similar to the command we discussed for text building. Again, however, it is important to remember that text building did not involve the use of BMS maps.

3. As the message is built, the program must recognize when a terminal page is full so that it can display the proper trailer map(s) and begin a new page. Remember that when the program is written, there is no way to know what type of terminal will be used to initiate the transaction. Therefore, *page full* can be detected only at execution time. When a message has exceeded the terminal's page size, CICS informs the program by raising an exceptional condition, OVERFLOW. This causes a condition-handling routine called the *overflow processing* routine to be invoked.

4. Building the message, as described in steps 2 and 3, is distinct from *displaying* the message. Once the complete message, called the logical message, has been built the program must transmit it to the terminal. It does so with a SEND command, using options that will be introduced later in the chapter. The application program SENDs an entire message at once. However the page-by-page display of multi-page messages is performed by BMS in response to paging control signals from the user. Thus, display of multi-page messages is a responsibility shared between the application program and BMS. The application program provides control fields in each page of the display to permit the user to enter paging commands. BMS interprets and responds to the commands entered in the control fields.

There is a final programming requirement that may not be immediately obvious. Consider a multi-page transaction in the context of resource utilization. It may take the user several minutes to study the detail information for each record in a page of the display. If the application program had to remain in the CICS region, waiting for the user to read the entire message, the memory resource would not be used efficiently. Therefore, the application program needs to be able to handle the paging in a pseudo-conversational manner.

The next sections of this chapter will discuss each of the programming requirements in detail.

Defining Maps that Share a Single Panel

You have used the DFHMDI macro to define individual BMS maps. In this section, we will introduce additional parameters that you will use with the DFHMDI macro when you define maps that will appear in page-formatted panels—that is, maps that will share a single panel.

Previously, you have described a map's position within a panel in *absolute* terms; for example, you specified the line number and column number of the map's upper left corner. However, a map's position can also be described in terms of *location relative to other maps*. Figure 9-3 shows a page-formatted panel made up of header, detail, and trailer maps. Clearly the header map appears "first"; that is, at the top of the display. However, each repetition of the detail map simply appears "next"—after whichever map precedes it. Thus, the first instance of the detail map follows the header map, and the second instance follows the first instance of the detail map. Similarly, the trailer map follows the "last" detail map. It may follow immediately, or it may be placed at the bottom of the display, leaving a gap if the detail maps didn't fill the rest of the screen. The application program is not required to keep track of where

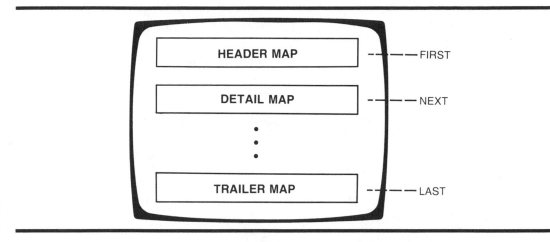

**Figure 9-3
Panel Showing
Relative Map
Positioning**

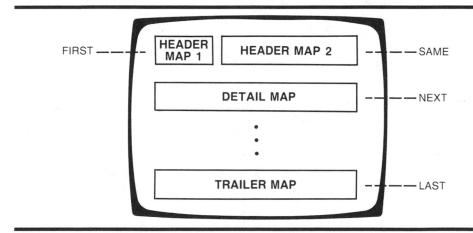

**Figure 9-4
Example of Page-
Formatted Panel**

each map is located on the display; it only needs to send the maps in order
left-to-right and top-to-bottom.

Figure 9-4 shows a somewhat more complex display. It illustrates that a
map doesn't have to fill a complete line of the display. It also illustrates that a
display may contain multiple header maps just as Figure 9-2 showed multiple
trailer maps. Notice also that the maps used in page-formatted panels are typically smaller than the maps you have used before. HEADER MAP 2, for
instance, might have a size of two lines by thirty columns.

Defining Map Position

A page-formatted panel need not contain either header or trailer maps; it
may be made up entirely of detail maps. However, if header or trailer maps
are used, they must be defined using the DFHMDI options HEADER = YES or
TRAILER = YES, respectively. Detail maps need not be identified in any special
way by the DFHMDI macro.

A map that has been defined as a header map must always be placed at the
top of a page. There may be more than one header map on a page; however, all
header maps must be SENT for mapping before any other type of map is sent.

If a program SENDs a header map *after* another type of map, BMS will start a new page with the specified header as the first map on the page.

The chapter "Advanced Terminal Control" introduced the JUSTIFY option of the DFHMDI macro to specify RIGHT or LEFT justification on the display. For page formatting, you can use a second argument of JUSTIFY to specify vertical justification. The complete option is written:

$$JUSTIFY = (\ LEFT \ ! \ RIGHT, \ FIRST \ ! \ LAST)$$

If the first argument value is omitted, LEFT is assumed. Figure 9-5 illustrates the effect of LEFT or RIGHT justification.

JUSTIFY = (,FIRST) indicates that a map is to be positioned as the first map on the page. Only one FIRST map can appear on a given page.

Maps defined with the JUSTIFY = (,LAST) option are always placed at the bottom of the page. Trailer maps are often defined with JUSTIFY = (,LAST) to force this positioning. More than one LAST map may appear on a page; however they may be positioned only *across* the page as shown in Figure 9-6.

Additional page formatting arguments may also be used in the LINE and COLUMN options of the DFHMDI macro. You may recall that the LINE option can be used to specify the absolute number of the line on which the map is to appear. Alternatively, it may specify a relative line location. The complete option is defined.

$$LINE = number \ ! \ NEXT \ ! \ SAME$$

Figure 9-5
Justifying a BMS
Map on the
Display Screen

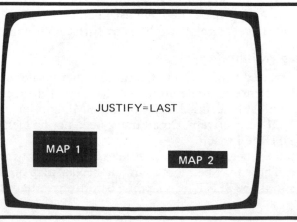

Figure 9-6
Using JUSTIFY =
LAST to Position
Two BMS Maps

LINE = NEXT indicates that the map is to begin on the next available line on the page. If no LINE option is specified in the DFHMDI macro, NEXT is assumed. If the first map SENT for a page specifies NEXT, the map will be positioned at line 1.

LINE = SAME indicates that the map is to be positioned at the same starting line used in the previous output request. This situation is illustrated in Figure 9-7.

Horizontal placement may also be specified in relative terms by using the option;

COLUMN = number ¦ NEXT ¦ SAME

Columns are counted from the left or right side of the page based on the JUSTIFY option. The effect of argument values NEXT and SAME is similar to the LINE case; it is illustrated in Figure 9-8.

Establishing Page Margins

Each time you place a map into a page-formatted panel, part of the panel becomes unavailable for use by other maps. The unavailable area includes the space filled by the map, but also a margin above and to the side of the map. This is because maps must be placed into the panel in order top-to-bottom, left-to-right and because BMS must save space at the bottom of the panel for a trailer map.

The LINE option determines a top margin. For example, once you've placed a map into line five of the panel, you cannot place another map into lines one through four. If you tried, you would be violating the *top-to-bottom* rule.

There is also a bottom margin determined by the depth (number of lines used) of the largest TRAILER map in the map set. For example, if the map set in use contains a trailer map that takes up six lines of a panel, BMS will not let you SEND a non-trailer map that extends into the panel's bottom six lines.

Left and right margins are determined principally by the JUSTIFY and COLUMN options. This will be discussed further below.

Let's look at the rules by which margins are established. We will begin with the top margin.

Because of the top-to-bottom, left-to-right rule, the LINE specification of the first map SENT determines the top margin for the page. Once the first map

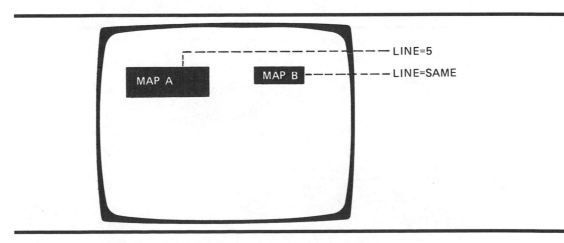

Figure 9-7
Using LINE = SAME
to Position BMS Map

has been sent, no other map can be sent that appears above it. As additional maps are SENT, the top line occupied by each map also makes unavailable any lines above it on the display. Figure 9-9, illustrates this rule.

The display shown contains two maps, MAPA and MAPB. Since the MAPB begins lower on the display than MAPA, it must have been SENT after MAPA.

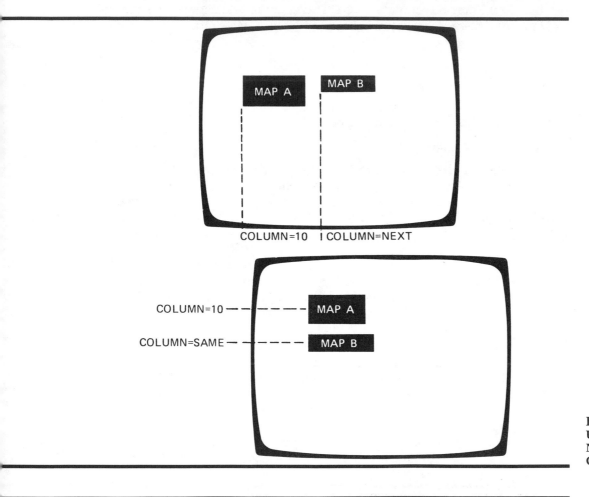

Figure 9-8
Using COLUMN = NEXT and COLUMN = SAME

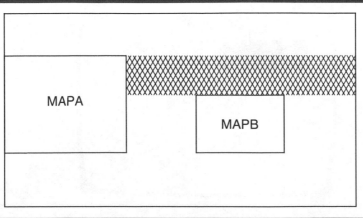

Figure 9-9
Top Border of Page-Formatted Panel

When the first map, MAPA, was SENT, it created a top margin as shown in the shaded area. When MAPB was SENT, it created an additional *unavailable area*, the hatched area shown in the figure. Now no map can possibly be placed in that area without violating the top-to-bottom rule.

As maps are SENT, BMS keeps track of the number of lines remaining at the *bottom* of the display to insure that there is room left for the trailer map(s). Because BMS has no way of predicting which trailer map(s) the application program will actually SEND, it reserves space for the longest single trailer map *defined in the map set.*

Earlier, we said that multiple trailer maps could appear on a single page. To make use of this feature, you must insure that BMS reserves adequate space at the bottom of the page for the longest combination of trailer maps that may be used. You must take care of this when you construct the map set, by including a trailer map whose length is the maximum that will be used by any *combination* of smaller trailer maps. Consider the case shown in Figure 9-10.

This represents a case similar to that shown in Figure 9-2. On a given page, the program may SEND TRAILER 1, TRAILER 2, or both. The depth of Trailer 1 is one line and of TRAILER 2, two lines. If the map set contained definitions only for TRAILER 1 and TRAILER 2, BMS would reserve two lines at the bottom of the page. However, this would be inadequate for the case when the program SENDs *both* TRAILER 1 and TRAILER 2. In order to cause BMS to reserve space for both TRAILER 1 and TRAILER 2, you would define a third TRAILER map whose depth is three lines. The third TRAILER is referred to as a "Dummy" TRAILER because it is never actually used; its only role is to define the "largest trailer length in the map set" as three lines.

When a map defined with the JUSTIFY = RIGHT option is placed on a display, it makes unavailable all area to the right of its right border. That is, it defines a right-hand margin for the lines it occupies. Similarly, a map defined with JUSTIFY = LEFT establishes a left-hand border for the lines it occupies. Figure 9-11 illustrates these effects.

In the case of Figure 9-11, both MAPA and MAPB occupy the same lines. If more complicated panels are constructed wherein different-sized maps share lines, the definition of *unavailable page areas* becomes somewhat more complex. The rule is: "When two or more maps are placed so that they share certain

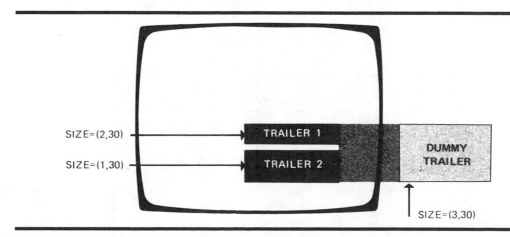

**Figure 9-10
Using a Dummy
Trailer to
Reserve Space**

lines, the left or right area made unavailable by the map that ends highest is extended to the depth of the map that ends lowest." This is illustrated by Figure 9-12.

Here, MAPA is the "map that ends lowest" and MAPB is the "map that ends highest." Both maps were defined with JUSTIFY=LEFT, so they each establish a left-hand margin. The margin established by MAPA is shown as hatched left to right. MAPB establishes a top margin, all lines above MAPB, and also makes unavailable the area left of MAPB *to the depth of MAPA*. The area made unavailable by MAPB is shown as hatched right to left.

You may want to experiment with these rules and verify for yourself that the *available display area* must always be in the shape of an L, a reversed L, a rectangle, or an inverted T.

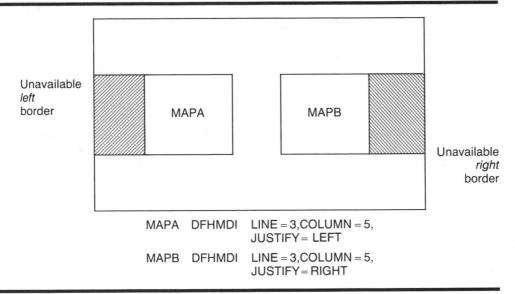

Unavailable *left* border

MAPA   MAPB

Unavailable *right* border

```
MAPA   DFHMDI   LINE = 3,COLUMN = 5,
                JUSTIFY = LEFT
MAPB   DFHMDI   LINE = 3,COLUMN = 5,
                JUSTIFY = RIGHT
```

**Figure 9-11
Left and Right
Borders of Page-
Formatted Panel**

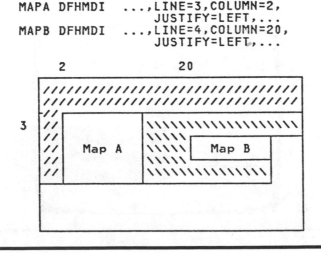

```
MAPA DFHMDI    ...,LINE=3,COLUMN=2,
               JUSTIFY=LEFT,...
MAPB DFHMDI    ...,LINE=4,COLUMN=20,
               JUSTIFY=LEFT,...
```

Map A   Map B

**Figure 9-12
Left and Right
Borders When BMS
Maps Share Lines**

Building Page-Formatted Messages

You build a page-formatted panel by issuing a series of SEND MAP commands, each specifying the ACCUM option and naming the BMS map to be sent. Each map has been defined to format a particular part of the page. The series of SEND commands must specify the maps in a top-to-bottom, left-to-right order. In this section, we will look first at how a single-page message is built and transmitted; then we will extend the discussion to multi-page messages.

Single Page Messages

Figure 9-13 shows an example of a single-page message and illustrates the steps an application program would perform to *build* the message.

Where the flowchart indicates a SEND operation, the program issues a SEND command of the form:

EXEC CICS SEND MAP(name) MAPSET(name) ACCUM ERASE...

Note: The command may be continued to include other options that we discussed previously.

Here, the ACCUM option has the same effect as the ACCUM option discussed in the previous chapter for text building with the SEND TEXT command. It indicates that this mapping request is part of a cumulative page-building operation.

The effect of the ERASE option is to erase the display, to clear MDT flags, and also to ensure that all areas of the display are made available in the sense discussed earlier in "Establishing Page Margins." BMS executes the ERASE only for the first SEND command for a page. If you specify the option in any subsequent SEND MAP commands for the same page, BMS will ignore all occurrences except the first. This permits you to place a a SEND MAP command that specifies ERASE in a loop that sends a series of detail maps.

For example, suppose that your program is to display detail information from 12 records in a single message. The program would probably contain a loop, to be executed 12 times, that included a SEND MAP command for the detail map. You can code the ERASE option on the command to insure that the screen will be cleared before the message is displayed. BMS will ignore the option for all except the first time through the loop unless a new page is started. (In the next section we will discuss how to begin a new page in a multi-page message.)

Once the complete page has been built, the program issues a SEND PAGE command to signal that the cumulative page building operation is finished, and to send the page to the terminal. The command is written:

EXEC CICS SEND PAGE

Notice that this is the same command that we introduced in the previous chapter to send a page of unformatted TEXT. A page may either include BMS maps as discussed in this chapter, or TEXT as discussed in the last chapter; the two may not be mixed.

Here we will introduce two additional options of the SEND PAGE command: RELEASE and TRANSID.

RELEASE indicates that the transaction is terminating; it is effectively the same as a SEND PAGE followed by EXEC CICS RETURN—"Over and Out" in the jargon of radio operators.

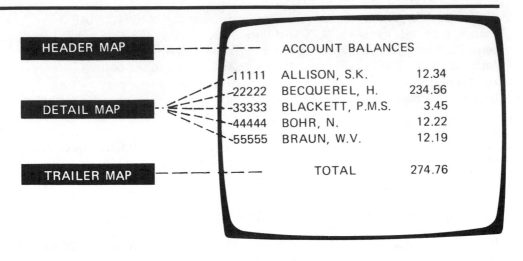

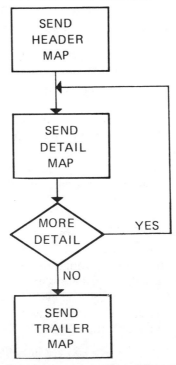

APPLICATION PROGRAM

Figure 9-13
Building a Single-Page Message

TRANSID may be specified *with* RELEASE to indicate that the transaction is to be terminated, and that the named transaction should be invoked if additional input is received from the user terminal. The effect of TRANSID is to establish pseudo-conversational mode.

Multi-Page Messages

Having seen how a single-page message is created, we look now at the multi-page case. We begin by describing the overall process.

Paging Overview

Consider again the flowchart shown in Figure 9-13. Assume that at some point in the illustrated page-building process—say during the fifteenth iteration through the loop—the accumulated output page exceeds the page size of the terminal device being used. BMS would recognize this when the application program attempted to SEND a map that would extend into the bottom margin—the area reserved for the largest trailer map. At this point, BMS would raise an OVERFLOW condition; thus, causing control to transfer to the application program's exception-handling routine for OVERFLOW.

This routine, called the overflow processing routine, must complete the page and *reissue the SEND command* for the map that caused the overflow. When the overflow processing routine "completes the page," BMS does not send the page to the display; instead, it places it into a temporary storage area. The overflow-handling routine may be executed several times before the complete message is built in temporary storage. For example, if the complete message requires five pages on the terminal display, the overflow-handling routine will be executed to complete pages one through four. We refer to the accumulated pages in temporary storage as the *logical message*.

When the entire logical message has been constructed in temporary storage, the application program issues a SEND PAGE command. This will cause the *BMS paging transaction* to be invoked. It is this transaction—not your program—that will display each page under the control of the user at the terminal. Therefore, your program doesn't have to include code to respond to the user's "next page, please" requests.

The logical sequence is:

1. Send a detail map. (SEND MAP)
2. Check to see whether this is the last detail record to be included in the message.
3. If more detail records are to be included, loop back to step 1.
4. When all detail records have been sent, issue a SEND PAGE command.

Building the Logical Message

You build a *multi-page* output message by using the SEND MAP command with the ACCUM option *and* an additional option: PAGING. The command is:

    EXEC CICS SEND MAP(name) MAPSET(name) PAGING ACCUM ...

The effect of the PAGING option is to cause the page to be placed in temporary storage rather than being displayed at the terminal. PAGING must be specified on each command for the logical message.

The opposite of PAGING is *TERMINAL*, which is the default for SEND MAP and SEND TEXT commands.

Overflow Processing

When BMS recognizes a page overflow, it raises the OVERFLOW condition as described in the Overview. The Overview stated that the overflow processing routine was responsible to *complete the page* and to reissue a SEND for the map that caused the overflow. Figure 9-14 shows how an overflow processing routine is related to the overall page-building process.

Notice that "completing the page" does not mean issuing a SEND PAGE command. The SEND PAGE is issued only once, as shown at the bottom of

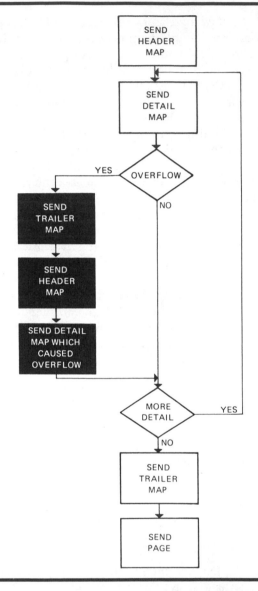

Figure 9-14
Overflow Processing

the flowchart, to transmit the complete *logical message*. The overflow processing routine completes a physical page by:

1. issuing SEND MAP for any trailer map(s) desired,
2. issuing SEND MAP for any header maps desired for the following page, and
3. reissuing SEND MAP for the map that created the overflow.

Each of the SEND MAP commands includes the ACCUM and PAGING options. BMS recognizes the start of a new page when it receives the first non-trailer map after an OVERFLOW. In the sequence above, step 2 would cause BMS to recognize a new page. If header maps were not used, BMS would begin a new page when the overflow processing routine reissued SEND for the detail map that had caused the overflow.

Completing the Logical Message

When the complete logical message has been built, the program must issue a SEND PAGE to initiate the actual display of the logical message. The command may include these options:

> RELEASE [TRANSID (name)] I *RETAIN*
> AUTOPAGE I *NOAUTOPAGE*
> *OPERPURGE*

In addition to the RELEASE and TRANSID options described for the single-page case, a new option, RETAIN, may be specified. RETAIN indicates that control is to be returned to the program when the paging operation is complete. Therefore, when this option is chosen, the application program will remain in the CICS region while the user receives the entire multi-page message. RELEASE indicates, as in the single-page case, that the application program is to be terminated. If neither RETAIN nor RELEASE is specified, the BMS paging transaction is *scheduled*, but control is returned immediately to the application. The logical message will not actually be displayed at the terminal until the user transaction has been terminated.

AUTOPAGE or NOAUTOPAGE indicate how the logical message is to be displayed. AUTOPAGE specifies that the logical message is to be displayed page-by-page without waiting for paging commands from the user. This is normally used when the terminal output device is a printer or other device that does not require user attendance. NOAUTOPAGE requires that the user's paging commands control the display of each page of the message. If neither AUTOPAGE nor NOAUTOPAGE is specified, the display will be controlled according to a paging status assigned by the system programmer for the type of terminal in use.

User Control of Paging

The multi-page message is physically displayed at the user terminal under the control of a BMS paging transaction. The transaction is scheduled for execution as discussed above in the description of the SEND PAGE command. Assuming that the terminal is a device type that does require user intervention (AUTOPAGE is *not* in effect), the BMS paging transaction displays each page as directed by the user. BMS displays a page and then waits for a *paging command* from the user to indicate that the next page may be displayed.

Each CICS installation can define its own system of paging commands. The system programmer defines the format, together with other system parameters, during CICS system generation. An installation may also define Programmed Function Keys to control paging so that the user doesn't have to type the paging commands. Therefore, the paging procedure is not the same in all CICS installations. We will illustrate the concept of paging commands by using the *standard default* format provided with the CICS system.

You should construct each page of the output message so that it contains a field into which the user can type a paging command. Often the field is placed in a TRAILER or HEADER map; the only requirement is that, when a READ is issued for the terminal, the paging command is the first input data received. Recall that, for IBM 3270 devices, only those fields whose MDT flags have been set are transmitted back to the computer. Therefore, to insure that the paging command field is transmitted, your BMS map should specify the *FSET* attribute for the field. To insure that the command field is read *first*, it should be the first unprotected field in the display.

Figure 9-15 illustrates a three-page message whose paging command field is in a TRAILER map. An initial value of P/N is placed in the field. This is the standard command for "next page, please." If the field had been defined with the DFHMDF FSET attribute to force the MDT "on," the user would have only to press the ENTER key in order to view the next page. Notice that in the final page of the message, the trailer map has been modified to contain the command P/1 for *display page 1*. If the user pressed the ENTER key after viewing page 3, BMS would redisplay page 1 of the message.

To allow the user to type a different command over the default command provided, the command field must be unprotected, and the cursor should be positioned under the paging command. Therefore, the DFHMDF macro for the paging command field should specify the UNPROT and IC attributes in addition to the FSET attribute.

Purging Logical Messages

As we have seen, a special BMS transaction is responsible for displaying the logical message under control of the user's paging commands. Besides the *next page* and *page n* commands we have discussed, the user may enter paging commands that suspend display of one message, while allowing another trans-action to be invoked to produce a different message. The rules for this *chaining* of messages determine when BMS considers a user to be finished with a particular message. Ordinarily, as soon as a user is finished with a message, BMS will automatically delete the message from temporary storage. However, particularly if several messages have been chained, the user could easily forget which messages are in the chain and take some action that would trigger automatic deletion of a message without the user's intending it. To prevent this, the application program can specify the OPERPURGE option with the SEND PAGE command for the message. OPERPURGE specifies that the message is to be retained until the user explicitly requests that it be purged.

Note that once the application program has SENT an output message, the program has no further control over the message. Depending upon the combin-ation of RETAIN and RELEASE specified, the program may or may not still be active when the message is displayed.

Until SEND PAGE has been issued, however, the application program does have control of the message. In particular, the program can delete a message that it has partially built in temporary storage. Typically, this would be done if the application program detected some abnormal condition during construction of the message. Rather than displaying an incomplete or possible erroneous message, the program would delete the message and send an error message to the user.

The command used to delete a logical message that has not yet been sent is:

EXEC CICS PURGE MESSAGE

The PURGE MESSAGE command should be issued whenever an application program terminates abnormally. Otherwise the partial message will remain in CICS temporary storage. The chapter "Transient Data and Temporary Storage" will discuss the management of temporary storage.

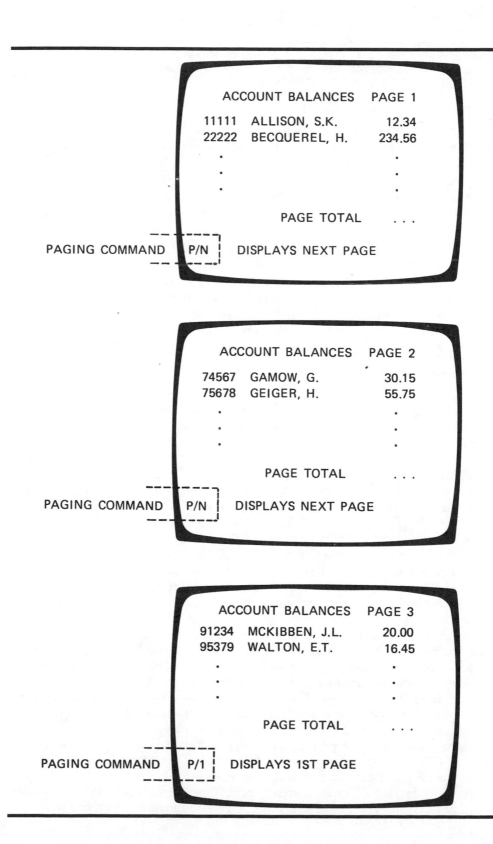

ACCOUNT BALANCES   PAGE 1

11111   ALLISON, S.K.   12.34
22222   BECQUEREL, H.   234.56
          .   .
          .   .
          .   .

                    PAGE TOTAL   . . .

PAGING COMMAND   P/N   DISPLAYS NEXT PAGE

ACCOUNT BALANCES   PAGE 2

74567   GAMOW, G.   30.15
75678   GEIGER, H.   55.75
          .   .
          .   .
          .   .

                    PAGE TOTAL   . . .

PAGING COMMAND   P/N   DISPLAYS NEXT PAGE

ACCOUNT BALANCES   PAGE 3

91234   MCKIBBEN, J.L.   20.00
95379   WALTON, E.T.   16.45
          .   .
          .   .
          .   .

                    PAGE TOTAL   . . .

PAGING COMMAND   P/1   DISPLAYS 1ST PAGE

**Figure 9-15
Multi-Page
Message With
Paging Commands**

Note: At this point, you are ready to begin Exercises 1 and 2 for this chapter. Part 2 of the chapter covers the material you will need to complete Exercise 3.

Part 2: Message Routing

So far, we have discussed CICS commands used by an application program to communicate with the *direct terminal*. By direct terminal we mean that:

1. The terminal is the same one used to initiate the transaction for which the program is executing.
2. The terminal receives output messages *immediately* in what appears to the user as a conversational mode. The user, having entered a transaction request, waits to receive a message in response to the request.

In practice, there are a variety of situations in which an application program may need to send output to a terminal other than the direct terminal. The requirement might be either to send a message to a physically different terminal, or to send a message *on a delayed basis* to the same terminal from which the transaction was initiated. We speak of a terminal used in either of these ways as a *routing terminal*, because BMS supports the requirement through a feature called *message routing*.

Applications

Suppose that you are designing a CICS application program to search a manufacturing parts data base for certain parts specified by the user. As we have discussed in earlier chapters, you must decide how to handle exceptional conditions that the program may encounter in reading from the data base. In particular, you will need exception-handling routines for the IOERR and NOTOPEN conditions.

Either of these conditions is potentially serious to a manufacturing operation, for—assuming that the problem is not in the logic of your program—they indicate that all or part of a critical data file has become unusable. In view of that, your program must make the condition known to someone who can take immediate corrective action. In most installations, that would be either the data base administrator or the central system operator. Therefore, your exception-handling routine should be programmed to send a message to be received immediately, not by the user at the direct terminal, but by the data base administrator and central system operator at their respective terminals.

As an example of delayed, non-conversational messages, consider an application program designed to format special financial reports. The user, probably a financial analyst, initiates the transaction and conversationally enters parameters which describe the required data and the report's format. Once the description is complete, the program sends the completed report to a terminal or terminals specified by the user. For example, the user might specify that the report be sent to a publication-quality output device for printing.

Two communication processes take place in parallel within such an application. One is a conversation, conducted via SEND and RECEIVE commands, with the user at the direct terminal. The other is the construction of the logical message that constitutes the output report. This message is built in temporary storage as the program issues SEND ACCUM commands. When the report has been completed, the program uses a SEND PAGE command to make the report available to the designated routing terminals.

Notice that the same terminal in use as the direct terminal may be designated as a routing terminal. For example, while the user is experimenting with "getting the format right," he or she will probably want to receive the report at a nearby printer. If there is a terminal with an attached printer available, the user might well choose to work from that terminal. In that case, the same physical device would be used both as the direct terminal, to control the transaction and describe the final report, and as a routing terminal, to receive the final report. However, the report will be sent to the terminal in the same manner as if the terminal had not been used to initiate the transaction. That is, the report will be received as soon as the terminal has been made ready *after the transaction has completed.* The display of the report will be entirely separate from the conversational communication between the application program and the direct terminal.

Message Routing Overview

To make use of the BMS message routing facility, your program must:

1. Build a list that identifies the destination(s) of the routed message.
2. "Establish the routing environment—that is, specify to BMS that certain SEND commands are associated with routing terminals and not with the direct terminal.
3. Construct the message. For multipage messages this includes providing, in the overflow processing routine, for page overflow where the receiving terminals may not all have the same page size.
4. SEND the message to the routing terminals.

The following sections will discuss each of these steps in detail.

The Route List

Recall that the Terminal Control Table (TCT) describes each CICS terminal. Each terminal has a four-character identifier that matches the terminal to a TCT entry. You can use this identifier to designate terminals you want to route a message to.

A CICS user may have a three-character *operator identifier* assigned according to the requirements of the particular installation. In most installations, an identifier is assigned to the data base administrator, and another to the central system operator responsible for CICS. The installation may also choose other "special users" who will be assigned identifiers. You can use the operator identifier to designate users you want to route a message to.

A route list may identify a destination for a routed message by specifying a terminal identifier, an operator identifier, or both. CICS interprets these designations as follows:

1. If the terminal identifier is specified, the message will be routed to the specified physical terminal as soon as the terminal is free to receive messages.
2. If an operator identifier is specified, CICS checks to see whether the designated user is signed-on to CICS. If the user is signed-on, the message will be sent to the terminal that he or she is using as soon as the terminal is free to receive messages. In this case, if the designated user leaves the physical terminal before receiving the message, the next user to sign-on at the same terminal could receive the message.

3. If both the terminal identifier and operator identifier are specified, the message will be sent to the designated terminal as soon as the designated user is signed-on to it and the terminal is free to receive messages.

The discussion above has used the phrase "free to receive messages." In order to receive a routed message, the terminal obviously must be signed-on to CICS, but also must be assigned a status that permits routed messages to be received. The status relative to routed messages may be set by the terminal user to RECEIVE, TRANSCEIVE, or TRANSACTION. If the terminal is in RECEIVE or TRANSCEIVE status, it can receive a routed message at any time that the terminal is not directing a transaction. If a terminal is in TRANSACTION state, it cannot receive a routed message unless the user explicitly requests the message. Typically, the user would periodically enter a query command to determine whether there are messages waiting and to read any title that has been included to describe a waiting message. (The section "Establishing the Routing Environment" below will discuss how titles are attached to routed messages.) The user could then request a particular message by entering its identifying code from the list.

A route list is made up of a series of 16-byte entries. Each entry has the format illustrated in Figure 9-16. We have not yet discussed the *status flag* byte; it is set by BMS and will be discussed in the next section—"Establishing the Routing Environment." The end of a terminal list is marked by an *end-of-list* indicator, a half-word whose value is -1. In COBOL you can define the end-of-list indicator with the following statement:

PICTURE S9(4) COMP VALUE -1.

Figure 9-17 shows a COBOL program's definition of an entire route list.

Operator Class Destinations

An installation may choose to establish *operator classes* so that each operator identifier can be assigned to one or more classes. Then an application program may define an operator class as a routing destination by building an operator class code field.

There may be a maximum of 24 operator classes, so the code field can be defined in three bytes, with each bit associated with an operator class. The bits are mapped in *reverse order*; that is, the bit for class 1 is the low-order

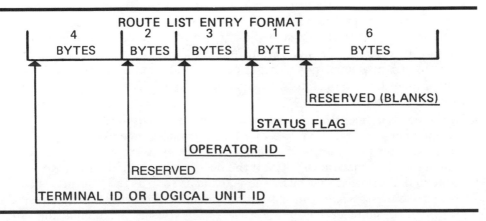

ROUTE LIST ENTRY FORMAT

4 BYTES	2 BYTES	3 BYTES	1 BYTE	6 BYTES

RESERVED (BLANKS)

STATUS FLAG

OPERATOR ID

RESERVED

TERMINAL ID OR LOGICAL UNIT ID

Figure 9-16
Route List
Entry Format

(rightmost) bit. If the operator class is to be designated as a routing destination, its corresponding bit should be set "on" (that is, equal to 1).

Setting bits in a COBOL program is not straightforward, but one approach is to convert the required bit configuration to a decimal number value. Figure 9-18 shows how a COBOL program might define an operator class code field designating classes 1, 8, and 10 as destinations. The numeric value 641, which is moved into BINARY-FIELD, has a hexadecimal representation of 281. Its binary representation is, therefore, 001010000001, in which bits 1, 8, and 10 (reading from right to left) are "on."

An application program may use either or both an operator class code field and route list to specify destinations.

Establishing the Routing Environment

The routing environment is established by the ROUTE command. The command makes the routing destinations known to BMS and, optionally, sets conditions for the delivery of the routed messages. The ROUTE command is said to *establish the routing environment* because it causes the next SEND

```
01    ROUTLST.
      02    ENTRY1.
            03    RTRM1    PIC X(4).
            03    FILLER   PIC XX      VALUE SPACES.
            03    ROPID1   PIC X(3).
            03    RFLAG1   PIC X       VALUE SPACES.
            03    FILLER   PIC X(6)    VALUE SPACES.
      02    ENTRY2.
            03    RTRM2    PIC X(4).
            03    FILLER   PIC XX      VALUE SPACES.
            03    ROPID2   PIC X(3).
            03    RFLAG2   PIC X       VALUE SPACES.
            03    FILLER   PIC X(6)    VALUE SPACES.
      02    ENTRY3.
            03    RTRM3    PIC X(4).
            03    FILLER   PIC XX      VALUE SPACES.
            03    ROPID3   PIC X(3).
            03    RFLAG3   PIC X       VALUE SPACES.
            03    FILLER   PIC X(6)    VALUE SPACES.
      02    ENDLST           PIC S9(4) COMP VALUE -1.
```

Figure 9-17
Route List Definition
In COBOL Program

```
WORKING-STORAGE SECTION.
01    BINARY-FIELD       PIC 9(8) COMP.
01    DUMMY REDEFINES BINARY-FIELD.
      02    FILLER        PIC X.
      02    OPER-CLASSES  PIC XXX.
                 .
                 .
                 .
PROCEDURE DIVISION.
                 .
                 .
                 .
MOVE 641 TO BINARY-FIELD.
```

Figure 9-18
Defining Operator
Class Code

PAGE commands to be interpreted as "send to routing destinations" as opposed to "send to direct terminal." The ROUTE command and its arguments are:

```
EXEC CICS ROUTE
[LIST (data-area)]
[OPCLASS (data-area)]
INTERVAL (0)    I
      INTERVAL (hhmmss)    I    TIME (hhmmss)
TITLE (data-area)
ERRTERM (name)
```

The LIST and OPCLASS arguments place in effect a route list or operator class code field that has been constructed as described above. If neither LIST nor OPCLASS is specified, the message is sent to *all* terminals as a general "broadcast." Normally, only the central system operator will be authorized to use transactions that use the broadcast feature.

The INTERVAL and TIME arguments can be used to specify that the message is to be delivered at a particular time. The time may be *relative* to the time the message was made available. In this case, the INTERVAL argument is used to specify the elapsed time delay (in *hhmmss* form, where *hh* represents a two digit hour field, *mm* is a two digit minute field, and *ss* is a two digit second field). INTERVAL(0), which is the default, specifies that the message is to be delivered as soon as the destination is available. Alternatively, you can use the TIME parameter to specify an absolute "time of day" for message delivery.

You use the TITLE option to specify a title for the message. We said that a user may enter a request to see a list of messages waiting to be received. The title you specify will appear in the list as further identification of the message. The argument may contain up to 62 characters of title identification that must be preceded by a two-byte length field. For example:

```
01 MSG-TITLE.
   02   TITLE LENGTH PIC S9(4) COMP VALUE (23).
   02   TITLE-DATA PIC X(23) VALUE 'QUARTERLY INCOME REPORT'.
```

If BMS determines that a message is undeliverable, it can construct and send an error message to a specified terminal. The ERRTERM argument specifies the identification of a terminal to receive the error message. Note that this error condition is detected at "delivery time," not at the time that the ROUTE command is issued.

Determining the Routing Destination

We have said that either or both a route list and an operator class code field may be specified in a ROUTE command. Additionally, the route list may specify a destination in three different ways: by operator identifier, by terminal identifier, and by both an operator and terminal identifier. We need now to look at how a destination is determined, given various combinations of specifications.

If only a route list is specified, there are three possible situations.

1. The list entry specifies only an operator identifier. In this case BMS determines where (that is, at what terminal) the identified user is signed-on. If the user is signed-on at a BMS-supported terminal, that terminal becomes the destination. If the user is not signed on when the ROUTE command is executed, a destination cannot be determined and the list entry will be skipped.

2. The list entry specifies only a terminal identifier. The terminal is the destination, and the message will be delivered as soon as the terminal is free to receive it.
3. The list specifies both a terminal and operator identifier. The message will be sent to the specified terminal as soon as the identified user is signed-on at that terminal and the terminal is free to receive messages.

If only an operator class code field is specified, the message will be sent to every BMS-supported terminal at which a user of the specified operator class is signed on *at the time the ROUTE message is executed*. If the user signs off between the time the ROUTE command is executed and the message delivery time, the message will be sent as soon as a user of the designated operator class signs on to the terminal.

If both a route list and an operator class code field are specified, there are two possibilities:

1. If a route list entry specifies only a terminal identifier, the terminal becomes a destination depending upon whether or not the signed-on user belongs to a designated operator class. Thus, the OPCLASS rules control the effect of this entry.
2. If a route list entry specifies an operator identifier, with or without a terminal identifier, the entry will be effective; the OPCLASS specification has no effect upon the entry.

Exceptional Conditions

At the time the ROUTE command is executed, BMS can detect certain error conditions. For example, a terminal identifier that appears in the route list might not be defined in the TCT—or might identify a terminal not supported by BMS. In either case, BMS would raise the INVERRTERM condition.

Route list entries that specify only an operator identifier require that the specified user be signed on to an eligible BMS terminal when the ROUTE command is issued. Otherwise the entry will be skipped. A route list entry may have been incorrectly coded so that it specifies neither an operator nor a terminal identifier; in this case also BMS will skip the entry.

The result of any of these errors is that some or all of the requested destinations are "ineligible receivers." BMS will raise either the RTEFAIL or RTESOME conditions depending upon whether *all* or only *some* of the destinations were ineligible. If a route list was specified, BMS will also set an error code in the status byte of each failed entry. Figure 9-19 lists various status byte codes.

Constructing the Message for Routing

The same procedure applies in building a message for routing as in building a message for the direct terminal. There is only one rule that must be remembered: each SEND TEXT or SEND MAP command must specify the ACCUM option.

Remember that a message may be either a TEXT message or a MAP message. If you attempt to combine the two, the INVREQ exception condition will be raised.

Overflow Processing

Recall that if your program builds a message that may exceed terminal page size, you must provide an overflow processing routine. When a message is

STATUS FLAG	BIT REPRESENTATION
ENTRY SKIPPED	X'80'
INVALID TERMINAL IDENTIFIER	X'40'
TERMINAL NOT SUPPORTED UNDER BMS	X'20'
OPERATOR NOT SIGNED ON	X'10'
OPERATOR SIGNED ON AT UNSUPPORTED TERMINAL	X'08'
INVALID LDC MNEMONIC	X'04'

Figure 9-19
Status Byte Codes for RTEFAIL and RTESOME

being built for the direct terminal, there is only one page size to consider—the size of the direct terminal page. However, in a routing environment, a message may ultimately be sent to several different types of terminal with different page sizes. BMS keeps track of page overflow for you, so you don't have to count lines for each terminal type. But if your program is keeping information like page subtotals, you will have to plan the overflow processing routine to be sure that you calculate subtotals correctly for each page size.

For example, consider a report format like the one illustrated in Figure 9-2. Here, a header map contains the page number, and a trailer map contains a "subtotal for page n." Suppose that you want to route this message to two terminals—one terminal device can display nine detail records (ALLISON through GAMOW) on a single page. The other device can display only six (ALLISON through COCKROFT) detail records on a page.

Then the page subtotal would be different for page 1 as formatted for these two different destinations. The overflow routine must know which destination type has caused overflow so that it can insert correct values into the header and trailer maps.

Notice from the discussion of "Determining the Routing Destination" that the ROUTE command causes each destination to be restricted to a particular terminal. The application program may have specified the terminal directly, or it may have specified an operator identifier. In the latter case ROUTE determines the terminal indirectly by finding where the specified user is signed-on. If the specified user isn't signed-on when the ROUTE command is executed, BMS rejects the destination specification. Therefore, once ROUTE has been executed, the set of all possible page sizes for the message is known.

After the ROUTE command is completed, you can find out how many different page sizes exist among the routing terminals you designated. You do this by examining the CICS field DESTCOUNT.

To do so, you use an ASSIGN command that names the CICS field (DESTCOUNT) you want to examine and a program variable into which you want the field's value to be placed.

The command is written:

EXEC CICS ASSIGN DESTCOUNT(variable name) END-EXEC.

The ASSIGN command moves the value of DESTCOUNT into the variable named as argument.

You may code several options in the same ASSIGN command. For example, you might request the value for PAGENUM (which is discussed below) in addition to DESTCOUNT.

As the program continues processing and builds the logical message, BMS signals overflow whenever any of the page sizes is exceeded. When overflow occurs BMS makes available:

1. in DESTCOUNT, the relative number of the destination type for which overflow has been raised. That is, if ROUTE had found five different page sizes represented, then at overflow time DESTCOUNT would contain an integer value from one to five depending upon which destination type had just overflowed.
2. in PAGENUM, also available through the ASSIGN command, the page number for the destination type that has just overflowed.

Given the three pieces of information described above—the number of possible page sizes, the relative number of the overflowing destination type, and the page number for the overflowing destination—you can design the required general overflow processing routine.

Sending the Routed Message

Once you have constructed the complete logical message, you issue a SEND PAGE command like the one you used to send a logical message to the direct terminal. The only difference is that if you code the RELEASE and RETAIN options, BMS will ignore them. Control will always be returned immediately to the instruction following the SEND PAGE. The program may then continue or it may terminate by issuing a CICS RETURN.

The SEND PAGE command terminates the routing environment that the ROUTE command established. If you issue another SEND PAGE without an intervening ROUTE command, it will be interpreted as a SEND to the direct terminal.

Summary

Often an application program needs to produce a message panel made up of several maps, or to produce messages that exceed a single page. BMS permits you to build messages of these types in temporary storage, using SEND MAP ACCUM commands. If the message may exceed a single page, you must also specify the PAGING option in the SEND MAP commands, and you must provide an overflow processing routine. The overflow processing routine will receive control when BMS raises the OVERFLOW condition, signifying that a SEND MAP command has caused the bottom page boundary to be exceeded.

When a complete *logical message* has been built in temporary storage, you issue a SEND PAGE command to send the message to the terminal. If the message is multi-page and is not being sent to an AUTOPAGE device, SEND PAGE causes a BMS paging transaction to be scheduled to display the message under the user's control. The user controls display by entering paging commands into fields that your application program provided in each page of the message. The actual display of the message may be performed pseudo-conversationally or while the application program waits, depending upon options you specified in the SEND PAGE command.

The terminal used to request a transaction is known as the *direct terminal* when it is used to converse with the transaction. In some situations, an application program may need to send output to another terminal, or to prepare a message to be sent later to the originating terminal. The BMS *message routing* facility supports these requirements.

A message for routing may be made up of BMS maps or unformatted text. (Unformatted text displays were discussed in the previous chapter.) The application program must construct lists that identify the destination(s) for each routed message. A route list identifies destinations by terminal identifier, operator identifier, or both. You may also specify an *operator class* as a routing destination by constructing an operator class code field.

Once the application program has constructed the destinations list or operator class code field, it issues a ROUTE command to establish the routing environment. So long as the routing environment is in effect, any SEND MAP or SEND TEXT command that specifies PAGING is understood to refer to the routing terminal. You use the SEND PAGE command to make the logical message available to the destination terminals. SEND PAGE also terminates the routing environment.

While the routing environment is in effect, the program may also issue SEND MAP or SEND TEXT commands without the PAGING option (that is, with the TERMINAL option that is the default). These commands send a message to the direct terminal. In this way, your program may conduct a conversation with the direct terminal while it is constructing a logical message to be sent to routing terminals.

If the routing message is a mapped, multi-page message, then you must provide an overflow routine. Since the routing destinations may not all have the same page size, you must allow for different page sizes when you build a logical message that includes page-dependent information (like page numbers and page-oriented subtotals). To allow this, the ROUTE command makes available a count of the number of different page sizes among the specified destinations. Later, when BMS detects overflow for a given terminal type, it makes available a number that identifies which page size has overflowed, and also a number giving the count of pages that have so far been mapped to the overflowed destination type. The application program can retrieve these values by using the ASSIGN command with the options DESTCOUNT or PAGENUM respectively.

DISCUSSION QUESTIONS

1. What is the effect of the following sequence of BMS commands? (The commands are abridged to show only critical options.)

                SEND TEXT TERMINAL
                ROUTE ...
                SEND TEXT
                RECEIVE MAP

```
            SEND TEXT PAGING ACCUM
            SEND TEXT
            SEND TEXT PAGING ACCUM
            SEND MAP(Y) PAGING ACCUM
            SEND MAP(Y) TERMINAL ACCUM
            SEND PAGE
            SEND TEXT TERMINAL
```

2. The following BMS maps have been sent. If the screen size is 50 columns by 30 rows, sketch the screen, indicating the area available for additional maps.

MAPA DFHMDI ..LINE = 3,COLUMN = 2,JUSTIFY = LEFT,SIZE = (15, 12) ...
MAPB DFHMDI ..LINE = 4,COLUMN = 5,JUSTIFY = RIGHT,SIZE = (4,12) ...

3. For the following SEND PAGE situations, indicate when the message will be received at a terminal, and state when and where control will return following execution of the SEND command.
   a. SEND PAGE TRANSID(NEXT) RELEASE...
   b. SEND PAGE RETAIN
   c. SEND MAP PAGING

      SEND PAGE
   d. SEND PAGE
   e. ROUTE
      SEND PAGE RETAIN
   f. ROUTE ...
      SEND PAGE TRANSID(NEXT) RELEASE

4. Two trailer maps are defined in a mapset. The first has SIZE = (2,80), the second has SIZE = (4,80). If the page size is 24 lines by 80 columns, how many lines are available for header and detail maps?

5. A map is defined with: COLUMN = 3,JUSTIFY = RIGHT. How many columns to the right of the map are blank?

6. A mapset includes maps defined as follows:

```
            HEAD     DFHMDI   HEADER = YES,SIZE = (8,40)
            TRAIL1   DFHMDI   TRAILER = YES,SIZE = (3,40)
            TRAIL2   DFHMDI   TRAILER = YES,SIZE = (7,40)
            DET1     DFHMDI   SIZE = (5,40)
            DET2     DFHMDI   SIZE = (8,40)
```

Describe the effect of the following statements assuming a screen size of 24 lines. Also assume that the overflow routine issues only a single SEND command.

```
            SEND MAP(HEAD),ACCUM
            SEND MAP(DET1),ACCUM
            SEND MAP(DET2),ACCUM
            SEND MAP(HEAD),ACCUM
```

EXERCISE

This exercise has three parts. In the first part, you will define a mapset with multiple maps and use the maps to create a single page formatted message. The second part requires you to create multi-page output to the terminal. In the third part, you will send a message to two routing terminals.

☐ *Part 1.*

Define a header map, a detail map, and a trailer map as shown in Figure 9-20. The X's represent data that must be supplied by your application program. Other information shown is constant. Use the following names for the mapset and maps:

mapset	CICMO1C
header map	HDRMAP
detail map	DTLMAP
trailer map	TRLMAP

Write a program to browse FILEA starting at the record whose key (a number) is entered by the user as input to the transaction request. If the user does not supply a key, begin the browse at the beginning of the file. If you need to review the structure of FILEA, refer back to the programming example in the preceding chapter, or to the exercise in Chapter 5, "Random Access of Data Files".

Use the maps from mapset CICMO1C to build a page as shown in Figure 9-21.

Complete the page after retrieving five records, or when the end-of-file has been reached. Send the page and terminate the task.

☐ *Part 2.*

Modify map HDRMAP to include the constant PAGE and a page number

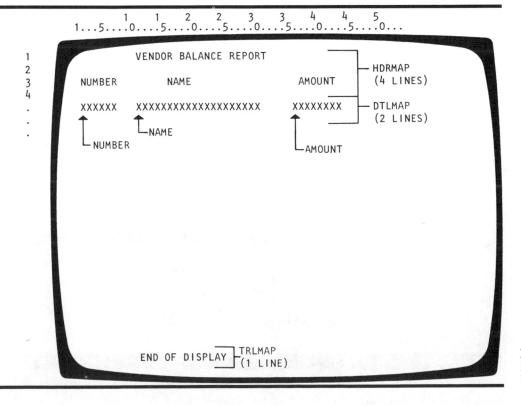

**Figure 9-20
Panel Layout for
Programming Exercise**

field (PAGENUM). Remove TRLMAP and create two new trailer maps, TRLMAP1 and TRLMAP2. TRLMAP1 and TRLMAP2 are shown in Figure 9-22, which illustrates the complete page format.

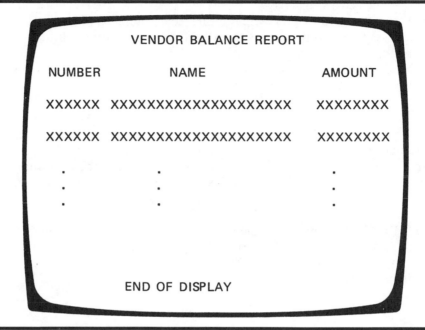

Figure 9-21
Page-Built Panel for
Exercise Part 1

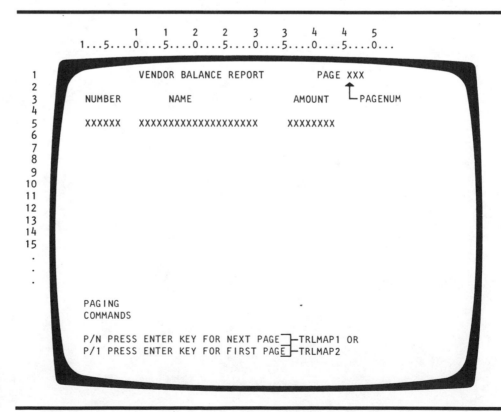

Figure 9-22
Page-Built Panel for
Exercise Part 2

Include the default paging command P/N in TRLMAP1 and P/1 in TRLMAP2. You must modify the application program from Part 1 as follows:

A. The browse should continue to end of file. Thus, the output message may exceed a single page.

B. Write an overflow processing routine that completes the current page and starts a new page, inserting the correct page number into HDRMAP.

C. When the logical message is complete, send it to the terminal in such a way that the program will terminate immediately.

□ *Part 3.*

Modify the application program to route the logical message to two terminals: the originating terminal, and a terminal whose identifier is specified in the transaction request. The transaction request *must* include the beginning record number that was previously optional. The transaction request is now of the form:

TTTT NNNNNN IIII

where TTTT is the transaction identifier, NNNNNN is the starting record key for the browse, and IIII is a terminal identifier. Remember that the overflow routine must provide for the situation in which the two routing terminals have different page sizes.

10 Data Security and Integrity

Introduction

In this chapter, we will turn our attention to the system environment in which your application programs will be used. In particular, we will see how application programs use system features designed to protect data integrity and security.

In the first chapter, we pointed out that a company's data is critical to the daily work that goes on within the company. Consider some of the example data files we have discussed so far. Without the *personnel file*, employee paychecks could not be prepared and distributed. A company that sells merchandise could not function without an *inventory file*. A manufacturing company could not keep its production going without the *parts file* to report how many of each part are on hand and where each part can be obtained.

Because the data base is necessary to keep the company in operation, it is critical that the information it contains always be usable, accurate, and complete. These factors are the goals of *data integrity*.

In addition to data integrity, the company must be concerned with the *security* of its data. Data security deals with the questions: who may use particular data, and in what way may they use it. That is, some people may be authorized to read a data file, and others authorized both to read and *change* the file. Still others may be authorized to change items in a file, but not to read the file as a whole. When "using data" includes authorization to *change* data, data security and data integrity are related. For changing data always carries with it the possibility of making the data incorrect or unusable.

Most DB/DC installations have a department or key person assigned to oversee security planning and procedures. In many of the data security procedures, the key roles are played by data base administrators, system programmers, and computer operators. However, as an application programmer, you need to understand the procedures because they affect the way in which users view an application program and the way in which you yourself may access data.

You have a more direct responsibility toward data integrity. When you design and program an application program that modifies data files, you have to keep in mind what would happen to the files if your program—or another part of the computing system on which the program depends—were to fail at any point. This chapter will discuss several types of program failures that can leave data files incorrect or unusable—i.e., failures that destroy data integrity. Then we will discuss what you can do in the CICS environment to prevent loss of data integrity and to allow for recovery when data does become lost, incorrect, or unusable.

Objectives

After completing this chapter, you will be able to:

- Discuss three general approaches to maintaining security in a DB/DC environment.

- Describe how the CICS sign-on table can be used to restrict access to CICS, CICS transactions, and CICS files.
- Describe the CICS journal facility, and discuss how it can be used to protect data integrity and security.
- Discuss the data characteristics an application program should include in validity checking.
- Discuss the significance of *logical unit of work* and *synchronization points* in protecting data integrity.
- Describe how the *dynamic log* and *system log* are used during data recovery operations.
- Define *inflight task*, and determine what data modifications will be backed out during a backward recovery operation.
- Use the CICS SYNCPOINT and JOURNAL commands.

Data Security

In many DB/DC installations, there are people who are specifically assigned to oversee the security of data. Even if you don't have a specific assignment like this, you need to be aware of security issues because they are an important concern to your company—and more important, to modern society as a whole. Keep in mind that many people who use computers don't fully understand the implications of *Data Base/Data Communications.* Computer users often propose new DB/DC applications because they see that "getting this file onto the computer" will allow work to be done better or faster. However, in the excitement of "computerizing the department," they may not think about what can happen if *anyone with a CICS userid* can access their file. As a data processing professional, it's up to you to be sure users think through the potential for both use and misuse of their computerized data.

When most people think about data security, they think about data that a company wants to keep secret from *outsiders*—often because the data would be helpful to competitors. For example, a manufacturing data base can reveal how products are assembled, what materials are used, and what new products the company is working to develop.

But there are other reasons for wanting to protect the security of data. Often files contain information that a company has been trusted to protect. Financial institutions and insurance companies, for example, have files that contain private information about their clients. An insurance company that allowed details of its clients' medical histories to become public, could expect not only to lose business, but possibly to be in serious legal difficulty as well. Perhaps you think such a company wouldn't deserve much sympathy in a case like this, particularly if the problem was caused by negligence. However, from a social perspective, most of us would sympathize with the company's clients, who could easily suffer both embarrassment and real injury as a result.

Perhaps on a smaller scale, every company that has employees also has private information that must be protected. For example, think about the information in a typical personnel file. It includes information like: the employee's salary, job rating, home address and phone number, marital status, and named insurance beneficiary. The company needs most of this information to administer salary and insurance plans, find a contact in case of emergency, etc. However, it is information the employee may not wish to be generally known. Therefore, the company has a *custodial responsibility* to limit the number of people, both inside and outside the company, who may see the information.

No matter what type of company you work for, you will find that some data files require special procedures designed to limit access to the information the files contain. Let's look at some of the factors that go into planning these procedures.

Security Planning

Although it sounds obvious, it's often forgotten that the best way to avoid losing data is not to collect it in the first place. Realizing this, for example, many companies have severely reduced the amount of data they store in their personnel files. When a new DB/DC application that deals with sensitive data is proposed, the most important question to be asked may be simply, "Are you sure you really *need* to collect this information?"

Put another way, the first consideration is whether the *value* of having the data outweighs the *cost* of collecting and maintaining it, and the *potential damage* that would be caused if the data became generally known or misused. Keep in mind that "potential damage" may not be primarily a matter of dollars—it may be ill-feelings or "bad publicity" for an organization that has collected and failed to adequately protect sensitive information.

Once an organization has decided to collect the sensitive data, it must then make a second evaluation: What level of protection does the data require? It's important to realize that there is no way to absolutely guarantee the security of any resource, whether the resource is computer-related or not. Normally, the strategy is to choose a level of protection based upon the value of the resource or the cost of its loss. The objective is to make it more time-consuming and expensive for a thief to obtain the resource than the resource is worth. This is the same strategy we use when we decide how to protect our home from burglary. If we invest in new furniture, we may also invest in sturdier locks. If we have valuable jewelry or paintings, we may install a burglar alarm.

The strategy breaks down, however, if someone decides to break into our home—or a computer system—not because there is anything of value to be taken, but simply to "break in and look around just to see if I can." In this case, the owner of the resource is forced to use a more expensive level of protection than would normally be required. In a home, the major cost of security protection is usually the cost of purchasing and installing a device. However, in the computer environment the major cost comes from two other factors: the added work that the computer must do in order to check security, and the delay and inconvenience to people who must use data to do their jobs.

Notice that we have been using the general term *protected resources*, because computer security does not apply only to protecting *data*. The following are examples of resources that a data center might wish to protect:

1. a specific computer or computer system
2. certain application programs
3. data bases or files
4. *portions* of a data base or file

As the last example suggests, it is often necessary to authorize a person to access *some* of the information in a file, but not to access all of it. In the CICS case, this can be accomplished by restricting the programs that an individual may use. This will be discussed in the section "CICS Data Security."

Generally speaking, a data center will use some combination of three methods to protect resources: access control, access monitoring (audit trails), and data encryption.

Access Control

The first method is *access control*; keeping the information away from unauthorized people. In our homes, we put a lock on the door and give keys only to people we trust. In the data center, we make a list of the people who are to be trusted with certain information. To access the data, someone must prove that he or she is on on the *authorization list*. If the data is on a computer, the authorization list usually contains "user ID's," and the person must prove his or her identity by knowing the password that matches an authorized user ID, by having an electronically coded badge with the user ID, or by some other computer-verifiable means of identification. These are examples of *system access control* methods; the computer system on which the data is stored is responsible for protecting the data.

Data centers also use *physical access control* methods. For example, a computer, its terminals, and the cables that connect them may be placed in a locked room that can be entered only with a special key or combination. The locks and the building's construction serve as *physical access controls*.

The operating system or DB/DC system include system access control as an optional function. In order to use system access controls, the data center must decide:

1. Which resources will be protected
2. Who will be authorized to access each resource
3. What *type* of access will be permitted to each authorized user.
   (For example, of the users permitted to *read* a protected file, only a few will also be authorized to *modify* the file.)

The function of system access control can be summarized as follows: whenever a program attempts to access a protected resource, determine whether the *requester* is authorized to perform the requested *operation* upon the requested *resource*.

Access Monitoring

The second security method is *access monitoring*; keeping track of when and under what circumstances a protected resource is accessed. This is like installing a television camera to continually view the door or cash register area of a store. The camera doesn't make it physically more difficult to break into the store, but it can prevent thefts by alerting the storekeeper that someone has attempted to break in. And, of course, it provides information that can be used after a burglary to find the responsible persons.

Assume that a data center has selected a file, which we call file TOMONITOR, to be monitored. Then each time a program attempts to access TOMONITOR, the system will record certain information about the attempt. The collected information is referred to as an *audit trail*. An audit trail record is written for both successful and unsuccessful requests for a protected resource. It contains information like: time and date, name of the program that requested the resource, name of user who invoked the program, terminal used to invoke the program, type of resource requested, file from which the resource was requested, type of request (e.g., READ or WRITE), etc. The system writes the information into a security data set called the "log." The audit trail records in the log can be analyzed to detect unusual patterns of activity or to report on specific types of activity.

Access monitoring is not usually used alone, but is most often used with access control to provide additional protection for selected resources. Consider what happens if file TOMONITOR is protected both by access control and access monitoring. If an unauthorized program attempts to read TOMONITOR, access control rejects the access request, and access monitoring records the request. Without access monitoring, the failed attempt would be unnoticed. Because of the audit trail, however, the data center is aware that access control rejected a request for information. Often the unsuccessful attempt is caused simply by an authorized user who has forgotten or misspelled a password. However, the log can be analyzed to detect the patterns of rejected requests that may show that someone is deliberately trying to obtain information for which they are not authorized.

Data Encryption

In the third security method, data is stored in the computer system in a coded (*encrypted*) form. In order to understand the data, a user or program must know the "key" to the code. Therefore, if an unauthorized person were able to get through the other levels of security and to *obtain* data, there would still be the problem of *understanding* it. The concept of coded messages is a familiar one; with computers, very complex codes can be used, yet the information can be coded and decoded relatively quickly when the code key is given.

From the user's point of view, encryption is flexible and easy to use. For example, consider a simple document that has been entered from a terminal. Typically, the document exists only in temporary storage until some type of SAVE command is executed. To use encryption, the user simply specifies a key at the time the document is saved. The SAVE operation then encodes the document as it is moved to permanent storage. The encoded document will be unintelligible to anyone who doesn't know the key.

When the user wishes to view or modify the data, he or she simply specifies the same key as an option of a DISPLAY or EDIT operation. The document is decoded, using the specified key, and displays the decoded version. The only catch is that, if the user has forgotten the key, the document cannot be decoded. If the user fears the key may be forgotten, and writes it down, then the effectiveness of the data's security depends upon the level of protection given to the key itself. Ultimately, therefore, encryption like other security techniques, depends upon human beings for its effectiveness.

CICS Security Facilities

In the CICS environment, some types of security protection are provided by the operating system and some by CICS itself. We will first discuss the facilities that CICS provides.

Assuming that the data center has installed the optional access control facilities, a CICS user encounters the first access control at sign-on time. A

CICS transaction requests a userid and a password. In order to sign-on to CICS, the user must enter a userid and password pair that match a valid entry in the CICS access control table. The first access control, therefore, protects access to the *CICS system* itself.

Once a user has successfully signed on, CICS reads the *security code* that has been assigned for the userid. Security codes are kept in a table called the *sign-on* table. There is an entry in the sign-on table for each userid authorized to use the system. The security code determines which CICS *application programs* the user may invoke. Since an application program is required to perform a transaction, this second access control protects access to *CICS transactions*.

Assume that the user has entered a transaction request that invokes a program for which the user is authorized. Suppose that the transaction is designed to copy a file to a printer, and that the user supplies the name of the file as part of the transaction request. When the program attempts to access the file, CICS performs a third access control check to determine whether the program is authorized to access the *file* that the user requested.

Therefore, by defining the programs a *user* can invoke and the files that a *program* can access, the data center indirectly controls the *files* that a *user* may access. To allow user A to access file F, the sign-on table entry for A must authorize use of a program that, in turn, has been authorized to access file F. If A needs to read file F but may not change the file, then A's security code should not authorize any program that modifies F.

CICS application programs may also contain their own security features. For example, suppose that the data center wants to make a rule that a certain transaction must be performed only from specific authorized terminals. If you are responsible for writing the program that performs this transaction, you could include instructions to read the TCT, find the identifier of the terminal that requested the transaction, and then compare the identifier with a list of authorized terminals. If the requesting terminal is on the "authorized" list, your program would continue with the transaction. If the requesting terminal is *not authorized*, your program would write an audit trail record into the security log (if one has been defined) and then terminate. Keep in mind that if the transaction involved message routing, you would have to check the authorization of all the routing terminals too.

As another example, you might want your program to perform its own access monitoring. You could conveniently use the CICS *journal* facility to do this. The journal is designed principally for use in recovering from lost data situations; the section "User Defined Journal Entries" describes how application programs may use the journal for other purposes as well.

CICS applications can also make use of security facilities provided by the operating system. For example, the data center may set up the operating system to require special passwords for using selected system resources, like data files. When a program or user attempts to access one of the protected resources, the operating system interrupts and requests the password associated with the resource.

Data Integrity

Data integrity is lost when a file or part of a file has become incorrect or unusable. In this situation we usually speak of "lost data," although really it is data *integrity* and not necessarily the physical data that has been lost.

There are three general ways in which data integrity can be lost:

1. A program writes incorrect data into a file. This might happen because a user has supplied incorrect data or because the program contains a logic error. In this situation, the data file can normally still be read, but it contains incorrect information. As application programmer, you have the major responsibility for preventing this type of error.

2. A program terminates abnormally while it is writing data into a data file. The abnormal termination could be caused by an error within the program itself, or by some condition outside the program. For example, CICS or the operating system might fail, the computer or the device on which the data is stored might fail, or the electrical power might be shut off. Abnormal terminations like these can cause errors in the *logical structure* of the data file, so that some or all of the data can no longer be read. Later in this section, we discuss some of the steps you can take to prevent data loss of this kind.

3. The medium (tape or disk) on which data has been recorded is lost or physically damaged. In this case, too, all or part of the data base becomes unreadable. This type of data loss is usually caused by factors outside the CICS system. The job of recovering data that has been lost in this way is primarily the responsibility of data base administrators, system operators, and system programmers. However, you need to understand the procedures that are used.

Validity Checking

Your first role in data integrity is to insure that your program does not write incorrect data into a data file. Although there's no way to guarantee that data provided by a user is *correct*, your program can often detect when data is incorrect (*invalid*).

For example, consider a merchandising data base that contains the following fields:

> Item Name
> Catalog Number
> Quantity on Hand
> Price
> Date Available
> Supplier's Name
> Supplier's City
> Supplier's Phone Number

If a user enters $13.20 as the price of an article, your program cannot detect that the correct price is actually $12.30. However, if the user enters $13.20 as the "Date Available," your program should detect an error. Likewise your program should recognize that CHICAGO is not a valid entry for "Supplier's Phone Number." In these examples, the *type* of data entered does not match the data type expected for a field.

Following is a list of some of the characteristics, or *attributes*, of data fields that an application program can check:

1. data *type* (character, integer, decimal, etc.)

2. the *range* of acceptable numeric values
3. number of characters or digits allowed
4. appearance in a *list* of "legal" values
5. *logical relationships* to other data items

A common example of logical relationship occurs when two fields in a record are *mutually exclusive*. That is, if fields A and B are mutually exclusive, the user may not supply a value for *both* field A *and* field B.

Some data management systems include validity checking facilities so that the programmer need only *describe* data field attributes; the system performs the actual checking. However in the case of CICS, each application program must perform its own validity checking. As an example, suppose that your program is designed to update a file whose records contain a field for the U.S. Social Security Number. The expected format of the number is three numeric digits, followed by a dash, then two numeric digits, a dash, and four numeric digits. When the program receives data to write into the file, it should check to see that the fourth and seventh characters of the social security number field are a "dash," and that all other characters are numeric digits. If the input value does not have that format, the program should reject the input.

Data Recovery Techniques

Earlier in this chapter, we listed abnormal program terminations ("crashes") as a potential cause of lost data. In this section, we will look at crashes that occur within an application program; later we will discuss the case in which CICS or the computer system itself crashes.

In Chapter 4 we introduced the HANDLE CONDITION facility. Recall that when CICS detects an exceptional condition, it will transfer control to the exception-handling routine you have provided for the condition or to your exception-handling routine for the general ERROR condition. If there is no exception-handling routine active either for the condition or for ERROR, CICS will take a default action. For many conditions, the default action is to abnormally terminate, ABEND, the task.

However, CICS can detect only exceptional conditions that occur within CICS commands. A task may also ABEND if an unrecoverable error occurs *outside* a CICS command. For instance, your program might perform an arithmetic operation using an undefined number, a "garbage value," as one of the operands.

When a CICS task ABENDs, control is given to the CICS ABEND processing routine. If the ABENDing task was modifying a file that the data center had designated as "recoverable," the ABEND processing routine will perform "dynamic transaction backout" in order to prevent data loss. What this means is that CICS must undo ("back out") any changes that the task had started to make to the file. In the next section we will describe how this is done.

Dynamic Transaction Backout

Consider a program designed to modify a single record of a data file and then to terminate. Figure 10-1 illustrates the major events that occur when such a program is executed.

First a task is initiated to execute the program. When the task is ready to modify the record, it issues a READ UPDATE command; then it updates the record with a REWRITE command. (Note that the task has exclusive control

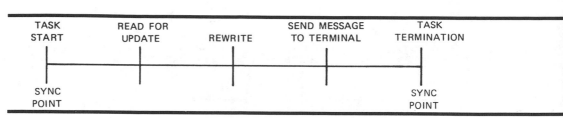

**Figure 10-1
Events During
Execution to Update
Record**

of the affected record between these two events. Exclusive control was discussed in the chapter "Random Access of Data Files.") The task then sends the user a confirming message, for example, "Update Completed for employee JOHNSON," and terminates.

Now let's assume that the task is updating a file that the data center has identified as *recoverable*. That is, the file is eligible for *dynamic transaction backout*. Then if an ABEND occurs while the task is performing the update, CICS will back out the change made by the REWRITE command. The effect is to return the files to the way they were when the task began.

The objective of dynamic transaction backout is always to restore files to the state they were in when "everything was OK" so that the transaction can be restarted from that point. To do this, CICS must keep track of two things. First, it must mark the points in time at which files are "OK." Second, whenever a task attempts to modify a recoverable file, CICS must make a copy of the record that is to be changed. That is, it saves a "before image" of the record.

A point in time at which the files are OK is called a *synchronization point* or, for short, a *sync point*. When we say that files are OK at a sync point, we mean that any updates have been completed successfully. The file may contain incorrect information (like the $13.20 price instead of $12.30); CICS has no way of detecting that.

CICS keeps track of sync points by writing a *syncpoint record* into a system data set called the *system log*. We will have more to say about the system log later in the chapter.

CICS assumes that files were OK when the task began. Therefore, one sync point is always the beginning of a task. CICS also assumes that if the task completes *normally*, any file updates it performed were done successfully. Therefore *normal task termination* is also a sync point. CICS records these two sync points automatically; these are the only sync points involved in the sequence shown in Figure 10-1.

Logical Unit of Work: The activity that a task performs between two sync points is called a *logical unit of work* (LUW). Since the task illustrated by Figure 10-1 has only two sync points, it consists of a single logical unit of work. This is the default case for every CICS task. Shortly, we will describe how you can declare additional sync points in order to segment a task into more than one logical unit of work (LUW). Figure 10-2 shows a task for which this has been done.

The program of Figure 10-2 is designed to update two records, RECORD1 and RECORD2, of a recoverable file. The intermediate sync point declares to CICS that "files are OK here" between the two updates. Instead of a single LUW, the task has been segmented into two shorter LUW's.

Before describing how to declare sync points and thus define LUW's, we

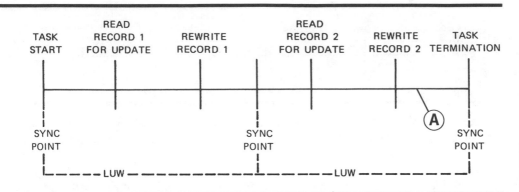

Figure 10-2
Synchronization
Point for Multiple
Record Update

need to discuss *why* you might want to do so. There are three principal reasons. To understand them, you need to know more about how dynamic transaction backout works.

We have said that CICS keeps a copy of the "before image" of each record modified in a recoverable file. CICS keeps these copies in an area called the *dynamic log* that is located in the CICS region. Since the purpose of keeping the copies is to be able to back out a change, CICS must keep a copy until it is sure that the files are OK. But that is exactly the definition of a sync point. Therefore, CICS keeps the "before images" for the period between sync points— that is, it cannot discard a copy until a LUW is complete. Keep in mind that the files we are discussing here are files that have been designated as "recoverable."

The first, though not the most important, reason for declaring intermediate sync points is to reduce the amount of CICS region space required to hold "before images." More sync points mean that LUW's are shorter, so that CICS can discard images more frequently. The more often CICS can discard the before images, the fewer will accumulate in the region.

A second reason has to do with exclusive control. Remember that the purpose of exclusive control is to be sure that, while one task is changing a file, no other task may attempt to change the same data. You may wish to review the discussion in Chapter 5 to recall why it is important that changes to the same data be done one at a time and in order.

However, until the LUW is complete, there is always the possibility that the task may ABEND, forcing CICS to back out any changes that have been made. This possibility requires that CICS handle exclusive control slightly differently for recoverable files than for files not designated as recoverable.

To see why, suppose a task called T1 has read a record containing the value 2600, rewritten the record with a value of 2400, then continued processing and ABENDed before completing the LUW. Meanwhile, a second task read the 2400 value from the file, subtracted 200 from it, and wrote the updated value 2200 into the file. CICS ABEND processing for task T1 must back out T1's change because the LUW had not been completed. The before image, containing the value 2600, will be written back into the file. In effect, CICS has backed out the work of *both tasks* although the second task has no way of knowing that this has occurred. In order to prevent this confusion, CICS *extends exclusive control* for recoverable files to the end of the LUW. That is, instead of releasing exclusive control when a REWRITE is performed, CICS leaves exclusive control in effect until the next sync point. This, then, is a second reason for declaring intermediate sync points—by creating smaller LUW's, you reduce the amount of time a task has exclusive control of the shared file.

Now look again at the task shown in Figure 10-2. It updates RECORD1 and then updates RECORD2. The program declares a sync point after the RECORD1 update. Therefore, CICS will discard the "before image" of RECORD1 at the intermediate sync point instead of keeping it until task termination. We will see that the sync point between updates is a good idea, but it will work only if the two records, RECORD1 and RECORD2, are *unrelated*. To understand, we need to look further at how CICS may use the copied records.

Let's assume that the task illustrated by Figure 10-2 ABENDS at the point labeled A. Because the task has updated a *recoverable* file, CICS must perform *Dynamic Transaction Backout*. To do this it reads the copied records from the dynamic log—starting with the last entry—and writes them back into the file. In the case of Figure 10-2, the dynamic log contains only a copy of RECORD2; the RECORD1 copy was discarded at the end of the first LUW. Therefore, CICS restores only RECORD2. If the intermediate sync point had not been declared, the copy of RECORD1 would still be in the dynamic log and CICS would have restored RECORD1 too. If a program updates several unrelated records, it's a good idea to have a sync point after each update so that an ABEND will cause only the most recent changes to be backed out. This is a third reason for declaring intermediate sync points—to prevent successful updates from being backed out needlessly.

But why must the records be unrelated? Let's look again at Figure 10-2, but assume that RECORD1 and RECORD2 are related. We'll see that in this case it is incorrect to declare the intermediate sync point.

Suppose that the two records are related in the following way. The file to be updated is a travel bureau file in which each record contains a list of people who have reservations for a particular tour. RECORD1 is for a January cruise to Hawaii; RECORD2 is for the same dates in Miami Beach. Client Sandsun has reservations for Miami Beach, but wants to switch to the Hawaii cruise. The program must remove Sandsun's name from RECORD2 and add it to RECORD1. Now follow along in Figure 10-2. The task successfully updates RECORD1 (Sandsun is going to Hawaii). The first LUW ends and the task begins to update RECORD2, but it ABENDs in the process. CICS performs Dynamic Transaction Backout as part of the ABEND processing. It restores RECORD2 to its initial state (Sandsun is going to Miami Beach). The change to RECORD1 was completed in the first LUW so it is not backed out. The result: Sandsun is scheduled for *both* Miami Beach and Hawaii.

Because the change to RECORD1 is logically related to the change of RECORD2, these two records must be kept in synchronization—either both changed or both backed out. The intermediate sync point is an error because the files are not OK until *both* changes have been completed...Sandsun added to RECORD1 *and* deleted from RECORD2.

Before leaving the subject of defining LUW's, we should point out one very practical consideration. The point of defining an LUW is to declare that files are OK so that a transaction can restart from this point. There's no point in having the LUW if you don't provide the user with a transaction or a transaction option that does, in fact, start from that point. In short, an LUW in the middle of a transaction makes no sense if the user can't request processing to begin there.

The Dynamic Log: We have said that CICS keeps "before images" in an area called the dynamic log. At this point, let's see what the dynamic log looks like.

Figure 10-3 shows a dynamic log for a task that is somewhat more complex than the task of Figure 10-2. This task not only modifies records, but also adds and deletes them. Notice that the second entry (labeled REC 2) in the log consists only of a key—it is not an image of an entire record. This entry is associated with an *Add Record* operation. When a task adds a record, CICS need to keep only the *key* of the new record, because if Dynamic Transaction Backout occurs, it needs only to delete the record that was to be added.

This completes our discussion of *why* and *where* to declare sync points. We need now to describe *how* you declare them.

The SYNCPOINT command: To define a sync point, you use the CICS command:

EXEC CICS SYNCPOINT

In the next section we will discuss an additional option of the SYNCPOINT command. First, let's review the connection between sync points and dynamic transaction backout.

If a task updates a recoverable file and then ABENDs, CICS backs out all the file changes performed since the task's last sync point. This process is called Dynamic Transaction Backout and is performed automatically by CICS during ABEND processing. If the application program did not declare intermediate sync points, then the only sync point in effect will be the *start of task* syncpoint and all the task's updates will be backed out. If there are points

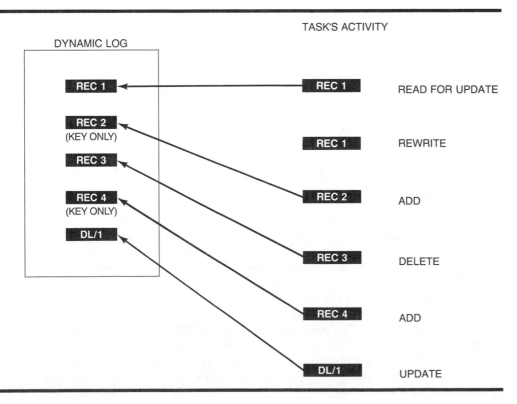

Figure 10-3
Dynamic Log,
Example of Contents

within the task's execution when the files are *all* OK *and* from which the user can restart processing, the program should declare these as intermediate sync points. This reduces the time during which the files are held under exclusive control and prevents Dynamic Transaction Backout from backing out updates that had been successful.

Exception-Handling Considerations: So far, we have discussed how CICS restores recoverable files when a task ABENDs. However, you know that ABENDs can often be prevented if you design and program effective Exception-Handling Routines. The primary objectives of an exception-handling routine are: first, to recover from the exception and continue processing, or as a second choice, to terminate in an orderly fashion. In neither case will an ABEND occur.

But suppose you are writing a program that updates recoverable files. Because your exception-handling routine prevents an ABEND from occurring, it also prevents Dynamic Transaction Backout from taking place. However, you are responsible for making sure that an exceptional condition does not interfere with the correct and complete update to the file. You must be sure that files are OK before your program terminates.

You can do this by *requesting* the same transaction backout that would have occurred automatically if your program had ABENDed.

There are two ways of doing this. First, consider the case when the exception-handling routine must terminate the task. Typically, it will SEND the user a message like "Transaction is Terminating. Please retry." Then it will issue a CICS RETURN command. To request transaction backout, you can replace the RETURN command with the command:

EXEC CICS ABEND

This will cause the CICS ABEND processing routine to be invoked and to perform Dynamic Transaction Backout before terminating the task.

As a second option, consider the case in which your exception-handling routine is able to recover and restart processing from some point in the program. Before transferring control to the restart point, you want to restore the files. To do this, you issue the SYNCPOINT command with an additional keyword:

EXEC CICS SYNCPOINT ROLLBACK

The command causes CICS to perform transaction backout and then *return control* to the instruction following the SYNCPOINT command.

Recovery Restart

The preceding section described how CICS restores recoverable files during ABEND processing for a task. But what if CICS itself, or another part of the system, ABENDs? That kind of failure would cause all the CICS tasks to be interrupted, and many of them might have been in the process of updating recoverable files. The dynamic log won't help in this case because it is in the CICS region and will be lost when CICS terminates.

To recover files after a system crash, CICS uses a technique called *Recovery Restart*. When CICS is restarted after the system crash, it will perform a backout process similar to that used for Dynamic Transaction Backout. The objective is the same; that is, to return all recoverable files to a state when they were OK. However, in this case, *many* tasks may be involved and the "before images" have to be found somewhere other than in the dynamic log.

To support Recovery Restart, the system programmer must define a sequential data set called the *system log*. While CICS is active, it records both sync points and before images in the system log. The process is called, *change logging* or simply *logging*. Figure 10-4 shows how information is logged for three CICS tasks.

The figure shows three tasks labeled A, B, and C that are active during a period that is represented in the system log. Notice that the first entry in the log is a sync point record generated when Task A begins. Later Tasks B and C begin and Task C terminates; each of these events produces a sync point record in the log. Each entry in the system log is associated with a particular

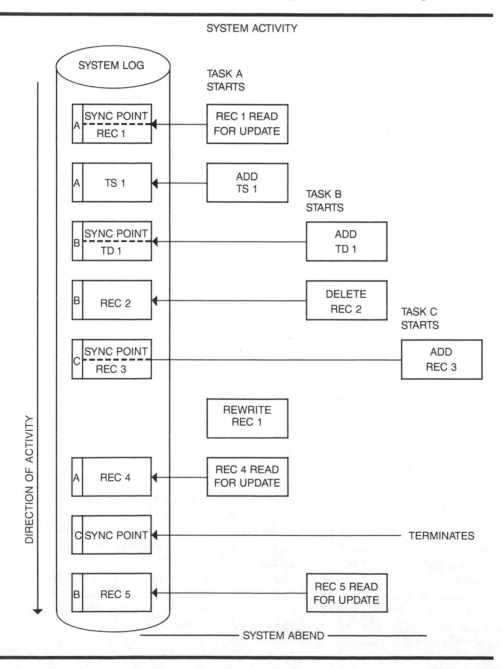

Figure 10-4
System Log with Three Tasks

task. In this example, a system crash occurs just after Task B has read a record (RECORD 5) for UPDATE. At the time of the crash, Task C had completed, but Tasks A and B were still active. Tasks active at the time of a crash are referred to as *inflight tasks*. When CICS is restarted, Recovery Restart will backout any update to a recoverable file that took place during the current LUW of an inflight task. Let's see how this is done.

When the system operator restarts CICS, the Recovery Restart processor will read the system log, beginning from the end. When it finds a before image created by an inflight task it will rewrite the image into the file. When it finds a sync point record for a task, it marks that task *not inflight.*" The effect is to remove every change made by a task during the task's current LUW. Look again at the system log illustrated in Figure 10-4. Which changes will be backed out?

Records 5, 4, 2, and 1 are restored; records TD1 and TS1 are removed. Record 3 is not restored because it was modified by Task C but in a *previous LUW*. Recovery Restart marked Task C "not inflight" when it read the sync point record (second from the end) for task C—before it read the before image for record 3.

Notice that Recovery Restart will work correctly only if application programs have correctly defined sync points. If sync points are declared at a point when the files are not OK, then some changes that should be backed out will remain in the file.

Forward Recovery Method

Recovery Restart and Transaction Backout are examples of *backwards recovery*. They begin with the data base at the point a problem occurs and read a log *backward*, rewriting record images until a correct version of the data base has been obtained.

A second method of recovering files is *forward recovery*. In this case, recovery starts with a copy of the file that was made at some time in the past. A file copy made for this purpose is called the *backup file*. Then all the changes that have been made to the file since its backup was created are *reapplied* to the backup file.

If you have done a lot of work on computers, you have probably found from experience that it's wise to copy your important files periodically, just in case they might be lost or damaged. The same principle applies in a DB/DC installation. The operations staff has a schedule for *backing up* (that is, making backup copies of) each recoverable file. They may copy a file daily, weekly, or on some other schedule depending upon how frequently the file is modified.

To perform forward recovery, the data center needs a valid backup copy *and* some way of knowing how the file has been modified after the copy was made. We know about the backup copy; but what about the modifications? This brings us to a facility called *automatic journaling*.

Automatic Journaling

Automatic Journaling (*journaling* for short) is a CICS facility that the data center can elect to use for certain files. It causes CICS to collect a copy of every change that is made to each selected file; the copies are kept in a sequential data set called a *journal*—each file is assigned to a specific journal. If journaling is to be used, the system programmer must define the sequential data sets to be used as journals, and must set certain fields in the File Control Table (FCT) entry for each file for which a journal will be kept. One field in the FCT entry specifies that changes to this file are to be journaled; another specifies which journal will be used for the file. Figure 10-5 shows how the FCT defines a separate journal for each of three files.

As the figure indicates, each journal is identified by a number. The number may be from 2 through 99. The number 1 is reserved for the system log that is known to CICS as journal #1. Keep in mind, though, that the system log is different from the other journals in that:

■ The system log is used to record changes to all the recoverable files.

■ CICS copies a record into the system log *before* the record is modified; the journal is used to collect the *new* (that is, *after update*) record image.

The FCT entry also specifies what type of file activity is to be recorded in the journal. For example, journal records might be written when a REWRITE, WRITE, DELETE, READ UPDATE, or READ command is issued for the file. But why would anyone want to record READ commands in the journal? A READ doesn't change the file, so recording it makes no sense for recovering the file.

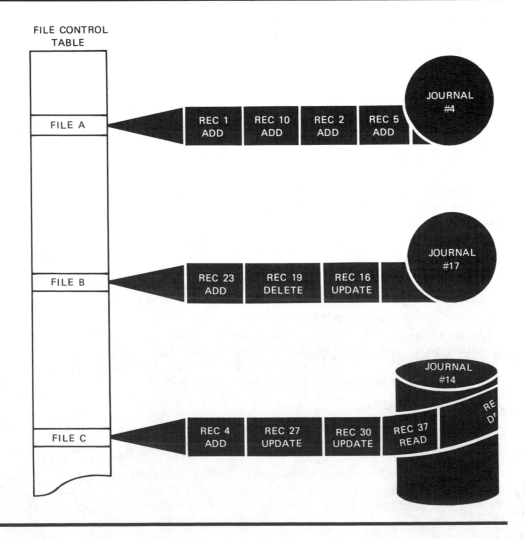

Figure 10-5
Journals Defined for Three Files

Recall the earlier discussion of access monitoring for data security. If a record is placed into the journal each time a file is read, this information can be used as a security check. In fact, the journal can be used for several other purposes besides data recovery. For example, it is often useful to know how active a particular file is (that is, how often it's accessed in a given period of time), or to know what types of transactions are used most often on the file (what proportion of transactions change the file as opposed to simply reading it). The data to answer these kinds of questions can conveniently be obtained from the journal.

User Defined Journal Entries

If journaling is specified in a file's FCT entry, CICS *automatically* writes standard data recovery records into the journal for that file. This is transparent to the application program; that is, you don't have to write any CICS commands to cause journaling to be performed.

The standard records are adequate for most data recovery purposes, but if an application is designed to use the journal for some additional purpose, the application programs may have to write their own type of records into the journal.

Here is the CICS command used to write a record into a journal file:

```
EXEC CICS JOURNAL JFILEID (data value)
          FROM (data area)   LENGTH (data value)
          TYPEID (data value)
          PREFIX (data value)   PFXLENG (data value)
```

The JFILEID keyword is used to specify the identifying number of the journal to be written. We have seen that a file's FCT entry gives the journal number to be used for a particular file.

As a matter of good programming practice, your program should obtain the journal identifier number from the FCT entry and specify it as the JFILEID argument. Why is this important? Suppose that you have written a program to use journal #2; that is, you have specified JFILEID(2) in a JOURNAL command. After your program has been in use for several months, the data center decides to move the application to another computer on which other CICS applications are supported. But on this new computer there is already a file that has been assigned to use journal #2. The system programmer should be able to take care of this problem by changing the FCT entry for your application's file to assign a new journal number, say 47. However, because your program ignores the FCT entry, it will continue to use journal #2. CICS will write the automatic data recovery journal entries to journal #47 as specified by the FCT, but your program's entries will continue to go to journal #2—the *wrong journal* in this new environment.

This text will not describe how to read the FCT. In practice, most installations will provide a subroutine for you to call in order to obtain the journal identifier number. When you complete the exercise for this chapter, keep in mind that you would be expected to use such a subroutine. However, for the exercise, simply use a variable name as the JFILEID argument—you may set the variable to a constant value before you issue the JOURNAL command.

The remaining options of the JOURNAL command define the contents of the record to be written into the journal. The FROM argument specifies a data area that contains the *user data* to be written.

LENGTH gives the length of the user data.

TYPEID specifies an optional two-character identifier to be placed in the record. This identifier tells what kind of record this is; the possible identifiers must be defined as part of the application program's design. This field will be used by programs that read the journal, so that they can determine what each record means.

PREFIX specifies an optional data area to be placed ahead of the user data in the record. PFXLENG specifies the length of the prefix area.

Figure 10-6 shows how a user-defined journal record is formatted.

If TYPEID was specified, the type identifying field appears first; it is followed by the PREFIX area if one was defined. The user data appears last in the record.

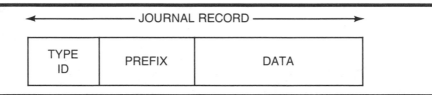

Figure 10-6
Format of
Journal Record

Summary

By definition, the information contained in data files is important in the daily business of the company. The data is, therefore, a company asset which, like any other asset, must be protected from damage and misuse.

"Protecting" data involves two separate issues. The first is *data security* which prevents information from being accessed by unauthorized individuals. Security is a concern when data files contain information that would be useful to the company's competitors or for which the company has custodial responsibility. The second issue is *data integrity*—insuring that data files remain usable and that the information they contain is complete and correct.

The degree of security protection required for a data file depends upon the damage the company would suffer if particular information became known to unauthorized people. This chapter discussed three general techniques for providing data security; they may be used singly or in combination.

Access control methods attempt to keep unauthorized individuals away from restricted data. Computer systems in which information is stored use *system security* features to control access to data by determining whether an access request is from a program or individual *authorized* to perform the *requested operation* upon the *requested data*. Access can also be controlled by *physical security* methods that are external to the computer on which the data is stored. For example, terminals from which data may be accessed may be kept in a locked room within a locked building.

Encryption techniques may be used so that data can be understood only by those who know the code and how to use it. Encryption techniques use both software and hardware to encode and decode the data when given the correct code information.

Finally, *access monitoring* can be used to record information about each access or attempted access of protected data. The information can be used to detect attempts at unauthorized access and to identify the source of such attempts.

The DB/DC system and operating system provide system security facilities that can be selected and defined by system programmers and data administrators. You don't have to change your application programs to take advantage of these standard security facilities. However, if an application requires it, you can program additional checking. To do this, your program may need to examine data in system control blocks or to make use of system facilities like the CICS journal.

Application programmers have a major responsibility in the area of *data integrity*. There are two things you must do in order to maintain data integrity:

1. Verify that data is correct before writing it into a data base.
2. Provide a way to recover when possible errors have been detected.

Data is verified by *validity checking*—testing an input value against a model of what it is expected to look like. In the CICS environment, you are responsible for coding the appropriate validity-checking logic into your application program.

When a data file has become damaged, it must be recovered so that work can resume. We discussed two general types of file recovery—backward and forward recovery. *Backward recovery* starts with the data base in its current (possibly erroneous) state and *removes* (backs out) changes recorded in a log until a usable version of the data base has been obtained.

You are responsible for segmenting a program into *Logical Units of Work* (LUW's) if the program modifies a file or other recoverable resource. You define a logical unit of work by declaring *synchronization points* within the program. Each synchronization point (*sync point*) declares to the system that "my files were OK at this point." The interval between two sync points is a logical unit of work. If the application program terminates abnormally, the system will perform *Dynamic Transaction Backout*—a backward recovery operation to restore the files to the state they were in at the most recent sync point. You use the SYNCPOINT command to declare a synchronization point.

You must also be sure that your exception-handling routines insure that files are OK before they restart or terminate the task. The routines can do this by requesting transaction backout—either indirectly by using the ABEND command to invoke the CICS ABEND processor, or directly by using the SYNCPOINT command with ROLLBACK option.

For *forward recovery*, the data center's operation staff make periodic backup copies of data files, and CICS keeps a journal of changes as they are made to the files. Data base recovery starts with the most recent usable backup file and *reapplies* the changes recorded in the journal after the backup file was made (but omitting any changes determined to be errors).

To support forward data base recovery, CICS provides a system journal facility controlled by File Control Table (FCT) fields that are set by the system programmer. A field in a file's FCT entry associates the data file with one of 100 journal files supported by CICS. Other control fields specify types of operations (like READ or READ for UPDATE) that are to cause a standard entry to be written into the assigned journal. The journal entries can be used for data base recovery, security monitoring, or as input for reports (like change summaries). You aren't involved with the CICS journals unless a specific application requires that non-standard journal entries be written. In this case, you use the CICS JOURNAL command to write an entry into the assigned journal.

DISCUSSION QUESTIONS

1. List the programming skills this chapter discussed for preserving data integrity.
2. Review the programs you wrote for the Exercise of Chapter 5. Assuming that the file updated by your programs was a recoverable file, what changes would you make to the programs based upon this chapter's discussion?

EXERCISE

The purpose of this exercise is to practice writing records into a journal file. Remember that the system will write *standard* data recovery records into the journal automatically if the FCT entry for a file specifies journaling. However, the design of some applications may require that you write non-standard records to be used instead of or in addition to the standard ones.

For this exercise, you will modify the program you wrote for the Exercise, Part 3 of the chapter "Random Access of Data Files." Assume that the specifications for the program have been changed to require that the program record every transaction request that causes the file to be changed.

Recall that the user's transaction request was 16 bytes long. It included the four-byte transaction identifier, a four-byte function request like UPDT or GDEL, and a six-byte record key. Your program should write the request into journal #44 whenever a record is updated, added to, or deleted from the file.

11 Test and Problem Determination Tools

Introduction

Most of our discussion up to this point has focused on the activity of *writing CICS application programs*. That is, we have focused on CICS commands and how to use COBOL language facilities in connection with those commands. We have also spent some time in discussing *program design* in the DB/DC environment.

Designing and writing programs are but two of the activities involved in the overall job of application development. In this chapter, we will focus on two additional activities—program testing and problem determination. The term *debugging* is sometimes applied to both of these activities, but in reality the two activities are separate and different.

Program testing is the systematic process of demonstrating that a program is correct. Its objective is to insure that no program is made available to users until the program is complete and reliable.

By this point in your programming career, however, you have probably learned that "there is no such thing as a bug-free program." In spite of our best efforts to observe all of the good program practices and to test programs thoroughly, we can expect that eventually an unusual combination of events will trigger a failure—sometimes in a program that has been working reliably for months or even years. *Problem determination* is the process of discovering what caused a program to fail and how the program must be changed to prevent the failure from happening again.

Both program testing and problem determination are extremely important in the DB/DC environment. The company depends upon being able to get accurate information quickly from the DB/DC system. As soon as a program has become a part of the CICS application system, a large number of people begin to rely upon it in order to do their jobs. A program that produces incorrect results or that crashes unpredictably is worse than no program at all. Good program testing prevents this situation.

On the other hand, when a program does fail, it's critical that the reason be discovered quickly—not only so the program can be fixed, but also so that users can be told what to do in order to avoid the problem. This is what problem determination is about.

This chapter discusses two CICS facilities that you can use in program testing or problem determination. The Execution Diagnostic Facility, usually referred to as EDF, is an example of an interactive debugging tool. It allows you to control a CICS task as the task executes and permits you to look at and change program variables *during task execution*. The second facility, the CICS transaction dump, can be used *after a task has terminated* to find out what values were stored in program variables and CICS control blocks at a particular point during the task's execution.

Objectives

After completing this chapter, you will be able to:

- Describe how the Execution Diagnostic Facility (EDF) is used in the *same-terminal* and *two-terminal* modes.
- Describe how the Execution Diagnostic Facility (EDF) can be used in *program test* and *program debug* situations.
- Use EDF to debug or to test a CICS application program.
- Interpret a CICS transaction dump.

Execution Diagnostic Facility (EDF)

A program fails when its logic is incorrectly or incompletely defined to handle a particular set of conditions. The conditions include inputs supplied by the user and data files, as well as factors in the processing environment—for example, contents of system control blocks and the mix of tasks in the system at a given time. To fix the program you need to trace through the logic, taking into account the conditions in effect when the program was run.

But, this is easier said than done. At best, it is time-consuming. At worst, it may be impossible to find out what the run-time environment was like. When you trace through a program's logic, it's also easy to make a mistake by losing track of what value has been assigned to a variable, or by taking the wrong path at a branch point. Sometimes you may pass over an instruction, feeling sure that you know its result, only to discover much later that the result was not what you assumed.

One debugging approach is to add *debug statements* that write out trace messages or the values of key variables at critical points in the program. These outputs help you trace the program's flow. But modifying and recompiling the program to insert the debug statements takes time, and you may make errors. Even worse, sometimes adding the debug statements changes the program so that the bug appears to "disappear," but returns when you take out the debug statements.

The ideal would be to be able to "get inside the computer" and *watch* as the program runs, so that you could see exactly how variables change and branches are taken. It would be even better if, when you saw a variable set to an incorrect value, you could stop the program, put the correct value into the variable, and then let the program continue. This technique is called *interactive debugging*. You may already have used interactive debugging facilities that are provided for various programming languages. The Execution Diagnostic Facility, EDF, is an interactive debugging facility designed especially for the CICS environment.

EDF Overview

You can use EDF both during program test and in problem determination situations. We'll look first at a problem determination case.

Suppose that you have written a CICS application program called PROG. PROG has been tested, found reliable, and made available for general use by CICS users. You have just received a call that PROG has failed during execution. Let's assume that the user who experienced the problem has done everything correctly, and the problem clearly lies in PROG. As we said earlier, you need to find out quickly what went wrong so that you can warn users how to avoid the problem while you work to fix PROG.

Using EDF, you can proceed in either of two ways. You can find out exactly what inputs the user supplied the program, start first EDF and then PROG from your own terminal, supplying the same inputs the user did. This approach is referred to as *same-terminal* debugging, because EDF and the application program to be debugged are run from the same terminal. As PROG runs, you will receive the same output messages the user did, but you will also receive message panels from EDF. As will be discussed in more detail below, the panels allow you to examine and/or modify storage locations in PROG and elsewhere in the CICS region.

The second approach is to start EDF from your terminal and request that it trace PROG as it runs *on the user's terminal*. In this case the user runs the program just as before, entering the same inputs and receiving the same messages. EDF will send message panels to your terminal at various points during PROG's execution. The user will receive only the messages produced by PROG—just as though EDF weren't involved. The user will receive the same messages and supply the same inputs as he or she did previously, but the program will appear to run more slowly, because EDF is interrupting it to send the EDF panels to you.

If you choose the second approach—that is, you let the user invoke PROG—you will start EDF with a transaction request like:

CEDF L77A

where L77A is the *terminal identifier* of the user's terminal.

In this case, you are requesting that EDF trace a transaction that is run from the specified terminal, but *your terminal* will receive the EDF panels. Your terminal is the direct terminal for EDF, and the user's terminal is the direct terminal for PROG. If there's already a transaction in process on the terminal when you start EDF, EDF will begin tracing that transaction. If there is not, EDF will begin tracing as soon as the user enters a transaction request.

If you decide to trace PROG as it runs on your own terminal, you start with the transaction request:

CEDF

In this case you don't specify a terminal-identifier, because EDF is to trace the next transaction invoked from *your terminal*. Therefore, your terminal will be the direct terminal for both EDF and PROG. After EDF has started, you will invoke PROG. You will then receive the first EDF panel informing you that PROG is about to begin. Once PROG begins to run, you will receive both EDF panels and the messages produced by PROG.

Whether PROG is run from your terminal or from the user's, EDF will send panels to your terminal at certain points during PROG's execution. You will receive the first EDF panel when PROG begins to execute. The panel informs you that execution is about to begin. At this point, you may use EDF facilities to look at storage locations and modify them if you wish. PROG will not begin to execute until you enter a *go ahead* command to EDF.

After execution has begun, EDF will interrupt PROG before each CICS command. At these points, EDF will display an ABOUT TO EXECUTE COMMAND panel that names the CICS command that PROG is about to execute. It also shows you which options were coded for the command and displays the current value of any arguments. Again, you may look at and change storage locations before giving the *go ahead* command.

When the CICS command has been completed, EDF will suspend PROG's execution again and display the results of the command. The results will not be returned to PROG until you have examined them and changed them if you desire.

Execution will continue in this manner until PROG terminates or until you terminate EDF, allowing PROG to continue without further interruptions.

Example EDF Session

Let's look at an EDF session panel-by-panel. Assume that you are about to trace a program named FCEXCOB1 that is invoked by the CICS transaction code FC01. In this example, you will trace FCEXCOB1 from your own terminal.

To begin the EDF session, you enter the transaction request:

CEDF

Once EDF has been initiated, you can enter the FC01 transaction request. Assume that the transaction request is:

FC01 DISP LS012

When the FC01 transaction request has been entered, EDF displays the EDF PROGRAM INITIATION panel shown in Figure 11-1

The first line of the panel displays the transaction ID, the program name and the sequential task identification number that CICS assigned when the task was started. Below the STATUS line that identifies the panel as the PROGRAM INITIATION panel, EDF displays the contents of the EIB. The EIB is displayed only on the PROGRAM INITIATION panel, although you may request to see the EIB from other EDF panels.

```
TRANSACTION:  FC01     PROGRAM: FCEXCOB1     TASK NUMBER:  0001592     DISPLAY:
STATUS:       PROGRAM INITIATION
EIBTIME   =  +0174857
EIBDATE   =  +0079086
EIBTRNID  =  'FC01'
EIBTASKN  =  +0001592
EIBTRMID  =  'LA1E'
EIBCPOSN  =  +00015
EIBCALEN  =  +00000
EIBAID    =  X'7D'                       AT X'001323D2'
EIBFN     =  X'0000'                      AT X'001323D3'
EIBRCODE  =  X'000000000000'             AT X'001323D5'
EIBDS     =  '. . . . . . . .'
EIBREQID  =  '. . . . . . . .'


ENTER: CONTINUE

PF1:    END EDF SESSION       PF2:   RE-DISPLAY            PF3:   SWITCH HEX/CHAR
PF4:    EIB DISPLAY           PF5:   WORKING STORAGE       PF6:   USER DISPLAY
PF7:    SUPPRESS DISPLAYS     PF8:   UNDEFINED             PF9:   STOP CONDITIONS
PF10:   OLDEST DISPLAY        PF11:  PREVIOUS DISPLAY      PF12:  UNDEFINED
```

Figure 11-1
EDF "Program
Initiation" Panel

Below the EIB display are the words: ENTER: CONTINUE. This lets you know that to let execution continue, you must press the ENTER key. Below that line is a list of all the Program Function (PF) keys that you may use while viewing this panel, together with an explanation of what function is assigned to each Program Function key. Program Function key assignments may differ between particular versions of CICS, so you may find that the EDF panels on your CICS system define the keys differently than shown in this chapter's illustrations.

The panel in Figure 11-1 indicates that Program Function key 4 (PF4) can be used to request display of the EIB. If your terminal has no PF keys, you can use the cursor and the ENTER key to request any of the functions listed here. For example, to request the function assigned to PF4, you would place the cursor under the PF4 label and then press the ENTER key.

Once you have viewed the panel and pressed ENTER to allow execution to continue, PROG will execute normally until the first CICS command is reached. At that point, EDF will interrupt execution and display the ABOUT TO EXECUTE COMMAND panel. It is shown in Figure 11-2.

The status line indicates that this panel is displayed because CICS is ABOUT TO EXECUTE COMMAND. In this example, the CICS command about to be executed is a HANDLE CONDITION command. The panel shows the command and the options: LENGERR, DSIDERR, NOTFND, NOTOPEN, and ERROR that were coded for the command. The panel also displays the value of arguments. In the case of the HANDLE command, the arguments are the names of program labels. Since FCEXCOB1 is a COBOL program, EDF represents the arguments as an empty pair of parentheses. If you were tracing a PL/1 program, you would see instead the absolute physical address of the program label. For Assembly language programs, the offset of the program label relative to the beginning of the program is displayed.

Notice the OFFSET field that is displayed about halfway down the panel.

```
TRANSACTION:  FC01     PROGRAM: FCEXCOB1     TASK NUMBER:  0001592     DISPLAY:
STATUS:    ABOUT TO EXECUTE COMMAND
EXEC CICS HANDLE     CONDITION
    LENGERR( )
    DSIDERR( )
    NOTFND( )
    NOTOPEN( )
    ERROR( )




OFFSET:     X'0005BA'     LINE:    00031       EIBFN = X'0204'

ENTER: CONTINUE

PF1:      END EDF SESSION     PF2:     RE-DISPLAY          PF3:     SWITCH HEX/CHAR
PF4:      EIB DISPLAY         PF5:     WORKING STORAGE     PF6:     USER DISPLAY
PF7:      SUPPRESS DISPLAYS   PF8:     ABEND USER TASK     PF9:     STOP CONDITIONS
PF10:     OLDEST DISPLAY      PF11:    PREVIOUS DISPLAY    PF12:    UNDEFINED
```

**Figure 11-2
EDF "About to
Execute Command"
Panel**

This gives the *relative address* (offset from the beginning of the program) of the CICS command that is about to be executed. LINE represents the line number of the CICS command in the translator listing. The third value in this line, EIBFN, is a *function number* that CICS uses to describe the command HANDLE CONDITION.

When you press ENTER to permit execution to continue, CICS executes the HANDLE command. As soon as execution is complete, and before CICS returns control to the program, EDF suspends execution and displays the COMMAND EXECUTION COMPLETE panel shown in Figure 11-3.

The values in the OFFSET line are the same as the previous panel. However, a new field, RESPONSE, appears just below OFFSET. It describes the completion status of the command. The EIBRCODE field that follows RESPONSE contains the completion code that will be made available to the program in the EIBRCODE field of the EIB. Notice that you can request to see the entire EIB from the COMMAND EXECUTION COMPLETE panel by pressing PF4.

When you allow PROG to continue, it will be executed without interruption until the next CICS command is encountered. In this example, the next command is RECEIVE. Figure 11-4 shows the ABOUT TO EXECUTE COMMAND panel for the RECEIVE command.

This ABOUT TO EXECUTE COMMAND panel shows that the INTO and LENGTH options were coded in the command. It also displays the current values of each argument. The value of the LENGTH argument is 15 at this time. Remember that the LENGTH argument will be modified when the RECEIVE command is executed.

EDF has two modes of display: character or hexadecimal.

The panels you have seen so far have been displayed in *character mode*. In character mode, numeric values are displayed as decimal numbers and each byte in a character field is displayed as an alphanumeric character. If a byte in a character field does not represent a displayable alphanumeric character, EDF displays the byte as a period.

```
TRANSACTION:  FC01    PROGRAM: FCEXCOB1    TASK NUMBER:  0001592    DISPLAY:
STATUS:   COMMAND EXECUTION COMPLETE
EXEC CICS HANDLE    CONDITION
    LENGERR( )
    DSIDERR( )
    NOTFND( )
    NOTOPEN( )
    ERROR( )




OFFSET:   X'0005BA'    LINE:    00031      EIBFN = X'0204'
RESPONSE: NORMAL                           EIBRCODE = X'000000000000'

ENTER:  CONTINUE

PF1:     END EDF SESSION      PF2:    RE-DISPLAY          PF3:    SWITCH HEX/CHAR
PF4:     EIB DISPLAY          PF5:    WORKING STORAGE     PF6:    USER DISPLAY
PF7:     SUPPRESS DISPLAYS    PF8:    ABEND USER TASK     PF9:    STOP CONDITIONS
PF10:    OLDEST DISPLAY       PF11:   PREVIOUS DISPLAY    PF12:   UNDEFINED
```

Figure 11-3
EDF "Command Execution Complete" Panel

```
┌─────────────────────────────────────────────────────────────────────────────
│  TRANSACTION:  FC01    PROGRAM:    FCEXCOB1    TASK NUMBER:  0001592    DISPLAY:
│  STATUS:    ABOUT TO EXECUTE COMMAND
│  EXEC CICS RECEIVE
│      INTO('. . . . . . . . . . . . . .')
│      LENGTH(+00015)
╵
~
╷
│  OFFSET:    X'000640'        LINE:    00035        EIBFN = X'0402'
│  ENTER:  CONTINUE
│
│  PF1:      END EDF SESSION       PF2:    RE-DISPLAY          PF3:    SWITCH HEX/CHAR
│  PF4:      EIB DISPLAY           PF5:    WORKING STORAGE     PF6:    USER DISPLAY
│  PF7:      SUPPRESS DISPLAYS     PF8:    ABEND USER TASK     PF9:    STOP CONDITIONS
│  PF10:     OLDEST DISPLAY        PF11:   PREVIOUS DISPLAY    PF12:   UNDEFINED
└─────────────────────────────────────────────────────────────────────────────
```

Figure 11-4
EDF Panel Showing
Argument Values

In *hexadecimal* mode, EDF displays each field as a string of hexadecimal digits enclosed in single quotes and preceded by the character X.

Figure 11-4 shows a panel displayed in character mode. If the panel were in hexadecimal mode, LENGTH would be represented:

$$X'000F'$$

In the illustrated panel, the value of the INTO field is shown as a series of periods. You can't be sure of what value is actually in the field since in character mode EDF uses the period to represent any byte that cannot be displayed as a character. In this case, you might guess that the INPUT field has not yet been set to any particular value. That is, the field may be *uninitialized*. To see whether or not you had guessed correctly—that is, to find out exactly what is in the INTO field—you could request that EDF display the panel in hexadecimal rather than character mode. You do this by pressing PF3 that is assigned to the function SWITCH HEX/CHAR. This would cause EDF to display this panel *and all the panels that follow* in hexadecimal mode until you use PF3 to switch mode back to character again.

Figure 11-5 shows a COMMAND EXECUTION COMPLETE panel displayed in hexadecimal mode. Notice the form of the values for DATASET, INTO, etc. Notice also that the *absolute address* of each argument value is displayed to the right of the value. For example, the phrase, AT X'001328AC' indicates that the INTO area can be found at absolute address 001328AC. You can use this address to request a display of the entire INTO area or to locate INTO in a transaction dump. Both these techniques will be described later in this chapter.

Program Control Options

When you have viewed the panel, you may press ENTER to allow PROG to continue. However, there are other execution control options you might choose instead.

```
TRANSACTION:  FC01    PROGRAM: FCEXCOB1     TASK NUMBER:  0001592    DISPLAY:
STATUS:    COMMAND EXECUTION COMPLETE
EXEC CICS READ
     DATASET(X'C3D3C1E2E2C4E240')                                 AT X'00132936'
     INTO(X'D3E2F0F1F2C7D9F5F440F5C2C1D5C440E2C8D6D9E3D640D9' . . .)   AT X'001328AC'
     LENGTH(X'004B')                                              AT X'0013287C'
     RIDFLD(C'D3E2F0F1F2')                                        AT X'0013288E'
     EQUAL

OFFSET:    X'000736'     LINE:    00043        EIBFN = X'0602'
RESPONSE: NORMAL                                EIBRCODE = X'000000000000'
ENTER:  CONTINUE

PF1:     END EDF SESSION     PF2:    RE-DISPLAY          PF3:    SWITCH HEX/CHAR
PF4:     EIB DISPLAY         PF5:    WORKING STORAGE     PF6:    USER DISPLAY
PF7:     SUPPRESS DISPLAYS   PF8:    ABEND USER TASK     PF9:    STOP CONDITIONS
PF10:    OLDEST DISPLAY      PF11:   PREVIOUS DISPLAY    PF12:   UNDEFINED
```

Figure 11-5
EDF Panel in
Hexadecimal Mode

You can *terminate PROG* by pressing PF8 (ABEND USER TASK). In this
case, EDF will terminate PROG and request a transaction dump. The second
part of this chapter describes transaction dumps and how to use them.

You can *terminate EDF* by pressing PF1 (END EDF SESSION). In this case,
PROG would continue to execute without interruption by EDF. You would
see no further EDF panels.

Finally, you could allow PROG to continue without interruption *until*
a particular *stop condition* occurs. A stop condition is not necessarily a
CONDITION like LENGERR or NOTFND. In this context *condition* is used
in a general sense to mean any situation that meets criteria you define.

For example, suppose you wanted to allow PROG to continue until it reached
the next SEND command. You would specify this in two steps: first, choose
the SUPPRESS DISPLAYS option; secondly, define the condition you want to
trigger the next EDF panel. SUPPRESS DISPLAYS means that EDF will
continue to trace PROG's execution, but it will not display any EDF panels
until the stop condition occurs. You choose SUPPRESS DISPLAYS by pressing
PF7. Then, to define the stop condition you are looking for, you press PF9
(STOP CONDITIONS). EDF displays a menu, as shown in Figure 11-6, that
allows you to set a stop condition for execution of the specific command. In
this case, you have decided that the SEND command is the one you want to
trigger the next EDF panel.

As shown in the illustration, you could also set a condition to stop only at
a *particular* SEND command, by giving the command's line number or offset.
Other possible stop conditions are:

- Any CICS error CONDITION
- Normal or abnormal task termination
- Transaction ABEND

Notice that for the menu panel, you use the ENTER key to return to the

228

current EDF display. In this case, the current panel is the one shown in Figure 11-4.

If you choose to allow the EDF session to continue normally—that is, you press ENTER from the ABOUT TO EXECUTE COMMAND panel; CICS will execute the RECEIVE command using the options and argument values displayed on the ABOUT TO EXECUTE COMMAND panel. When execution is complete, and before control returns to PROG, EDF will interrupt and display the COMMAND EXECUTION COMPLETE panel. This panel is illustrated by Figure 11-7.

```
TRANSACTION: XABC        PROGRAM: UPDATE      TASK NUMBER: 0000111        DISPLAY: 00.
DISPLAY ON CONDITION:

        COMMAND:                EXEC CICS SEND
        OFFSET:                 X'......'
        LINE NUMBER:            ........
        CICS EXCEPTIONAL CONDITION:
        ANY CICS ERROR CONDITION        YES
        TRANSACTION ABEND               YES
        NORMAL TASK TERMINATION         YES
        ABNORMAL TASK TERMINATION       YES




ENTER: CURRENT DISPLAY
PF1 : UNDEFINED                 PF2 : UNDEFINED                 PF3 : UNDEFINED
```

Figure 11-6
EDF Menu for
Setting Stop
Conditions

```
TRANSACTION:  FC01    PROGRAM:    FCEXCOB1    TASK NUMBER:   0001592    DISPLAY:
STATUS    PROGRAM
EXEC CICS RECEIVE
   INTO('FC01 DISP LS012')
   LENGTH(+00015)



OFFSET:   X'000640'     LINE:   00035       EIBFN = X'0402'
RESPONSE: EOC                               EIBRCODE = X'000000000000'
ENTER: CONTINUE

PF1:     END EDF SESSION    PF2:    RE-DISPLAY          PF3:    SWITCH HEX/CHAR
PF4:     EIB DISPLAY        PF5:    WORKING STORAGE     PF6:    USER DISPLAY
PF7:     SUPPRESS DISPLAYS  PF8:    ABEND USER TASK     PF9:    STOP CONDITIONS
PF10:    OLDEST DISPLAY     PF11:   PREVIOUS DISPLAY    PF12:   UNDEFINED
```

Figure 11-7
EDF "Command
Execution Complete"
Panel Showing
INTPUT Area

The panel shows that the data:

FC01 DISP LS012

has been placed in the INTO field. Recall that this was the transaction request you used to invoke PROG. The LENGTH value remains 15, the length of the transaction request.

The response message is EOC for *End of Command*. If the message received from the terminal had exceeded 15 characters, the response message would be LENGERR.

Modifying Working-Storage

So far, we have discussed the program control options you can select from an EDF panel. Let's look now at how you would go about displaying and modifying storage locations.

In general, you may change any value shown in an unprotected area of the panel. That is, if you can type over the value from your terminal, you may change the value. In particular, at this point, you could change:

the characters in the INTO field
the response code
the value of LENGTH

Refer back to the ABOUT TO EXECUTE COMMAND panel shown in Figure 11-4. From that panel you could have changed:

the command name RECEIVE to NOP or NOOP to suppress execution
the value of LENGTH to be *passed to the RECEIVE command*

Let's discuss these two possibilities in a little more detail.

Suppose that you are tracing PROG as it runs on the user's terminal, but you want PROG to use input data that you enter from your terminal instead of letting the user enter the data. If you change the command name from RECEIVE to NOP, CICS will not attempt to read from the user's terminal. When the command (NOP) is completed, EDF will display the COMMAND EXECUTION COMPLETE panel. At that point, you can modify the panel to provide PROG any data you wish. To do so, you simply type over the values displayed for the INTO, LENGTH, and RESPONSE fields.

We have said that you could modify the value of LENGTH from both the ABOUT TO EXECUTE COMMAND panel and the COMMAND EXECUTION COMPLETE panels. However, the modification would work a little differently in the two cases.

When a command is about to be executed, the argument values displayed are *copies* of the corresponding locations in working-storage. Remember that when you code a RECEIVE command, the argument of the LENGTH option is a *variable name*. Suppose that, in this case, the variable is named HOWLONG. Then the command as it appears in your COBOL program is:

EXEC CICS RECEIVE INTO(field) LENGTH(HOWLONG) END-EXEC.

Somewhere in PROG's working-storage is a location that corresponds to the variable name HOWLONG. When EDF displays the ABOUT TO EXECUTE COMMAND panel, it takes the value from HOWLONG, places it in another location, and displays the contents of the new location. That is, it displays a *copy* of HOWLONG. If you type over the LENGTH argument on the ABOUT TO EXECUTE COMMAND panel, you will modify the copy, but you will not modify the value of HOWLONG in working-storage. When the command executes, it will use the modified value you typed into the panel. After execution, the COMMAND EXECUTION COMPLETE panel displays the value produced by the command. You may modify this value. After you press ENTER to permit execution to continue, the value from the panel will be moved into HOWLONG.

Therefore, modifying the value in the ABOUT TO EXECUTE COMMAND panel causes the command to use the new value, but does not change HOW-LONG itself. If you type over the LENGTH argument from the COMMAND EXECUTION COMPLETE panel, the value you type will replace the HOWLONG value in working-storage.

Displaying and Modifying Working-Storage

You may also request to see other areas of storage. We have already pointed out that you may press PF4 to see the contents of the EIB. If you press PF5, you will obtain a display of working-storage. Figure 11-8 shows an example.

Notice that the second line of the display gives the address, 0013287C, of the first working-storage location displayed.

Each line of the working-storage display shows an *absolute address*, a *relative address* that gives the offset of storage within working storage, the hexadecimal value of four full words of storage, and a character mode display of the same full words.

In the illustrated case, working storage begins at absolute address 0013287C. Because every working-storage display begins at a "double double" word location, the absolute address shown for the first line is 00132870. However, since locations 00132870 through 0013287B are not part of working storage, their values are not displayed—the first three full word positions are blank. The first

```
TRANSACTION:   FC01    PROGRAM: FCEXCOB1    TASK NUMBER: 0001592    DISPLAY:
ADDRESS: 0013287C

00132870   00000000                                     00000000           ....
00132880   00000004   00000000   D3C1C3F9   40C4C9E2   D740D3E2   ....LAC9 DISP LS
00132890   00000014   F0F1F200   00000000   00000000   00000000   012............
001328A0   00000024   00000000   00000000   00000000   D3E2F0F1   ...........LS01
001328B0   00000034   E3E640D9   C5C3C5C9   E540C3C8   C9F1F7F7   TW RECEIV CHI177
001328C0   00000044   0000F7F8   40F0F1F3   F0D3C1E7   40F7F8F1   ..78 0130LAX 781


ENTER:   CURRENT DISPLAY

PF1 : SWITCH HEX/CHAR      PF2 : RE-DISPLAY         PF3 : END EDF SESSION
PF4 : SUPPRESS DISPLAYS    PF5 : WORKING STORAGE    PF6 : USER DISPLAY
PF7 : SCROLL BACK          PF8 : SCROLL FORWARD     PF9 : STOP CONDITIONS
PF10: REMEMBER DISPLAY     PF11: PREVIOUS DISPLAY   PF12: ABEND USER TASK
```

**Figure 11-8
Working Storage
Display from EDF**

working storage location has a hexadecimal value X'00000000' as shown for the fourth full word in the first line of working storage displayed. Since the location contains no displayable characters, the character representation of the word shows periods.

The second line of the working-storage display begins at absolute location 00132880. This is the fourth byte of working-storage, so the *relative location* column shows the address X'000004'. These addresses are shown in the first two fields of the line. Next appear four hexadecimal fields, each displaying a full word of working storage. The second full word contains the value X'D3C1C3F9'. This value represents the characters LAC9 that appear in the character mode display shown at the right side of the panel.

When you press the WORKING STORAGE key from an EDF menu, you obtain a panel that displays storage beginning with the first locations in working storage. If you want to see locations that follow those displayed, you can use the Scroll Forward PF key (PF8 in the illustrated panel). You can return to the beginning of working storage by pressing the Scroll Back PF Key (PF7 in the illustrated panel.)

You may also type over the values shown in this panel.

You may type over the ADDRESS field shown in the second line of the panel. By changing this address, you can request to see any location in working-storage. For example, earlier you saw a panel in hexadecimal mode that gave the address of an INTO area as X'001328AC'. To look at the INTO area from the WORKING-STORAGE panel, you would type this address over the value, X'0013287C', shown in the ADDRESS field.

You may also modify a working-storage location directly by typing a new value into either the hexadecimal or character display of the location. For example, suppose that the relative location X'000014' should contain the characters 013 in place of the characters 012 shown. You could place the correct value into working-storage by changing the character 2 in the character mode display of the third byte of this full word to a 3.

You can modify a working-storage location by typing over either the hexadecimal or character mode display of the location. If you needed to change relative location X'000004' from the integer 0 to 1, you would change the last position of its hexadecimal mode display from 0 to 1, so that the full word had the hexadecimal value X'000001'.

Other EDF Features

At this point, we have discussed the basic EDF features you need to know in order to test a CICS program. In addition to these, there are several options that you may want to use in certain situations.

Refer to the PF Key listing at the bottom of the panel shown in Figure 11-8. The following are options we haven't yet discussed.

1. RE-DISPLAY

Note: In some EDF panels, this option is labeled CURRENT DISPLAY instead of RE-DISPLAY.

The *current display* refers to the panel that EDF displayed when it last interrupted program execution. For example, suppose that EDF has interrupted execution to display an ABOUT TO EXECUTE COMMAND panel.

You view this panel and then request to see a WORKING-STORAGE panel. At this point you are viewing the panel shown in Figure 11-8. However, the *current panel* is ABOUT TO EXECUTE COMMAND. If you select this option, the current panel will be redisplayed, including any changes that you have made to the values shown.

2. USER DISPLAY

This option is only available when you are doing same-terminal debugging. It causes EDF to display the panel most recently displayed by the program being tested—that is, the panel a user would ordinarily be viewing at this point in the program's execution.

3. REMEMBER DISPLAY

You request this option if you want EDF to keep an image of this panel for your future reference. For example, suppose you are viewing the section of working-storage that contains a large input area. You would like to see how these values change as execution progresses. To do so, you would display working-storage and request REMEMBER DISPLAY. You can then redisplay this copy for comparison after storage has been altered by other CICS commands or COBOL statements. You do not see this option on panels associated with CICS commands—that is, on ABOUT TO EXECUTE or COMMAND EXECUTION COMPLETE panels—because EDF automatically remembers these panels.

Refer now to Figure 11-7. Notice the options OLDEST DISPLAY and PREVIOUS DISPLAY that are associated with PF Keys 10 and 11. You use these options to review earlier panels that have been remembered by EDF. When you are examining these earlier panels, the NEXT DISPLAY option is also available to allow you to request the remembered panel that followed the panel currently in view.

Program and Task Termination

Assume now that your program has reached its normal end and is ready to return to CICS. You will receive an ABOUT TO EXECUTE COMMAND panel like the one shown in Figure 11-9. Notice that the command that is about to be executed is EXEC CICS RETURN.

After the RETURN command has been completed, you receive a PROGRAM TERMINATION panel in place of the usual COMMAND EXECUTION COMPLETE panel. If you allow execution to proceed, the next panel you receive will be a TASK TERMINATION panel.

Figure 11-10 illustrates a TASK TERMINATION panel. Notice in the lines above the PF Key assignments, the message TO CONTINUE EDF SESSION REPLY YES... REPLY:NO. If you are debugging a pseudo-conversational transaction, you do not want to discontinue EDF until the end of the last transaction in the chain. For example, assume that PROGRAM FCEXCOB1 concludes with a pseudo-conversational RETURN command naming a second transaction to be invoked when the user enters the next terminal input. In this case, you want EDF to continue and to trace the new transaction when it is invoked. To request this you type over the REPLY:NO at the far right of the panel, so that it reads REPLY:YES.

```
TRANSACTION:  FC01    PROGRAM: FCEXCOB1    TASK NUMBER:  0001592    DISPLAY:
STATUS     ABOUT TO EXECUTE COMMAND
EXEC CICS RETURN




OFFSET:    X'0007EC'    LINE:    00051       EIBFN = X'0E08'
ENTER: CONTINUE

PF1:    END EDF SESSION     PF2:    RE-DISPLAY          PF3:    SWITCH HEX/CHAR
PF4:    EIB DISPLAY         PF5:    WORKING STORAGE     PF6:    USER DISPLAY
PF7:    SUPPRESS DISPLAYS   PF8:    ABEND USER TASK     PF9:    STOP CONDITIONS
PF10:   OLDEST DISPLAY      PF11:   PREVIOUS DISPLAY    PF12:   UNDEFINED
```

**Figure 11-9
Panel Before
Executing Return
Command**

```
TRANSACTION:  FC01    PROGRAM: FCEXCOB1    TASK NUMBER:  0001592    DISPLAY:
STATUS:    TASK TERMINATION




TO CONTINUE EDF SESSION REPLY  YES                              REPLY:NO
ENTER: CONTINUE

PF1:    END EDF SESSION     PF2:    RE-DISPLAY          PF3:    SWITCH HEX/CHAR
PF4:    EIB DISPLAY         PF5:    WORKING STORAGE     PF6:    USER DISPLAY
PF7:    SUPPRESS DISPLAYS   PF8:    UNDEFINED           PF9:    STOP CONDITIONS
PF10:   OLDEST DISPLAY      PF11:   PREVIOUS DISPLAY    PF12:   UNDEFINED
```

**Figure 11-10
EDF "Task
Termination" Panel**

Problem Determination with EDF

Now that you're familiar with the EDF panels, let's see how you might use EDF in a debugging situation.

Refer back to the program you wrote for the exercise of the chapter "BMS Input/Output Commands." The program reads an input map containing AMOUNT values for up to three invoices. The values are received into BMS map fields INVAM1I, INVAM2I, and INVAM3I respectively. The program then calculates the total of these three values, accumulating the result in a program variable called TOTAL. Next TOTAL is moved into the BMS map field ITOTALO, and a SEND MAP command is issued to display the calculated total.

Suppose a user reports that whenever only a *single invoice number* is entered, the program displays a total of 0. You realize that the error could occur for one or more of the following reasons:

1. Incorrect values are read from the input map AMOUNT fields.
2. An incorrect value is calculated for TOTAL.
3. A correct value is calculated, but it is not placed into the output map field before the SEND MAP command is issued.

To use EDF you need a compiler listing of the program, including the Data Division Map (DMAP) section that gives the location of each program variable. Taking the listing to your terminal, you start EDF and then the transaction that invokes your program.

You will receive panels when your program is started and as each CICS command is encountered. Eventually, you will receive an ABOUT TO EXECUTE COMMAND panel for the first SEND MAP command. At this point, you may want to see what value is in the program variable TOTAL. To do so, request WORKING STORAGE. Referring to the DMAP from the compiler, find the offset of TOTAL within working-storage. You find the offset by looking under the DISPL column opposite the SOURCE NAME entry for TOTAL. Suppose the DISPL column entry is 02C. Then to find TOTAL in the working-storage display, you would look for the line in the panel that contains relative location X'00002C'. Locate the correct full word in the hexadecimal mode display and make a note of the value you see there. Do the same for the program variables, INVAM1I, INVAM2I, and INVAM3I. Then allow the program to continue.

Next you will receive panels for COMMAND EXECUTION COMPLETE, ABOUT TO EXECUTE COMMAND (for the RECEIVE MAP command), and COMMAND EXECUTION COMPLETE (for the RECEIVE MAP command). Now you can display working-storage again and see the value your program will receive for INVAM1I, INVAM2I, and INVAM3I. If they don't appear to be correct, you can fix them and see whether the program will now function correctly.

When you allow execution to continue, your program will begin calculating a total. The next EDF panel you receive will be an ABOUT TO EXECUTE COMMAND panel for the SEND MAP command that displays the total for the user. When you see this panel, you will want to request working-storage again and look at both TOTAL and ITOTALO. If TOTAL is incorrect, you will want to check the three "amount variables" again to see whether they may have been modified after they were received. Assuming that they are correct, the part of your program that calculated TOTAL must be incorrect. Perhaps it wasn't executed at all—if so, TOTAL will still contain the same value you observed at the beginning of the session.

If TOTAL is correct but ITOTALO is incorrect, you know that the bug must lie in the part of your program that placed TOTAL into the BMS map field ITOTALO. You can correct ITOTALO now, before the SEND MAP is executed, to confirm that the program will then display a correct result.

Notice that EDF allows you to examine and change program variables or interrupt program execution only at each CICS command. This allows you to determine that the program failed somewhere between two CICS commands. If a large number of COBOL instructions are executed between the CICS commands, you may need to use additional debugging tools to find the problem more exactly.

Testing with EDF

At the beginning of this chapter, we said that EDF was useful for both problem determination and program testing. For program testing, EDF is most often used to force an exceptional condition to occur so that you can verify that the exception-handling routine works correctly. Suppose you have coded an exception-handling routine for INVREQ. This exceptional condition occurs in a variety of situations, but it is difficult to construct a test case that will cause it to occur. To test the exception-handling routine you can simply run your program under EDF, and enter INVREQ into the RESPONSE field of a COMMAND EXECUTION COMPLETE panel. When you permit execution to continue, CICS will raise the INVREQ condition and control will transfer to your program's exception-handling routine.

The Transaction Dump

As discussed above (*Program Control Options*), one option you may choose when debugging a program under EDF is to terminate the program and obtain a *transaction dump*. A transaction dump is a listing that shows all the areas of the CICS region that are related to the particular transaction. This is useful when you aren't yet sure exactly what program variables may be involved in a problem, or when a problem may be related to the contents of areas outside working storage.

Obtaining a Transaction Dump

You request a transaction dump from EDF by pressing the PF key assigned to Abend User Task. EDF will respond with the message ENTER ABEND CODE AND REQUEST ABEND AGAIN. The ABEND code is a four-character code to be printed in the heading of the dump as an identification field. To request the transaction dump, you enter the four-character code and press the same PF Key you used to specify ABEND USER TASK. You may wish to ABEND the task without getting a transaction dump. To do so, you type NO in place of the ABEND code.

A transaction dump is also produced whenever a CICS task terminates abnormally. As we discussed in the preceding chapter, abnormal task termination may occur when a CICS command detects an exceptional condition for which you have not provided an exception-handling routine, or when an unrecoverable error occurs outside a CICS command.

A CICS program can also issue a command that requests a transaction dump. In this case, a dump is produced but the task is not terminated. The format of this command is:

EXEC CICS DUMP DUMPCODE (name)

The argument of the DUMPCODE option specifies the four-character code to be printed in the heading of the dump.

CICS writes transaction dumps into a sequential file called the *dump data set*. There is a single dump data set assigned for the CICS system. Therefore, the dump data set normally contains dumps from many CICS transactions. The entire dump data set is printed when the CICS system is shut down. However, most installations also have procedures that allow transaction dumps to be printed while CICS is running. It may be possible to copy a transaction dump into a direct access file so that you can examine it from your terminal. In practice, you must consult with the central system operator to find out how to obtain a transaction dump that has been written from one of your programs.

Using A Transaction Dump

The transaction dump is most commonly used in the following four ways:

1. To find the value of working-storage variables and data areas at the time the dump was written

2. To find which COBOL statement of your program is located at a particular absolute address shown in the transaction dump

3. To determine the location of an instruction that caused an ABEND

4. To determine what CICS command had been executed by the task just prior to an ABEND

Later in this chapter, we will describe how to use the transaction dump for each of these purposes. Following the discussion is an Exercise that will lead you through these techniques, using an example COBOL program and transaction dump. First, we'll see what a transaction dump looks like.

Format of a Transaction Dump

A transaction dump begins with a *header area* that contains general information about the task and the reason for the dump. Following the header is a series of storage areas shown in a format similar to the working-storage display you saw with EDF.

Dump Header Area

Figure 11-11 shows the first page of an example transaction dump. The dump header area consists of the four lines beginning with CUSTOMER INFORMATION CONTROL SYSTEM STORAGE DUMP and ending with REGS 5-11.

Line 1 of the header area contains four fields intended to help you identify the dump. (Remember that the dump tape contains dumps from many transactions and may contain several dumps from a single transaction showing failures that occurred at different times.)

The first field, CODE, indicates the reason for the dump. If you requested the dump from EDF or with the CICS DUMP command, you specified the code that appears here. If the dump was caused by abnormal task termination, the code tells you something about the type of ABEND that occurred. In Figure 11-11 the code is ARSA, the general code for program errors not associated with a CICS command (for example, a division by zero). You can find the meaning of other codes in the manual *CICS: Messages and Codes*.

The next field, TASK, is somewhat misnamed—it contains the *transaction* identifier.

```
CUSTOMER INFORMATION CONTROL SYSTEM STORAGE DUMP    CODE=ASRA    TASK=CCOM        DATE=04/07/81   TIME=11:02:21   PAGE    1

PSW              03AD0007   D06565EA

REGS 14-4        505FAF80   00000000   0061EE5C   0061F174       50656536   0065645C   0061F268

REGS 5-11        50656814   0061EE5C   0061F15B   0061F15C       006567E4   00656020   00656020


TASK CONTROL AREA (USER AREA)  ADDRESS  61E900  TO  61EE0F     LENGTH  000510

000000   0061E800 005E9A34 015EF790 005E9CF0    0061EA10 005E4F3A 80000100 C43100A0   *./Y..;...;7..;.0./...;..h....D...*   61E900
000020   405FB532 0068C9A0 00000000 0068CBE4    005FB6D4 005FBAA8 00656008 005FACC0   * .....I........U...M...y..-....*      61E920
000040   0061E800 0061E800 005E4F14 005FBAEA    005FB760 005EF020 505FAF80 0061F400   *./Y../Y..;......-..;0...../4.*        61E940
000060   405FAE0E C1E2D9C1 0061EE5C 00006000    005FB6D4 0065645C 0061F268 005FACC0   * ...ASRA../.*..-....M...*./2....*     61E960
000030   FE00F408 E3C5D4D7 C3404040 C1E2D9C1    03AD0007 D06565EA 00000000 00000000   *..4.TEMPC  ASRA................*      61E980
0000A0   505FAF80 00000000 0061EE5C 0061F174    50656536 0065645C 0061F268 50656814   *.......*./*./1.........*./2....*     61E9A0
0000C0   0061EE5C 0061F15B 0061F15C 006567E4    00656020 00656020 0A020000 00014000   *./.*./15./1*...U..-....-.......*     61E9C0
0000E0   0061F400 8C0000A8 24F40000 00000000    00000000 00000000 00000000 00000000   */4...y.4......................*      61E9E0
000100   00000000 00000000 D3C9C6D6 E2E3D6D9    42000090 00000000 FF61EAA0 60605514E   *.......LIFOSTOR........./...-.4*     61EA00
000120   006052S8 00140000 0061F174 0061EEF4    0061EF1E 0061EEDC 00000000 0061F41C   *.-..q...../1../.4./...../...4.*      61EA20
000140   00000000 006156F8 0060604F70 00619E56   0061F1A0 0061E900 005E90F0 FE61EAA0   *...../.8.-.../.../1../Z..;q0./..*     61EA40
000160   F000D2C3 005EED54 00000000 00000000    8B000028 00000000 00000000 00000000   *0.KC.;.d......................*      61EA60
000180   00000000 00000000 00000000 00000000    00000000 018000028 00000000 00000000  *.............................*       61EA80
0001A0   48000078 0061EA10 FF61ED58 405F43D8    00000000 0000000C 0061EB34 FE61EAA0   *....../.../...Q......../...*        61EAA0
0001C0   00000000 005FD918 405F4374 805F43A6    0061E800 0061E000 00000000 015EF790   *......R......w./Y../......;7.*       61EAC0
0001E0   005EF020 0061E900 005E90F0 FE61EB18    F700E3E2 00605370 00000000 00000000   *.;0.../Z..;q0././.7.TS.-........*    61EAE0
000200   4961F408 E3C5D4D7 C3404040 00000000    00000000 00040000 00000000 00000000   *./4.TEMPC  ...................*      61EB00
000220   00000000 00000000 00000000 00000000    00000000 000C0000 00000000 005FD918   *......................R.*          61EB20
000240   00000000 00000000 00000000 015EF790    005EAD5C 00000000 400000D8 FE61EAA0   *..............;7..;.*........./..*   61EB40
000260   00000000 00000000 00000000 00000000    00000000 00000000 00000000 00000000   *.............................*       61EB60
000280   00000000 00000000 00000000 00000000    00000000 00000000 00000000 00000000   *.............................*       61EB80
0002A0   00000000 FE61EC10 E500E7E2 00616634    00000000 00000000 00000001 00000000   *......../..V.XS./............*       61EBA0
0002C0   00000000 00000000 00000000 00000000    00000000 00000000 00000000 00000000   *.............................*       61EBC0
0002E0   00000000 00000000 00000000 00000000    00000000 00000000 00000000 00000000   *.............................*       61EBE0
000300   00000000 00000000 00000000 00000000    00000000 00000000 00000000 00000000   *.............................*       61EC00
000320   LINES TO 0004E0 SAME AS ABOVE                                                                                       61EC20
000500   00000000 00000000 8A040608 0061F400                                          *.........../4.            *           61EE00


TASK CONTROL AREA (SYSTEM AREA) ADDRESS  61E800  TO  61E8FF     LENGTH  000100

000000   8A040608 0061F400 0061F4B0 0061F4B0    8000008C 005FD918 0061C080 00000000   *...../4../4../4.......R../...*       61E800
000020   005EA060 00000000 00000000 00000000    00000000 FF5E4F14 00000000 0061EF64   *.;-...............;.............;../.*   61E820
000040   0061EE10 0061EA70 00000000 00000000    00000000 00000000 00000000 00000000   *.....///.....................*       61E840
000060   00000000 00000000 00000000 C1E2D9C1    00000000 00000000 00000000 0061F1A0   *...............ASRA........../1.*     61E860
000080   FE61EC10 00000000 FE61EA00 FE61EE08    00000000 00000000 00000000 00000000   *./.......//../...............*        61E880
0000A0   005EF790 00000000 00000000 00000000    C3C3D6D4 00000000 00000000 00000000   *.;7................CCOM.......*      61E8A0
0000C0   C1E2D9C1 00000000 0061F400 00000000    00000000 00000000 00000000 00000000   *ASRA...../4.................*        61E8C0
0000E0   00000000 00000000 00000000 00000000    00000000 00000000 00000000 00000000   *.............................*       61E8E0
```

Figure 11-11
Transaction Dump
With Header Area
and TCA

```
CUSTOMER INFORMATION CONTROL SYSTEM STORAGE DUMP    CODE=ASRA    TASK=CCOM        DATE=04/07/81   TIME=11:02:21   PAGE    3

CSA OPTIONAL FEATURE LIST      ADDRESS  5E9CF0  TO  5E9F53     LENGTH  000264

0001C0   00000000 00000000 00000000 00000000    00000000 00000000 00000000 00000000   *.............................*       5E9EB0
0001E0   00000000 00000000 00000000 00000000    00000000 00000000 00000000 00000000   *.............................*       5E9ED0
000200   999C000C 000C000C 000C001C 000C000C    000C000C 001C000C 000C000C 000C001C   *r............................*       5E9EF0
000220   000C000C 000C001C 001C000C 000C000C    000C001C 000C000C 000C000C 001C000C   *.............................*       5E9F10
000240   000C000C 000C001C 000C000C 000C000C    001C000C 000C000C 000C001C 000C000C   *.............................*       5E9F30
000260   000C000C                                                                     *....                       *          5E9F50


TRACE TABLE                    ADDRESS  681AC0  TO  6820FF     LENGTH  000640

TRACE HDR     00681F10   00681AC0   006820F0   00682120

TRACE TABLE   ID REG14   REQD TASK FIELD A  FIELD B              TRACE TYPE

681F20        F1 5FAE0E CC04 0007 00000098 015EF790    ......7.  SCP GETMAIN-INIT
681F30        C8 5ED27E 0004 0007 0061EAD0 8C0000A8    ........  SCP ACQUIRED USER STORAGE
681F40        F4 5FAF80 FE04 0007 00000000 C1E2D9C1    ....ASRA  DCP TRANSACTION
681F50        F0 65568C 4004 0007 00000000 00000000    ........  KCP WAIT
681F60        FD 00002C 0104 0007 003C9FF4 003C9FF8    ...4...8  ... REPEAT 00002 TIMES
681F70        F0 5F32BE 4004 TC   00000000 00000000    ........  KCP WAIT
681F80        F1 5FB94A 4004 0007 0061E790 015EF790    ..X...7.  SCP FREEMAIN
681F90        C9 5ED374 0004 0007 0061E790 8C0002A8    ..X.....  SCP RELEASED USER STORAGE
681FA0        F2 5FB03A 0204 0007 C4C6C8C1 C3D74040    DFHACP    PCP XCTL
681FB0        F1 5FB476 8804 0007 00610193 015EF790    ......7.  SCP GETMAIN
681FC0        C8 5ED27E 0004 0007 00657000 88001000    ........  SCP ACQUIRED PGM STORAGE
681FD0        F0 5FB532 4004 0007 00000000 00000000    ........  KCP WAIT
681FE0        F0 5F32BE 4004 TC   00000000 00000000    ........  KCP WAIT
681FF0        F0 5FBBF8 4004 0007 00000000 00000000    ........  KCP WAIT
682000        DC 657092 0004 0007 C1C3D700 C1E2D9C1    ACP.ASRA  ACP
682010        E0 657A76 0003 0007 012207D5 815EF790    ...N..7.  MGP DFH 02005 TERM TIOA
682020        F1 67EE8E C304 0007 0040013B 015EF790    .....7.   SCP GETMAIN-INIT
682030        C8 5ED27E 0004 0007 0061F000 85400148    ..0.. .   SCP ACQUIRED TERMINAL STORAGE
682040        FC 680238 0103 0007 00456000 005EF790    ......7.  ZCP ZARQ APPL REQ WRITE WAIT SAVE COND
682050        F0 5F35F4 4004 0007 00000000 00000000    ........  KCP WAIT
682060        F0 5F32BE 4004 TC   00000000 00000000    ........  KCP WAIT
682070        FD 00001C 0104 TC   003CA01F 003CA01F    ........  ... REPEAT 00001 TIMES
682080        F0 5F5AE6 0804 0007 0061E100 01000007    ........  KCP RESUME
682090        F0 5F32BE 4004 TC   00000000 00000000    ........  KCP WAIT
6820A0        FC 5F3534 0105 0007 00000000 0061F000    ......0.  ZCP RETN ZARQ APPL REQ
6820B0        E0 67EB42 0005 0007 012207D5 8161F000    ...N..0.  MGP DFH RETN 02005 TERM TIOA
6820C0        F2 65790A 8104 0007 C4C6C8D7 C5D74040    DFHPEP    PCP LINK-CONDITIONAL
6820D0        F1 5FB7D0 8904 0007 0061004C 015EF790    ......7.  SCP GETMAIN
6820E0        C8 5ED27E 0004 0007 0061E790 89610058    ..X.....  SCP ACQUIRED RSA STORAGE
6820F0        F2 67302C 1004 0007 C4C6C8D7 C5D74040    DFHPEP    PCP RETURN
```

Figure 11-12
Transaction Dump
Showing Trace Table

```
CUSTOMER INFORMATION CONTROL SYSTEM STORAGE DUMP    CODE=ASRA   TASK=CCOM     DATE=04/07/81  TIME=11:02:21   PAGE    4

    681AC0         F1 5FB8EC 4004 0007 0061E790 015EF790   ..X...7.   SCP FREEMAIN
    681AD0         C9 5ED374 0004 0007 0061E790 85610058   ........   SCP RELEASED RSA STORAGE
    681AE0         E0 657A76 0003 0007 018007D5 815EF790   ...N..7.   MGP DFH 02005 CSMT
    681AF0         F1 67EF02 CC04 0007 0040013B 015EF790   ......7.   SCP GETMAIN-INIT
    681D00         C8 5ED27E 0004 0007 0061E790 8C400148   ..X.. ..   SCP ACQUIRED USER STORAGE
    681B10         F1 67EF26 4404 0007 0061E790 015EF790   ..X...7.   SCP FREEMAIN
    681B20         C9 5ED374 0004 0007 0061E790 8C400148   ..X.. ..   SCP RELEASED USER STORAGE
    681B30         E0 67EB42 0005 0007 018007D5 00000000   ...N....   MGP DFH RETN 02005 CSMT
    681B40         F2 657720 1004 0007 C4C6C0C1 C3D74040   DFHACP     PCP RETURN
    681B50         F0 5FB89C 8004 0007 13000000 015EF790   ......7.   KCP DETACH
    681B60         D8 5EBEA0 0203 0007 02005890 00000000   ........   SPP SYSTEM
    681B70         FC 5FD14E 0D03 0007 03000000 005EF790   ......7.   ZCP ZISP ISC FREE
    681B30         FC 5F42E4 0D05 0007 03000000 005EF790   ......7.   ZCP RETN ZISP ISC FREE
    681B90         D8 5FD2CE 0005 0007 03000000 005EF790   ......7.   SPP RETN
    681DA0         F0 5EDEAA 0304 0007 015EF790 00000000   ..7.....   KCP DEQALL
    681BB0         F1 5EBFCE 4A04 KC   0061E000 00000000   ........   SCP FREEMAIN
    681BC0         C9 5ED374 0004 KC   0061EAD0 8C0000A8   ........   SCP RELEASED USER STORAGE
    681BD0         C9 5ED374 0004 KC   0061EA40 8C000008   ... ....   SCP RELEASED USER STORAGE
    681BE0         C9 5ED374 0004 KC   0061E610 8C000178   ..W.....   SCP RELEASED USER STORAGE
    681BF0         C9 5ED374 0004 KC   0061E000 8A040608   ........   SCP RELEASED TCA STORAGE
    681C00         F1 5F5480 6004 TC   00000000 805EF790   ......7.   SCP FREEMAIN ALL
    681C10         C9 5ED374 0004 TC   0061F000 85400148   ..0.....   SCP RELEASED TERMINAL STORAGE
    681C20         F1 5F5378 E404 TC   00000087 005EF790   ......7.   SCP GETMAIN-COND-INIT
    681C30         C8 5ED27E 0004 TC   0061E000 84000088   ........   SCP ACQUIRED LINE STORAGE
    681C40         F0 5F32BE 4004 TC   00000000 00000000   ........   KCP WAIT
    681C50         FD 00001C 0104 TC   003CA0EB 003CA0EB   ........   ... REPEAT 00001 TIMES
    681C60         FD 00001C 0204 TC   E3C5D4C5 1102135F   TIME....   TIMING TRACE 11/02/13.5
    681C70         F0 5F32DE 4004 TC   00000000 00000000   ........   KCP WAIT
    681C80         FD 00001C 0104 TC   003CA2E2 003CA2E2   ...S..S    ... REPEAT 00001 TIMES
    681C90         F0 5F999A 0704 TC   D3F7F7C1 C3C3D6D4   L77ACCOM   KCP ATTACH-CONDITIONAL
    681CA0         F1 5EBA6E EA04 TC   00000600 805EF790   ......7.   SCP GETMAIN-COND-INIT
    681CB0         C8 5ED27E 0004 TC   0061E800 8A040608   ..Y.....   SCP ACQUIRED TCA STORAGE
    681CC0         F0 5F32BE 4004 TC   00000000 00000000   ........   KCP WAIT
    681CD0         E5 5F43D8 0C03 0008 C3C3D6D4 00540000   CCOM....   XSP SECURITY
    681CE0         F2 5F4598 0204 0008 E7C4C6C8 C3C3D6D4   XDFHCCOM   PCP XCTL
    681CF0         F1 5FB476 8804 0008 00000134 015EF790   ......7.   SCP GETMAIN
    681D00         C8 5ED27E 0004 0008 00656000 88001000   ........   SCP ACQUIRED PGM STORAGE
    681D10         F0 5FB532 4004 0008 00000000 00000000   ........   KCP WAIT
    681D20         F0 5F32BE 4004 TC   00000000 00000000   ........   KCP WAIT
    681D30         F1 5FC0BE 8C04 0008 00650374 015EF790   ......7.   SCP GETMAIN
    681D40         C8 5ED27E 0004 0008 0061EE10 8C650388   ........   SCP ACQUIRED USER STORAGE
    681D50         F1 614E2A CC04 0008 00000170 015EF790   ......7.   SCP GETMAIN-INIT
    681D60         C8 5ED27E 0004 0008 0061F1A0 8C000178   ..1.....   SCP ACQUIRED USER STORAGE
    681D70         E1 656524 0004 0008 0061EE5C 00000204   ........   EIP HANDLE-CONDITION ENTRY
    681D80         F1 614628 CC04 0008 0000007F 015EF790   ......7.   SCP GETMAIN-INIT
    681D90         C8 5ED27E 0004 0008 0061F320 8C000088   ..3.....   SCP ACQUIRED USER STORAGE
    681DA0         F1 61473E 4004 0008 00000040 015EF790   ......7.   SCP GETMAIN-INIT
    681DB0         C8 5ED27E 0004 0008 0061F3B0 8C000048   ..3.....   SCP ACQUIRED USER STORAGE
    681DC0         E1 656524 00F4 0008 00000000 00000204   ........   EIP HANDLE-CONDITION RESPONSE
    681DD0         E1 656590 0004 0008 0061EE5C 00000402   ........   EIP RECEIVE-TC ENTRY
    681DE0         F1 5F26B2 4404 0008 0061E000 005EF790   ......7.   SCP FREEMAIN
    681DF0         C9 5ED374 0004 0008 0061E000 85000088   ........   SCP RELEASED TERMINAL STORAGE
    681E00         E1 656590 00F4 0008 00000000 00000402   ........   EIP RECEIVE-TC RESPONSE
```

CUSTOMER INFORMATION CONTROL SYSTEM STORAGE DUMP   CODE=ASRA   TASK=CCOM   DATE=04/07/81 TIME=11:02:21   PAGE   5

```
CUSTOMER INFORMATION CONTROL SYSTEM STORAGE DUMP    CODE=ASRA   TASK=CCOM     DATE=04/07/81  TIME=11:02:21   PAGE    5

    681E10         E1 6565E4 0004 0008 0061EE5C 00000A02   ........   EIP WRITEQ-TS ENTRY
    681E20         F1 6050D8 8E04 0008 00610014 015EF790   ......7.   SCP GETMAIN
    681E30         C8 5ED27E 0004 0008 0061F400 8E610028   ..4.....   SCP ACQUIRED TEMPSTRG STORAGE
    681E40         F7 60514E 4903 0008 E3C5D4D7 C3404040   TEMPC      TSP PUTQ
    681E50         F1 6050DE F804 0008 00000020 015EF790   ......7.   SCP GETMAIN-COND-INIT
    681E60         C8 5ED27E 0004 0008 0061B350 93000020   ........   SCP ACQUIRED TSTABLE STORAGE
    681E70         F1 6053F8 B704 0008 0061E028 015EF790   ......7.   SCP GETMAIN-CONDITIONAL
    681E80         C8 5ED27E 0004 0008 0061B870 97610030   ........   SCP ACQUIRED TSMAIN STORAGE
    681E90         F7 6059BA 0065 0008 0061B870 97610030   ........   TSP RETN NORMAL
    681EA0         F1 60516A 4004 0008 0061F400 015EF790   ..4...7.   SCP FREEMAIN
    681EB0         C9 5ED374 0004 0008 0061F400 8E610028   ..4.....   SCP RELEASED TEMPSTRG STORAGE
    681EC0         E1 6565E4 00F4 0008 00000000 00000A02   ........   EIP WRITEQ-TS RESPONSE
    681ED0         F2 5E73A8 6004 0008 C1E2D9C1 00000000   ASRA....   PCP ABEND
    681EE0         F1 5FAE0E CC04 0008 00000098 015EF790   ......7.   SCP GETMAIN-INIT
    681EF0         C8 5ED27E FE04 0008 0061F400 8C0000A8   ..4.....   SCP ACQUIRED USER STORAGE
    681F00         F4 5FAF80 FE04 0008 00000000 C1E2D9C1   ....ASRA   DCP TRANSACTION
    681F10         F0 68568C 4004 0008 00000000 00000000   ........   KCP WAIT


    TRANSACTION STORAGE -USER       ADDRESS 61F400 TO 61F4AF      LENGTH  0000B0

    000000   8C0000A8 0061F3B0 00000000 00001840    C4C6C8E3 C1C3C240 80600000 C1E2D9C1   *...y./3........ DFHTACB .-..ASRA*   61F400
    000020   E7C4C6C8 C3C3D6D4 00000000 00000000    00000000 00000000 00000000 00000000   *XDFHCCOM.......................*   61F420
    000040   00000000 00000000 D7E3E661 D9C5C7E2    03AD0007 D06565EA 0061EE5C 0061F174   *........PSW/REGS........./.*./1.*   61F440
    000060   50656536 0065645C 0061F268 50656814    0061EE5C 0061F15B 0061F15C 006567E4   *......*./2....../.*./15./1*...U*   61F460
    000080   00656020 00656020 0061E900 005E98F0    506565E4 00000000 00000000 00000000   *..-...-../Z..:q0...U...........*   61F480
    0000A0   00000000 00000000 8C0000A8 0061F3B0                                          *..........y./3.                *   61F4A0


    TRANSACTION STORAGE -USER       ADDRESS 61F3B0 TO 61F3FF      LENGTH  000050

    000000   8C000048 0061F320 50656524 0061515C    0061EE5C 0061F174 00656850 005FBAA8   *.....y3......./.*./.*./1.......y*   61F3B0
    000020   0061F268 50656814 0061EE5C 0061F15B    0061F15C 006567E4 00656020 00656020   *./2...../.*./19.1*...U..-...-.*   61F3D0
    000040   00656450 0061F64F 8C000048 0061F320                                          *...../......./3.               *   61F3F0


    TRANSACTION STORAGE -USER       ADDRESS 61F320 TO 61F3AF      LENGTH  000090

    000000   8C000088 0061F1A0 0061F36E 007F0302    00000000 00000000 00000001 00000000   *...h./1../3....................*   61F320
    000020   00000000 00000000 00000000 00300000    00000000 00000000 00000000 00000000   *...............................*   61F340
    000040   00000000 00000000 00000000 00000000    00000000 C0000161 F3B00461 EF640261   *........................./3../.*/*   61F360
    000060   F3B00461 EF640000 00000000 00000000    00000000 00000000 00000000 00000000   *3../...........................*   61F380
    000080   00000000 0000FF00 8C000088 0061F1A0                                          *..........h./1.                *   61F3A0


    TRANSACTION STORAGE -USER       ADDRESS 61F1A0 TO 61F31F      LENGTH  000180

    000000   8C000178 0061EE10 0061F2D0 00000000    00000000 00000000 00000000 00000000   *..../.../2.....................*   61F1A0
    000020   40404040 005EF790 00000000 00000000    00000000 00000000 00000000 00000000   *   .;7......................*   61F1C0
    000040   00000000 00000000 00000000 00000000    00000000 00000000 00000000 00000000   *...............................*   61F1E0
    000060   00000000 00000000 00000000 00000000    00000000 00000000 0061F268 8061F26C   *......................./2../2.*   61F200
    000080   0061F400 B06050BA 00000000 00000000    00000000 00000000 00000000 00000000   *./4.-..........................*   61F220
    0000A0   00000000 00000000 00000000 0061F320    00000000 00000000 00000004 00000000   *.............../3..............*   61F240
```

Figure 11-13 Continuation of Trace Table

Figure 11-14 Transaction Dump With Storage Area

```
CUSTOMER INFORMATION CONTROL SYSTEM STORAGE DUMP    CODE=ASRA    TASK=CCOM    DATE=04/07/81   TIME=11:02:21   PAGE    6


TRANSACTION STORAGE -USER       ADDRESS  61F1A0  TO  61F31F      LENGTH  000180

0000C0  00000000 00000000 0061F2D0 FF000000   0061EF64 0061EE5C 00000000 005FBD4C   *........./2......./.../.*.......*  61F260
0000E0  0061EF64 40614FDE 40656022 005FBD4C   0061F268 006560F0 0061EE20 00656068   *./.. /.. .-....../2...-0./....-.*  61F280
000100  005FBDC8 0061E800 00656020 00614DE4   006564E6 FF5E4F14 0061F1A0 0061E900   *...H./Y..-../(U...W.;.../1../Z.*  61F2A0
000120  80000000 00000000 40C4C6C8 C5C9C240   0110221C 0081097F C3C3D6D4 0000003C   *........ DFHEIB ...a...CCOM....*  61F2C0
000140  D3F7F7C1 0000000F 0007D0A 02000000     00000000 00000000 00000000 00000000   *L77A...'.....................*   61F2E0
000160  000000E3 C5D4D7C3 40404000 00000000   00000000 00000000 8C000178 0061EE10   *...TEMPC  ...................../..*  61F300


TRANSACTION STORAGE -USER       ADDRESS  61EE10  TO  61F19F      LENGTH  000390

000000  8C650388 0061E800 00656020 0065682C   00656850 005FDAA8 00000000 005FDAA8   *...h./Y....../.........y*
000020  006566FC 50656814 00656120 0065641F   00656420 006567E4 00356020 00656020   *............./.......U..-..-.*   61EE30
000040  00656450 00656228 005FC088 E2E3C1D9   E340D6C6 40E6D6D9 D2C9D5C7 40E2E3D6   *...........hSTART OF WORKING STO*  61EE50
000060  D9C1C7C5 000F0000 00000000 00000000   00000000 00000000 00000000 00000000   *RAGE..........................*  61EE70
000080  00000000 00000000 00000000 00000000   00000000 00000000 00000000 C3C3D6D4   *..............................CCOM*  61EE90
0000A0  00000000 00000000 00000000 00000000   00000000 00000000 00000000 C3C3D6D4   *............................CCOM*  61EEB0
0000C0  40E4D7C4 E340F0F0 F0F0F100 00000000   00000000 0A02E000 04000000 00000000   * UPDT 00001...................*  61EED0
0000E0  00000000 0A02E000 04000049 00404040   40404040 40404040 40404040 40400000   *..........................*  61EEF0
000100  00000000 00000000 00000000 0000E3C5   D4D7C340 40400000 00000000 00000000   *................TEMPC  .......*  61EF10
000120  00000000 00000000 00000000 C0001000   00000000 00000000 00000000 00000000   *..............................*  61EF30
000140  00000000 00000000 00000C00 00400000   00000000 00000000 00000000 0061F278   *......................../..*  61EF50
000160  506565E4 0061515C 0061EE5C 0061F174   50656536 0065645C 0061F268 50656814   *...U./.*./.*./1......*./2...*  61EF70
000180  0061EE5C 0061F15B 0061F15C 006567E4   00656020 00656020 00656450 2010004B   *./.*./1$./1*...U..-..-........K*  61EF90
0001A0  00000000 00000000 00614F74 00656764   00000000 00000000 00000030 00000000   *.........................*  61EFB0
0001C0  00000000 00000000 00000000 00000000   00000000 00000000 00000030 00000000   *........................*  61EFD0
0001E0  LINES TO 0002C0 SAME AS ABOVE                                                                                  61EFF0
0002E0  00000000 00000000 00000000 00000000   00000000 00000000 00000000 C5C4E4C3   *.......................EDUC*    61F0F0
000300  D7C7D4C3 0C656020 00000000 00000000   00000000 00000000 00000000 00000000   *PGMC..-......................*   61F110
000320  00000000 00000000 00000000 00000000   00000000 00000000 00000000 00000000   *..............................*  61F130
000340  00000000 00000000 0061EE5C 00000000   0061F2D0 FF000000 0061F168 005E93F0   *.........../*........../2....../1...iq0*  61F150
000360  00000000 0061EEF4 0061EF1E 0061EECC   8061EF3D 00000000 00000000 00000000   *......../4../......./.........*  61F170
000380  00000000 00000000 8C650388 0061E800   00000000 00000000 00000000 00000000   *..........h./Y.              *  61F190


TERMINAL CONTROL TABLE          ADDRESS  5EF790  TO  5EF87F      LENGTH  0000F0

000000  D3F7F7C1 99F20404 005EF794 00000000   0061E900 00000000 00000000 00000000   *L77Ar2...;7m......./Z........*  5EF790
000020  00000000 0C000000 00000100 C0000980   000F7DB0 00000000 00000000 00000000   *..............'..............*   5EF7B0
000040  00000000 00000000 07801850 00000000   00000000 00F00000 00000000 00000000   *..............0.............*   5EF7D0
000060  00000000 00000000 005EF634 005EF86A   00000000 00000000 00000000 00000000   *.........i6..i8.............*   5EF7F0
000080  00000000 005EF888 00000000 001B0000   00000000 00000000 00540000 0000006C   *......i8h...............d....*  5EF810
0000A0  0000005C 00000C00 0C6C0000 0C008100   00400000 00000000 00000000 00000000   *...*..........a..............*  5EF830
0000C0  00000000 00010000 00000000 00000000   00000000 00000000 00001600 00000100   *...........................*   5EF850
0000E0  00185000 00820000 03D4D400 00000000   00000000 00000000 00001600 00000100   *.....b...MM.....         *    5EF870
```

**Figure 11-15
Continuation of
Storage Area Dump**

```
CUSTOMER INFORMATION CONTROL SYSTEM STORAGE DUMP    CODE=ASRA    TASK=CCOM    DATE=04/07/81   TIME=11:02:21   PAGE    7


PROGRAM STORAGE                 ADDRESS  656008  TO  65699F      LENGTH  000998

000000  C4C6C8C5 58F0F00C 07FF58F0 F00A07FF   005FC224 00615790 00700700 900EF00A   *DFHE.00....00.....B../..0....0.*  656008
000020  47F0F082 005FBD4C 0061F268 006560F0   0061EE20 00656068 005FBDC8 0061E800   *.00b....../2...-0./.....-...H./Y.*  656028
000040  00656020 00614DE4 006564E6 FF5E4F14   0061F1A0 0061E900 0061F278 00614FDE   *..-../(U...W.;.../1../Z../2 /.*   656048
000060  00656120 5065682C 00656850 005FBAA8   006566FC 50656814 00656120 0065641F   *../..........y............./.*  656068
000080  00656450 00656228 005FC088 58C0F0C6   00000000 00000000 00000000 00000000   *...........h..0F              *  656088
0000A0  58E0C000 58D0F0CA 9500E000 4770F0A2   9610D048 92FFE000 47F0F0AC 98CEF03A   *..0.n...0so..k....00.q.0.*     6560A8
0000C0  90ECD00C 185D989F F0BA9110 D0480719   07FF0700 00656764 00656020 00000000   *.)q.0.j..............-..*       6560C8
0000E0  00656450 0061EF64 006564E6 006567CA   C3D6C2C6 F2F5F5F1 C5C4E4C3 D7C7D4C3   *..........W....COBF2551EDUCPGMC*  6560E8
000100  00656424 F0F461F0 F761F8F1 F1F04BF5   F64BF4F3 00000000 E2E3C1D9 E340D6C6   *....04/07/8110.56.43....START OF*  656108
000120  40E6D6D9 D2C9D5C7 40E2E3D6 D9C1C7C5   00000000 00000000 00000000 00000000   * WORKING STORAGE.............*   656128
000140  00000000 00000000 00000000 00000000   00000000 00000000 00000000 00000000   *.............................*   656148
000160  LINES TO 0001E0 SAME AS ABOVE                                                                                  656168
000200  00000000 00000000 00000000 0C000000   00000000 00000C00 00400000 00000000   *..............................*  656208
000220  00000000 005FBD4C 00000000 00000000   00000000 00000C00 00400000 00000000   *.......<.....................*   656228
000240  00000000 00000000 00000000 00000000   00000000 00000000 00000000 00000000   *............................*   656248
000260  00000000 00000000 2010004B 00000000   00000000 005FC088 00000000 00000000   *...........K...........h.....*   656268
000280  00000000 00000000 00000000 00000000   00000000 00000000 00000000 00000000   *.............................*   656288
0002A0  LINES TO 0003A0 SAME AS ABOVE                                                                                  6562A8
0003C0  00000000 00000000 C5C4E4C3 D7C7D4C3   00656020 00000000 00000000 00000000   *.......EDUCPGMC..-............*   6563C8
0003E0  00000000 00000000 00000000 00000000   00000000 00000000 00000000 00000000   *.............................*   6563E8
000400  00000000 00000000 00000000 00000000   00000000 00656120 00000000 00000000   *........................./...*   656408
000420  00000000 00000000 00000000 00000000   00000000 00656020 00000000 00000000   *......................-..*      656428
000440  00000000 00000000 00656850 00656012   00656850 006566C8 006566FC 006566FC   *...........y..-..H....*          656448
000460  000F0010 0120C0C0 500C2802 04C00004   0D010000 00656020 00000000 00020402   *...............-..*             656468
000480  C0000400 00001400 00000000 00E3C5D4   D7C7D4C3 00656670 C903C5C1 00000000   *............TEMPC....FILEA*      656488
0004A0  0602F000 04000080 00049430 00040000   00010000 40000000 E080000 04000010     *..0........ ...k.........*       6564A8
0004C0  00E2D1C3 F10E0C80 00040000 600005D6   40D9C5C3 D6D9C440 C6D6E4D5 C4005840   *.SJC1....NO RECORD FOUND....*    6564C8
0004E0  D0045840 40185310 40005010 D1FC5810   40045010 D200D211 6098C023 924060A4   *...J.....K.K-q..k --..*          6564E8
000500  D20660AB 60A4A110 6098D010 D2109680   D2104110 D21058F0 C00405EF 58E0D1FC   *K.-.-..q..K.o.K..K.0.....J.*     656508
000520  4810E014 4130C00C 4910C034 05204720   201E8B10 000147C0 201E4811 20180910   *......................i.*       656528
000540  00025011 300007F1 00020001 D2016018   C018D20E 6098C036 924060A7 D20960A8   *.....1...K-..K-q..k -xK-q.*     656548
000560  60A74110 60985010 D201C410 60705010   D2144110 60985010 D2189680 D2184110   *-x..-q..K.....-..q..K....*       656568
000580  D21058F0 C00405EF D20460C2 C0459240   60C7D201 60C860C7 D2016E01 C01AD208   *K.0....-.K-B..k -GK-H-GK.-...K.*  656588
0005A0  6098C04A 924060A1 D20F60A2 60A14110   60985010 D2104110 60C25010 D2144110   *-q..k -K.-s-..q..K.....-B..K..*  6565A8
0005C0  60705010 D2184110 60E15010 D21C9680   D21C4110 D21058F0 C00405EF FA22601C   *-...K..-..-..K.o.K..K.0.....-*   6565C8
0005E0  C01CD201 601AC01F D20460C2 C0539240   60C7D201 60C860C7 D2086098 C0589240   *..K.-...-.K-B -GK-H-GK--q..k *   6565E8
000600  60A1D20F 60A260A1 41106098 5010D210   41106098 5010D214 41106020 5010D218   *-.K.-s-..q..K..-.......-..K..*   656608
000620  4110601A 5010D21C 4110607A 5010D220   9680D220 4110D210 58F0C004 05EF9200   *-..K.....K..K.o.K..K.0......*    656628
000640  6070D226 60716070 D2276070 6020D201   60E1C021 D20E6098 C0619240 60A7D209   *-.K.-.-.K-..K-..K-..-q./k -xK..*  656648
000660  60A860A7 41106098 5010D218 41106101   5010D21C 4110D210 58F0C004 05EFD208   *-y-x..-q..K.......K.....K.0..K..*  656668
000680  5010D21C 410060E1 5010D220 9680D220   4110D210 58F0C004 05EFD208 6098C070   *...K.....-.K..K.o.K..K.0....K.-q.*  656688
0006A0  924060A1 D20F60A2 60A14110 60985010   D2109680 D2104110 60C25010 D2144110   *k -..-K-q.'k -.K-s-..q..K..*     6566A8
0006C0  60D05010 D2149680 D2144110 D21058F0   D20F60A2 60A14110 60985010 D2104110   *K-..K.o.K..K.0...K-q.'k -.K-s-..q..K.*  6566C8
0006E0  C00405EF D20E6070 D2144110 D21058F0   60405EF D20E6070 D2144110 60607D217   *..K.o.K..K-..K.-s-....fk -.K*    6566E8
000700  6086607F D2016E01 C018D20E 6098C061   924060A7 D20960A8 60A74110 6098D217   *-.-..K.-.-.K-..K-q./k -xK..-q..K*  656708
000720  D2104110 61015010 D2144110 60FF5010   D2184110 60705010 D21C4110 60E15010   *K...-..K..-...K...-..K.-..*      656728
000740  D2209680 D2204110 D21058F0 C00405EF   D2086098 C0709240 60A5D207 60A260A4   *K.o.K..K.0....K-q..k -.K.-s-.*   656748
000760  41106098 5010D210 9680D210 4110D210   58F0C004 05EF5010 58E0D180 9110D048   *-..K...K.o.K..K.0...K....0,.J.j...*  656768
000780  900EE048 47E0F02E 94FFD048 5810C000   90000010 1B1158F0 C00805EF 58E0D1D0   *.....0.m.......k.......J.*       656788
0007A0  980EE00C 07FE58D0 D00498EC D00C07FE   05F058E0 D1B09110 D0484710 F01A900E   *q.........0..J.j....0..*         6567A8
0007C0  E04850D0 50085050 D0045820 C0009500   20000779 92FF2000 9610D048 50E0D054   *........./....n....k...o......*   6567C8
```

**Figure 11-16
Transaction Dump
With Program Storage**
```
240
```

```
CUSTOMER INFORMATION CONTROL SYSTEM STORAGE DUMP    CODE=ASRA    TASK=CCOM       DATE=04/07/81   TIME=11:02:21   PAGE   8

PROGRAM STORAGE                    ADDRESS  656008  TO  65699F      LENGTH 000998

0007E0   05F09120 D04847E0 F0165800 B048982D    B05058E0 D05407FE 96200048 41600004   *.0j.....0......q.........o....-..*   6567E8
000800   4110C00C 4170C018 06700550 58401000    1E4B5040 10008716 50004180 D1F44170   *.............  ..... ..g.....J4..*   656808
0008C0   D1F70510 58008000 1E0B5000 80008786    1000580 D1F458E0 D1B0906D E06058E0   *J7.............gf...-J4..J.....-..*   656828
000840   D05407FE 00000000 FFF5F7F4 F660C3C2    F140C3D6 D7E8D5C9 C7C8E340 C9C2D440   *........5746-CB1 COPYRIGHT IBM *     656848
000860   C3D6D9D7 4B40F1F9 F7F3F5F7 F4F660D3    D4F440C3 D6D7E8D9 C9C7C8E3 40C9C2D4   *CORP. 19735746-LM4 COPYRIGHT IBM*    656868
000880   40C3D6D9 D74B40F1 F9F7F3C6 C540F2F4    F6F3F5F6 C6C540F2 F4F6F3F5 F7000000   * CORP. 1973FE 246356FE 246357...*    656888
0008A0   47F0F018 C9D3C2C4 E3C3F2F0 F2F5F0F0    F1F261F2 F061F7F8 90EDC00C 05A05890   *.00.ILBDTC20250012/20/78........*    6568A8
0008C0   A09E1299 4780A054 91109000 4710A05A    96109000 50D09080 18BD41D0 907C50D8   *...r....j.......o............Q*      6568C8
0008E0   00081211 4780A02E 58110000 91C09000    4780A04C 58F0A096 05EF941F 90001211   *...........j........0.o..m....*      6568E8
000900   4770A04C 58F0A092 05EF58D0 908094EF    900098EC D00C07FE 91809001 4710A086   *.....0.k....m...q.....j.....f*       656908
000920   96809001 58C0A08E 58F0C090 9210C094    50D09080 18BD41D0 907C50D8 000805EF   *o.......0..k..m........Q....*        656928
000940   58D09080 47F0A054 00000000 00000000    00000000 00000000 00000000 00000000   *....0.........................*      656948
000960   00000000 00000000 00000000 00000000    00000000 00000000 00000000 00000000   *..............................*      656968
000980   00000000 00000000 00000000 00000000    00000000 00000000                     *......................   *          656988

END OF CICS/VS STORAGE DUMP
```

**Figure 11-17
Continuation of
Program Storage**

The third and fourth fields of the first line contain the date and time when the dump was written.

The second line of the header contains the PSW (Program Status Word) value at the time of ABEND or when the dump was requested. The Messages and Codes manual refers you to the PSW in order to determine the cause of some types of ABENDS. You can also use the PSW to determine which instruction in your program caused an ABEND.

Lines three and four of the dump header display the contents of the general registers 0 through 11, 14, and 15. Notice that the registers are shown in the order 14, 15, 0 through 11. Although you can't determine the contents of registers 12 and 13 from the dump header, this is rarely a problem in debugging a CICS program.

Storage Area Dumps

The first storage area shown in Figure 11-11 is the TASK CONTROL AREA (USER AREA). Notice that the title line for this part of the storage dump gives the area's beginning and ending *absolute addresses* and the area's length in bytes. (The length is expressed as a hexadecimal number.) The first column of the storage display gives the *offset* within the storage area (in this case, the offset within the user area of the TCA) of the first byte of storage shown in each line of the dump. Each line of the dump contains eight full words of storage, shown first in hexadecimal form and then, to the right, in character form. The rightmost column of each line gives the *absolute address* of the first byte shown in the line. The storage areas that you will use most often are the TRANSACTION STORAGE and PROGRAM STORAGE areas. We will also refer to the TRACE TABLE and the TASK CONTROL AREA (SYSTEM AREA).

Finding Working-Storage Locations

To find a working-storage location in a transaction dump you need the compiler's Data Definition Map (DMAP) output. In the dump, you will need to refer to the TRANSACTION STORAGE area and the general registers in the dump header.

As an example, suppose that you wish to find the area TERMINAL-MSG defined in the program shown in Figure 11-18. You will first consult the DMAP output from the program's compilation. The DMAP is shown in Figures 11-22 and 11-23. Find the entry for TERMINAL-MSG and make a note of the values shown in the BASE and DISPL columns of the DMAP. Remember that when you used the EDF working-storage display to locate a program variable, you used the DISPL value. In using the transaction dump you will need both the BASE and DISPL values.

First use the BASE value (BL = 1) by referring to the REGISTER ASSIGNMENT section of the DMAP. It appears just before the CONDENSED LISTING and is shown in Figure 11-24. In this example, there is a single entry that equates BL = 1 to REG 6. This means that, at execution time, general register 6 will contain the BASE address for any program variable whose BASE entry in the DMAP is BL = 1.

To find the absolute address of TERMINAL-MSG, you must add its DISPL value (070) to the absolute address contained in general register 6. Referring to the general registers shown in the dump header, you find that register 6 contained the address X'61EE5C'. Adding this base address and the offset for TERMINAL-MSG you obtain the absolute address X'61EECC'. Now search through the TRANSACTION STORAGE areas until you find the area that contains this address. (It appears in Figure 11-15.) Remember that the rightmost column of the storage dump gives the absolute address of the storage shown in each line of the dump. Use this column to find location X'61EECC'. You should be looking at a full word containing the characters CCOM. Compare this and the following bytes to the definition of TERMINAL-MSG in the program and verify that the contents appear to be reasonable.

Finding The Program Statement Located at a Given Absolute Address

Often you will be able to find the absolute address of an instruction that has caused an ABEND. The next section of this topic will discuss how to do this. Once you have found this instruction in the dump, you will need to determine which of your COBOL program statements is associated with the instruction.

Suppose that you have determined that a program failure was caused by execution of the instruction located at absolute address X'656554'. Notice that this address is shown in the PROGRAM STORAGE section of the dump which appears in Figure 11-16.

PROGRAM STORAGE is the area that contains the reenterable program itself. It is essentially a picture of the phase module or load module produced when you link-edited your program. (The discussion below uses the DOS/VSE term *phase module*. If you are using an OS/VS-based CICS system, you can substitute the OS/VS term *load module*.) To find the program statement associated with an absolute address, you will need to refer to the compiler listing of the program (Figures 11-19–11-21), the CONDENSED LISTING (Figure 11-24), and the LINKAGE EDITOR output (Figure 11-25).

The first step is to convert the absolute address X'656554' to an offset within PROGRAM STORAGE. Since PROGRAM STORAGE is a picture of the phase module, the offset relative to the beginning of PROGRAM STORAGE will be the same as the offset relative to the beginning of the first program location in the phase module.

To find the offset, subtract the absolute address of the first location in PROGRAM STORAGE from the absolute address X'656554'. The title line

```
CICS/VS COMMAND LANGUAGE TRANSLATOR VERSION 1.5                              TIME 10.56 DATE 7 APR 81    PAGE 1

              CBL LIB,CLIST,SXREF

     LINE        SOURCE LISTING

     00001           ID DIVISION.
     00002           PROGRAM-ID. EDUCPGMC.
     00003           ENVIRONMENT DIVISION.
     00004           DATA DIVISION.
     00005           WORKING-STORAGE SECTION.
     00006           77  FILLER PIC X(24) VALUE 'START OF WORKING STORAGE'.
     00007           77  MSG-LENGTH PIC S9(4) COMP VALUE 0.
     00008           77  RECORD-LENGTH PIC S9(4) COMP VALUE 0.
     00009           77  TOTAL-FIELD PIC S999V99 COMP-3.
     00010           01  FILE-IOAREA.
     00011               05 PATIENT-NO PIC X(6).
     00012               05 ROOM-NO PIC X(5).
     00013               05 ILLNESS PIC X(20).
     00014               05 DOCTOR-NO PIC X(10).
     00015               05 FILLER PIC X(39).
     00016           01  TERMINAL-MSG.
     00017               05 MESSAGE-OUT PIC X(40).
     00018               05 MESSAGE-IN REDEFINES MESSAGE-OUT.
     00019                  10 TRANSID PIC X(4).
     00020                  10 FILLER PIC X.
     00021                  10 FUNCTION-CODE PIC X(4).
     00022                  10 FILLER PIC X.
     00023                  10 PATIENT-NUM PIC X(6).
     00024           PROCEDURE DIVISION.
     00025               EXEC CICS HANDLE CONDITION NOTFND(NORECORD)
     00026                  ERROR(BADREAD) END-EXEC.
     00027               MOVE 15 TO MSG-LENGTH.
     00028               EXEC CICS RECEIVE INTO(TERMINAL-MSG)
     00029                  LENGTH(MSG-LENGTH) END-EXEC.
     00030               EXEC CICS WRITEQ TS QUEUE ('TEMPC')
     00031                  FROM(MESSAGE-IN) LENGTH(16) MAIN END-EXEC.
     00032               ADD 12 TO TOTAL-FIELD.
     00033               MOVE 80  TO RECORD-LENGTH.
     00034               EXEC CICS READ INTO(FILE-IOAREA) DATASET('FILEA')
     00035                  RIDFLD(PATIENT-NUM) LENGTH(RECORD-LENGTH) END-EXEC.
     00036               MOVE LOW-VALUE TO MESSAGE-OUT.
     00037               MOVE FILE-IOAREA TO MESSAGE-OUT.
     00038               EXEC CICS SEND FROM(MESSAGE-OUT) LENGTH(40) END-EXEC.
     00039               EXEC CICS RETURN END-EXEC.
     00040           BADREAD.
     00041               EXEC CICS ABEND ABCODE('SJC1') END-EXEC.
     00042           NORECORD.
     00043               MOVE 'NO RECORD FOUND' TO MESSAGE-OUT.
     00044               EXEC CICS SEND FROM(MESSAGE-OUT) LENGTH(15) END-EXEC.
     00045               EXEC CICS RETURN END-EXEC.
     00046               GOBACK.
```

**Figure 11-18
Source Listing of
CICS Application
Program**

```
     1  IBM DOS VS COBOL                      REL 2.5 + PTF51  PP NO. 5746-CB1              10.56.43  04/07/81

        CBL LIB,CLIST,SXREF
     00001           ID DIVISION.
     00002           PROGRAM-ID. EDUCPGMC.
     00003           ENVIRONMENT DIVISION.
     00004           DATA DIVISION.
     00005           WORKING-STORAGE SECTION.
     00006           77  FILLER PIC X(24) VALUE 'START OF WORKING STORAGE'.
     00007           77  MSG-LENGTH PIC S9(4) COMP VALUE 0.
     00008           77  RECORD-LENGTH PIC S9(4) COMP VALUE 0.
     00009           77  TOTAL-FIELD PIC S999V99 COMP-3.
     00010           01  FILE-IOAREA.
     00011               05 PATIENT-NO PIC X(6).
     00012               05 ROOM-NO PIC X(5).
     00013               05 ILLNESS PIC X(20).
     00014               05 DOCTOR-NO PIC X(10).
     00015               05 FILLER PIC X(39).
     00016           01  TERMINAL-MSG.
     00017               05 MESSAGE-OUT PIC X(40).
     00018               05 MESSAGE-IN REDEFINES MESSAGE-OUT.
     00019                  10 TRANSID PIC X(4).
     00020                  10 FILLER PIC X.
     00021                  10 FUNCTION-CODE PIC X(4).
     00022                  10 FILLER PIC X.
     00023                  10 PATIENT-NUM PIC X(6).
     00024           01  DFHEIVAR COPY DFHEIVAR.
     00025 C         01  DFHEIVAR.                                                04000000
     00026 C             02  DFHEIV0  PICTURE X(26).                              08000000
     00027 C             02  DFHEIV1  PICTURE X(8).                               12000000
     00028 C             02  DFHEIV2  PICTURE X(8).                               16000000
     00029 C             02  DFHEIV3  PICTURE X(8).                               20000000
     00030 C             02  DFHEIV4  PICTURE X(6).                               24000000
     00031 C             02  DFHEIV5  PICTURE X(4).                               28000000
     00032 C             02  DFHEIV6  PICTURE X(4).                               32000000
     00033 C             02  DFHEIV7  PICTURE X(2).                               36000000
     00034 C             02  DFHEIV8  PICTURE X(2).                               40000000
     00035 C             02  DFHEIV9  PICTURE X(1).                               45000000
     00036 C             02  DFHEIV10 PICTURE S9(7) USAGE COMPUTATIONAL-3.        50000000
     00037 C             02  DFHEIV11 PICTURE S9(4) USAGE COMPUTATIONAL.          55000000
     00038 C             02  DFHEIV12 PICTURE S9(4) USAGE COMPUTATIONAL.          60000000
     00039 C             02  DFHEIV13 PICTURE S9(4) USAGE COMPUTATIONAL.          65000000
     00040 C             02  DFHEIV14 PICTURE S9(4) USAGE COMPUTATIONAL.          70000000
     00041 C             02  DFHEIV15 PICTURE S9(4) USAGE COMPUTATIONAL.          75000000
     00042 C             02  DFHEIV16 PICTURE S9(9).                              80000000
     00043 C             02  DFHEIV17 PICTURE X(4).                               81000000
     00044 C             02  DFHEIV18 PICTURE X(4).                               82000000
     00045 C             02  DFHEIV19 PICTURE X(4).                               83000000
     00046 C             02  DFHEIV97 PICTURE S9(7) USAGE COMPUTATIONAL-3 VALUE ZERO.85000000
     00047 C             02  DFHEIV98 PICTURE S9(4) USAGE COMPUTATIONAL VALUE ZERO. 90000000
     00048 C             02  DFHEIV99 PICTURE X(1)  VALUE SPACE.                  95000000
     00049           LINKAGE SECTION.
     00050           01  DFHEIBLK COPY DFHEIBLK.
     00051 C         *   EIBLK EXEC INTERFACE BLOCK                               02000000
     00052 C         01  DFHEIBLK.                                                04000000
```

**Figure 11-19
Translator Listing of
CICS Application
Program**

```
      2       EDUCPGMC        10.56.43        04/07/81

00053 C      *         EIBTIME       TIME IN 0HHMMSS FORMAT              06000000
00054 C                02 EIBTIME    PICTURE S9(7) USAGE COMPUTATIONAL-3. 08000000
00055 C      *         EIBDATE       DATE IN 00YYDDD FORMAT              10000000
00056 C                02 EIBDATE    PICTURE S9(7) USAGE COMPUTATIONAL-3. 13000000
00057 C      *         EIBTRNID      TRANSACTION IDENTIFIER              16000000
00058 C                02 EIBTRNID   PICTURE X(4).                       19000000
00059 C      *         EIBTASKN      TASK NUMBER                         24000000
00060 C                02 EIBTASKN   PICTURE S9(7) USAGE COMPUTATIONAL-3. 29000000
00061 C      *         EIBTRMID      TERMINAL IDENTIFIER                 34000000
00062 C                02 EIBTRMID   PICTURE X(4).                       37000000
00063 C      *         DFHEIGDI      RESERVED                            40000000
00064 C                02 DFHEIGDI   PICTURE S9(4) USAGE COMPUTATIONAL.  43000000
00065 C      *         EIBCPOSN      CURSOR POSITION                     46000000
00066 C                02 EIBCPOSN   PICTURE S9(4) USAGE COMPUTATIONAL.  49900000
00067 C      *         EIBCALEN      COMMAREA LENGTH                     52000000
00068 C                02 EIBCALEN   PICTURE S9(4) USAGE COMPUTATIONAL.  55000000
00069 C      *         EIBAID        ATTENTION IDENTIFIER                70000000
00070 C                02 EIBAID     PICTURE X(1).                       73000000
00071 C      *         EIBFN         FUNCTION CODE                       76000000
00072 C                02 EIBFN      PICTURE X(2).                       79000000
00073 C      *         EIBRCODE      RESPONSE CODE                       82000000
00074 C                02 EIBRCODE   PICTURE X(6).                       85000000
00075 C      *         EIBDS         DATASET NAME                        88000000
00076 C                02 EIBDS      PICTURE X(8).                       91000000
00077 C      *         EIBREQID      REQUEST IDENTIFIER                  94000000
00078 C                02 EIBREQID   PICTURE X(8).                       97000000
00079        01  DFHCOMMAREA PICTURE X(1).
00080        01  DFHBLLSLOT1 PICTURE X(1).
00081        01  DFHBLLSLOT2 PICTURE X(1).
00082    PROCEDURE DIVISION USING DFHEIBLK DFHCOMMAREA.
00083    *    EXEC CICS HANDLE CONDITION NOTFND(NORECORD)
00084    *      ERROR(BADREAD) END-EXEC.
00085             MOVE '            ' TO DFHEIV0 CALL 'DFHEI1' USING
00086         DFHEIV0 GO TO NORECORD BADREAD DEPENDING ON DFHEIGDI.
00087         MOVE 15 TO MSG-LENGTH.
00088    *    EXEC CICS RECEIVE INTO(TERMINAL-MSG)
00089    *      LENGTH(MSG-LENGTH) END-EXEC.
00090             MOVE '            ' TO DFHEIV0 CALL 'DFHEI1' USING
00091         DFHEIV0 TERMINAL-MSG MSG-LENGTH.
00092    *    EXEC CICS WRITEQ TS QUEUE ('TEMPC')
00093    *         FROM(MESSAGE-IN) LENGTH(16) MAIN END-EXEC.
00094         MOVE 'TEMPC' TO DFHEIV3 MOVE 16 TO DFHEIV11 MOVE ' \
00095         TO DFHEIV0 CALL 'DFHEI1' USING DFHEIV0 DFHEIV3 MESSAGE-IN
00096         DFHEIV11.
00097         ADD 12 TO TOTAL-FIELD.
00098         MOVE 80 TO RECORD-LENGTH.
00099    *    EXEC CICS READ INTO(FILE-IOAREA) DATASET('FILEA')
00100    *      RIDFLD(PATIENT-NUM) LENGTH(RECORD-LENGTH) END-EXEC.
00101             MOVE 'FILEA' TO DFHEIV3 MOVE '  0      ' TO DFHEIV0 CALL 'DF
00102  -      'HEI1' USING DFHEIV0 DFHEIV3 FILE-IOAREA RECORD-LENGTH
00103         PATIENT-NUM.
00104         MOVE LOW-VALUE TO MESSAGE-OUT.
00105         MOVE FILE-IOAREA TO MESSAGE-OUT.
```

**Figure 11-20
Translator Listing,
Page 2**

```
      3       EDUCPGMC        10.56.43        04/07/81

00106    *    EXEC CICS SEND FROM(MESSAGE-OUT) LENGTH(40) END-EXEC.
00107             MOVE 40 TO DFHEIV11 MOVE '              ' TO DFHEIV0 CALL '
00108  -      'DFHEI1' USING DFHEIV0 DFHEIV99 DFHEIV98 MESSAGE-OUT
00109         DFHEIV11.
00110    *    EXEC CICS RETURN END-EXEC.
00111             MOVE '            ' TO DFHEIV0 CALL 'DFHEI1' USING DFHEIV0.
00112    BADREAD.
00113    *    EXEC CICS ABEND ABCODE('SJC1') END-EXEC.
00114             MOVE 'SJC1' TO DFHEIV5 MOVE '      - ' TO DFHEIV0 CALL 'DFH
00115  -      'EI1' USING DFHEIV0 DFHEIV5.
00116    NORECORD.
00117         MOVE 'NO RECORD FOUND' TO MESSAGE-OUT.
00118    *    EXEC CICS SEND FROM(MESSAGE-OUT) LENGTH(15) END-EXEC.
00119             MOVE 15 TO DFHEIV11 MOVE '              ' TO DFHEIV0 CALL '
00120  -      'DFHEI1' USING DFHEIV0 DFHEIV99 DFHEIV98 MESSAGE-OUT
00121         DFHEIV11.
00122    *    EXEC CICS RETURN END-EXEC.
00123             MOVE '            ' TO DFHEIV0 CALL 'DFHEI1' USING DFHEIV0.
00124         GOBACK.
```

**Figure 11-21
Translator Listing,
Page 3**

**Figure 11-22
Data Definition Map,
Page 1**

```
4     EDUCPGMC      10.56.43      04/07/81
```

INTRNL NAME	LVL	SOURCE NAME	BASE	DISPL	INTRNL NAME	DEFINITION	USAGE	R O Q M
DNM=1-061	77	FILLER	BL=1	000	DNM=1-061	DS 24C	DISP	
DNM=1-077	77	MSG-LENGTH	BL=1	018	DNM=1-077	DS 1H	COMP	
DNM=1-097	77	RECORD-LENGTH	BL=1	01A	DNM=1-097	DS 1H	COMP	
DNM=1-120	77	TOTAL-FIELD	BL=1	01C	DNM=1-120	DS 3P	COMP-3	
DNM=1-144	01	FILE-IOAREA	BL=1	020	DNM=1-144	DS 0CL80	GROUP	
DNM=1-168	02	PATIENT-NO	BL=1	020	DNM=1-168	DS 6C	DISP	
DNM=1-188	02	ROOM-NO	BL=1	026	DNM=1-188	DS 5C	DISP	
DNM=1-208	02	ILLNESS	BL=1	02B	DNM=1-208	DS 20C	DISP	
DNM=1-225	02	DOCTOR-NO	BL=1	03F	DNM=1-225	DS 10C	DISP	
DNM=1-244	02	FILLER	BL=1	049	DNM=1-244	DS 39C	DISP	
DNM=1-263	01	TERMINAL-MSG	BL=1	070	DNM=1-263	DS 0CL40	GROUP	
DNM=1-288	02	MESSAGE-OUT	BL=1	070	DNM=1-288	DS 40C	DISP	
DNM=1-309	02	MESSAGE-IN	BL=1	070	DNM=1-309	DS 0CL16	GROUP	R
DNM=1-332	03	TRANSID	BL=1	070	DNM=1-332	DS 4C	DISP	
DNM=1-349	03	FILLER	BL=1	074	DNM=1-349	DS 1C	DISP	
DNM=1-368	03	FUNCTION-CODE	BL=1	075	DNM=1-368	DS 4C	DISP	
DNM=1-391	03	FILLER	BL=1	079	DNM=1-391	DS 1C	DISP	
DNM=1-410	03	PATIENT-NUM	BL=1	07A	DNM=1-410	DS 6C	DISP	
DNM=1-431	01	DFHEIVAR	BL=1	098	DNM=1-431	DS 0CL106	GROUP	
DNM=1-452	02	DFHEIV0	BL=1	098	DNM=1-452	DS 26C	DISP	
DNM=1-469	02	DFHEIV1	BL=1	0B2	DNM=1-469	DS 8C	DISP	
DNM=1-486	02	DFHEIV2	BL=1	0BA	DNM=1-486	DS 8C	DISP	
DNM=2-000	02	DFHEIV3	BL=1	0C2	DNM=2-000	DS 8C	DISP	
DNM=2-017	02	DFHEIV4	BL=1	0CA	DNM=2-017	DS 6C	DISP	
DNM=2-034	02	DFHEIV5	BL=1	0D0	DNM=2-034	DS 4C	DISP	
DNM=2-051	02	DFHEIV6	BL=1	0D4	DNM=2-051	DS 4C	DISP	
DNM=2-068	02	DFHEIV7	BL=1	0D8	DNM=2-068	DS 2C	DISP	
DNM=2-085	02	DFHEIV8	BL=1	0DA	DNM=2-085	DS 2C	DISP	
DNM=2-102	02	DFHEIV9	BL=1	0DC	DNM=2-102	DS 1C	DISP	
DNM=2-119	02	DFHEIV10	BL=1	0DD	DNM=2-119	DS 4P	COMP-3	
DNM=2-137	02	DFHEIV11	BL=1	0E1	DNM=2-137	DS 1H	COMP	
DNM=2-155	02	DFHEIV12	BL=1	0E3	DNM=2-155	DS 1H	COMP	
DNM=2-173	02	DFHEIV13	BL=1	0E5	DNM=2-173	DS 1H	COMP	
DNM=2-191	02	DFHEIV14	BL=1	0E7	DNM=2-191	DS 1H	COMP	
DNM=2-209	02	DFHEIV15	BL=1	0E9	DNM=2-209	DS 1H	COMP	
DNM=2-227	02	DFHEIV16	BL=1	0EB	DNM=2-227	DS 1F	COMP	
DNM=2-245	02	DFHEIV17	BL=1	0EF	DNM=2-245	DS 4C	DISP	
DNM=2-263	02	DFHEIV18	BL=1	0F3	DNM=2-263	DS 4C	DISP	
DNM=2-284	02	DFHEIV19	BL=1	0F7	DNM=2-284	DS 4C	DISP	
DNM=2-305	02	DFHEIV97	BL=1	0FB	DNM=2-305	DS 4P	COMP-3	
DNM=2-323	02	DFHEIV98	BL=1	0FF	DNM=2-323	DS 1H	COMP	
DNM=2-341	02	DFHEIV99	BL=1	101	DNM=2-341	DS 1C	DISP	
DNM=2-359	01	DFHEIBLK	BLL=2	000	DNM=2-359	DS 0CL51	GROUP	
DNM=2-380	02	EIBTIME	BLL=2	000	DNM=2-380	DS 4P	COMP-3	
DNM=2-397	02	EIBDATE	BLL=2	004	DNM=2-397	DS 4P	COMP-3	
DNM=2-414	02	EIBTRNID	BLL=2	008	DNM=2-414	DS 4C	DISP	
DNM=2-432	02	EIBTASKN	BLL=2	00C	DNM=2-432	DS 4P	COMP-3	
DNM=2-453	02	EIBTRMID	BLL=2	010	DNM=2-453	DS 4C	DISP	
DNM=2-471	02	DFHEIGDI	BLL=2	014	DNM=2-471	DS 1H	COMP	
DNM=2-489	02	EIBCPOSN	BLL=2	016	DNM=2-489	DS 1H	COMP	

**Figure 11-23
Data Definition Map,
Page 2**

```
5     EDUCPGMC      10.56.43      04/07/81
```

INTRNL NAME	LVL	SOURCE NAME	BASE	DISPL	INTRNL NAME	DEFINITION	USAGE	R O Q M
DNM=3-000	02	EIBCALEN	BLL=2	018	DNM=3-000	DS 1H	COMP	
DNM=3-018	02	EIBAID	BLL=2	01A	DNM=3-018	DS 1C	DISP	
DNM=3-034	02	EIBFN	BLL=2	01B	DNM=3-034	DS 2C	DISP	
DNM=3-049	02	EIBRCODE	BLL=2	01D	DNM=3-049	DS 6C	DISP	
DNM=3-067	02	EIBDS	BLL=2	023	DNM=3-067	DS 8C	DISP	
DNM=3-082	02	EIBREQID	BLL=2	02B	DNM=3-082	DS 8C	DISP	
DNM=3-100	01	DFHCOMMAREA	BLL=3	000	DNM=3-100	DS 1C	DISP	
DNM=3-121	01	DFHBLLSLOT1	BLL=4	000	DNM=3-121	DS 1C	DISP	
DNM=3-142	01	DFHBLLSLOT2	BLL=5	000	DNM=3-142	DS 1C	DISP	

for the PROGRAM STORAGE section of the dump tells you that the first byte of PROGRAM STORAGE is located at X'656008'. The offset, then, is X'054C' (X'656554' minus X'656008').

Next, you will use the Linkage Editor output to see where this offset lies relative to the beginning of your program. The Linkage Editor output shown in Figure 11-25 is from a DOS/VSE CICS system. However, you can easily locate the equivalent information for an OS/VS based system. The important information is that the COBOL program (CSECT) EDUCPGMC appears at offset X'033090' and the first CSECT (LABEL), DFHECI appears at X'033078'. Relative to DFHECI, EDUCPGMC appears 18 hexadecimal (X'033098' minus X'033078') or 24 decimal bytes into the phase module. The offset of the instruction you are looking for, relative to the *beginning* of EDUCPGMC is then, X'054C' minus X'018' = X'0534'.

```
        8        EDUCPGMC        10.56.43      04/07/81


    LITERAL POOL (HEX)

    00448 (LIT+0)      000F0010  01200C00  50002802  04C00004  0D010000  0000000L
    00460 (LIT+24)     00000000  00020402  C0000400  00001400  00400000  00E3C5D4
    00478 (LIT+48)     D7C30A02  E0000400  004900C6  C9D3C5C1  0602F000  04000080
    00490 (LIT+72)     00040030  00040000  00010000  40000000  0E080000  04000010
    004A8 (LIT+96)     00E2D1C3  F10E0C80  00040000  6000D5D6  40D9C5C3  D6D9C440
    004C0 (LIT+120)    C6D6E4D5  C4


                 PGT                     00430

                 OVERFLOW CELLS          00430
                 VIRTUAL CELLS           00430
                 PROCEDURE NAME CELLS    0043C
                 GENERATED NAME CELLS    00448
                 SUBDTF ADDRESS CELLS    00448
                 VNI CELLS               00448
                 LITERALS                00448
                 DISPLAY LITERALS        004C5
                 PROCEDURE BLOCK CELLS   004C6


    REGISTER ASSIGNMENT

    REG 6     BL =1

    WORKING-STORAGE STARTS AT LOCATION 00100 FOR A LENGTH OF 00104.

                                         CONDENSED LISTING

       82    VERB  1  0004C6        85    VERB  1  0004DE        85    VERB  2  0004EE
       86    VERB  1  000504        87    VERB  1  000534        90    VERB  1  00053A
       90    VERB  2  00054A        94    VERB  1  000570        94    VERB  2  000580
       94    VERB  3  000586        95    VERB  1  000596        97    VERB  1  0005C4
       98    VERB  1  0005CA       101    VERB  1  0005D0       101    VERB  2  0005E0
      101    VERB  3  0005F0       104    VERB  1  000626       105    VERB  1  000630
      107    VERB  1  000636       107    VERB  2  00063C       107    VERB  3  00064C
      111    VERB  1  000682       111    VERB  2  000692       114    VERB  1  0006A8
      114    VERB  2  0006AE       114    VERB  3  0006BE       117    VERB  1  0006DC
      119    VERB  1  0006EC       119    VERB  2  0006F2       119    VERB  3  000702
      123    VERB  1  000738       123    VERB  2  000748       124    VERB  1  00075E


    *STATISTICS*        SOURCE RECORDS =    124    DATA ITEMS =      61    PROC DIV SZ =      34
    *STATISTICS*        PARTITION SIZE =3504008    LINE COUNT =      56    BUFFER SIZE =     512
    *OPTIONS IN EFFECT* PMAP RELOC ADR =   NONE    SPACING    =       1    FLOW        =    NONE
    *OPTIONS IN EFFECT* NOLISTX        APOST       SYM     NOCATALR    LIST      LINK     NOSTXIT      LIB
    *OPTIONS IN EFFECT* CLIST          FLAGW       ZWB     NOSUPMAP    NOXREF    ERRS     SXREF        NOOPT
    *OPTIONS IN EFFECT* NOSTATE        TRUNC       SEQ     NOSYMDMP    NODECK    NOVERB   NOSYNTAX     NOLVL
    *OPTIONS IN EFFECT*                NOCOUNT                      NOVERBSUM  NOVERBREF
    *LISTER OPTIONS*        NONE
```

**Figure 11-24
Register Assignment
Area of Data
Definition Map**

```
    04/07/81 PHASE    XFR-AD  LOCORE  HICORE  DSK-AD    LABEL    LOADED  REL-FR OFFSET INPUT

             XDFHCCOM 033090  033078  033A0B  0FE 09 07                                   RELOCATABLE
                                                       DFHECI   033078  033078 000000 DFHECI
                                                      *DFHCBLI  03307C
                                                      +DFHEI1   033082
                                                      *DFHAICBA 03308C
                                                       EDUCPGMC 033090  033090 000018 SYSLNK
                                                       ILBDMNS0 0338C0  0338C0 000848 ILBDMNS0
                                                       ILBDTC20 033918  033918 0008A0 ILBDTC20

    UNRESOLVED EXTERNAL REFERENCES                     WXTRN     ILBDTC00
                                                       WXTRN     ILBDTC01
                                                       WXTRN     ILBDDBG0
                                                       WXTRN     ILBDDBG7
                                                       WXTRN     ILBDDBG8
                                                       WXTRN     ILBDTC30

    UNRESOLVED ADCON  AT OFFSET 000339D0
    UNRESOLVED ADCON  AT OFFSET 000339D4
    UNRESOLVED ADCON  AT OFFSET 000339C0
    UNRESOLVED ADCON  AT OFFSET 000339C4
    UNRESOLVED ADCON  AT OFFSET 000339C8
    UNRESOLVED ADCON  AT OFFSET 000339CC

    006 UNRESOLVED ADDRESS CONSTANTS
```

**Figure 11-25
Linkage Editor
Output for Phase
Module**

Refer to the CONDENSED LISTING to find which program statement is closest to the offset X'0534'. It is statement number 87 that appears exactly at this offset. In most cases a single program statement generates several computer instructions, so the program offset you calculate from the absolute address will often lie between the offsets for two COBOL statements. In this case the first of the two statements is the one you are looking for.

Statement 87 is the COBOL statement: MOVE 15 TO MSG-LENGTH. We have found that it is associated with the instruction at absolute address X'656554'. Let's take a look at that absolute address in the transaction dump. Remember that the rightmost column of each line in the transaction dump gives the absolute address of the first byte of storage displayed in the line. Using this as a guide, you should find that the full word beginning at X'656554' contains the hexadecimal value X'D2016018'. If you are familiar with IBM 370 object code, you will recognize that this is the first part of a MOVE instruction that moves two bytes of storage into a location at offset X'018' plus the contents of general register 6. Remember that, according to the DMAP, register 6 is the BASE for BL = 1 variables. You can return to DMAP to confirm that the variable located at BL = 1 plus X'018' is MSG-LENGTH. Since program statement 87 moves a value into MSG-LENGTH, this is a good indication that program statement 87 is the statement associated with absolute address X'656554'.

Notice that absolute address X'656554' lies at offset X'054C' within PROGRAM STORAGE. To find the instruction in the dump you could have used either the absolute address column at the right of each line or the offset column at the left of the line. Practice finding this location by using the offset X'054C' instead of the absolute address. You should reach the same location as before.

Finding the Instruction that Caused an ABEND

Whenever you see an ABEND code of ASRA you know that either the computer itself or the operating system has rejected an instruction or a request. To determine the cause of the problem, you will usually begin by finding the absolute address of the instruction that caused the ABEND. Then, if the address is within PROGRAM STORAGE, you will use the technique we've just described to associate that instruction with a statement in your program. If the address lies outside your program, you will need to use a different procedure to find which was the last statement your program executed.

First, let's see how to find the absolute address of the instruction that caused the ABEND. To do so you will look at the PSW in the dump header. The last three bytes of the PSW give the address of the *next instruction* that would have been executed if the ABEND hadn't occurred. Therefore, the locations *preceding* this instruction contain the instruction that failed. For example, if statement 87 of EDUCPGMC had caused an ASRA-type ABEND, the last three bytes of the PSW would contain X'65655A'. To discover that the error occurred in statement 87, you would first observe that the absolute address lies within PROGRAM STORAGE. You would then use the technique we've just described to find the program statement associated with this absolute address.

Practice this once again. You would first calculate an offset (X'65655A' minus X'656008' = X'0552') from the beginning of PROGRAM STORAGE or the phase module. Next, refer to the Linkage Editor map and convert X'0552' to an offset within the program EDUCPGMC. The result should be X'053A'. (X'0552' minus X'018'. Remember that the X'018' came from subtracting the beginning offset for EDUCPGMC from the beginning offset for DFHECI.) Now compare this to the program statement offsets listed in the CONDENSED LISTING. You should find that statement 90 is the statement that would have been executed next had the ABEND not occurred. Look back at the program listing. Statement 90 is the first statement generated by the compiler to issue the CICS command shown in lines 88 and 89 (which are comments). Therefore, you know that the previous statement, statement 87, was the program statement that failed.

Determining the CICS Command Your Program Last Executed

Suppose that when you look at the address in the PSW, you find it does not lie within PROGRAM STORAGE. This means that the ABEND occurred after your program transferred control to:

1. a CICS command
2. a system routine
3. a random storage location as a result of a "wild" branch instruction

The last two possibilities are outside the scope of this text. We will consider the case in which your program has invoked a CICS command that subsequently failed.

In this situation, you would like to know which CICS command your program last invoked and which program statement invoked the command. You have already seen how to find a program statement, given the absolute address of an instruction. Now we will describe how you may be able to find the last CICS command your program issued, and the absolute address in PROGRAM STORAGE that invoked the command.

To do this, you will make use of an area in the CICS region called the *Trace Table*. CICS uses the trace table to record the activity of every task in the system. Whenever a CICS module receives control, it places an entry into the table.

Figures 11-12 through 11-14 show the trace table as it is formatted in a transaction dump. Notice that the title line for the trace table gives the beginning and ending absolute addresses for the table and the table's length in hexadecimal. The local system programmer decides how much space in the CICS region will be set aside for the trace table.

The table is used in a "wraparound" manner. That is, once the table becomes full each new entry overwrites the oldest entry. CICS maintains a pointer that is always set to the most recently used entry slot in the table. This address is shown in the first field of the *trace table header*, just under the title line. In Figure 11-12, the most recent trace table entry is at address X'00681F10'. Since each entry requires 16 bytes, this means that the next entry will be written to location X'00681F20', which is the first entry location shown in the dump. (If X'00681F10' were the last entry in the table, the next entry would be written into the table's first location at X'681AC0'.) This illustrates that the table is shown in the dump beginning with the *oldest entry*. Therefore, the *most recent entry* appears at the end of the trace table dump.

Remember that the trace table contains information for all of the CICS tasks in the system. In order to use the table, you have to know how to identify the entries associated with the task executing your program. Notice the fifth column, labeled TASK, in the trace table dump. It contains the *task sequence number* of the task that caused each entry. When CICS initiates each new task, it assigns a sequence number to the task.

If you requested the transaction dump from EDF you saw the task sequence number for your task in the heading line of each EDF panel. You could also have read the number from the EIBTASKN field of the EIB display. If you don't know the sequence number of the task you are debugging, you can find it by looking in the TCA (SYSTEM AREA) section of the transaction dump. Relative location X'0011' of this area contains the three-byte task sequence number in packed decimal form. In packed decimal, each digit of the decimal number is represented in four bits of storage. The rightmost four bits contain a sign code.

Look at the three bytes at offset X'0011' of the TCA (SYSTEM AREA) dump shown in Figure 11-11. They contain X'00008C'. The rightmost four bits contain the number's algebraic sign—you can ignore them for this purpose. Then the remaining 20 bits of the field represent the number 8. This is the sequence number of the task shown in this dump. Suppose that the field contained the value X'00132C'. Then the task sequence number would be 132.

To see a history of the CICS requests made by your task, you would begin at the most recent (end of the TRACE TABLE dump) trace table entry and look backwards, selecting only those entries with an 8 in the TASK column. Examine each entry by looking at the decoded TRACE TYPE field to the right of each line. Notice that this field begins with the name of a CICS module. For example, the most recent entry was made by KCP, the CICS Task Control Program. Usually you will be most interested in entries made by the Execution Interface Program (EIP). An EIP entry is made in the trace table at the beginning and end of each CICS command. Notice that the most recent EIP entry is labeled WRITEQ-TS RESPONSE. This entry records the *completion* of a CICS WRITEQ-TS command. Trace backward in the trace table until you find the EIP entry labeled WRITEQ-TS ENTRY. This records the *beginning* of the same CICS command. The intervening trace table entries were made by CICS modules that were invoked during execution of WRITEQ-TS.

As you can see, a single command may generate many trace table entries. When you consider that hundreds of CICS tasks may be in the system at a time, you can see that the trace table may be filled quite quickly. You may find that the entries you would like to see had been overwritten by new entries before your task failed. If this is the case, you may have to try other debugging techniques or run the program again when fewer tasks are active.

Let's assume, however, that you are able to find the trace table entry for the most recent CICS command that your program invoked. Then look in the column labeled REG14 for the entry. This contains the absolute address of the *next sequential instruction* of the application program. In this example, the command WRITEQ-TS was invoked by the instruction *preceding* absolute address X'6565E4'. This is the address shown for register 14 in the EIP trace table entry. When the WRITEQ-TS command is completed, control will return to this address.

Once you have found this absolute address, you may use the technique we've discussed above to find the program statement that generated the instruction. If the most recent EIP entry was for a command ENTRY, you know that the program statement you found invoked the CICS command, and that the ABEND occurred during execution of the command. You will want to look carefully at the argument values your program specified to the command.

On the other hand, if the most recent EIP entry was for a command RESPONSE, you know that CICS completed the command and execution continued beyond that point in your program. Since the problem instruction lies outside your program, the failure probably occurred in a non-CICS system routine invoked by your program. You will need to look carefully at the program logic between the CICS command just completed and the next CICS command you expected your program to execute. In this situation, the trace table has allowed you to pin the failure down to a point between execution of two CICS commands.

Summary

This chapter has described the use of two tools for testing or trouble-shooting CICS application programs. The Execution Diagnostic Facility (EDF) is an *interactive debugging* tool that permits you to monitor a CICS task as it performs a user transaction. The transaction dump is a printed listing of the areas in the CICS region associated with a transaction at a given point during execution.

You may use EDF in either of two modes. In *same-terminal* mode you invoke first EDF and then the transaction to be tested. You will receive normal transaction messages and EDF panels at the same terminal. In *two-terminal* mode you invoke EDF to monitor a transaction as it runs on a second terminal. You receive EDF panels while the user receives normal transaction messages.

When EDF monitors a transaction, it interrupts execution whenever any of several event types occur. It then displays an EDF panel that contains information about the event. Events which trigger EDF displays include:

1. Task Initiation
2. Invocation of a CICS command
3. Completion of a CICS command
4. Abnormal or Normal Task Termination
5. Transaction Completion

When you receive an EDF display you may:

1. Modify information displayed in a panel
2. Request to see areas of working-storage
3. Request to see the EIB
4. Save the panel for future reference
5. Skip a command about to be executed
6. Terminate the task
7. Terminate the task and request a transaction dump

Transaction dumps are written into a sequential file called the dump data set when:

1. A dump is requested from EDF
2. A program issues an EXEC CICS DUMP command
3. A task terminates abnormally (ABEND)

A transaction dump consists of several sections:

1. The dump header gives information that helps you identify the dump. It includes a code describing the reason for the dump, the transaction identifier, the time and date on which the dump was written. The header also shows the contents of the Program Status Word (PSW) and the contents of general registers 1-11, 14, and 15 at the time of ABEND.
2. Transaction Storage shows the contents of working-storage and data areas associated with the transaction.
3. Program Storage shows the reenterable program, consisting of the CSECT's linked together by the Linkage Editor.
4. Trace Table shows the current trace table entries, beginning with the oldest and ending with the most recent entry.
5. Task Control Area (TCA)—including both the system and user sections.

You use the transaction dump together with the compiler listing of a program, including the Data Definition Map (DMAP) and condensed listing, and the Linkage Editor map. This chapter described how to use the transaction dump to:

1. Find the contents of a variable in working.storage.
2. Find the program statement associated with an instruction at a particular absolute address.
3. Find the instruction that caused an ABEND.
4. Determine which CICS command your program executed most recently.

EXERCISE

1. You have learned to modify a location in working-storage by typing over either the hexadecimal or character mode representation of the location in an EDF panel. Devise an experiment to find out what happens if you modify *both* the hexadecimal and character mode display of the location, specifying a different value in each.

2. Return to the program you wrote for the chapter "Random Access of Data Files." Run the program under EDF and force the following exceptional conditions:
   a. LENGERR
   b. NOTOPEN
   c. INVREQ

3. Figures 11-11 through 11-25 include the compiler output, linkage editor map, and a transaction dump for a COBOL program. (Some pages of the complete listing have been omitted in order to save space. However, the figures contain all the information you will need to complete this exercise.) Using these figures, answer the following questions:
   a. What is the transaction ID of the task that abended?
   b. What is the reason for the transaction dump?
   c. What is the absolute address of the instruction at which the ABEND occurred?
   d. At what absolute address is the CSECT DFHECI located?
   e. At what absolute address is the CSECT EDUCPGMC located?
   f. What is the offset of EDUCPGMC within program storage?
   g. If the ABEND occurred within program storage, what is the line number of the program statement that caused the ABEND?
   h. What was the last CICS command issued by the program? Was the command completed? How do you know?
   i. What is the line number of the program statement that invoked the last CICS command?
   j. List the task sequence numbers of each task with an entry in the trace table. What is the task sequence number of the task shown in this dump?

4. In the previous exercise you should have identified a COBOL statement in EDUCPGMC that caused an ABEND. In this exercise you will determine the cause of the ABEND more exactly.
   a. Write the statement that caused the ABEND.
   b. What program variable(s) does the statement use?
   c. Find each variable and write down its contents.
   d. Can you tell whether the values appear reasonable?

12 Transient Data and Temporary Storage

Introduction

The CICS application programs you have written so far have been independent of one another, and have followed a typical flow of execution. This flow can be summarized in the following steps:

1. User enters transaction request.
2. CICS determines which application program performs the requested transaction, and initiates a task to execute the application program.
3. Application program optionally receives input from user.
4. Application program performs transaction, possibly reading from or writing to a direct access file.
5. Application program sends output to user and, optionally, to specified routing terminals.
6. Transaction is complete. Application program returns control to CICS, which terminates task.

Notice that the program receives input only from the user who initiates the transaction, and sends output only to user terminals.

The only variation in this pattern has occurred with pseudo-conversational transactions where, before terminating, the application program arranges for a second program to be invoked to handle the user's next input.

Except in the pseudo-conversational case, the program is completely independent of other application programs in the CICS application library. Functionally, a pseudo-conversational transaction can also be viewed as a single independent transaction. It converses with a single user at a single direct terminal. The flow of control from program to program is controlled by logic internal to the transaction. When one program gives up control it has already determined which program will be executed next. There is no way for control to flow to an application program that is not known within the transaction.

In practice, most application programs are not quite so independent. Usually an application program is part of a larger *application system*. For example, you will often hear about "the accounts payable *system*" or the "inventory control *system*."

In an application system, each transaction is related to others. A transaction within an application system can:

1. Receive input from another transaction
2. Produce output to be processed by other transactions
3. Initiate other transactions
4. Be initiated by other transactions

In this chapter we will discuss two major CICS facilities, *Transient Data* and *Temporary Storage*, that can be used to pass data between transactions. We will also describe two ways in which a transaction can be initiated *without* a transaction request from a user terminal.

Objectives

After completing this chapter, you will be able to:

- Distinguish among *intrapartition transient data, extrapartition transient data,* and *temporary storage* queues.
- Use the CICS WRITEQ, READQ, and DELETEQ commands for transient data and temporary storage.
- Discuss the naming conventions required when an application program accesses a temporary storage queue.
- Describe how the ENQ and DEQ commands can be used to insure that nonsharable resources are used serially.
- Describe how an *intrapartition transient data queue* can be used to trigger automatic transaction initiation.
- Use the CICS START command to initiate a CICS transaction.

Transient Data

The transient data facility is designed to allow a CICS transaction to produce, or to accept as input, a sequential file of data. The data may be produced by one CICS transaction for processing by another CICS transaction. In this case, the data is referred to as *intrapartition* transient data. It is both *produced and processed* within the CICS region.

Alternatively, the sequential data file may be produced by programs *outside CICS* for processing by a CICS transaction. Or a CICS transaction can produce the file for processing *outside CICS*. In these cases, the data is referred to as *extrapartition* transient data.

We begin by introducing those features of transient data that apply to both the intrapartition and extrapartition cases.

We have already said that transient data is *sequential* in organization. Because transient data must be processed sequentially, it is said to reside in a transient data *queue*.

Recall that each direct access file that can be processed by CICS is defined in the File Control Table (FCT). In a similar way, each transient data queue that can be produced or read by a CICS transaction must be defined in a table called the *Destination Control Table (DCT)*. Each separate transient data queue is referred to as a transient data *destination*, and has a one- to four-character symbolic name called the *destination ID*.

Extrapartition Transient Data

Let's look at a situation in which you might use an extrapartition transient data destination. Suppose that a company uses CICS to handle telephoned orders for merchandise. As each call is received, a clerk uses a CICS *order-entry* transaction to update the inventory file and enter billing information into an invoicing file. Both the inventory and invoicing files are direct access files described in the File Control Table (FCT). The transaction updates these files online as the clerk takes the order from the caller.

The company also wants to keep data about each call for statistical purposes. Monthly, a data analysis program is run to analyze the following information about each call:

1. Time of day and day of the week received

2. Customer's city and zip code
3. Item(s) ordered
4. Dollar amount of the sale
5. Where the customer heard about the company

The analyzed information is then made available to planners in marketing and advertising.

To support the statistics-gathering requirement, the order-entry transaction records the information listed above, adding it to a sequential file that will be processed later by the data analysis program. The sequential file is a *transient data queue*. The data analysis program is not run as a CICS transaction—there is no need for the analysis to be done online, so the program is run as a batch job. Because the data analysis program is not a CICS transaction, the sequential file containing the data is an *extrapartition* transient data queue. The queue may be a sequential file on a direct access storage device or it may be a file on magnetic tape. (Later we will see that an extrapartition transient data queue may also be a sequential output device, like a printer. However, such an output device would not satisfy the requirements of this example.)

Notice the following factors that allow the transient data facility to be used in this example:

1. The data will be processed sequentially.
2. There is no need to separate the data according to the terminal used to enter the order.

The second factor deserves some further thought. Assuming that there are many clerks available to process phone orders, there will normally be many copies of the order entry transaction in execution at any time. The application program that performs the transaction contains CICS commands to write data to the transient data destination assigned for this purpose. As we mentioned earlier, each destination is identified by a one- to four-character destination ID. The program uses the destination ID in the CICS command to write data into the queue. Each copy of the program uses the same destination ID; therefore, each transaction will write to the same queue, and data about orders taken by different clerks at different terminals will be intermixed in the queue.

The two factors listed above apply to any transient data destination. In this particular example, the destination must be an *extrapartition* destination because a CICS transaction (the order-entry transaction) is producing data for processing *outside* the CICS region (by the batch data analysis program).

The following are additional characteristics that apply only to *extrapartition* transient data destinations:

1. Each destination is a separate physical file.
2. The destination may be a sequential file on a direct access device, on magnetic tape, or on a physical device like a printer or plotter.
3. The Destination Control Table (DCT) entry defines the destination as either an input or output destination.
4. The records within the file may be either fixed or variable length, and the DCT entry specifies the record format.
5. The central system operator may open or close a destination. An attempt to read from or write to a destination that is not open raises the NOTOPEN exceptional condition.

Intrapartition Transient Data

Now that we've seen how an extrapartition transient data queue might be used, let's expand the previous example to use an *intrapartition* transient data destination as well.

Suppose that, as an additional part of its processing, the order-entry transaction produces a warehouse "pick list" for each phone order. The pick list contains the catalog number, description, and quantity of each item ordered, and an order number that allows all of the items for a single order to be gathered together for shipping. At a CICS terminal in the warehouse, a transaction is run to read the pick list and print out the items needed, their location in the warehouse, and the order number associated with the item. The warehouse transaction might be fairly sophisticated, particularly if the warehouse is large. For example, the warehouse might be divided into several zones, with one or more CICS terminals in each zone. Then as the warehouse transaction reads each pick list from the intrapartition transient data queue, it can determine where each required item is located and use BMS routing facilities to print the pick list item at the terminal in the correct zone.

In order to use the intrapartition transient data facility, the following conditions must be met:

1. The warehouse transaction must read from the intrapartition queue in sequential order. Once it reads a record from the queue, the record cannot be read again. In effect, each record is removed from the queue as it is read.
2. The intrapartition queue must be on a direct access storage device assigned to hold intrapartition data. Intrapartition queues cannot be on magnetic tape or sequential devices, as can extrapartition queues.
3. The records in the intrapartition queue must be variable length records.
4. If the order-entry transaction attempts to place a record in the intrapartition queue, but the queue is full, the NOSPACE exceptional condition will be raised.

The preceding list indicates a few important differences between intrapartition and extrapartition transient data destinations.

The two are alike in that they are *sequential* and that each destination must be defined in the Destination Control Table (DCT).

However, where each extrapartition queue is a separate file, all intrapartition queues share space in a single file that can be thought of as the intrapartition data area. This area must be on direct access storage volumes—it cannot be on tape or on a sequential device. As each record is written into an intrapartition queue, it is assigned space in the single intrapartition data area, and the preceding record in the same queue (destination) is linked to the new record.

As each record is read from an intrapartition queue, it becomes "lost." There is no way to find the record and read it again. Therefore, a transaction that reads from an intrapartition queue must be able to handle each record as it is read.

The system operators must pay particular attention to the amount of space available in the intrapartition transient data area, because all of the intrapartition transient data queues share its space. If all of the space allocated to the intrapartition transient data area is full, transactions that attempt to write to an intrapartition transient data queue will receive the NOSPACE exceptional condition.

A queue will grow within the intrapartition transient data area if its records are not read as fast as they are written. In an application system like the order-entry warehouse case the queue may grow throughout the day as records are written from online terminals. In the evening when activity on the online terminals slows down, the processing transactions can "catch up" and empty the queue.

The system programmer may set the DCT to define an intrapartition queue as "reusable." In this case as each record is read, its space becomes available to be written into. When all of the records in a reusable queue have been processed, the queue occupies no space in the intrapartition transient data area. The queue has been "cleaned-up."

If a queue is *non-reusable*, each record is *logically* removed from the queue as the record is read, but its space remains allocated. When all of the records in a non-reusable queue have been processed, the queue still occupies just as much space in the intrapartition transient data area as if no records at all had been processed. If special steps are not taken to clean up the queue, it will eventually fill all the direct access storage space available in the intrapartition transient data area.

To clean up a non-reusable queue, the queue must first be *drained* by allowing the processing transactions to execute while the transactions that write into the queue are made unavailable. Once the queue has been *drained*—that is, all of its records have been processed—it consists entirely of obsolete records. Then a program can be run to *delete* the queue. This causes the storage allocated to processed records to be released. The discussion of Transient Data commands, which follows, describes how to delete an intrapartition transient data queue.

Transient Data Commands

Now that you've seen examples of Transient Data queues in use, let's look at the CICS commands you can use to write and read transient records.

In general, each command consists of a name, like WRITEQ or READQ, followed by a space and the characters TD that stand for Transient Data. Be careful not to omit the TD characters. If TD is omitted, CICS assumes that the command is intended for Temporary Storage instead of for a Transient Data queue. Temporary Storage will be discussed later in this chapter.

Writing Transient Data Records

The WRITEQ TD command is used to write a record into a transient data queue. The command is written:

```
EXEC CICS WRITEQ TD
          QUEUE (name)
          FROM (data-area)
          LENGTH (data-value)
```

Notice that the form of the command is the same for either an extrapartition destination defined for output or for an intrapartition destination. This allows your program to be independent of the DCT definition, so that an application program need not be changed if a decision is made to use an intrapartition queue rather than an extrapartition one.

QUEUE specifies the one- to four-character destination ID by which the queue is defined in the DCT.

FROM identifies the area that contains the data to be written.

LENGTH is the number of bytes of data to be written.

You should always code a LENGTH argument, even if you expect the queue to contain fixed length records. Remember that, at some later time, the application system designers might decide to modify the DCT to specify variable length records. This would cause your program to fail if you had omitted LENGTH.

The following exceptional conditions may be raised by the WRITEQ TD command:

1. IOERR   The write command has failed due to an unrecoverable output error.
2. QIDERR   The destination ID given as the QUEUE argument cannot be found in the DCT.
3. NOSPACE   There is no room available on a requested *intrapartition* queue.
4. NOTOPEN   The requested destination is closed.
5. LENGERR   May occur for any of the following reasons:

   ■ The LENGTH option was omitted and the queue contains variable length records.
   ■ The LENGTH argument is greater than the maximum record length defined in the DCT.
   ■ The queue contains fixed length records, and the LENGTH argument gives an incorrect length.

Reading A Transient Data Queue

The READQ TD command is used to read a record from a transient data destination. The command is written:

```
EXEC CICS READQ TD
          QUEUE (name)
          INTO (data-area)   I   SET (pointer reference)
          LENGTH (data-area)
```

The QUEUE parameter is as defined above for the WRITEQ command.

INTO identifies the area into which data should be read.

SET specifies a pointer reference identifying a BLL Cell to be set to the location of the input in a CICS buffer. If SET is specified, CICS obtains an input buffer, moves the input into the buffer, and sets the pointer reference to the address of the buffer. The buffer is retained until the next transient data command is executed.

LENGTH identifies a halfword binary value giving the length of the input area. CICS will set the LENGTH argument to the number of bytes of input read.

The following exceptional conditions may occur during execution of the READQ TD command:

1. QZERO   The requested queue is empty. This is equivalent to an "end of file" condition.
2. QBUSY   For an *intrapartition* queue, the queue is being written into or deleted by another task. The CICS default action for this condition is to suspend the task until the queue becomes free.
3. IOERR   The write command has failed due to an unrecoverable input error.

4. QIDERR   As described above for WRITEQ TD.
5. NOTOPEN   As described above for WRITEQ TD.
6. LENGERR   May occur for any of the following reasons:

- The LENGTH option was omitted and the queue contains variable length records.
- The record read from the queue is longer than the length specified by the LENGTH parameter. CICS truncates the record to fit into the size specified by LENGTH, but then sets LENGTH to the *actual* record size.
- The queue contains fixed length records, and the LENGTH argument gives an incorrect length.

Deleting an Intrapartition Transient Data Queue

As discussed above, an intrapartition transient data queue that is not defined as reusable will continue to grow until the entire queue is deleted. The queue will then begin to grow again when the first WRITEQ TD command for the queue is executed.

To delete the queue, you use this command:

DELETEQ TD QUEUE (name)

QUEUE is as defined above for the WRITEQ TD and READQ TD commands. The QIDERR exceptional condition will be raised if the QUEUE argument names a destination ID that is not defined in the DCT.

Temporary Storage

The Temporary Storage facility allows a CICS application program to create a sequential file that can be read or modified by other CICS transactions. Temporary Storage data is similar to intrapartition transient data in that it is created and used only within the CICS region. However, Temporary Storage is unlike transient data in several important ways:

1. Whereas a transient data destination must be predefined in the DCT, a queue in temporary storage is named and created dynamically by the program that first writes into a given queue. As will be discussed later in this section, this allows separate queues to be created by copies of the same transaction running from different terminals.
2. Records in a temporary storage queue can be either read in sequential order, or directly accessed by relative record number. (Because data in temporary storage need not be processed sequentially, the term *queue* may be misleading. As will be discussed later, the term *message set* is often used in place of queue.)
3. Records in temporary storage can be read and reread, or modified and rewritten. Once written, a record remains accessible in temporary storage until it is explicitly deleted.
4. Temporary storage queues may be on direct access storage or in main memory.

These differences make temporary storage more suitable than transient data for certain types of applications. For example, the fact that temporary storage may be located in main memory means that records can be accessed very quickly. In the intrapartition example above, there was no requirement that the warehouse transaction print the pick file entry instantaneously. Several minutes or hours might pass between the time a record was written into the intrapartition transient data queue and the time the warehouse transaction processed the same record. Within an application system, however, instantaneous processing is often a requirement.

For example, let's look again at the order-entry process we've been discussing. So far, we've assumed that the process proceeds in an orderly sequence as shown in Figure 12-1.

When a telephone order is received, the clerk begins by obtaining the customer's name and address. Next the customer provides a list of items to be ordered. As the clerk enters each item, the program updates the inventory file and writes the item request into the warehouse transient data destination. When the customer has no more items to order, the clerk presses a key to signal "that's all," and the order entry program sends the list, including the total price, to the invoicing file. The transaction is complete.

In practice, however, it's unlikely that many telephone orders proceed in this way. At any point the customer may decide to cancel or modify an item previously requested. The customer may want to review the partial order, find out the total cost of items ordered so far, find out what the current account balance is, specify a different shipping address than billing address, or correct any information given to the clerk so far.

If you designed an order-entry program according to Figure 12-1 flowchart, the program would force the customer and clerk to conduct their conversation in a rigidly defined sequence. In effect, they would be working for the program rather than the program working for them. To handle the real world requirement a more flexible design is required.

Figure 12-2 shows a different view of the order-entry process. Instead of a single transaction, the process is implemented by a set of separate, but related transactions:

1. *Start New Order* is always the first transaction of the process. It creates an initial order form in temporary storage. The initial form could contain information like date and time the order was received, name of clerk handling the order, etc.
2. *Enter "Bill To" or "Ship To"* places into the order form the name and address of the party to be billed for the order or to receive the order.
3. *Enter Item Request* writes a description of one order item and its price into the order form.
4. *Edit Item List* displays the current order form including total price. The user may request to modify any information displayed.
5. *Process Order* is the last transaction of the process. It updates the inventory and billing files, writes statistical data to the extrapartition transient data queue, writes the pick list to the intrapartition transient data queue, and deletes the order form from temporary storage.

In Figure 12-2, the sequence of processing is controlled by the customer and the orders clerk, not by a program design. The only requirement is that the first transaction is Start New Order and that the last transaction is Process Order. The customer can now provide information in any sequence, and the clerk simply invokes the appropriate transaction at each step. If the customer wants to interrupt the order to ask whether the company has received the latest payment on the account, the clerk can invoke a completely unrelated

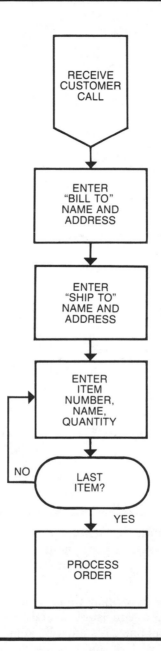

Figure 12-1
Idealized Order
Entry Process

transaction to answer that question. Once the question has been answered the order process can continue.

We have described these transactions as interrelated. They are related to one another because they are working on the same data structure—the order form for this particular phone call.

The order-entry process needs to be conversational from the user's view. Therefore, each transaction must be able to read the order form as soon as the transaction is requested and to modify the form instantaneously. To satisfy

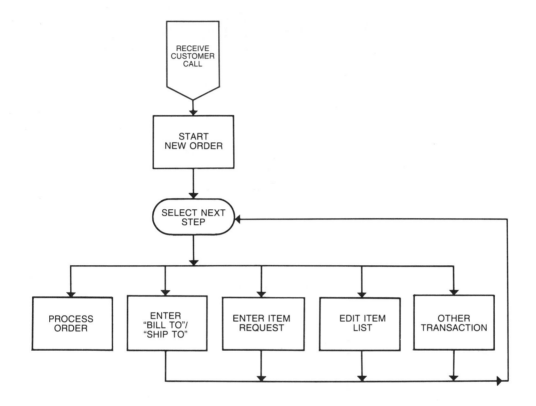

**Figure 12-2
Modular Programming
Approach to Order
Entry Transaction**

these requirements the records that make up the order form can be written into temporary storage assigned to main memory.

The newly designed transaction must satisfy the following additional requirements:

1. There is no way to know how many items a customer will order. Therefore, the order form may need to consist of several records.
2. The data from different phone calls must be kept separate. Keep in mind that if there are seventeen clerks, each using the order-entry transactions to handle a telephone order, there will be seventeen order forms being constructed. Each time the clerk invokes a new transaction, the new program must be able to find the correct order form in temporary storage.
3. Because the customer may want to change an item requested much earlier in the conversation, the programs must be able to retrieve records from temporary storage in any order and to read a given record several times. We have seen that records can be read from a message set by relative number, and that records remain in temporary storage until they are explicitly purged.

Now that we've discussed some of the functions that the temporary storage facility provides, let's look more closely at the facility itself.

We've said that Temporary Storage may exist either in main memory (MAIN) or on direct-access storage (AUXILIARY). In either case, the data in temporary storage is in the form of variable length records. Records are accessed *by name* in temporary storage. The record names are not predefined, but are generated dynamically by the program that writes a record into temporary storage. Records with the same name make up a *temporary storage queue* or *message set*. A message set may contain only one record or many records. Once written, records in a message set can be retrieved sequentially or directly by their relative number. A record may be read more than once. It remains accessible in temporary storage until a program purges the record (or message set) by name. In case of a system or CICS crash, temporary storage records on direct access volumes can be recovered.

Naming Conventions for Temporary Storage

When a program writes a record into temporary storage it assigns a one- to eight-character *name* to the record. In order to read or purge the record from temporary storage, another program must request the record by name.

This arrangement implies three requirements:

1. All programs in an installation must use a naming standard, so that two programs do not inadvertently use the same name for their records.
2. When multiple copies of the same program are executing, the name assigned to a temporary storage record must be different for each copy of the program. Otherwise, the records associated with different terminals will become intermixed in the same message set.
3. In order to read a record from temporary storage, a program must be able to discover the record name used by the program that wrote the record.

To see how this can work, we will return to the order-entry example. The Start New Order transaction constructs an initial order form for the customer order and writes it into temporary storage. To do so, it must specify a name for the record that represents the order form.

The first requirement is that the name must be different from any name used by any other CICS application in the installation. To meet this requirement, an *installation standard* must be defined so that every application program defines names according to the same rule. Let's assume that each program that creates a temporary storage message set must be assigned a three-character code by some central administrator—perhaps a system programmer or data base administrator. The three-character code will be the first three characters of the record name used to create the message set.

Suppose that you request a code for your Start New Order program, and are assigned the code P01. Then the CICS command you use to write the initial order-entry form into temporary storage must specify a record name that begins with the characters P01. As long as the administrator is careful not to assign the code P01 to any other program, your program cannot write into a message queue belonging to any other program.

The next requirement is that if multiple copies of the Start New Order transaction are running at the same time, each must use a different name for its order forms. Otherwise, the items ordered through a clerk at terminal A would become intermixed with items ordered through a clerk at terminal B.

A good way to satisfy this requirement is to use the direct terminal's terminal identifier as part of the record name. Your program can get the terminal identifier from the TRMID field of the EIB.

Remember that the terminal identifier may be up to four characters long. If the terminal identifier is the last four characters of the record name and the code P01 is the first three characters, you have free only one character position of the eight-character record name. You can make use of this remaining position if your program needs to write into more than one message set in temporary storage. For example, you could use P011 for the first message set written and P012 for the second message set.

Let's suppose that, following these rules, your program writes the order form into a record named P011tttt where tttt stands for the terminal identifier.

Then the programs that read the order form must also use the name P011tttt when they issue their read command. You will have to tell the programmers who write these programs that the first four characters of the record name for the order form are P011. Given that information, their programs can read the correct order form by taking the terminal identifier from EIBTRMID and appending it to P011.

Temporary Storage Commands

We have discussed three operations that can be performed upon a message set in temporary storage: write a record, read a record, delete a message set. The CICS commands used for these operations are similar to the Transient Data commands described in the first part of this chapter. Each command consists of a command name, like WRITEQ or READQ, followed by a space and the characters TS which stand for Temporary Storage. The TS distinguishes the command from a Transient Data command. However, if you omit the TS characters, CICS treats Temporary Storage as the default.

Writing Data To A Temporary Storage Queue

You use the WRITEQ TS command to write a record into temporary storage. The command is written:

```
EXEC CICS WRITEQ TS QUEUE (name)
    FROM (data-area)
    LENGTH (data-area)
    [REWRITE ]   [ITEM (data-area)
    [MAIN I AUXILIARY]
```

QUEUE gives the one- to eight-character record name. If there is currently no record in temporary storage with the specified name, a new temporary storage message set (or queue) will be established and this record will be its first record. If there are already one or more records (that is, an existing message set) in temporary storage with the specified name, this record will be added to the existing message set.

FROM specifies the data-area that contains the record to be written.

LENGTH specifies the number of bytes in the record. Remember that records in temporary storage message sets are variable length records, so the LENGTH parameter is required.

REWRITE specifies that the record is to *replace* a record that already exists in the message set. If REWRITE is specified, ITEM must be coded and must indicate the relative record number of the record to be replaced.

If REWRITE is *not* specified, the ITEM parameter may be coded to *receive* the relative position (record number) of this new record in the message set. When CICS adds the record to the message set, it will set the ITEM argument to the record's relative record number.

Code MAIN in order to assign the message set to main memory. The default is AUXILIARY that assigns the message set to direct-access storage.

Suppose that you wish to write a new record to a temporary storage queue whose eight-character name is in the variable UNIQNAME. The data to be written is in data-area MESSAGE and the variable LENGTH contains the length of the record in bytes. Your command would be written:

```
EXEC CICS WRITEQ TS QUEUE (UNIQNAME) FROM (MESSAGE)
    LENGTH (LENGTH) ITEM (DREF)
```

When the command is complete, the variable DREF will contain the relative record number, within the message set, of the new record. If the record is the first record of a new message set, DREF will contain 1.

Suppose that, later, you wish to replace this record with a modified version. The modified data is in a data-area called DATAFLD, and the new record is to contain 40 bytes. Your command would be written:

```
EXEC CICS WRITEQ TS QUEUE (UNIQNAME) FROM (DATAFLD)
    LENGTH (40) REWRITE ITEM (DREF)
```

The following exceptional conditions can be detected during execution of a WRITEQ TS command:

1. INVREQ   The length of the specified data area is zero or exceeds an installation-defined maximum.
2. IOERR   There is an unrecoverable output error in writing a record to AUXILIARY storage.
3. ITEMERR   The item number specified with the REWRITE option is invalid. For example, it might be zero or a number greater than the number of records in the message set.
4. QIDERR   The queue specified for a REWRITE option cannot be found.
5. NOSPACE   There is not enough space in the temporary storage area to contain the data. The CICS default for this condition is to place the task in a wait state until space becomes available. Therefore, you should define a condition-handling routine for NOSPACE if immediate response to the transaction must be guaranteed.

Reading Data From Temporary Storage

You use the READQ TS command to read data from a temporary storage message set. The command is written:

```
READQ TS QUEUE (name)
        SET (ptr-ref)  I  INTO  (data-area)
        LENGTH (data-area)
        [NEXT]  I  [ ITEM (data-value) ]
```

QUEUE is as defined above for WRITEQ TS.

SET, INTO, and LENGTH are as defined above for READQ TD.

The ITEM and NEXT options specify which record (item) is to be read from the message set. If ITEM is specified, its argument must contain the relative record number to be read. NEXT is the default. It causes the record after the record last retrieved *by any task* to be read. Notice that, if more than one task will be reading from the same message set, you should code the ITEM option. Otherwise one task could execute a READQ TS command, resetting the relative record counter and causing a second task that specifies READQ TS NEXT to skip records inadvertently.

The following exceptional conditions can be detected during execution of a READQ TS command:

1. IOERR   There is an unrecoverable input error reading from an AUXILIARY temporary storage queue.
2. ITEMERR   The item number specified is invalid; or when NEXT is specified, the record most recently read from the queue was the queue's last record.
3. LENGERR   The length of the record exceeds the value specified by the LENGTH option.
4. QIDERR   The specified queue cannot be found.

Deleting a Temporary Storage Queue

You use the DELETEQ TS command to delete an entire temporary storage queue. In the order-entry example above, the *Process Order* transaction would use this command to erase the order form from temporary storage once it has completed all other processing. It is important to remember to delete temporary storage as soon as possible within a transaction in order to avoid filling up memory and direct-access space allocated to temporary storage.

The command is written:

DELETEQ TS QUEUE (name)

The QUEUE parameter contains the name of the message set to be deleted.

The QIDERR exceptional condition occurs if the specified queue cannot be found.

The ENQ Facility

In the chapter "A CICS Transaction," we discussed how reenterable programs can be shared by several CICS tasks. We have also discussed several types of resources, such as files, that cannot be shared but must be used *serially* or "in turn" by multiple tasks. CICS uses the exclusive control mechanism to insure that only one task may update a file at a time, and it raises the QBUSY condition if a task attempts to read from an intrapartition transient data queue while another task is in the process of updating or deleting the queue. Both are examples of mechanisms for insuring that a nonsharable resource is used serially.

Occasionally, you may need to access a nonsharable resource that is not controlled by CICS. For example, an application system may use a table in memory that can be accessed only serially. Or you may need a different level of control for a nonshared resource that CICS does control.

As an example of this second case, suppose that an application needs to write two records into an extrapartition transient data queue, but must guarantee that these records appear together in the queue. CICS will guarantee that, while a program is writing any single record into the queue, other tasks may not attempt to add records. But in this case, you must prevent other tasks from adding records until your program has written both of its records.

This type of requirement should be avoided whenever possible, because it is always undesirable to force CICS tasks to wait while your task executes multiple CICS commands. However, we will assume that it is a necessary requirement in this particular situation.

When CICS controls a nonsharable resource, it takes advantage of the fact that the resource can be accessed only by executing a CICS command. Therefore, CICS is in a position to intercept each attempted access.

Your program lacks this advantage. It is not in position to intercept WRITEQ TD commands executed by other tasks. Therefore, it can control access to the queue only with the cooperation of all other programs that use the queue. In effect, all programs must agree to "check first" to see whether they may issue their WRITEQ TD command. The ENQ facility is used for this purpose.

The first step in using the ENQ facility is to define a standard name for the nonsharable resource. The name can be anything at all, so long as it is not longer than 255 characters. It is desirable, but not necessary that the name be descriptive. All that is really necessary is that all programs use the same name for the resource, and that no other CICS program use the same name for any other resource. Notice that this is another example in which an *installation standard naming convention* must be defined and observed by all CICS application programs. Otherwise, programmers for entirely separate application systems might inadvertently make up the same name for two different resources.

Once a resource name has been defined, each program that uses the resource must perform these three steps:

1. Issue the ENQ command to see whether the resource is free, and to gain exclusive control of it when it is free.
2. Access the resource as required. This should be done as soon as possible after the ENQ command and should be completed as quickly as possible.
3. Issue the DEQ command to free the resource for use by other tasks. This should be done as quickly as possible after the program has finished using the resource.

The ENQ command is written:

> EXEC CICS ENQ RESOURCE (data-area) LENGTH (data-value)

RESOURCE identifies a constant or data-area that contains the resource name. LENGTH specifies a halfword binary value that defines the number of characters in the resource name.

If the resource is not available, CICS raises the ENQBUSY condition. If you have not coded an exception-handling routine for ENQBUSY, CICS will place your task in a wait state until the resource becomes available.

The DEQ command is written:

> EXEC CICS DEQ RESOURCE (data-area) LENGTH (data-value)

RESOURCE and LENGTH are as defined above for ENQ.

The following sequence shows how ENQ and DEQ are used to control access to a resource whose name is a nine-character string located in the variable SERIAL.

EXEC CICS ENQ RESOURCE (SERIAL) LENGTH (9) END-EXEC.
    [one or more statements that access the resource named by SERIAL]
EXEC CICS DEQ RESOURCE (SERIAL) LENGTH (9) END-EXEC.

Automatic and Programmed Transaction Initiation

Our discussion of transient data and temporary storage has covered the first two requirements of application systems: receiving input from another transaction, and producing output for processing by another transaction. We have yet to discuss how transactions can be initiated without a transaction request from the user terminal.

The first method is called *Automatic Transaction Initiation*.

It uses an intrapartition transient data queue to "trigger" a transaction whenever the queue reaches a specified length.

In the second method, *Programmed Transaction Initiation*, a CICS application program executes a CICS command to initiate another transaction.

Automatic Transaction Initiation

To see how an intrapartition transient data destination can be used to trigger a transaction, we return to the warehouse transaction in the example order-entry application system. We haven't yet discussed how this transaction gets started. One way would be to require someone in the warehouse to start the transaction each day. The transaction could then remain permanently active, entering a timed wait whenever a READQ TD command results in the QZERO condition, and then trying another READQ TD when the timed wait expires.

An alternative method is to use the Automatic Transaction Initiation facility. To do so, the system programmer defines a non-zero *trigger level* in the DCT entry for the transient data destination. The DCT also specifies the name of a transaction, in this case the warehouse transaction, which is to be started whenever the number of records in the destination reaches the trigger level. Once activated, the warehouse transaction program can read from the transient data queue until the QZERO condition is raised and then terminate. It will be automatically reinitiated when the trigger level for the intrapartition transient data queue is reached.

Normally a transaction is associated with a terminal—its direct terminal—when the user enters a transaction request from that terminal. In the case of automatic transaction initiation, there is no explicit transaction request. Instead, the request is indirect and is triggered by the intrapartition transient data queue. If the transaction is to be associated with a terminal, the *queue name* must be the same as the *terminal identifier* of the transaction's direct terminal.

Programmed Transaction Initiation

CICS also provides a command that you can execute to initiate a new transaction. You may request that the transaction begin immediately or at a specified time in the future. The requested transaction may use either the same terminal as the transaction that initiated it, or it may use a different terminal.

The command is written:

EXEC CICS START TRANSID (name)
    TERMID (name)
    [INTERVAL (data-value)]   I   [TIME]

TRANSID specifies the one- to four-character transaction identifier. This is the same identifier that a user would enter to request the transaction from a terminal.

TERMID specifies the one- to four-character terminal identifier of the terminal to act as the transaction's direct terminal.

The INTERVAL and TIME options specify when the requested transaction is to start. If you want the transaction to start immediately you specify INTERVAL (0). If you want the transaction to start after some interval of time you specify the time interval in the form *hhmmss*, where *hh* stands for hours, *mm* stands for minutes, and *ss* stands for seconds. For example, if you wanted the transaction to start in an hour and a half, you would specify

INTERVAL (013000)

You use the TIME option to specify a specific time of day at which the transaction is to start. This argument is also specified in the form *hhmmss*. To start a transaction at two o'clock in the afternoon, you would specify

TIME (140000)

The TERMIDERR and TRANSIDERR exceptional conditions occur if, respectively, the terminal identifier or transaction identifier are specified incorrectly.

Using INTERVAL to Specify Time of Day

In the next chapter, you will see that the START command may be used to start a CICS transaction in an entirely different computer system. When you do that, the TIME option can be confusing if the other system is in a different time zone. Suppose you want the transaction to begin at 3 p.m. with respect to your time zone. If you specify TIME (150000), the receiving system will interpret the time value according to its own time zone. In many cases, it is more convenient to calculate the time interval between "now" and the time you want the transaction to begin. Then you can use this value as the argument of the INTERVAL option.

Suppose that your program is running at half past noon, or 123000. Then to start a transaction at 3 p.m. in your time zone, you could specify INTERVAL (023000). To use this technique, you need a convenient way to find out what time it is. CICS provides the ASKTIME command for this purpose.

The command is written:

EXEC CICS ASKTIME

After the command is completed, the *current* time can be found in the TIME field of the EIB. Remember that, when a task is initiated, EIBTIME is set to the current time of day—that is, the time of day at which the task was initiated. You may use the ASKTIME command to update EIBTIME at any point in your program.

Variations of the START Command

You may start a transaction that is not associated with a CICS terminal. To do so, you simply omit the TERMID option.

You may pass data to the transaction to be started. To do so, you code the options:

> FROM (data-area) LENGTH (data-area)

FROM specifies the data-area containing data to be passed to the new transaction, and LENGTH specifies the length of the data in bytes.

The transaction initiated by the START command can access the data passed by the FROM option *only* by executing a RETRIEVE command.

The command is written:

> RETRIEVE INTO (data-area) I SET (pointer reference)
> LENGTH (data-area)

You may code either the INTO option, to specify an area into which the data is to be moved, or the SET option, to specify a BLL Cell to be set to the data's address.

LENGTH specifies a data area that contains the maximum length of data that the program can accept. After completion of the RETRIEVE command, the specified data area is set to the actual length of the data. If INTO is coded and the data's length exceeds the maximum length the program can accept, CICS will place the maximum number of bytes in the INTO area. In this case, LENGTH will be set to the original length of the data.

Summary

CICS application systems are made up of many application programs that communicate with one another. A transaction that is part of an application system must be able to:

1. Pass data to another transaction
2. Receive data from another transaction
3. Initiate another transaction
4. Be initiated by another transaction

The transient data facility permits a CICS program to prepare or process a sequential file of data. *Extrapartition* transient data queues are sequential files that are either created by a CICS program for use outside the CICS system, or are created outside the CICS system for use by a CICS program. *Intrapartition* transient data queues are queues within a sequential file that are created by a CICS program for processing by another CICS program.

Both intrapartition and extrapartition transient data queues (also called transient data *destinations*) must be processed sequentially. Each queue (destination) must be defined in a CICS table called the Destination Control Table (DCT).

Extrapartition transient data queues may be assigned to a direct-access storage volume, a magnetic tape, or a sequential device like a printer.

Intrapartition transient data queues are always on direct-access storage. As each record is read from an intrapartition transient data queue, the record becomes "lost" and cannot be accessed again. If the system programmer has defined the queue as "reusable," the space occupied by the record becomes available space in the intrapartition transient data-area. If the queue is not reusable, the queue will continue to grow and must periodically be deleted so its space can be reclaimed.

The commands WRITEQ TD, READQ TD, and DELETEQ TD are used to create and process transient data queues.

A CICS transaction can also write data into Temporary Storage for access by other CICS transactions. Each record in temporary storage is named, and the set of records with the same name make up a temporary storage queue (also called a *message set*). The names are not predefined like transient data destination names. Application programs must observe an installation-defined naming convention to insure that each queue in temporary storage is named uniquely.

A temporary storage queue may be assigned either to direct-access storage (called an AUXILIARY queue) or to memory (called a MAIN queue). Records in a temporary storage queue can be retrieved either in sequential order or directly, according to their relative record number. A record remains in temporary storage until it is explicitly deleted. Therefore, it may be accessed more than once.

The WRITEQ TS, READQ TS, and DELETEQ TS commands are used to process records in temporary storage.

Sometimes CICS applications must use a resource that cannot be shared and that is not controlled by CICS. The ENQ and DEQ commands are used to, respectively, request exclusive control and release exclusive control of such a resource. All application programs that use a resource of this kind must include ENQ and DEQ commands that refer to the resource by an installation-defined name.

Most CICS transactions are initiated by a user who enters a transaction request from a CICS terminal. However, a CICS transaction can also be initiated automatically when an intrapartition transient data queue reaches a predefined length (trigger level). The system programmer uses the DCT entry for the intrapartition transient data queue to define the trigger level and the transaction to be initiated.

A transaction may also be initiated under program control. A CICS application program can issue the START command naming the transaction to be initiated and, optionally, specifying a time of day or time interval when the transaction should be initiated.

DISCUSSION QUESTIONS

1. Assume that a program has been written to prepare a sequential file for processing by a batch job. A decision is made to process the file instead with a CICS transaction. The file typically contains 150 records, and the processing transaction does not require a rapid response time.
   a. As the application is presently programmed, where does the sequential file reside?
   b. Where will the file reside if the requested change is made?
   c. As the application is presently programmed, what is the record format of the data?

  d. If the requested change is made, what will be the data's record format?

  e. What programming change will be required in the program that creates the data?

2. Indicate whether each of the following statements refers to extrapartition transient data (E), intrapartition transient data (I), or temporary storage (T) data. (Some statements may describe more than one type of data.)

  a. May be assigned to a physical device like a printer

  b. Used in automatic transaction initiation

  c. Contains only variable length records

  d. May contain fixed length records

  e. Records must be read in sequential order

  f. Records may be read only once

  g. Each queue makes up a separate file

  h. Defined in a Destination Control Table (DCT) entry

  i. Each queue has a one- to eight-character name

  j. May be on a direct-access storage volume

  k. Records may be read in random order (by relative record number)

  l. May be kept in internal storage (memory)

3. You are asked to write a program for a transaction that can be initiated either by a programmed START command or by a pseudo-conversational transaction. The preceding transaction must provide data to your transaction.

  Where should the preceding transaction place the data?

EXERCISES

1. This exercise is to practice the use of an intrapartition transient data queue. You will write two transactions:

> A01C receives input data from a terminal and writes data into an intrapartition transient data queue named LA1P.

> B01C reads data from the LA1P queue and sends it to the user terminal.

To test your programs, run the transaction A01C from your terminal several times to write several records into the queue. Then run B01C to obtain a display of the entire queue.

Assume that A01C is invoked by a transaction request of the form:

> A01C ITEMX NO Description

ITEMX represents a five-character item number

NO represents a two-digit number (quantity)

Description may be up to 20 characters long.

For example:

> A01C LAX01 12 LEATHER HIKING BOOTS

A01C should handle the following exceptional conditions:

1. "Transient Data Area Is Full."
   Send this message and terminate.

2. "Input Data Is Too Long."
   Send this message and terminate.

Transaction B01C may send the records one at a time to your terminal. When all of the records have been processed, send the message *End of Data* and terminate.

2. This exercise is to give you practice in use of the Temporary Storage area. You will write two programs as follows:

   A. Transaction A01C is initiated from a user terminal with the following transaction request:

   A01C xxxxxx xxxxxxxx

   The second field is called TS-NUMB and is 6 characters long. The third field, 8 characters in length, is called TS-PHONE.

   For example:

   A01C 135928 984-1427

   Write the data into a temporary storage queue called TSCOB1.

   If the input message is too long, or there is no space in the temporary storage area, display a suitable error message and terminate.

   B. Transaction B01C is also initiated from a user terminal. It is similar to transaction B01C in Exercise 1, except that it reads records from the temporary storage queue TSCOB1. When all of the records have been read, delete the queue and terminate.

13 Communicating with Other CICS Systems

Introduction

The previous chapter discussed several ways in which a CICS transaction can communicate with other CICS transactions. You learned to use the transient data and temporary storage facilities to prepare sequential files for processing by another transaction. You also learned how one transaction can initiate another transaction.

In this chapter, we will discuss how to perform these same functions when the two transactions involved are in different CICS systems. The other CICS system could be in the same computer, or in a remote computer connected by transmission lines to the computer in which your transaction is executed.

The first case, in which more than one CICS system is running in the same computer, is referred to as *Multiregion Operation* or MRO. We will discuss two reasons that might prompt a CICS installation to run more than one CICS region in the same computer.

The second case, in which an entirely separate computer is involved, is referred to as *Intersystem Communication* or ISC.

The chapter will begin by describing the ways in which two transactions can communicate in a multiregion situation. We will then see how similar communication can be performed in the intersystem case.

You will not be able to practice the programming skills discussed in this chapter unless your CICS system has been specifically set up to permit communication with other CICS systems.

Objectives

After completing this chapter, you will be able to:

- Discuss how multiple CICS regions can be used to improve system reliability or performance.
- Describe the CICS facilities for Transaction Routing and Function Request shipping.
- Describe how a CICS program can initiate a transaction in another CICS system.
- Distinguish between Multiregion Operation (MRO) and Intersystem Communication (ISC).
- Describe how CICS transactions in different CICS systems can conduct conversational (synchronous) processing.
- Explain the programming requirements for maintaining synchronization between two CICS transactions running in separate CICS systems.

Multiregion Operation

The first two chapters described how CICS fits into a typical computing environment. We said that CICS resided in a middle layer of software and served as a "go-between," translating service requests from application programs into a form that the operating system could process. We also described how the operating-system schedules work, allocating CPU service and other resources among CICS, other terminal systems, and batch jobs. A computing environment like this is shown in Figure 13-1. The figure shows two online systems: CICS and TSO, that are competing for resources with five batch jobs.

In many CICS installations, the computing environment would look more like the one shown in Figure 13-2.

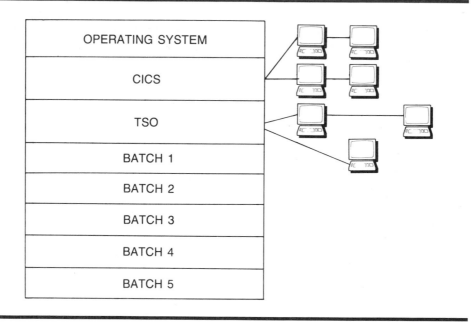

Figure 13-1
Central System With CICS, TSO, and Batch Jobs

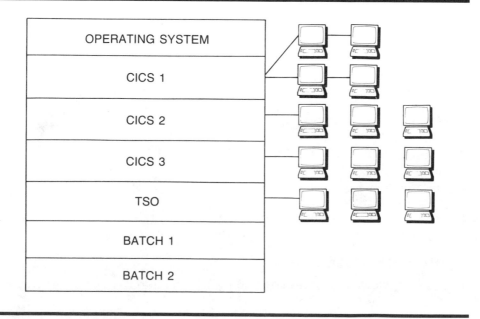

Figure 13-2
Central System With Three CICS Regions

Here there are *three* CICS systems, as well as the TSO and batch regions shown before. Each CICS region represents a complete CICS system. That is, each region has its own CICS tables (TCT, PCT, FCT, DCT, etc.). Each "owns" a set of terminals defined in its Terminal Control Table (TCT), a set of files defined in its File Control Table (FCT), a set of transient data queues defined in its Destination Control Table (DCT), and so on. To the operating system, each CICS region appears as a completely separate task. Each CICS region can, and usually does, have a different priority for the operating system's use in scheduling work.

Applications of Multiregion Operation

An installation may decide to use multiregion operation (MRO) for either of two major reasons. The first is for system reliability, particularly while new application programs are being tested or developed. The second is to improve system performance. Let's see how multiregion operation works toward these two goals.

System Reliability

As we have said, most CICS installations have a large number of applications that have been thoroughly tested and are in daily use to run the business. At the same time, there are a number of new applications in various stages of test and development. During development, application programs fail more often than not. And occasionally they fail spectacularly, bringing the entire CICS system down with them. Or they may fail in less obvious ways that can also affect other CICS transactions. For example, a program may enter a processing loop, locking out other CICS application programs for very long periods of time. Or it may exhaust a shared resource, for example, by entering an infinite loop that writes into an intrapartition transient data queue.

No business that relies upon its CICS system can tolerate incidents that interrupt normal processing of CICS transactions. Nevertheless, every business needs the new applications even though developing, or even installing, them involves reliability risks. The objective then is to take every possible measure to insure that failures during development do not affect the *production* system— those applications required to run the business.

A common approach is to define a CICS *test region* for use in developing and testing new applications. This region is separate from the *production CICS* region in which only well tested applications are permitted to run.

The reliability of the test region is not expected to be high because, by definition, the application programs that run there are unreliable. However, because the unreliable applications are isolated in their own region, the reliability of the *production* region is improved.

System Performance

Remember that, while CICS schedules work in its own region, the operating system schedules work among CICS, other similar online systems, and individual batch jobs. The operating system schedules work according to the priority of each competing task. And, to the operating system, each CICS region represents a single task.

However, CICS applications can be very different in the amount and frequency of service they require. Some applications need very rapid response and execute for short periods of time before becoming inactive. Other applications perform more computation, running for a longer period of time, but not requiring quite so rapid a response time. The CICS scheduling method takes these different requirements into account by allowing a different priority level to be assigned to each transaction. In many cases, however, overall system performance can be improved if transactions with similar response requirements are run in the same CICS region.

Installations that use this approach will define a *quick response* region, and one or more regions that require less rapid response. Figure 13-3 shows a possible environment. The response time shown for each region is a *response time goal* established for transactions that run in the region.

Capabilities of Multiregion Operation

Now that you've seen two ways in which Multiregion Operation (MRO) is used, let's identify some capabilities that must be present in order to support these uses.

First, think about MRO from the user's point of view. We have said that each CICS region "owns" a set of terminals. But you've also seen that a transaction may be assigned to a region on the basis of its response time requirement. A user who needs many different transactions can't be expected to move from terminal to terminal, entering each transaction from a terminal assigned to the correct CICS region. From this, you can conclude that one required capability is that *a CICS transaction can be invoked from any CICS terminal, no matter which region owns the terminal.*

Again from the standpoint of multiple CICS regions designed for performance, think about the application *systems* discussed in the previous chapter. In an application system, transactions pass data to other transactions. If a transaction

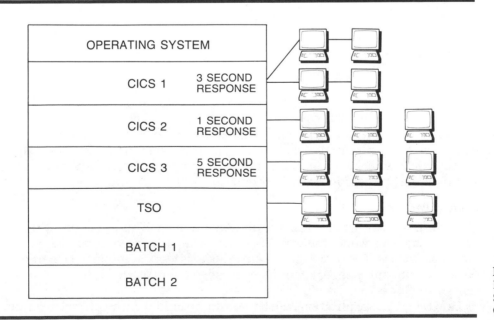

Figure 13-3
Performance-Oriented
Specification of
CICS Regions

could pass data only to transactions in the same region, then all of the transactions in an application system would have to be assigned to the same region, no matter what their response time requirement. This would defeat the whole purpose of an MRO environment defined to improve performance. This leads to two more required capabilities:

1. *A CICS program must be able to access resources such as data files, transient data queues, and temporary storage "owned by" any CICS region.*
2. *A CICS transaction must be able to start a transaction in any CICS region.*

Finally, think about MRO from an installation management point of view. Assume that, to improve reliability, the installation has defined a CICS test system separate from the production CICS system. Suppose that a new application program has been tested thoroughly in the CICS test region. The users, operators, and programmers all agree that the application is reliable and can be made a part of the production CICS system. If this use of MRO is to work, it must be possible to move the application *without changing the program.* If the program had to be changed, it would no longer be reliable and the step from test region to production region would always be a risky one.

This leads to a final required capability: *a CICS program must be able to do all of the things we have discussed without any special programming for MRO.*

Now let's look at each of these capabilities in turn.

Transaction Routing

Transaction Routing is the facility that allows a CICS transaction to be invoked from any CICS terminal, no matter which CICS region owns the terminal. A user who enters a transaction request doesn't have to know which CICS region the transaction will run in. If the transaction is in a region other than the one that owns the terminal, CICS routes the request to the region that owns the transaction. The transaction runs just as though it were in the region that owns the terminal.

CICS does this by initiating a *relay program* in the region that owns the terminal. The function of the relay program is illustrated in Figure 13-4.

The relay program routes terminal input to the CICS region that owns the requested transaction. When the transaction, running in its own region, sends output to the terminal, the CICS Terminal Control Program in the transaction's region sends it to the relay program, which passes it on to the terminal.

Function Request Shipping

Function Request Shipping allows a transaction to access resources in another CICS region. In particular, a transaction can:

■ Access files owned by another CICS system.
■ Transfer data to or from transient data queues and temporary storage in another CICS region.

When a CICS program issues a command that accesses a resource, CICS determines whether the resource is owned by the same region in which the program is executing. If it is not—that is, if the resource is owned by a *remote* region—CICS translates the command into a *function request* and "ships" the request to the remote region.

For example, suppose your program executes a READ command for a file

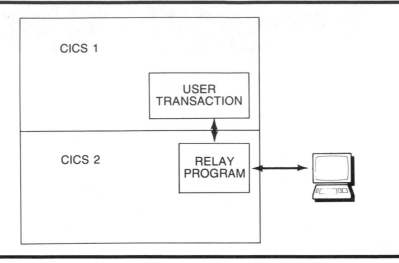

**Figure 13-4
Relay Program Used
in Transaction
Shipping**

named FILEA. CICS consults the File Control Table and finds that the entry for FILEA defines the file as a *remote* file owned by a CICS system called REG1. CICS then ships the READ request to REG1 where it is executed by a special transaction called a *mirror transaction*. The mirror transaction recreates your READ command, executes it, and returns the results to the CICS system in your program's region.

Starting a Remote Transaction

The previous chapter described the use of the START command that your program can use to invoke another transaction. If the transaction named in your START command is located in another CICS region, the command is handled as described above for Function Request Shipping.

Remember that CICS uses the Program Control Table (PCT) to find the program that performs a named transaction. If CICS determines that the required program is located in a remote region, it ships the START request to that region. A mirror transaction then issues the START command in the remote region. If you coded the FROM option on your START command, CICS ships the data in the FROM area along with the START request. The mirror transaction then makes it available to the transaction that will be initiated. When the requested program begins to execute in the remote region, it may use the RETRIEVE command to access the passed data—just as though the data had come from a transaction in the same region.

When you invoke a transaction with the START command, control returns to your program as soon as the command has been processed. The transaction itself has not necessarily started to execute. If you coded the TIME option or the INTERVAL option with a non-zero argument, the transaction may not begin execution until some time after your program has terminated. In any case, there is no coordination between your program and the transaction you are starting. We say that the two transactions execute *asynchronously*—without synchronization. If the transaction your program invokes is located in a remote region, we call this an example of *Asynchronous Distributed Processing. Distributed* because the total process is carried out in two separate CICS systems—

the processing is *distributed* between the two CICS systems.

In the section on Intersystem Communication, we will describe additional forms of Distributed Processing. Unlike the Asynchronous Distributed Processing described here, these forms require special programming. They can be programmed for the Intersystem Communication environment in such a way that they will also run in the MRO environment. However, they are usually thought of as Intersystem Communication facilities.

Programming Considerations

The CICS support for Multiregion Operation allows an application program that uses standard CICS commands to access resources in other CICS regions with no special programming. As an application programmer, you can write CICS programs without considering whether the resources they use are owned by the CICS system in whose region the program will run or by another CICS region.

This means that CICS transactions can be moved from region to region without reprogramming. What *is* required is that the system programmer modify the tables that define each region's resources. For example, if a data file is owned by the REGA system, then the FCT for REGA defines the file as a *local* resource and gives its location. If a transaction that uses the file is moved to REGB, then the system programmer must create an entry for the file in REGB's FCT. The REGB FCT must define the file as *remote* and give the name of the region, REGA, which owns the file. The other tables that define resources used by the program—the Terminal Control Table, for example—must be modified in similar ways.

Intersystem Communication

The Multiregion Operation facility supports linkage between transactions running in different CICS systems *within the same computer*. You may see the term *region-remote* used for this environment, because it is another *CICS region* that contains the remote transaction. Intersystem Communication is the facility that supports linkage between CICS transactions *in different computers*. The term used for this environment is *domain-remote*. The term *domain* comes from the System Network Architecture (SNA) in which different computers are referred to as separate *SNA domains*. Intersystem Communication uses SNA-based communications systems, such as the Virtual Telecommunications Access Method (VTAM), to transmit data and messages between the separate computers.

Figure 13-5 illustrates a typical network of computers in which Intersystem Communication might be used. In this illustration, there is a central computer at a headquarters location. This central computer supports a centralized and integrated data base. The other computers are located in *satellite* computers at branch offices or support centers. The satellite computers also use CICS systems to process data files associated with work processed locally.

In the illustrated network, Intersystem Communications can be used to permit the following:

1. Transactions running in one computer can access resources in another computer.
2. A transaction running in one computer can use the START command to initiate a transaction that runs in another computer.

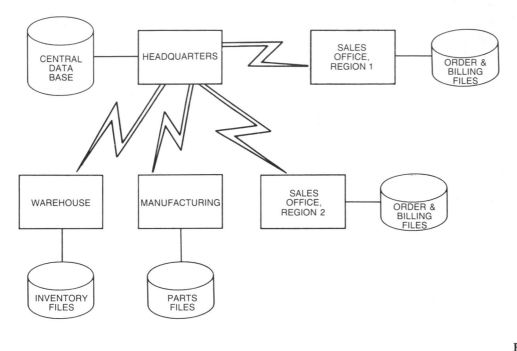

Figure 13-5
Example Network for
Intersystem
Communication

3. A transaction running in one computer can conduct a conversation with a transaction running in another computer.

Notice that the first two capabilities are also supported in the Multiregion Operation environment. In the discussion of MRO we referred to them respectively as *function request shipping* and *asynchronous distributed processing*. CICS application programs that use these capabilities can be moved, without change, from an MRO environment to an ISC environment.

CICS handles Function Request Shipping in the ISC environment in basically the same way we described for the MRO environment. That is, CICS initiates a mirror transaction in the remote computer. The mirror transaction performs the same processing whether it is in a remote computer or merely a remote region. However, in the ISC environment, communication between the two CICS systems involves a telecommunications link.

The third capability listed, permitting transactions running in different CICS systems to hold a conversation, is called *Distributed Transaction Processing* (DTP) or *Synchronous Distributed Processing*. The term, synchronous is used because the transactions involved must be kept in *synchronization* as they execute. That is, the transactions execute cooperatively. One transaction passes data to the other transaction that uses the data in its own processing and then passes information back to the first transaction. The first transaction will use this information as it continues to process. Neither transaction can run without the other, and each must receive data from the other at predefined points in processing. In this sense, the application is *distributed* between the two transactions. Unlike the other ISC capabilities we have listed, Distributed Transaction Processing requires special programming. Later in this chapter, we will discuss the commands and techniques involved.

We have said that Distributed Transaction Processing (DTP) must be programmed for the ISC environment. However, programs that have been written for ISC can also be run in an MRO environment. That is, communication between transactions that have been programmed according to ISC rules will function correctly whether the transactions are in separate computers (domain-remote) or merely in separate regions of the same computer (region-remote). This compatibility is provided, not by CICS itself, but by the telecommunications access method VTAM that includes an *application-to-application* processing facility.

To complete the comparison of MRO and ISC capabilities, notice that there is no ISC counterpart to the Transaction Routing capability offered by MRO. That is, in the Figure 13-5 configuration, a user who has signed on to a computer at the headquarters site cannot run a transaction in one of the other computers.

Distributed Transaction Processing

Before introducing the CICS commands used for programming DTP applications, we will describe the steps involved when two transactions perform synchronized processing. We describe the processing from the standpoint of the transaction that will initiate the conversation. This is referred to as the *front-end transaction*, and the computer in which it runs is the *local* system. The front-end transaction must initiate the second transaction—it may not begin a conversation with a transaction that is already in progress. Not surprisingly, the transaction that will be initiated is called the *back-end transaction*, and the computer in which it runs is the *remote system*.

The first step is for the front-end transaction to establish a communications link to the remote computer. In SNA terms, this is referred to as *acquiring a session*. Once the session has been acquired, the front-end transaction can send messages and data across the communications link. The first message contains the request to initiate a transaction in the remote computer.

Once the back-end transaction has been initiated, the two transactions can converse across the communications link. The front-end transaction must begin the conversation. That is, as the conversation begins, the front-end transaction is in a *Send* state. It can send, but not receive, messages. The back-end transaction is in a *Receive* state; it cannot send messages.

At any point in processing, only one transaction can be in Send state. Only the transaction in Send state can cause a change of state, in effect, it controls the conversation. A transaction in Receive state can *request* the transaction in Send state to change the states. However, the Send state transaction is not forced to do so. This *please change state request* is not supported in the MRO environment, and will not be discussed in this text.

The transaction in Send state can *flip-flop* the states of the two transactions by inviting a response from the other transaction. When it does this, it enters the Receive state and the other transaction enters the Send state. When a transaction in Send state invites a response, therefore, it effectively gives up control of the conversation.

Processing continues in this manner until either one of the transactions terminates, or until the transaction currently in Send state issues a command to terminate the session.

The next sections will describe the process in detail.

Acquiring a Session

To begin synchronous processing, the front-end transaction must first *acquire a session*—that is, establish a communications link. It does so by issuing an ALLOCATE command.

The command is written:

> ALLOCATE SYSID (name)
> [NOQUEUE]

SYSID specifies the name of the CICS system in which the back-end transaction is to execute. The system name is a one- to four-character name assigned by the system programmer.

CICS raises the SYSIDERR condition if the named system is not defined, either as a CICS system in the local computer (MRO) or as a system in another computer with which the local computer can communicate.

If all of the communication links between the local computer and the computer named in SYSID are in use, CICS raises the SYSBUSY condition. Control will transfer to your SYSBUSY exception-handling routine if you have coded one.

If SYSBUSY is raised and you have not provided an exception-handling routine for this condition, CICS checks to see whether you coded the NOQUEUE option. If NOQUEUE was coded, CICS returns control to the next statement in your program. You can detect that SYSBUSY occurred only by testing the EIBRCODE field in the EIB. Therefore, if you code the NOQUEUE option, your next statement should check EIBRCODE for the SYSBUSY code (hexadecimal D3). If you did not code NOQUEUE, CICS will place your transaction in the wait state until a communication link becomes available. Since there is no way to predict how long your transaction must wait until ALLOCATE can complete, you will probably use either a SYSBUSY exception-handling routine or the NOQUEUE option for most applications.

When the ALLOCATE command has completed successfully, the EIB field EIBRSRCE will contain the four-character name assigned to your session. You will use this session name in all of the commands that send or receive data to the remote computer. Since the EIBRSRCE field can be modified by other CICS commands, your program must move the session name from the EIB into a working-storage location as soon as ALLOCATE has completed.

Initiating a Transaction

To request that a transaction be initiated at the remote computer, you simply send a transaction request as the *first* message of the session. The transaction request has the same form you would use if you were to invoke the transaction from a terminal. That is, it begins with the one- to four-byte *transaction identifier* and may be followed by any data expected by the back-end transaction.

Transmitting Data To A Remote Transaction

Your program may use either of two commands to send data. The first is the SEND command, used with key words designed especially for the ISC environment.

The SEND Command

The SEND command is written:

```
SEND SESSION (name)
    FROM (data-area)
    LENGTH (data-value)
    [INVITE]
```

This form of the SEND command is essentially the same as you have used previously to send messages to the terminal user. There are only two new options:

SESSION gives the four-character session name assigned by CICS when the ALLOCATE command was completed. Remember that you should have moved this name from the EIB into your program's working-storage for use in transmission commands like SEND.

If the SESSION name doesn't match the name of a session allocated to your transaction, the NOTALLOC condition is raised.

Your program can issue the SEND command only if your transaction is in the Send state.

You code the INVITE option if you wish to *flip-flop* the communication states after sending this data. You are "inviting" the remote transaction to transmit, and to permit it to do so, you must place it in the Send state. Since communication is always in *flip-flop* mode, placing the remote transaction in Send state causes your transaction to enter the Receive state.

The CONVERSE Command

You may also transmit data by coding the CONVERSE command. The CONVERSE command is a *combination command*. It performs a series of functions that you could also accomplish by coding several separate commands.

CONVERSE performs the following:

1. Sends data to the remote transaction
2. Flip-flops the communication states
3. Waits for data from the remote transaction
4. Receives data transmitted by the remote transaction

Notice that to issue the CONVERSE command, a transaction must be in the Send state. However, in step 2, the CONVERSE command places the transaction in the Receive state. As soon as the remote transaction has received the data sent in step 1, it enters the Send state. It will remain in Send state unless it takes some action to change states. If your transaction needs to transmit after it executes a CONVERSE command, it must rely upon the remote transaction to flip-flop the communication states.

If the remote transaction replies with another CONVERSE, then its CONVERSE will flip-flop the communication states again. In this case your transaction will be in Send state after the Receive step (step 4) of its CONVERSE command has completed.

Figure 13-6 shows two transactions that are using the CONVERSE command

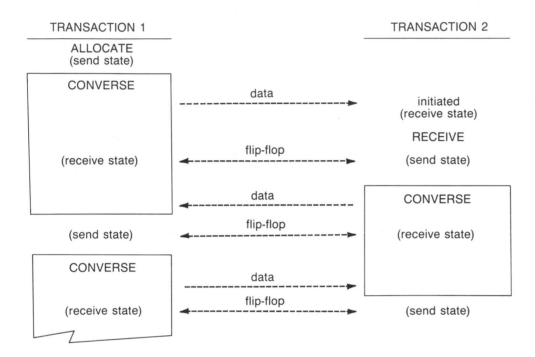

**Figure 13-6
Conversational
Processing With
the CONVERSE
Command**

to communicate. Notice that each CONVERSE flip-flops the communication states so that the conversation proceeds smoothly in a "listen to me and then you can talk" fashion.

The CONVERSE command is written:

```
CONVERSE SESSION (name)
    FROM (data-area)
    FROMLENGTH (data-value)
    INTO (data-area) I SET (pointer reference)
    TOLENGTH (data-area)
```

You are already familiar with the SESSION, FROM, INTO, and SET options. Remember that CONVERSE combines the functions of SEND and RECEIVE. The FROMLENGTH and TOLENGTH options take the place of the LENGTH option for, respectively, the SEND and RECEIVE commands.

Receiving Data From the Remote Transaction

As illustrated in Figure 13-6, once a conversation has started, it can be conducted exclusively with CONVERSE commands. However, the back-end transaction must initially use a RECEIVE command to receive the front-end transaction's first transmission. It must listen before it can talk.

Alternatively you can use only the SEND and RECEIVE commands for the entire conversation, never using CONVERSE at all.

The RECEIVE command is written:

```
RECEIVE SESSION (name)
    INTO (data-area) I SET (pointer reference)
    LENGTH (data-area)
```

You are already familiar with the SESSION option. The INTO, SET, and LENGTH options are coded just as for the RECEIVE commands you have used previously.

Terminating a Session

A session is terminated whenever either of the transactions terminates, or when a transaction issues the FREE command.

The command is written:

```
FREE SESSION (name)
```

A transaction may issue the FREE command at any time that it is in Send state. A transaction in Receive state may issue the FREE command if, after issuing a RECEIVE, it finds the EIBFREE field set to "on" or "Free Pending" (hexadecimal FF). This text will discuss only one case in which the EIBFREE field will be on. (See *Programmed Asynchronous Processing* below).

Session Control

Now that you have seen the commands that can be used in programming DTP transactions, let's look again at a conversation and focus on what each transaction must do to remain synchronized with the other.

The transaction that will initiate the conversation is called the front-end transaction. It begins by issuing the ALLOCATE command to acquire a session between the local and remote computers. The session is given a name that must be retrieved immediately from the EIBRSRCE field of the EIB. Once the session has been acquired, the front-end transaction is in the Send state.

The front-end transaction uses either the SEND or CONVERSE command to transmit data to the remote computer. The first transmission contains, in its first four bytes, the name of a transaction to be initiated in the remote computer.

At any point in processing, only one of the transactions can send data. It is said to be in the Send state. The other transaction is in the Receive state; it can only receive data.

When the back-end transaction begins executing, it is always in Receive state. After it receives the first transmission, it may be in either Send or Receive state depending upon whether or not the front-end transaction flip-flopped the states as part of its transmission.

The transaction in Send state can flip-flop the Send and Receive states by using the INVITE key word on the SEND command, or by using the CONVERSE command to transmit.

After each RECEIVE command, a transaction should check the EIBRECV field of the EIB. If the field is "on" (hexadecimal FF), the transaction is in Receive state and cannot transmit. If the transmitting transaction has flip-flopped the communication states, the EIBRECV field will be off.

A transaction should also examine EIBRECV after executing a CONVERSE command. Remember that after transmitting data, CONVERSE flip-flops the communication states in preparation for receiving the reply. In order to see whether the other transaction has flip-flopped the communication states again, the transaction must check the EIBRECV field after its CONVERSE command has completed.

Earlier, we said that a transaction in Receive state could issue the FREE command if the EIBFREE field in the EIB was "on." In fact, if EIBFREE is on, the transaction *should* issue the FREE command. It may not execute any other SESSION command. Like EIBRECV, EIBFREE should be checked after each RECEIVE or CONVERSE command.

Your program should always check EIBFREE *before* checking EIBRECV. If EIBFREE is on, your program must free the session. If it is off, the program can check EIBRECV and continue communicating across the communications link, issuing session commands appropriate to its state.

Figures 13-7, 13-8, and 13-9 illustrate the programming requirements for a transaction in any of these three states:

1. Front-end transaction before session has been acquired
2. Transaction in Send state
3. Transaction in Receive state

If a transaction is in Send state it may issue the FREE command at any time, whether it is the front-end or back-end transaction.

Programmed Asynchronous Processing

The discussion of MRO described how Function Request Shipping could be used to initiate a remote transaction for asynchronous processing. This requires no special programming in either the MRO or ISC environment. The initiating transaction simply issues a START command, and CICS takes care of sending the START command to the correct CICS system.

We have discussed the ISC session commands in the context of synchronous processing between two transactions. However, you can use these same commands to achieve asynchronous processing.

To do so, the front-end transaction acquires a session, as described above, and uses the SEND command to transmit the name of the requested transaction and any data that the transaction expects. However, this SEND command should also specify the LAST option.

The command would be written:

SEND SESSION (name) FROM (data-area) LENGTH (data-value)
    LAST

The LAST keyword causes the EIBFREE field in the back-end transaction's EIB to be set. As discussed above, the transaction should check EIBFREE after executing the initial RECEIVE command. Since EIBFREE is on, the transaction cannot use the communications link again, and should issue the FREE command as quickly as possible so that the link can be made available to other transactions.

Beginning State: Session not Allocated

Commands you can issue	Conditions/Codes	Resulting State
ALLOCATE	SYSIDERR	no change
	SYSBUSY	no change
	none	Send

**Figure 13-7
Summary of "Session
Not Allocated" State**

Beginning State: Send

Commands you can issue	Conditions/Codes	Resulting State
SEND	—	Send
SEND INVITE	—	Receive
CONVERSE	EIBFREE	must free
	EIBRECV (on)	Receive
	EIBRECV (off)	Send
FREE		Session not allocated

**Figure 13-8
Summary of
"Send" State**

Beginning State: Receive

Commands you can issue	Conditions/Codes	Resulting State
RECEIVE	EIBFREE (on)	must free
	EIBRECV (on)	Receive
	EIBRECV (off)	Send

**Figure 13-9
Summary of
"Receive" State**

Summary

An installation may run more than one CICS system in a single computer. Each of the systems is a complete CICS system. It has its own tables; for example: Program Control Table, File Control Table, Terminal Control Table, and Destination Control Table. The tables define the resources that may be accessed by the transactions that run in this CICS region. Each resource is defined as *local* (owned by this region) or *remote* (owned by another, named system). This environment is referred to as Multiregion Operation (MRO) or *region-remote* and may be used to improve CICS reliability and/or performance. There is no special programming required to support the MRO functions that include:

1. A transaction can be invoked from a terminal owned by any of the CICS systems.

   This is called Transaction Routing and is implemented by means of a *relay program* that CICS starts in the terminal-owning region to relay communication between the terminal and the system in which the requested transaction runs.

2. A transaction can refer to a resource owned by any of the CICS systems.

   This is called Function Request Shipping and is implemented by means of a *mirror transaction*, which CICS starts in the region that owns the requested resource.

3. A transaction can use a START command to initiate another transaction to run in any of the CICS systems.

   This is a form of Asynchronous Distributed Processing and is handled as a special case of Function Request shipping.

A computer may also be linked to several other computers by means of telecommunication lines. Each of the computers may support one or more CICS systems. This is referred to as an Intersystem Communication (ISC) or *domain-remote* environment. Function Request Shipping, including Asynchronous Distributed Processing with the START command, is supported in this environment just as in the MRO environment.

A third capability, Distributed Transaction Processing (DTP) or *Synchronous Distributed Processing*, must be programmed using CICS commands designed for the domain-remote environment.

CICS uses a telecommunication system such as VTAM (Virtual Telecommunications Access Method) to conduct transmission over the telecommunication lines. VTAM also includes an *application-to-application* facility which permits applications programmed for the domain-remote environment to run in the *region-remote* environment too.

In Distributed Transaction Processing, two CICS transactions conduct a synchronized conversation. One transaction, called the front-end transaction, must initiate the conversation by acquiring a session between the local and remote computers, and then transmitting a transaction request across the acquired communications link. From that point on, conversation proceeds in a *flip-flop* manner. At any time, one transaction is in Send mode and the other in Receive mode. The transaction in Send mode can *flip-flop* the communication states by using the INVITE keyword on a SEND command, or by issuing a

CONVERSE command. The CONVERSE command transmits data, flip-flops the communication states, waits for a reply, and receives the reply.

Whenever a transaction has completed a RECEIVE or CONVERSE command, it should check the EIB fields EIBFREE and EIBRECV. If EIBFREE is set, the transaction must issue the FREE command to free the session. If EIBRECV is set, the transaction is in Receive state.

DISCUSSION QUESTIONS

1. Complete the following statements:
   a. A relay program is used to support _____.
      CICS starts this program in _____
      when _____.
   b. A mirror transaction is used to support _____.
      CICS starts this transaction in _____
      when _____.

2. A transaction, which runs in a CICS system called REG1, uses a transient data queue TR01, a file FILEA, and starts a transaction TRN1. All of these resources are owned by the REG1 system.
   a. What changes to the *program* must be made to move the transaction to another CICS system REG2 that runs in the same computer as REG1?
   b. What changes to the CICS systems must be made to move the program as defined in part a?
   c. Go back and answer parts a and b assuming that the REG2 system is in another computer.

3. A transaction, TRN2, is part of a DTP application. There are two transactions in the application, and the first is always invoked from a user terminal. What *user* change will be required if:
   a. The transaction is a back-end transaction and is moved to a different CICS system in the *same computer.*
   b. Same as part a, except the transaction is a front-end transaction.
   c. The transaction is a back-end transaction and is moved to a CICS system in a *different computer.*
   d. Same as part c, except the transaction is a front-end transaction.

4. For each of the following capabilities, indicate whether they are supported in a region-remote (R) or domain-remote (D) environment, or in both (B) or neither (N) the domain-remote and region-remote environments:
   a. Function Request Shipping
   b. Asynchronous Distributed Processing *without* special programming
   c. Transaction Routing
   d. Distributed Transaction Processing (conversational, synchronous)
   e. Distributed Transaction Processing (conversational, synchronous) *without* special programming

5. Which of the following statements correctly describe Distributed Transaction Processing:
   a. Supported only in an MRO environment
   b. Supported only in a domain-remote environment
   c. Always requires a telecommunications access method

   d. Always requires special programming

   e. Involves synchronous communication between transactions

6. A program that is to act as a front-end transaction in a DTP application contains the following sequence of COBOL statements:

```
EXEC CICS ALLOCATE SYSID ('REG2') NOQUEUE END-EXEC.
EXEC CICS WRITEQ TD QUEUE ('TD01') FROM (OUTBUF)
        LENGTH (40)   END-EXEC.
MOVE EIBRSRCE TO SESSNAME.
CONVERSE SESSION (SESSNAME) FROM (OUTBUF2)
        LENGTH (40) INTO (INBUF) TOLENGTH(80)
        END-EXEC.
CONVERSE SESSION (SESSNAME) FROM (OUTBUF3)
        LENGTH (40) INTO (INBUF) TOLENGTH (80)
        END-EXEC.
```

You may assume that all data-areas and working-storage variables are correctly defined, and that the first four bytes in OUTBUF contain the name of a transaction to be initiated. You may also assume that REG2 is the name of a CICS system that has been correctly defined.

   a. The program fails on the first CONVERSE command, which raises the NOTALLOC condition. Why?

     (See if you can find *two* errors that cause this symptom. One will cause NOTALLOC to be raised *every time* the program runs. The second will cause only occasional failures due to NOTALLOC. In your answer, identify which causes the consistent failure and which causes occasional failures.)

   b. The second CONVERSE command causes unspecified failures. Why?

14 Accessing DL/I Data Bases

Introduction

In Chapter 1 we pointed out the distinction between data files and data bases. Strictly speaking, most of your work with CICS will probably involve data files rather than data bases. However, CICS can also be used to access several types of data bases. In this chapter, we will describe how CICS is used to access *hierarchical data bases* that have been defined and created using the IBM Information Management System (IMS).

IMS includes a data base management facility called Data Language/1 (DL/1) that is used to define, create, access, and maintain the data base. Because IMS and DL/1 are so closely associated, you may hear the data bases themselves referred to either as DL/1 or IMS data bases.

As a CICS programmer you may become involved with IMS and DL/1 in two ways:

First, your installation may use CICS to manage online access to its IMS data bases. That is, the installation may use IMS as its data base manager (the *DB* of DB/DC), but use CICS as the data communication (*DC*) manager. In this case, your CICS programs will use DL/I to access the IMS data base.

Secondly, your installation may use both CICS and IMS as DB/DC systems. In this case, you may be called upon to write CICS programs that communicate with IMS. This type of communication is similar to the intersystem communication facilities we discussed in the preceding chapter.

We begin our discussion by introducing the basic concepts and terminology of a *hierarchical* data base structure. We will then look at the concepts and terminology used in IMS and DL/I as a specific implementation of a hierarchical data base system.

Next we will describe how to write a CICS program that uses DL/I to read or update an IMS data base. Our examples and exercises will describe CICS programs that run under the DOS/VSE operating system. Programs that run under the MVS/SP operating system use COBOL CALL statements rather than the EXEC commands you are accustomed to. However, the concepts involved are the same whether your program will run under DOS/VSE or MVS/SP.

The final section of the chapter describes how CICS and IMS systems can communicate by using intersystem communication facilities described in the preceding chapter.

Objectives

After completing this chapter, you will be able to:

- Describe the structure of a hierarchical data base.
- Discuss the use of the Data Base Definition (DBD) and the Program Specification Block (PSB) to define a DL/I data base and an application program's *view* of the data base.

- Write a CICS program to read and update a DL/I data base.
- Distinguish between *direct control* and *queued* data communication systems.
- Describe how a CICS program can communicate with an IBM Information Management System (IMS).

Hierarchical Data Base Structure

In working with data files, you have read, replaced, updated, and deleted data *records*. To do so you needed to know the physical structure of the record. The record is the smallest unit of data that can be read from or written into a data file. A data file is made up of a sequence of records, each of which has the same basic structure.

In a hierarchical data base, the unit of data is a *segment*. When you read from the data base, you read a *segment* that contains one or more data fields. Segments are related, according to rules we will discuss later, and a group of related data segments make up a data base record.

Data Base Segment

A data base record can contain several distinct segment types. However, each data base record can contain the segment types in different combination. For example, assume that three segment types, called segment type A, B, and C are defined within a data base. One data base record might contain three data segments of type A, one of type B, and none of type C. Another record might contain one segment of each type.

To process a hierarchical data base, you need to know only the structure of those data segment types that your program will process. You do not need to know the structure of each data base record, and you don't need to know about all of the segment types that can appear in a record.

Hierarchical Relationships

Figure 14-1 illustrates a typical data base record.

The illustrated data base record contains four segment types: the PART, STOCK, ORDER, and DETAIL segments. The figure shows the relationships among the segment types by depicting them within a "tree structure." The basic relationship is one of dependency, usually referred to as the "parent-child" relationship.

In Figure 14-1, the STOCK segment is *dependent* upon the PART segment. The DETAIL segment is dependent upon the ORDER segment, which is dependent upon the PART segment. Stated another way, the STOCK segment is the *child* of the PART segment. The DETAIL segment is the child of the ORDER segment. The ORDER segment is the *parent* of the DETAIL segment and the *child* of the PART segment. The PART segment is parent of both the STOCK and ORDER segments, and it is dependent upon no other segment. That is, the PART segment has no parent segment. A segment, like PART, that has no parent segment is called the *root* segment of the data base record.

As shown in the figure, the root segment is said to be at *level 1* of the data base record. Each child segment appears at the level next higher than its parent's level. For example, the STOCK and ORDER segments, which are the children of the root segment PART, are at *level 2*. DETAIL, which is the child of ORDER, is at *level 3*. There may be up to 15 levels in a data base record.

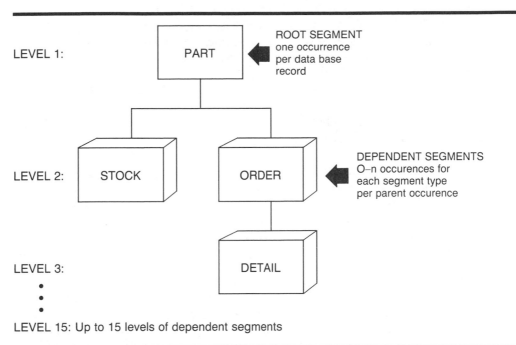

LEVEL 1: **PART** ◄ ROOT SEGMENT
one occurrence
per data base
record

LEVEL 2: **STOCK** **ORDER** ◄ DEPENDENT SEGMENTS
0–n occurences for
each segment type
per parent occurence

LEVEL 3: **DETAIL**

•
•
•

LEVEL 15: Up to 15 levels of dependent segments

**Figure 14-1
Model of
Hierarchical Data
Base Record**

Because each segment must appear at a well-defined level within a data base record, the data organization is said to be *hierarchical*.

Data Base Record

A data base record is made up from data segments according to two basic rules:

1. No segment can appear in a data base record unless its parent appears.

   This implies that the root segment must appear in every data base record. It also implies that a given segment type always appears at the same level within a data base record.

2. Each dependent segment (that is, every segment except the root segment) may appear any number of times—including zero times.

   For example, one record of the data base illustrated by Figure 14-1 might contain seven *occurrences* of the STOCK segment, while another data base record contained no STOCK segments at all.

   Keep in mind that the structure shown in Figure 14-1 describes the *application program's view* of a data base record. We mentioned earlier that to write an application program you don't need to know the *physical structure* of a data base record. Besides the four segment types shown, there might be several additional segment types within the data base record that your program has no need to access or to know about. We say that your program is "not sensitive" to these other segment types.

Accessing Data Segments

Normally, one of the data fields within the root segment is designated as a *key*. Sometimes a key field is also defined within one or more of the dependent segments.

You can access a data record directly by specifying a value for the root segment's key field. If a key field has been defined for a dependent segment, you can access that segment directly by specifying a value for its key field, *in addition* to the value for the key field of those segments upon which the target segment is dependent.

For example, in Figure 14-1, assume that a part number field is defined as the root segment's key, and that a warehouse location field is defined as a key in the STOCK segment. Then you could directly access a particular STOCK segment by specifying both a part number and a warehouse location.

Once you have directly accessed a particular segment, you may sequentially access the remaining segments. The sequential order within a data-base record is defined as *top-to-bottom*, then *left-to-right*.

Figure 14-2 shows a data base record within the data base illustrated in Figure 14-1. Notice that there are three occurrences of the STOCK segment and two occurrences of the ORDER segment. The first ORDER segment has two occurrences of DETAIL. The two DETAIL segments are referred to as "twins," multiple occurrences of a particular segment type under the same parent. The second ORDER segment has no DETAIL segment.

Figure 14-3 shows how this data base record can be thought of in terms of sequential process. If you were to retrieve segments sequentially, beginning from the root segment of record *n*, you would first retrieve the three STOCK segments in order. Next you would retrieve the first ORDER segment and both of its dependent segments, before retrieving the second ORDER segment. Remember that the physical data record may actually contain segments that are not known to your program. The sequential retrieval process simply skips over these—they remain "invisible" to your program.

Let's compare Figures 14-2 and 14-3 to see how the sequential retrieval can

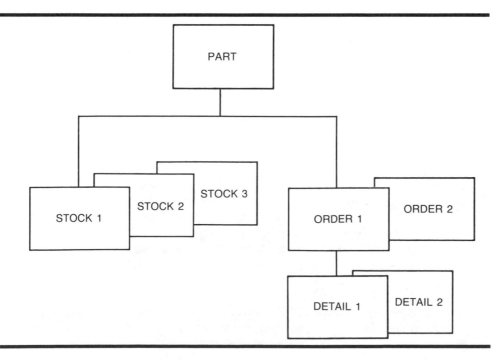

**Figure 14-2
Example Data
Base Record**

be seen from the tree structure diagram. Beginning from the root segment, you move first top-to-bottom to reach the second level of the structure. Then you move left-to-right, remaining at the same level to access each of the STOCK segments. After the third STOCK segment you retrieve the first ORDER segment (still moving left-to-right at the same level). Before moving left-to-right to look at the next ORDER segment, you move top-to-bottom to look at the DETAIL segment below ORDER1. You then move left-to-right, at the same level, to retrieve both of the twin DETAIL segments. Finally, you retrieve the second ORDER segment.

The general rule is, therefore, that sequential retrieval moves top-to-bottom whenever possible. When it has reached the deepest level along a branch, it then moves left-to-right.

Defining an IMS Data Base

Now let's look at the details of defining and accessing a hierarchical data base in the IMS environment. First, we'll very briefly describe how the physical data base structure is defined to IMS. Then, in somewhat more detail, we'll look at the definition of the application program's view of the physical data base. And finally, we'll describe the basic commands that DL/I provides for accessing the data base.

Defining the Data Base Structure

The data base designer must consider a great many factors in order to decide how the physical data base will be structured. The details are beyond the scope of this text. However, some general considerations are: the data base operations that are to be required, the mechanics of accessing the data, the required performance characteristics, security requirements, and the ways in which usage can be expected to change over time.

Since the physical structure of the data base is defined separately from the application program's view of the data base, many physical characteristics of the data base can be changed without forcing application programs to be changed. Nevertheless, the design must be done very carefully and can easily require several months of work.

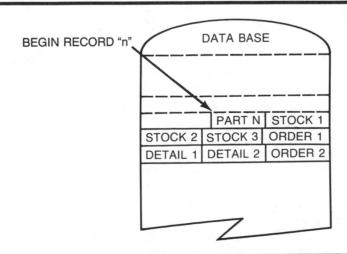

**Figure 14-3
Sequential View of
Hierarchical Data
Base Record**

Once the data base has been designed, it must be described to IMS. This is done by constructing a table called the *Data Base Description* (DBD). The DBD consists of DL/I statements in the form of assembler-language macro instructions. The DBD is assembled, link-edited, and placed in an IMS library. This process is called DBD Generation, or *the DBD Gen*.

The DBD Gen completely defines the data base. In particular, it defines each segment that may appear in a data base record and the hierarchical relationships among segments. It also defines each field that may be used as a key within a segment.

Defining the Application Program's View

Each application program may have its own view of the data base. This view is defined in a table called the *Program Specification Block* (PSB). The PSB lists the data bases that a program can access, and it specifies which segments in each data base the program will be "sensitive to" (that is, will be permitted to access). For each sensitive segment, the PSB also defines which processing options the program may perform. For example, a program might be permitted to retrieve (or *get*) a segment, but not to replace it. Your starting point, in writing a program to access an IMS data base, is to be sure that a PSB is constructed that fits the program's requirements.

Like the DBD, the PSB is constructed from a series of DL/1 statements in the form of assembler-language macro instructions. A *PSB Gen* process, similar to that for generating a DBD, is used to assemble the PSB and link-edit it into an IMS library.

PSB Structure

Figure 14-4 illustrates the overall structure of a PSB.

Each PSB contains one or more *Program Communication Blocks* (PCB). Each Program Communication Block (PCB) defines the communication your program is permitted with a particular data base. Therefore, if your program needs to access four data bases, the PSB must contain four PCB's.

The PCB defines a name by which your program will refer to the data base. This name is called a DBDNAME, and it is defined in the DL/I PCB statement. Following each PCB statement is a series of SENSEG statements. Each SENSEG statement names a data base segment type to which your program may refer. Each segment name specified in a SENSEG statement must match a segment name that has been defined for the data base in the DBD. Figure 14-4 shows a PCB that defines the application program view illustrated in Figure 14-1. The DBDNAME is DBONE. The PCB statement is followed by four SENSEG statements—one each for the PART, STOCK, ORDER, and DETAIL segments.

The hierarchical structure of the data base record is defined by the PARENT field of the SENSEG statement. For example, the SENSEG statement for DETAIL names ORDER as the parent segment.

The SENSEG statement also defines the processing options your program may use to access the particular segment. Possible options are *get*, *insert*, *replace*, and *delete*.

Advantages of DBD-PSB Structure

By separating the definition of a data base structure from a program's view

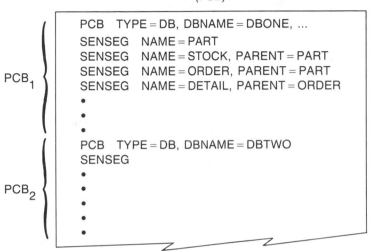

PROGRAM SPECIFICATION BLOCK
(PSB)

PCB$_1$ {

PCB   TYPE = DB, DBNAME = DBONE, ...
SENSEG   NAME = PART
SENSEG   NAME = STOCK, PARENT = PART
SENSEG   NAME = ORDER, PARENT = PART
SENSEG   NAME = DETAIL, PARENT = ORDER
•
•
•

PCB$_2$ {

PCB   TYPE = DB, DBNAME = DBTWO
SENSEG
•
•
•
•
•

**Figure 14-4
Example Program
Specfication Block
(PSB)**

of the data base, IMS permits a greater degree of data independence than can be achieved with simple data files. It is possible to change the data base structure quite significantly without modifying the program's view of the data base. And so long as the program's view remains the same, there is no need to modify the program.

Data independence is further increased because each program's view includes only those data base segments actually used within the program. New data base segments can be added to the data base without requiring program change. Contrast this with the data *file* situation in which a few data fields are added to the standard file record. In most cases, such a change to a data file will require change to all of the application programs that access the file.

The PSB is usually generated for you by a data base administrator or system programmer. We'll point out two advantages to having a central point of control for all of the DBD's and PSB's generated in a given installation.

The first advantage has to do with *data security*. The administrative function that controls the PSB's can determine exactly which programs can access a given segment of data. For example, it is important to be certain of which programs can access the SALARY segment of the PERSONNEL data base.

A second advantage is to permit orderly change to data bases. Usually, a company doesn't build an entire integrated data base at once. Rather, the data base is constructed a piece at a time, beginning with the pieces that are most important to the company. For example, data segments having to do with Purchasing might be implemented first. When the Purchasing applications are in production, the data base might be expanded to include Inventory

Control applications. As the data base grows, some structural changes may be required that do affect some application programs. If the PSB's are centrally maintained, the central administrator can determine how many programs would be affected by a proposed data base change.

CICS Access to IMS Data Bases

Let's look now at the situation in which CICS is used as the data communications (DC) manager for accessing IMS data bases. In this case, DL/1 runs within the CICS region as shown in Figure 14-5.

To access an IMS data base, your CICS application program issues access requests to DL/I. A request is processed first by the DL/1 interface that verifies the request is correct. The DL/I interface then passes the request on to the DL/I processing routines that handle the request and return data and status information to the DL/1 interface. The DL/I interface, in turn, makes the data and status available to your application program.

To access an IMS data base, your application program goes through a three-step process:

1. Schedule a PSB.

   This is simply a request to begin processing for those data bases listed in the named PSB. DL/I checks each PCB entry to determine the type of data base access it specifies. If each data base is available for the specified access, the schedule request can be granted.

2. Issue DL/I requests to access the data base.

   Requests are issued either in the form of CALL statements or of EXEC DLI statements, depending upon what operating system CICS is running under. Upon return from each DL/I operation, your program must check status codes returned by DL/I. The status codes are used to indicate any error

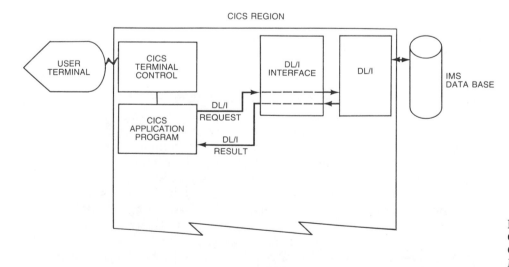

Figure 14-5 CICS as Communication Manager for DL/I Access

conditions, and also to report information such as the name of a segment retrieved by the operation.

3. Terminate the PSB.

The PSB is automatically terminated when the CICS task terminates, so in most cases your program need not explicitly terminate the PSB. Explicit termination of a PSB requires consideration of data recovery factors that will not be discussed in this text.

Issuing DL/I Requests

If you are using a DOS/VSE system, your requests to DL/I will be written as DL/I commands in an EXEC form similar to that you have been using throughout this text for CICS commands. For example, the statement:

EXEC DLI SCHEDULE (psbname) END-EXEC.

requests DL/I to schedule a PSB.

If your CICS system runs under MVS/SP, you must issue explicit CALL statements to interface with DL/I. For example, to schedule a PSB, you would write:

CALL 'CBLTDLI' USING PCB-FUN, PSB-NAME, UIB-PTR.

Here, PCB-FUN and PSB-NAME are working-storage variables that specify the function to be performed ('PCB ' in this case), and also the name of the PSB to be scheduled. UIB-PTR is a BLL Cell to contain the address of a User Interface Block that DL/1 uses to communicate with your program.

In this text, we will discuss only the DOS/VSE interface for DL/I processing.

Checking DL/I Status

In the DOS/VSE environment, the DL/1 interface uses a control block called the *DL/I Interface Block* (DIB) to return information to your application pro-ram. The CICS Command Translator automatically defines the DIB within your program's working-storage as it translates your CICS and DL/I commands.

Figure 14-6 shows the four fields of the DIB. You will use the DIBSTAT field most often. It is a two-byte field that contains values in character format.

You should check DIBSTAT after completion of each EXEC DLI command. This text will not discuss all of the possible error conditions. However, there are two codes you should be aware of. Successful completion is indicated by a

SYMBOLIC NAME	DESCRIPTION
DISFLAG	FLAG INDICATING THAT AN ONLINE TASK WAITED FOR A RESOURCE OWNED BY AN MPS BATCH TASK.
DIBSEGLV	INDICATES THE HIERARCHICAL LEVEL OF THE SEGMENT RETRIEVED.
DIBSEGM	CONTAINS NAME OF THE SEGMENT RETREIVED.
DIBSTAT	DL/I STATUS CODE.

**Figure 14-6
Fields in DL/I
Interface Block (DIB**

DIBSTAT value of two blank characters (' '). A DIBSTAT value of GE indicates that no data has been retrieved by a GET operation.

The meaning of the other DIB fields shown are:

- DIBFLAG, when set to hexadecimal X'FF', indicates that your program had to wait for a resource currently owned by a batch task °
- DIBSEGLV gives the *level* of the lowest level segment retrieved
- DIBSEGM gives the *name* of the lowest level segment retrieved

Scheduling a PSB

You use the following command to schedule a PSB.

EXEC DLI SCHEDULE PSB (name)

The command is terminated by END-EXEC just as for CICS commands. We omit the END-EXEC in the command description in order to be consistent with our description of CICS commands.

Name is an eight-byte field containing the name of the PSB to be scheduled. The person who generates the PSB must tell you the name by which you can refer to it.

Issuing An Access Request

The general form of an access request is:

EXEC DLI option USING PCB (value)
SEGMENT (data-value) SEGLENGTH (data-value)
arguments

Option is the name of the access operation to be performed. We will discuss three operations: GET UNIQUE, GET NEXT, and REPLACE.

USING PCB specifies which PCB within the PSB defines the data base to be accessed. For example, to access the data base named by the first PCB, you specify USING PCB (1). If your PSB defines only one data base, you don't need to code USING PCB.

The SEGMENT argument gives the name of the segment type to be retrieved. The segment name should match a name defined in the requested PCB, and it may be up to eight characters long.

SEGLENGTH gives the length of the segment area in bytes.

Arguments represents additional arguments that may be required for a particular operation. We will discuss three specific operations: GET UNIQUE, GETNEXT, and REPLACE. The description of each operation will describe any additional arguments required.

In the following discussion, we will use the data base record illustrated in Figure 14-1 as an example. We will also assume that a part number field named PARTNO has been identified as the key field for the root segment, PART.

GET UNIQUE Segment

The GET UNIQUE option is used to retrieve a segment according to a specified key value. This form of the command is written:

EXEC DLI GET UNIQUE USING PCB (value)
SEGMENT (data-area) SEGLENGTH (data-value)
WHERE (expression) FIELDLENGTH (data-value)
INTO (data-area)

The additional arguments are:

WHERE (expression) specifies the search condition that will identify the unique segment to be retrieved. The expression defines a relation between a key field and a specified value. For example, to retrieve a PART segment, for part number X012-A, you would specify a value of PART for SEGMENT, and code the WHERE expression as follows:

WHERE (PARTNO = VALUE)

Here we assume that the value X012-A has been moved into a working-storage variable named VALUE.

FIELDLENGTH specifies the number of bytes to be compared within the key field.

INTO specifies the data area into which the segment is to be moved.

GET NEXT Segment

This operation retrieves the *"next" segment* from the data base. *Next* is defined according to the rules discussed above for sequential access within a hierarchical data base.

The command is written:

```
EXEC DLI GET NEXT USING PCB (value)
SEGMENT (data-area) SEGLENGTH (data-value)
INTO (data-area)
```

The arguments are as described above.

REPLACE a Segment

This option is used to replace the *"current" segment* with data from your program's working-storage. The command is written:

```
EXEC DLI REPLACE USING PCB (value)
SEGMENT (data-area) SEGLENGTH (data value)
FROM (data-area)
```

The segment to be replaced is defined as the most recently accessed segment of the type named by SEGMENT.

FROM specifies the data-area containing the data that will replace the segment within the data base.

Example Program

Figure 14-7 shows a partial COBOL program that uses the SCHEDULE, GET UNIQUE, and REPLACE operations.

Communicating With IMS Systems

Having completed our discussion of CICS as DC manager for an IMS data base, we will look at the second situation in which a CICS programmer may encounter IMS.

In this case, both CICS and IMS are used within a company or installation. CICS transaction requests may involve change to an IMS data base, and IMS transactions may involve change to data files managed by CICS.

Generally speaking, you handle these requirements in much the same way

```
        IDENTIFICATION DIVISION.                             00010000
        PROGRAM-ID. 'EXDLICX'.                               00020010
        * * * * * * * * * * * * * * * * * * * * * * * * *    00030010
        * THIS PROGRAM SCHEDULES THE PSB, READS AND UPDATES *   00040010
        * A SEGMENT, AND TERMINATES.                     *   00050010
        *                                                *   00060010
        * PROGRAM IS INCOMPLETE AND WILL NOT EXECUTE     *   00070010
        * * * * * * * * * * * * * * * * * * * * * * * * *    00080010
         ENVIRONMENT DIVISION.                               00090001
         DATA DIVISION.                                      00100001
         WORKING-STORAGE SECTION.                            00110001
        * INPUT AREA *                                       00120005
         01 INPUT-AREA.                                      00130002
            02 TYPE PIC X(10).                               00140003
                      .                                      00170008
                      .                                      00180008
        * AREA TO RECEIVE DATA BASE RECORD *                 00190005
         01 DATA-AREA.                                       00200001
            02 FIELD1 PIC X(5).                              00210010
            02 FIELD2 PIC X(25).                             00220010
         PROCEDURE DIVISION.                                 00230001
                      .                                      00240001
                      .                                      00260001
        * SCHEDULE THE PSB *                                 00270010
            EXEC DLI SCHEDULE (PSBNAME) END EXEC.            00280010
        *                                                    00290005
        * CHECK THE DL/I STATUS CODE *                       00300010
            IF DIBSTAT NOT EQUAL TO SPACES THEN              00310010
        *                                                    00320005
        * ERROR DIAGNOSTIC CODE *                            00330010
                      .                                      00340007
                      .                                      00350007
        * ACCESS THE DATA BASE - GET A SEGMENT FOR UPDATE *  00370007
            EXEC DLI GET UNIQUE SEGMENT (SKILL)              00380010
                   WHERE (SKILTYPE=TYPE) FIELDLENGTH (10)    00380020
                   INTO (DATA-AREA)                          00390010
                   SEGLENGTH (30) END-EXEC.                  00400010
        *                                                    00410007
        * CHECK THE DL/I STATUS CODE *                       00420010
            IF DIBSTAT NOT EQUAL TO SPACES THEN              00430010
        * ERROR DIAGNOSTIC CODE *                            00440010
                      .                                      00460007
                      .                                      00470007
        * DISPLAY THE DATA ON THE TERMINAL *                 00400010
                      .                                      00500007
                      .                                      00510007
        * READ CHANGES WHICH MAY HAVE BEEN MADE *            00520010
                      .                                      00530007
                      .                                      00540007
        * MOVE THE CHANGED DATA TO DATA-AREA FIELDS *        00550010
                      .                                      00560007
                      .                                      00580007
        * UPDATE THE DATA BASE *                             00590010
            EXEC DLI REPLACE SEGMENT (SKILL)                 00600010
                   FROM (DATA-AREA)                          00610010
                   SEGLENGTH (30) END-EXEC.                  00620010
        * CHECK THE DL/I STATUS CODE *                       00630010
            IF DIBSTAT NOT EQUAL TO SPACES THEN              00640010
        * ERROR DIAGNOSTIC CODE *                            00650010
                      .                                      00660007
                      .                                      00680007
        * SEND A CONFIRMING MESSAGE TO THE TERMINAL *        00710010
                      .                                      00720007
                      .                                      00740007
            EXEC CICS RETURN END-EXEC.                       00750007
            STOP RUN.                                        00760007
```

Figure 14-7
Example Program,
SCHEDULE, GET
UNIQUE, and
REPLACE

as you would handle intersystem communication requests between two CICS systems. However, a synchronized conversation between IMS and CICS must always be initiated by CICS. That is, if distributed transaction processing (DTP) is required, CICS must always be the front-end system.

As we discuss intersystem communication between CICS and IMS, you should keep in mind an important difference in the architecture of CICS and IMS.

As you know, when a CICS user enters a transaction request, CICS invokes an application program to handle the required processing. The program performs the required processing under control of the user at the terminal. The processing is performed in a conversational manner (although, from an internal view, it may have been programmed as a pseudo-conversational transaction). The user's terminal is dedicated to the transaction until the transaction has been completed.

Systems like this, where the user's terminal is "connected" to the transaction until the transaction completes, are called *direct control systems*.

IMS, on the other hand, is an example of a *queued system*.

When an IMS user enters a transaction request, the request is analyzed and "scheduled" for processing by the appropriate *message processor* program. By "scheduled," we mean that the request (called a *message*) is placed in a work queue for the processing program. The user's terminal is then free. When the transaction has been completed, the message processor sends a response to the user's terminal.

The IMS user may have the impression that the transaction was performed "immediately," because a well-tuned IMS system can handle a large number of transactions very quickly. However, from a programming point of view, there is no way to predict how quickly the processing program will service the queued request.

Asynchronous Processing

We will look first at the case in which either the CICS or IMS system need only to *initiate* a process on the other system. In Chapter 13, we referred to this type of requirement as Asynchronous Distributed Processing.

When a CICS transaction initiates a process in the IMS system, this is referred to as the *CICS front-end case*. IMS is the *back-end system* for this intersystem communication.

Alternatively, you may need to program a CICS transaction that can be invoked by an IMS system. This is the *CICS back-end case*. IMS is the *front-end system* for this intersystem communication.

CICS Front-End Communication

When your CICS program is to initiate an IMS process, you can use the CICS START command in much the same way as discussed in the preceding chapter. CICS will use the telecommunications system to ship your START command to the IMS system. As an option of your START command, you can name a CICS transaction for IMS to initiate when processing is completed.

Figure 14-8 illustrates the overall communications flow.

In this figure, a CICS transaction (labeled TRAN A) issues a START command to initiate an IMS process. The START command is shipped to the IMS system that queues the request for the appropriate IMS message processing

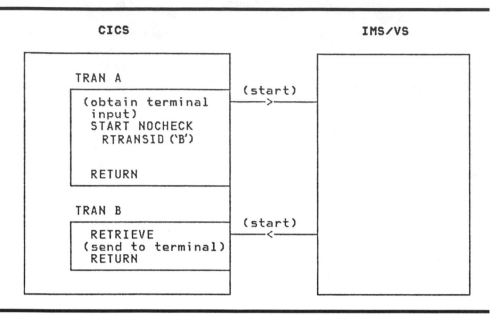

Figure 14-8
Overall Flow, CICS to
IMS Communication

program. Remember that IMS is a *queued system*, so the message processing program will process your request after it has completed all of the requests that precede your request in the queue.

After IMS processing is complete, a START command is sent by IMS to the CICS transaction named in the initial START command. In the figure, this transaction is referred to as TRAN B. If the IMS process is to return data to TRAN B, the TRAN B transaction can use the CICS RETRIEVE command to access the data.

When you use the CICS START command to initiate IMS processing, you code it as follows:

```
EXEC CICS START NOCHECK
[TRANSID (data-value)] [TERMID [data-value)]
[FROM (data-area) LENGTH (data-value)]
[RTRANSID (data-value)] [RTERMID (data-value)]
```

The NOCHECK option must always be specified. It indicates that no response to the START command itself is expected. As discussed above, your program may expect a response upon completion of *processing*. This is different from a response by IMS to *receipt of the START command*. The RTRANSID and RTERMID options are used to arrange for a processing response. They are discussed below.

Normally you will not code the TRANSID option. Instead you will accept the default value, ISCEDT, as the name of an *IMS editor* to which your transmission is to be directed. The IMS editor processes the transmission and then passes it to the IMS control region that enqueues the processed message for the correct message processor. The section *CICS Back-End Transaction* discusses a situation in which you do code the TRANSID option.

TERMID specifies the *primary resource name* that is to be assignd the IMS process. In CICS terms, the primary resource name is like a tranaction identifier.

Normally, you will not code the TERMID option. Instead you include the primary resource name in the first eight characters of your FROM data area, just as you do for starting a remote CICS transaction. The section *CICS Back-End Transaction* discusses a situation in which you do code the TERMID option.

The FROM and LENGTH options are specified if your program is passing data to the IMS process. They are coded just as described in the preceding chapter for CICS to CICS communication.

You code the RTRANSID option to specify the name of the CICS transaction for IMS to initiate after completing your request. The RTRANSID argument is a one- to four-character transaction identifier.

If the transaction named by RTRANSID is to be attached to a terminal when it is initiated, you code RTERMID to specify the identifier by which the terminal is known in the CICS Terminal Control Table.

Figure 14-8 illustrates a situation in which two different transactions, TRAN A and TRAN B, are used. The first, TRAN A, initiates an IMS process. The second, TRAN B, processes the response from IMS. The two transactions could be combined within a single program. In this case, the program would begin by checking to see whether it was initiated from the user terminal or from a START request. (After completing the description of the overall process, we will describe how a program can find out how it was initiated.)

If the transaction was initiated from a user terminal, the program should perform the steps described above for TRAN A. That is, it issues a START command, naming itself as the transaction to be initiated by IMS when IMS processing has completed. After issuing the START command, the program terminates.

If the program was initiated by a remote request from IMS, it should perform the steps described above for TRAN B. That is, it should issue a RETRIEVE command to access data sent by IMS, perform other required processing, and then terminate.

In effect, what we have just described is a pseudo-conversational process except that the second transaction is initiated by a message from IMS, rather than by input from the CICS user. The process could also be programmed conversationally—that is, the program could simply wait for reply from IMS. This is generally not recommended, since it is difficult to predict how long your request may have to wait in the IMS message processor's queue.

To determine how it was initiated, a CICS program can issue the following command:

EXEC CICS ASSIGN STARTCODE (data-area)

This causes a two-byte character code value to be placed in the data-area specified by STARTCODE. The possible code values are:

TD Initiation by transaction request from CICS user terminal.
S   Initiation by a START command with no data.
SD Initiation by a START command with data.

The data can be accessed only by issuing a RETRIEVE command.

QD Automatic initiation by a transient data queue trigger level.
U   Initiation by another CICS task (as by ATTACH command).

The ASSIGN command has a large number of options besides the STARTCODE option discussed here. It can be used to inquire about many conditions outside your program. You may want to refer to the *Application Programmer's Reference Manual* to see the complete list of options.

CICS Back-End Transaction

If an IMS processing program initiates a CICS transaction, CICS receives the request in the form of a START command. If the IMS request includes data, the initiated CICS program can issue the RETRIEVE command to access that data.

The RETRIEVE command is written:

```
EXEC CICS RETRIEVE
[INTO (data-area  I   SET (pointer-ref) ]
[LENGTH (data-area)]
[RTRANSID (data-area) ]   [RTERMID (data-area) ]
```

The INTO, SET, and LENGTH options are used as described in Chapter 12.

If your program is to send a response to IMS after processing has been completed, you will use a START command, as described above for the CICS front-end case, to initiate an IMS message processor to handle the response. In order to determine what IMS process to name in your START command, you code the RTRANSID and RTERMID options.

The RETRIEVE command sets the RTRANSID argument to the name of an IMS process to be named in your START command's TRANSID parameter. Similarly, the RTERMID argument will be set to a *primary resource name* to be specified as the TERMID parameter of your START command.

The following example shows how the RETRIEVE and START commands would be coded in the CICS back-end case.

```
EXEC CICS RETRIEVE RTRANSID (tran-name) RTERMID (res-name)
     END-EXEC.
     ...
  [statements to perform transaction-specific processing]
EXEC CICS START NOCHECK TRANSID (tran-name) TERMID (res-name)
     END-EXEC.
EXEC CICS RETURN END-EXEC.
```

Notice that the value *tran-name*, retrieved by the RTRANSID parameter, becomes the argument of the START command's TRANSID parameter. Similarly, the value *res-name* is retrieved in the RTERMID parameter, and it becomes the START command's TERMID argument.

Distributed Transaction Processing

In Distributed Transaction Processing, which is always synchronous or conversational in nature, CICS must be the front-end system. IMS cannot initiate a conversational process with CICS.

Once initiated, a conversation between CICS and IMS proceeds in the same manner as a conversation between two CICS systems. That is, your program uses the CONVERSE or SEND-RECEIVE commands according to the flip-flop rules described in the preceding chapter for communication status. As the front-end program, your program must initiate the conversation by issuing an ALLOCATE command to *acquire a session*. It can then use the SEND or

CONVERSE command to send the first message to the back-end (IMS) process. If you use the CONVERSE command, the communication states are flip-flopped, placing the back-end process in SEND state and your program in RECEIVE state. You can also cause the communication states to flip-flop by coding the INVITE option on your SEND command. In this case, the next command in your program would be a RECEIVE command.

Figure 14-9 reviews the overall flow, using the SEND and RECEIVE commands.

There is really only one difference between coding a DTP program that converses with an IMS system and coding a similar program that converses with another CICS system. The difference lies only in the content of the messages that are transmitted. In particular, you must send messages in a format that can be recognized by the IMS editor used for intersystem communication.

This text will not discuss the message formats in detail. In practice, you would work out the details together with an experienced IMS programmer. We will, however, introduce one new CICS command that you will use to construct the *first* message to be sent to IMS.

The first transmission from your program must include a control block called an *attach header*. The attach header names the IMS process that is to be initiated, and it also defines additional information required for the particular session.

You don't need to know the format of an attach header because CICS provides a command, BUILD ATTACH, to build the header for you. The options you code in the BUILD ATTACH command determine values that will be placed into the attach header.

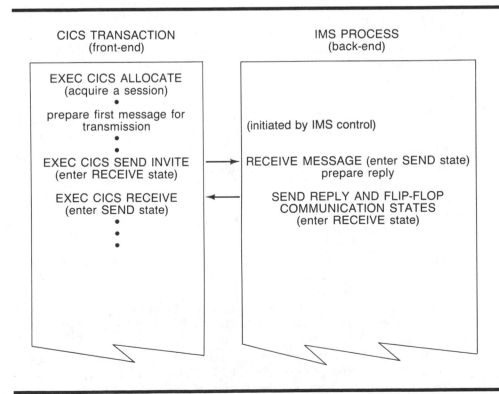

**Figure 14-9
Command Detail,
CICS to IMS
Communication**

The command is written:

BUILD ATTACH
[ATTACHID (name)]   [RESOURCE (name)]
[... other options ...]

ATTACHID specifies a name that the Command Translator will assign to the attach header. You will use the name later when you issue the SEND or CONVERSE command to transmit the first message to IMS.

RESOURCE names the primary resource to be assigned the remote IMS processing. As discussed above for Asynchronous Distributed Processing, the primary resource name corresponds to a CICS transaction identifier. Normally you do not code the RESOURCE option, but place the resource name in the first eight bytes of the first message you send.

To completely define a particular CICS-IMS session, you may need to code additional options that are not discussed in this text.

Once the BUILD ATTACH command has been completed, you issue either a SEND or CONVERSE command to transmit the first message. When you code this command, you include an ATTACHID parameter that names the attach header constructed by the BUILD ATTACH command.

For example, you would code the SEND command as follows:

EXEC SEND ATTACHID (name)
[FROM (data-area) LENGTH (data-area)]
[INVITE]

The name specified in the ATTACHID parameter must be the same name specified in the ATTACHID parameter of the BUILD ATTACH command.

The remaining parameters are as discussed in the preceding chapter for CICS to CICS communication. Remember that the first eight bytes of the FROM area should contain the name of the IMS *primary resource* (transaction identifier) to be invoked.

Summary

This chapter has described two ways in which CICS programs can be used to access hierarchical data bases created by the IMS Information Management System (IMS).

An installation may use CICS as the data communications manager for accessing IMS data bases. CICS application programs in this environment interface directly with Data Language/I (DL/I), the IMS data management facility. The programs interface with DL/I by using EXEC DLI commands (in the DOS/VSE environment), or by executing CALL statements to CBLTDLI (in the MVS/SP environment).

An installation may also use both CICS and IMS DB/DC systems. In this case, CICS application programs can use intersystem communication facilities to send transaction requests to the IMS system.

In a hierarchical data base, the unit of data is the *data segment*. A data base record is made up of one or more data segments. Within every record of the data base, segments are related according to a defined "parent-child" structure. The root segment is the data segment that has no parent segment. The root segment is said to reside in *level 1* of the hierarchy. Each child segment resides in the hierarchical level next higher than its parent segment's level.

Within a data base record, no segment (except the root segment) can appear without its parent segment. A segment that does appear may appear any number of times.

To write an application program, you need to know only the structure of data segments that your program will reference. You don't need to know about all the segment types that may appear in a record. In IMS, the complete data base structure is defined in a table called the Data Base Definition (DBD). An application program's view of IMS data bases is defined in another control block called the Program Specification Block (PSB).

The PSB defines which data bases, and which segments within each data base, an application program can reference. If a given segment type is defined in your program's PSB, the program is said to be "sensitive to" that segment type. The PSB also defines the type of access the program is permitted for each data segment type.

Before issuing any DL/I commands to access a data base, you must issue a DL/I command to schedule a PSB that defines your program's view of the data base. You may access a data segment directly by using a DL/I GET UNIQUE option and specifying a key value for each parent segment leading to the target segment. Once you have accessed a data base record, you may also access data segments sequentially using the DL/I GET NEXT option. Sequential access within a hierarchical data base record is defined in a top-to-bottom, left-to-right sequence. During sequential access, segment types to which your program is not sensitive are skipped over.

You may also use the DL/I REPLACE option to write new data into a particular data segment.

In an intersystem environment, CICS programs can initiate IMS processes, and IMS processes can initiate CICS transactions. Your CICS program uses the START command to initiate an IMS process in much the same way it would start a remote CICS transaction. If your CICS program is invoked by an IMS process, it uses the CICS RETRIEVE command to access any data sent by the IMS process.

A CICS program can use the ASSIGN STARTCODE command to determine how it was invoked. For example, the program might have been invoked by a CICS user's transaction request, by a START command, or by a transient data queue trigger level.

When communicating with an IMS system, you should keep in mind that IMS is not a *direct control system* like CICS, but is a *queued system*. This means that an IMS processing program takes its work from a queue, rather than directly from a user terminal. The IMS user's terminal is not connected to the processor program.

A CICS program can initiate conversational processing (Distributed Transaction Processing) with an IMS system. In synchronous intersystem communication between CICS and IMS, the IMS system must always be the *back-end system*.

Distributed Transaction Processing with an IMS processor is conducted according to the same rules as Distributed Transaction Processing with another CICS system. The only difference is that the messages your CICS program transmits must be in a format that IMS can interpret. In particular, your first message must include an *attach header* that you can build using the CICS BUILD ATTACH command.

DISCUSSION QUESTIONS

A data base is defined as illustrated in Figure 14-10. A program's view of the same data base is defined by the following PSB. (The DL/I statements shown include only those fields necessary for answering the Discussion Questions.)

PCB DBDNAME = PARTSDB
SENSEG NAME = PARTMAST
SENSEG NAME = STOKSTAT
SENSEG NAME = CYCOUNT
SENSEG NAME = BACKORDS

Assume that a data base record contains two occurrences of the STANDARD DATA segment and four occurrences of the STOCK STATUS (STOKSTAT) segment. The first STOKSTAT segment has two CYCLE COUNT (CYCOUNT) and no BACK ORDERS (BACKORDS) segments. The second STOKSTAT segment has one occurrence each of the CYCOUNT and BACKORDS segments. The third STOKSTAT segment has one BACKORDS segment and zero CYCOUNT segments. The fourth STOKSTAT segment has two BACKORDS segments and one CYCOUNT segment.

1. Write the PARENT definition required for each SENSEG statement in the PSB.

2. Show how the data base record described above would be stored within the data base.

3. Sketch a tree structure showing the application program's view of the *data base.*

   Show the level of each segment type in your sketch.

4. Sketch a tree structure showing the application program's view of the *data base record* described above.

   Show the level of each segment type in your sketch.

5. Suppose that the program issued a DL/I GET UNIQUE command that retrieved the root segment of the data base record described above. The program then issued five DL/I GET NEXT commands that name the BACKORDS segment. Summarize the result of each GET NEXT command.

EXERCISE

For this exercise, you will write an application program that reads and updates segments in an IMS data base. The exercise assumes that you are using a CICS system that runs under DOS/VSE.

Figure 14-10 illustrates the data base as it is defined in the DBD.

Your program's PSB is named DLZPSB3. It defines only a single data base. Your program is sensitive to the PART MASTER segment type (named PARTROOT) and the STOCK STATUS segment type (named STOKSTAT). Figure 14-11 shows the structure of these two segment types.

Notice that the PARTKEY field is defined as the segment key for the root segment, and STOCKEY is a key field for the STOKSTAT segment.

Your program is invoked by a user transaction request of the form:

A01C ffff kkkkkkkkkkkkkkkkk

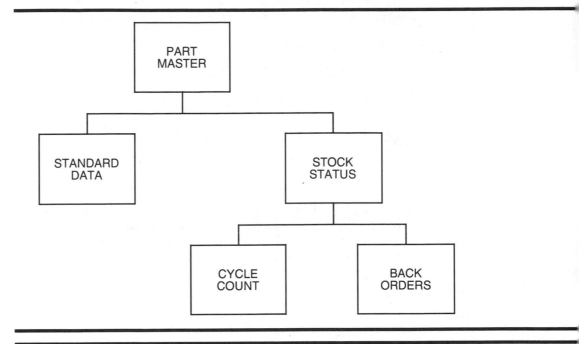

Figure 14-10
Data Base Definition
for Programming
Exercise

SEGMENT NAME	FIELD NAME	NUMBER OF BYTES	COMMENTS
PARTROOT		50	
	PARTKEY	17	SEGMENT KEY
		9	UNUSED
	DESC	15	DESCRIPTION
		9	UNUSED
STOKSTAT		160	
	STOCKEY	16	SEGMENT KEY
		89	UNUSED
	SSONORD	8	ON ORDER
	SSONHAND	8	ON HAND
		39	UNUSED

Figure 14-11
Segment Format for
Programming
Exercise

ffff represents a four-character function code. The code may have the following values:

1. DISP indicates a *display only* request for a segment.

2. UPDT indicates that a segment is to be replaced with data.

The *k* characters represent a PARTKEY value to be used as a search key. For both the DISP and UPDT functions, your program will first get the root segment with the specified key, and then get the *next* STOKSTAT segment from the data base. Then you are to display the STOKSTAT segment at the terminal.

If there is no STOKSTAT segment, display a message like:

NONE   XXXXXXXXXXXXXXX

where the *X* characters represent the description found in the root segment.

If a STOKSTAT segment is found, display a message like:

QQQQQQQQ XXXXXXXXXXXXXXX KKKKKKKKKKKKKKKKK

The *Q* characters represent the SSONORD field of the STOKSTAT segment. The *X* and *K* characters represent, respectively, the root segment's description and key fields.

If the function is UPDT, the user may then modify the displayed quantity (SSONORD). Your program is to read the modified data from the user terminal, and, to write it into the data base where it will replace the STOKSTAT segment whose SSONORD quantity you displayed for the user.

Your program should check for the following errors:

1. Illegal function code received in transaction request

2. Requested segment cannot be found

3. Unsuccessful update operation

If an error is detected, display an appropriate error message and terminate.

If an UPDT request is successfully completed, display a message, UPDATE COMPLETE before terminating.

The flowchart shown in Figure 14-12 summarizes the required program flow.

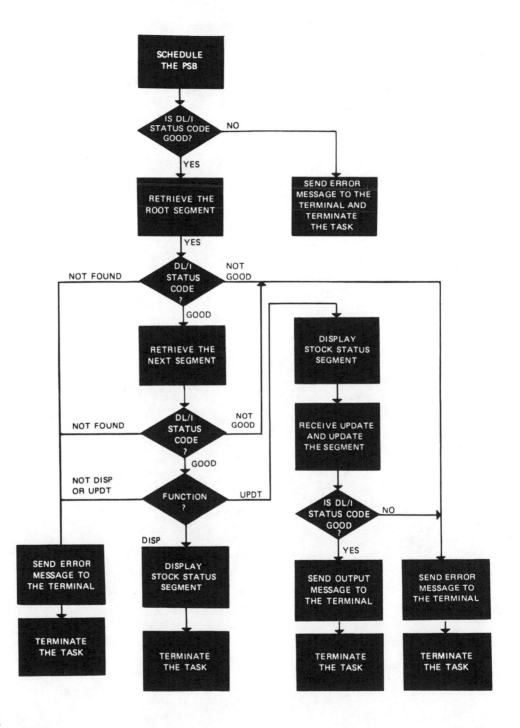

Figure 14-12
Overall Flow of
Programming Exercise

315

Acknowledgments

The following illustrations are reproduced or adapted with permission:

Figure 2-1 reprinted by permission from *Customer Information Control System*/Virtual Storage (CICS/VS), General Information. GC33-0155-1. Second Edition (December 1982). © Copyright International Business Machines Corporation 1982.

Figures 2-3, 3-2, 3-3, 3-4, 3-5, 3-7, 3-8, 4-3, 4-6, thru 4-14, 4-18 thru 4-23, 5-1, 5-2, 5-3, 5-5, 5-6, 6-1, 6-2, 6-5, 7-1, 7-2, 7-3, 7-5, 7-8, 7-9, 7-10, 7-12, 7-13, 7-19, 8-1, 8-2, 8-3, 8-4, 8-10, 9-1 thru 9-8, 9-10, 9-13 thru 9-19, 10-1 thru 10-6, 11-1 thru 11-5, 11-7, 11-8, 11-9, 11-10, 14-6 and 14-7 reprinted by permission from *Command Level Coding for CICS/VS*, Textbook. I0086. Major Revision (July 1981). © Copyright International Business Machines Corporation 1979.

Figures 4-1, 5-9, 6-12, 7-15, 7-16, 7-21, 9-20, 9-21, 9-22, 11-11 thru 11-25, 14-10, 14-11, 14-12 reprinted by permission from *Command Level Coding for CICS/VS*, COBOL Exercises. I0086. Reprinted July, 1981. © Copyright International Business Machines Corporation 1979.

Figures 4-2, 4-15, 5-4, 5-8 reprinted by permission from *Customer Information Control System/Operating System/Virtual Storage (CICS/OS/VS)*, Version 1, Release 6. Application Programmer's Reference Manual (Command Level). SC33-0161-0. First Edition (December 1982). © Copyright International Business Machines Corporation 1977, 1978, 1980, 1981, 1982.

Figures 4-16 and 4-17 reprinted by permission from *Customer Information Control System/Virtual Storage (CICS/VS)*, Version 1, Release 5. Application Programmer's Reference Manual (Command Level). SC33-0077-3. Fourth Edition (July 1981). © Copyright International Business Machines Corporation 1977, 1978, 1979, 1980, 1981.

Figures 6-6, 6-7, 7-4 and 7-6 reprinted by permission from *Customer Information* Control System/Virtual Storage (CICS/VS), Version 1, Release 5. System Programmer's Guide (OS/VS). SC33-0071-2. © Copyright International Business Machines Corporation 1978.

Figures 6-10 and 6-11 reprinted by permission from *Customer Information Control System/Virtual Storage (CICS/VS)*, Version 1, Release 5. System Application Design Guide. SC33-0068-2. Third Edition (May 1980). © Copyright International Business Machines Corporation 1977, 1978, 1979, 1980.

Figure 14-1 reprinted by permission from *IMS/VS Primer for CICS/VS Users*. Document Number GG24-1530. First Edition (February 1981). © Copyright International Business Machines Corporation 1980.

Figure 14-8 reprinted by permission from *Customer Information Control System/Operating System/Virtual Storage (CICS/OS/VS)*, Version 1, Release 6. SC33-0133-0. First Edition (December 1982). © Copyright International Business Machines Corporation 1977, 1978, 1979, 1980, 1982.

Index